Growing Up
in Medieval London

GROWING UP IN MEDIEVAL LONDON

The Experience of Childhood in History

BARBARA A. HANAWALT

New York   Oxford
OXFORD UNIVERSITY PRESS
1993

Oxford University Press

Oxford   New York   Toronto
Delhi   Bombay   Calcutta   Madras   Karachi
Kuala Lumpur   Singapore   Hong Kong   Tokyo
Nairobi   Dar es Salaam   Cape Town
Melbourne   Auckland   Madrid

and associated companies in
Berlin   Ibadan

Copyright © 1993 Oxford University Press, Inc.

Published by Oxford University Press, Inc.
200 Madison Avenue, New York, New York 10016

Oxford is a registered trademark of Oxford University Press

Library of Congress Cataloging-in-Publication Data
Hanawalt, Barbara.
Growing up in medieval London:
the experience of childhood in history
Barbara A. Hanawalt.
p.   cm.   Includes bibliographical references and index.
ISBN 0–19–508405–5
1. Children—England—London—History.
2. Youth—England—London—History.
I. Title.
HQ792.G7H27 1993   305.23′09421′2—dc20   92–45682

2 4 6 8 9 7 5 3 1
Printed in the United States of America
on acid-free paper

. . . We may begin with children's sports,
Seeing we all have been children.
John Stow's version of
Fitzstephen's description of London,
in *The Survey of London*

Preface

The pleasures of being a modern historian consist in two activities: the archival research and the presentation of a coherent story. History is a remarkably flexible discipline in that it permits a number of ways to tell its tale and, at its best, uses the devices most suited to the types of sources that must carry on the narrative. To think of narrative as being only a progression of events that tells the outcome of an election, a battle, a struggle for liberty, or a murder trial is too limited. Historians construct narratives through pictures, tables, regression analysis, and even chaos-theory models. The one constant in spinning out or computer-generating or imagining the historical past is that all historians who try to create a coherent narrative start with data from the past. They do not, as a philosopher might, posit a past and argue from it or, as a novelist might, create an imaginary past and people it with characters. Historians are trained to footnote the past. This process is a constraining art, a bit like writing a sonnet. It is a damn hard way to write fiction. This book explores a variety of techniques for telling the story of growing up in medieval London all of which are footnoted.

In the process of interpretation, historians seldom claim in these "postpositivist" days that they are writing "historical truths" that are devoid of the interpretations of individual writers or the times in which they live. One of the secondary comforts of history is that it can always be rewritten for a new time by another historian who takes a fresh look at the archival materials. It is a very comforting profession because it is hard to be scooped and hard to be obsolete. On the other hand, it is hard to have the last word and become a classic.

Although some historians set themselves up as arbiters of the best forms for telling a historical tale and urge earnest young historians to avoid some types of arguments, the nature of the sources and the material they contain are the truest guide in reconstructing the past as clearly and, one hopes, as faithfully to the events as possible. Some devices are better for some sources than others. It is, for instance, pointless to ignore the possibilities of quantification in repetitive records, such as court cases, censuses, parish registers, and tax listings, and instead to pull out the remarkable case and develop an atypical narrative on this basis without looking at what the average occurrences were. Thus to build demographic history on "woman gives birth to triplets" tells us little about ordinary birth patterns, other than that this one configuration made headlines in a medieval chronicle or a modern newspaper. Likewise, interpretations of the cultural significance of such an unusual event fall short without some investigation into how a society might view multiple births.

The more we wish to penetrate into the lives of ordinary people, the more complex our use of sources becomes. With this increasing complexity, the challenge of writing and of holding the attention of nonspecialists becomes even greater. Historians must learn to reach out to a broader readership among an interested public in order to keep the discipline alive. Keeping in mind multiple audiences and diverse sources, I have chosen a variety of narrative styles to spell out the history of London's children and youth. Some of the archival material is remarkable for its laborious recording of repetitive detail and is more readily accessible in numerical and tabular form. The wardship accounts, for instance, record the orphans, their names, their fortunes, and the person awarded wardship. None of the clerks, scribes, or city officials went back and did a tabulation of what was happening to city orphans in the aggregate. They used their archives to trace individual orphans, and individuals wishing to locate a particular orphan could ask that the record be searched. But none of the city officials issued numerical statements taking note of the peculiar fact that there were fewer female than male orphans in the wardship records or that the value of holdings that accrued to orphans had risen subsantially during the late fourteenth and early fifteenth centuries. Indeed, China today would not know of its shortfall of females compared with males if the World Health Organization did not ferret out the information.

We are very concerned these days with forms of historical argument. Some find it hard to conceive of a context for numbers. Historical data in numerical form are convincing in many ways, but we feel an unease with them. If these people did not use numbers in the same way as we do, should we use numbers because they present only part of the picture? Others argue that we are violating history by using terms such as "feudalism" and "adolescence" in discussions of the medieval period because they imply modern behavior that was not equivalent to the medieval practice. The argument against such a "purist" position is much the same as that against those who oppose numerical analyses. We try to write history in terms that are understandable to us, but we are not writing fiction. We cannot put ourselves back into that past, but we have terms and analytical tools that are useful to us and should not be dismissed lightly.

If, to purists of the historical profession, numerical data, as full of gaps as they are, and the use of modern terms such as "adolescence" are taboo, what are such purists to say to the composite characters and short stories about them that appear in this text? Can historians presume, on the basis of hours of research and a full life of study, to construct characters and short stories that are only partly to be found in the records? I came to the experimentation with narrative in the course of archival work. I thought that the material was so disparate, having been collected from so many different records, that it might be hard to follow. At the time, I was reading A. J. P. Taylor's autobiography for relaxation, and I was struck by his comment that social history is harder to write than political or diplomatic history because it lacks an immediate narrative. But books that I have much admired, such as Eileen Power's *Medieval People* and Jonathan Spence's *The Death of Woman Wang,* interlace larger social histories with individual biographies and tales. Whereas Spence has envied my access to quantitative data from abundant sources that are not available for an equivalent period of Chinese history, I have envied his ready-made short stories from contemporary writers' pens. So I have turned the tables. I have used my superior data and have written my own narratives, which are based on the lives of real people but which are made up of composite experiences. The narratives are set off by quotation marks so as to be readily recognizable. The chapters tell a traditional historical narrative without these explorations of individual experiences.

The stories summarize information in the chapters. They also serve to redress an imbalance in the records. We always know more about the elite and about middle-class males because they leave records, are involved in disputes, run the government and the economy, and so on. We often know only bits and pieces about the poor and the women and children. The composite stories help to bring a completeness to sparse and scattered narratives that would otherwise be missing. In this regard, they are much like quantitative narratives or those based on more traditional methods of putting archival materials into a framework for the public to read and enjoy.

Minneapolis   B. A. H.
January 1993

Acknowledgments

This book has been a pleasure to write in part because of its subject matter and in part because of the support I have received in writing it. I have had the occasion to learn from, instruct, and interact with some of the most interesting experts, graduate students, and colleagues in the course of writing this book on medieval London. My interest in writing on London came both from my long acquaintance with the city and from my work with my mentor, Sylvia L. Thrupp. Having moved from a general overview of fourteenth-century crime and late medieval English peasant families, I have found London to be a welcome retreat to a local environment. Entrance into studying London, however, could not have been so inviting without the generosity of the medievalists studying it. It is difficult moving into new archives, but I had remarkably generous guides. Caroline M. Barron told me about the various records that would help me look at youth and dower recovery. I, and many other scholars, have benefited from her generosity in encouragement and guidance in approaching London archival materials. She is a model of academic generosity. Janet Loengard, during a walk on a pleasantly warm day in Kalamazoo, Michigan, told me where to start and who to see and, on a miserably wet January day in London, suggested that my work was not done until I looked at yet one more set of records in the Guildhall. She was, of course, correct. My feet finally dried out. Martha Carlin, Vanessa Harding, and Derek Keene, speaking from their great knowledge of the London records, also directed me to various sources that helped fill in the picture of London childhood and youth. And then there were the seminars and the fellowship at the Institute of Historical Research, and the excellent archival help and warm welcome at the Corporation of London Record Office, the Guildhall, and the familiar Public Record Office on Chancery Lane.

Graduate students at both Indiana University and the University of Minnesota have contributed greatly to this study. Katherine Workman did the initial bibliographical work for the project at Indiana with the help of a grant from Indiana University. Katherine French did much of the statistical work on dower and orphans accounts, and Douglas Biggs and Eleanor Congdon worked on wills, wardmoots, and other records. Ulrike Strasser helped on the final bibliography and notes. I learned a great deal from these new scholars. They will make their own great contributions to the study of history.

Funding for this project has also been generous. The Guggenheim Foundation awarded me a fellowship in 1988 and 1989 for a year of research in London. Additional assistance was provided by the British Academy, through an exchange with the Newberry Library. A Fulbright Travel grant paid for transportation and provided appreciated hospitality while I did the research. The University of Minnesota made me feel very welcome as a new professor in 1988 with a generous grant from the Graduate School for research assistance, a summer faculty fellowship in 1988, and a match for my Guggenheim Fellowship from the College of Liberal Arts. All this research aid made the laborious process of gathering and processing the archival material much swifter than would otherwise have been possible. I emphasize this benefit by way of encouragement to funding agencies and universities to continue support for obscure fields in the humanities. To fellow faculty members of review panels with whom I have served, I can say that even medieval history can be on the cutting edge and expeditious funding can advance completion of important research.

It falls into the life of an academic to once in a while live the life of the "ivory tower," a mythical benefit of the profession. My "ivory tower," for this book was the Wissenschaftskolleg zu Berlin, where I spent the academic year 1990/1991. It was a great year for German wines (the 1990 vintage will reflect that beautiful glow of a warm autumn), for the unification of the two Germanies, and for a book on medieval London written in Berlin. The staff certainly made one feel that a myth could come true. Comfortable surroundings and time to write are only part of my gratitude for the year. I learned much about the Middle Ages on the other side of Europe both from extensive travel and from contacts that I have made with German and eastern European colleagues. My intellectual life is substantially enriched and enlarged by the experience.

For all the advantages of the "ivory tower"—myth and reality— scholarly writing is a lonely life. But support arises in surprising places. In March, as I was toiling away with German and the chapter on childhood,

Louise Scott suggested, in English, that I write a book about it. I felt liberated. When I began exploring various narrative techniques, I appreciated the input of Stuart Schwartz, who suggested that I start with a narrative of a ceremony; Sara Evans, who said she knew of a book that interspersed a narrative in the midst of a chapter; Joel Rosenthal and Lee and Arabella Patterson, who put up with my initial enthusiasm in London for a new type of "telling history" without squelching me; and Luise White, who sustained my struggle to persevere in the experiment. Luise also brought sophistication as a historian to give a critical reading to portions of the manuscript. Oxford University Press, particularly my editor, Nancy Lane, has taught me much about making a manuscript readable and accessible to a broader public. As I was trying to assemble the illustrations with only a month to get permissions and copies, I asked Wayne Howell, the artist-custodian in my office building, if he had ever illustrated a book. This led to the remarkable artistic renditions of late medieval manuscripts and early-sixteenth-century paintings that grace this book. Not only had he illustrated a book, but he also had a real interest in medieval art.

At the core of writing on family is my own domestic unit. My Gordon Setter, Scotland's Do Declare ("Doody"), has accompanied me to both the Institute for Advanced Study in Princeton and the Wissenschaftskolleg zu Berlin. She has become an international olfactory expert. Although an unpublished hound, she has not perished. She has overseen the writing of two books and reinforces my obedience to the task of writing by taking her place in my study before I do. But, above all, what has made my life as a scholar so fulfilling and so enjoyable is the shared life with my companion, Ronald Giere, in ivory towers, universities, homes, walks with the dog, and travel. He is an internationally recognized philosopher of science who is published and, therefore, will not perish. I dedicate this book to him.

Contents

Growing Up
in Medieval London

A boy watches a procession from a good vantage point. (Drawing by Wayne M. Howell, from "Essenwein, Medieval Housebook," Victoria and Albert Museum MS. 90.0.1)

1

Introduction

The priest had told the story of 1392 many times and had even written it down in a chronicle, but this time he was entertaining a diverse audience of children and servants who had gathered in his brother's house in Cheapside on St. Nicholas's Day to await the visit of the "boy bishop." "King Richard," he explained, "was no longer the dear boy-prince he was at his coronation. Those were the good old days, fifteen years ago. Most of you weren't alive then. He turned into a spoiled tyrant and moved his law courts to York to punish London. But neither he nor London could make a profit from the legal business way up there. And, of course, he could not afford to have a conspiracy arising in London while he was at York. So in a show of contrition, the mayor, aldermen, sheriffs, and all the worthy city dressed out in their ceremonial best and went to meet the king and queen." Here the chronicler recited the glories of the welcomers' livery—the colors of bright red and black, the gold and silver ornaments, the hats with their badges, the fine and spirited horses.[1] These were not simply merchants going out to welcome their prince; they were nobles by virtue of their wealth, if not their lineage. When these grand men had escorted the king and queen to London Bridge, they showed their magnificence by presenting the king with a milk-white steed saddled and bridled and trapped with white cloth of gold and red parted together, and the queen had a palfrey all white and in the same array. The saddlers, goldbeaters, silk women, tailors, drapers, and other craftspeople had been occupied with these luxurious productions. Richard loved such ornament and display. The chronicler explained that Richard was quite young, only eleven, when London held the coronation pageant and presented him with rich gifts. It had been a mistake. Now he expected bigger and better shows each time.

The moralizing comments made, the priest continued reminiscing about London's displays for Richard: "The reconciliation pageant was grand, magnificent, dazzling. To be sure, they used some of the equipment from the coronation parade and Queen Anne's entry into London as a bride. Then, the goldsmiths had erected a castle in Cheapside for young Richard's delight. On each tower was a beautiful maiden, who blew leaves of gold on the king and threw counterfeit gold florins before him and his horse. Wine ran forth from the two sides of the castle, and a gold angel, through a marvel of machinery, bowed down from atop the castle to give Richard a crown."

For the reconciliation, the chronicler explained, the city put up a stage between St. Paul's and the Cheap. The old angel was taken out of storage and refurbished with silver and gold leather—the hand of the carpenters and the leatherworkers was obvious here. Thanks to a system of pulleys, the angel bent down and actually crowned both Richard and Anne with magnificent gold crowns, embellished with gems. The goldsmiths, of course, had contributed to this part of the show. A chorus of little angels— little London boys and girls like themselves—sang while the large angel performed its ingenious feats. As usual, the conduits ran with wine (here the vintners had a hand).[2]

Having recited the events so often, the priest easily tailored them to his current audience: when his listeners' eyes opened wide at his description of the splendid wafer-thin gold and silver leaves floating down on the royal couple, he pointed out that a small boy, trying, out of avarice, to get as many of the leaves as possible, got crushed in the mob. A little girl of eleven was left in her house with a serving maid by her careful parents while they went off to Cheapside, but the silly servant left the house as soon as her master and mistress had, and the girl climbed up to the solar, leaned out the garret window, and, trying to catch a glimpse of the king and queen, fell out of the window. "Ohhh. Sorry mistress. She died, of course." Then the priest turned to Thomas Seint John, an apprentice, and said, "You were just a baby then, though you are a strapping lad now. You wouldn't remember, since you were at your nurse's breast. She would remember, if you asked the dear old lady." An aspiring young mercer was in the audience, but the seasoned priest had no trust of him. William

Bothe—he was taking in all the talk of power and wealth. Nothing good about him. He needed to learn something of humility. So the chronicler went on to tell how good Queen Anne, although she was a foreigner from faraway Bohemia, was a good friend of London. She said it was like Prague, being on a river (and getting infected with Wycliffite heresies, he thought to himself). When the party arrived at Westminster, she got down on her knees and interceded with the king to let London have its privileges back again. He relented (for more gifts), and the joyful celebrants returned to London for feasts.

The chronicler now had his sharp old eyes on the young men and women in the household audience: "Did I tell you about young John Toly? He came back from drinking all the wine he could out of the conduits. He managed to make his way up the ladders to the solar and fell into a drunken sleep. Well, early in the morning, he woke up with a desperate call of nature. Was he going to go down those ladders in his tipsy state and risk breaking his neck? No. He'd do it out the window. But he was so drunk he fell out and broke his neck. He had great plans, he did. He was going to earn money and go home and marry his village sweetheart."

Which reminded the old man of the maiden who remained chaste, but drowned in the great river. She was in a churchyard after coming out from vespers when a young man accosted her with a knife. He wanted her to have sex with him, but she refused. When he brandished the knife, she fled toward the Thames. He continued his pursuit, and she threw herself into the river. The moral, the chronicler pointed out to his terrified audience of young women, was that preservation of virginity was worth even death. God would approve. "Well," ventured one of the servant girls, "was the man hanged for homicide, as he should have been under the king's good laws and the king's—Richard's—good peace?" The London chronicler was lost for words. Being a priest, not a romance writer, he had to answer that the young man had gotten off because he fled or perhaps because he was the king's own poulterer.[3] "Damn women," thought the clerical chronicler to himself. "They can ruin any moral tale."

Approaches to Studying Childhood and Youth

The thesis of this book is simple. The Middle Ages did recognize stages of life that corresponded to childhood and adolescence. These two life stages, as we shall see, appeared in learned medical and scientific texts, in literary works of the "ages of man," and in the folk terminology of the period. Londoners, when they contrasted these stages with adulthood, spoke of youth as "wild and wanton" and adulthood as "sad and wise." The society had formal and informal mechanisms for marking the entry and the exit of individuals as they passed through the stages of life.

By the late Middle Ages, English society became preoccupied with rearing and educating children and youth so that they could successfully pass into the adult world. Advice manuals proliferated, and laws expanded to include young people. The court records, particularly those of London, recount the activities of children and their treatment during their childhood and adolescent years and show a concern with protecting their interests. When a child or youth wanted to gain the hearing of an official, he or she couched the request in terms such as "I was but a child then" or "I was a youth and new to the city" or "being of tender years" or in other phrases that evoked a sympathetic and sentimental picture of helplessness in his or her adult listeners.

Every indicator reveals a preoccupation, even an obsession, with early life stages and the successful passage of individuals through them. This book draws on a variety of archival and literary sources to present the case for childhood and adolescence in medieval London and to give the reader a sense of what growing up meant to the individuals who were going through the process. On the basis of this evidence, one can argue for a growing concern about children and adolescents.

A reader might quite rightly be skeptical of the need for a book that proves the existence of childhood and adolescence in an earlier time. After all, it is certainly observable that it is hard for a society to turn children into little adults simply by dressing them in adult clothing or putting them to adult tasks. Children cannot do adult tasks. It is also difficult to suppress the disruptions of puberty, so that awareness of adolescence must have existed. Biology, in other words, must have some relevance to the maturation and acculturation process.

Proponents of the nonexistence of childhood and adolescence in the Middle Ages, however, have widespread support among professional historians, as well as among the general public. The view is consistent with our folkloric myths about the Middle Ages. In our folklore, the term "dark ages" stands for everything bad that happened before the twentieth century; it is a way of making our own times look good by comparison. We have an inherent "Whigism" in our historical thinking that dictates that life must have gotten steadily better. Therefore, the people who lived during the "mid-evil" period, as my students call it, could not have known of the delights of childhood or the heartaches of adolescence; infanticide must have been rampant because medieval parents did not value children; all marriages were arranged, so there was no romantic love; nuclear families did not exist because there were no family values and affection. Americans have an additional bias against the "old country" as well—a place that one's forebears had to leave because it was too "medieval." As one woman said when she heard the topic of my book, "Childhood? But children worked in factories during the Middle Ages. There wasn't childhood." By pushing the industrial revolution back 500 years, she was able to come up with a very good folkloric explanation for the lack of childhood and adolescence in the Middle Ages.

Historians have perpetuated the folkloric theory that the Middle Ages did not have a concept of childhood or adolescence. Philippe Ariès's *Centuries of Childhood* sparked the considerable current interest in the study of childhood in history. With very little evidence from the medieval period, he argued that medieval illustrations of children pictured them as little adults and that the very language of the period did not use terms such as "adolescent," as we do. Words like "boy," "girl," and "child" could refer to a person of any age. If people of the Middle Ages did not have a word for it, they must not have had it. He contended that medieval "children were mixed with adults as soon as they were considered capable of doing without their mothers or nannies." By the age of seven, he concluded, they entered directly into the "great community of men."[4] In short, the modern period invented the definitions of childhood and adolescence and the sentimental attitudes toward them.

The dominant view of historians still holds, with Ariès, that childhood and adolescence were unknown as distinct categories in the Middle Ages. Historians of early modern Europe, such as Lawrence Stone and Edward Shorter, took Ariès's position as an unexamined certainty in the works they published in the 1970s.[5] Starting their studies in 1500 or later, they did not need to examine whether Ariès was right about the Middle Ages. Painting a negative, but not a jarring, picture of medieval practice was a useful foil for Ariès and for them. If political history has revolutions, social history must as well. The invention of childhood and adolescence was a convenient revolution. It is, of course, preposterous to argue that people woke up on the morning of January 1, 1500, and found that their family structure and their social values about the little adults or little monsters in their households had undergone a revolution. There is much to be said for a picture that presents social evolution rather than revolution, but one does have to read medieval Latin manuscripts or learn archaic legal systems to establish change over time rather than simply invent a past.

Medievalists have been laboring against the early modernists' construction of a medieval period without concepts of childhood and adolescence. Shulamith Shahar's *Childhood in the Middle Ages* is a notable effort in this field.[6] It is a detailed investigation of the prescriptive literature and anecdotal accounts of individuals and families during the medieval period.

Shahar's interpretation is largely a psychoanalytical one, and her conclusions are quite definite about the existence of a sentimental attitude toward children. Although she accepted Ariès's analysis initially, she saw, on looking more closely at the same type of evidence that he might have used, that his interpretation was wrong. But her reliance on literature that reflects the views of moralists and the upper classes leaves too much to speculation about how the rest of society functioned. And putting a strongly psychological interpretation on such evidence can lead a reader to wonder about a too modernist reading of sources, albeit of a different nature than Ariès's.

But the question, an oddly medieval, almost nominalist one, remains: If the medieval world did not have names for these stages of life, did they exist?[7] Readers of Aristotle, Augustine of Hippo, and other commentators on the "ages of man" know that medieval society recognized distinct periods of young life and had a variety of labels for them.[8] While it has been correctly argued, for instance, that the medieval word *adolescencia* did not mean the same thing as the modern term "adolescence," one of the objects of this book is to investigate the variety of ways in which the life stages were defined.[9] Writers on medieval society have long discussed formal institutions and informal mechanisms, such as apprenticeship, fostering, and squirehood, for acculturating youth to the adult world, but they have done so without defining the stages of life at which these occurred.[10]

The fight over terminological turf seems quite barren. Societies can have institutions without labeling them, as anthropologists have long known. Medievalists should also know this; they have been studying feudalism for years, but it is not a medieval term. Medieval society did not have a word equivalent to the modern usage of "family." *Familia* referred to the larger household of kin-related inhabitants, servants, and other dependents. But nuclear families, extended families, and other sorts of familial connections were well established. More complex word structures served. Thus Matilda, wife of William, and Alison and Thomas, daughter and son of William, worked quite well to identify a nuclear family.

One does not have to use modern labels, such as "childhood" and "adolescence," with the presumption that they meant exactly the same thing then as they do now. Much of the current literature on historical adolescence is hobbled by the assumption that adolescence can be defined only the way that social scientists began to define it in the early twentieth century. Historians are not usually accustomed to giving sociologists credit for their tendency to label everything, but in the case of adolescence they have been willing to dismiss the existence of the phenomenon until sociology came up with names for it. Likewise, the tendency of early modern historians to use only the existence of youth subcultures of riot and misrule as the sole permissible evidence for a concept of adolescence has created an unnecessary limitation on historical discussion. To find the correct elements to fit these definitions, historians have molded their evidence to establish youth subcultures and mentalities in the early modern period.[11] A historian's task is to find out how society at the time perceived these stages of life and how it defined them, rather than simply accepting a present-day definition. Modern social scientists did not invent stages of life.

In venturing into the issues of categories and definitions, however, I want to go armed with something more than folkloric theories, assumptions of either revolutionary change or a simple parity with the past, or psychoanalytical presumptions about universal human responses. One of the advantages of studying medieval Europe is that it gives the writer an ability to step back and look at the culture as distantly familiar yet alien. One of the first appeals of studying the Middle Ages is that it is exotic (for this reason it is used shamelessly for futuristic science fiction), but at the same time there is a common root with contemporary culture. One gets a perspective on a distant past and the awareness that many of our institutions, particularly the legal ones, grew out of that past. Approaching this culture as an anthropologist does a new people helps to give a fresh perspective not bound solely by modern language and definitions.[12] Historians are happy, thoughtless poachers of methodologies and often fail to treat them as they were intended—as hypotheses to be enlarged on or rejected rather than slavishly followed and confirmed. I will use my poached methodologies as suggestions, rather than trying to fit my own reading of the evidence into them.

The most basic question for investigating stages of life in any people, in any period of history, is nurture versus nature: Is culture or biology more important? I have argued elsewhere, and Shahar has pushed this argument further than I would, that biology plays a very basic role in shaping the cultural parameters of childhood.[13] For children to survive, they need not only to be nursed, fed, and kept warm (biology), but also to be played with and talked to (culture), or they cannot be socialized. It matters not whether a mother or her surrogate performs these basic tasks or whether or not a sentimental attitude toward a childish state is present; it is simply that these activities must take place for the child to survive. Likewise, it is very difficult to set children of seven to skilled labor such as smelting, plowing, or carpentry. They may be set to some tasks and may even be married at such a young age, but no one really anticipates that they will have the physical capacity to perform adult roles. Similarly, as we shall see, it was very difficult for medieval society to ignore the physical changes that occurred with puberty, try as it certainly did to suppress puberty's effects on behavior.

As one moves beyond childhood into adolescence, culture begins to play an even stronger role. Arnold van Gennep in *The Rites of Passage* distinguished between "physical puberty" and "social puberty," a distinction that helps to point out the limitations of a purely biological approach.[14] Physical puberty is marked by the development of both primary and secondary sexual characteristics, whereas social puberty is a cultural phenomenon. He saw the two processes as very distinct and not necessarily coinciding. He therefore urged that the phrase "puberty rites" not be used. In his analysis, he wished to place the emphasis on the cultural or social aspects of adolescent initiation. While preserving his distinction, I will argue that the correspondence between biological and social puberty varied by social class, gender, and the historical period. Young women might very well be married near biological puberty or experience sexual initiation and even pregnancy. This very fact can have a considerable influence on compressing a period of "social puberty" for females. Indeed, female sexuality was so important to medieval thinking that social puberty and physical puberty tended to merge. On the other hand, the merchant and artisanal classes of fifteenth-century London enforced a social construction of male adolescence that extended adolescence into the late twenties— well beyond exit from physical puberty.

Borrowing from van Gennep, Victor Turner in *The Ritual Process* emphasizes the liminal nature of transitions from childhood to adolescence to adulthood. The initiates are separated from the past stage, but must go through a period of "liminality" (or being on the threshold) before they are integrated into the next stage. The prescribed behavior he describes for the period of passage incorporates humility and passivity. The inductee is separated from familiar surroundings, abased, and placed in a state of expectant waiting for new, adult roles. The description fits well with the expectations that medieval adults had for their apprentices, servants, and children. Starting with the ceremony of baptism, the purpose of which was to separate the infant from primal sin and to induct it into the world of the Christian community, separation and induction were part of the movement from one life stage to the next. The physical movement of a servant or an apprentice from the natal home to that of the master was another type of separation. Acceptance of punishment without complaint, an outgrowth of the medieval adage that to spare the rod was to spoil the child, might very well have ground down the neophytes of medieval society so that they reached "a uniform condition" and could be "fashioned anew and endowed with additional powers to enable them to cope with their new station in life."[15]

Turner's model, however, is too limited for a general discussion of adolescence because it is concerned with the rituals of passage rather than with the whole period of adolescence. His view is one of days, not years. The medieval world, as we shall see, observed some of these ceremonies of passage, but the emphasis was on years of training rather than on brief rituals. Liminal passages is an incorrect concept, even though the behavioral descriptions seem very applicable to adult expectations for medieval adolescents. Van Gennep's distinction between culture and biology and Turner's concept of liminality are helpful, but too static; they are fixed too closely to a ceremony, rather than a process. Not one ceremony but a whole range of changes defines a life stage.

Defining the parameters of a life stage when they vary with time period, sex, and social class presents further complications because biology and culture may be interrelated in a bewildering fashion. The sociologist Glen Elder, Jr., has made a number of astute observations about the transitions from childhood to adolescence and from adolescence to adulthood. The definition of the life stage varies with the historical period under investigation; with the setting, whether urban or rural, and with the social and economic status of the individual labeled child, adolescent, or adult. In order to understand or define the periods, reference must be made to the adjacent life stage (or stages, in the case of adolescence). The boundaries marking entry into the adolescent period are, on the whole, more difficult to establish than are those marking the transition out of it.[16] For exit markers, for instance, one might cite concrete behaviors, such as assuming adult roles, including that of spouse, or adult attributes, such as economic independence, or even folkloric definitions, such as "doing a man's job."

Since culture may play a larger role than biology in shaping the adolescent experience, some basic questions concerning the relationship between society and adolescents arise. A natural tension exists between the aspirations of youths and the demands of adults. The adult population wants to establish a transition from adolescence to adulthood and consequently seeks to direct, train, and control adolescent behavior. The adolescent, on the other hand, seeks to establish a personal identity and independence. In the socialization process of youth, the question arises whether family, an adult-based surrogate for the family, or peers will be most influential as socializers. Elder observes that the process may be reciprocal, with youth to some extent educating adults.[17]

It is perhaps the question of influence that most distinguishes between adolescence then and now. No full-fledged youth subculture in which peers were the chief influence on an adolescent's life existed in the Middle Ages. While youth occasionally rioted, dressed in distinctive styles, and had some holidays reserved for its own fun, these activites were neither organized nor pervasive cultural events, as they became in late-nineteenth- and twentieth-century Europe and America. There was no "youth culture," as opposed to a broader societal culture; nor were there "juvenile delinquency" and "juvenile sentencing," as opposed to adult criminal behavior and punishment. Mature and married adults, the "sad and wise," did not aspire to become "wild and wanton" in imitation of carefree youth. To have a real youth culture, youth must have both independent income from wages and freedom to decide how to dispose of its leisure time.[18] London youth, as we shall see, had neither. The young lived in a master's household and relied on wages that the master controlled. They had neither extensive discretionary powers over their living arrangements nor personal wealth.

Left out of these approaches to the study of childhood and adolescence are gender differences. For instance, Turner posits a series of binaries that contrast the characteristics of the period of liminality and those of the "status system"—that is, behavior permitted the mature. His binary discriminations—"silence/speech, absence of property/property, sexual continence/sexuality"—well describe the differences between the male adolescent and the male adult in medieval society.[19] But if one adds a gendered reading to Turner's binaries, they prove less useful. Like the medieval "ages of man" literature, they describe a male experience. For males, a number of rituals demarcated entry into higher levels of society. Patrician males went through more ceremonial passages than did lower-status males. But the ceremonials and realities of passage were greater for even lower-class males than for females.

Females did not fall into the easy opposition of neophyte or initiate. For women, for instance, Turner's binary of absence of property or property ownership was largely meaningless. A woman's property passed from one male holder to another when she married. Silence or speech was a matter of degree, rather than license. Women, whether they were adolescents or adults, were to be reticent. An adult woman's voice might be more prominent in the home or even in a small business, but it did not have access to the public forum to which a male was entitled. Likewise, the binary of domestic space or public space was less significant for females because it changed only by degree. Young women moved from one domestic, household setting to another either by marrying or by becoming apprentices or servants. Their space was primarily that of the house and the city quarter, not that of the larger marketplace.

The most significant change for females was related to their sexual availability. The binary of sexuality was far more complex for females than simply continence or sexuality, because females' very entry into physical puberty changed their moral and market status. With the most common female exit from adolescence being marriage, control over girls' sexuality took on major significance. Adults, as we shall see, sought to manipulate female sexuality in ways that they did not with males. Whereas for males, sexuality was only one variable in the adolescent experience, for females, it became the central theme defining the adolescent years. It was a quality that could be marketed in marriage, illicit fornication, and seduction or sold in prostitution. Medieval society clearly saw loss of virginity as a passage, but not necessarily one that brought respect or adult status.

My process of investigation is eclectic. I have used sociology and anthropology where they help in seeking for definitions and categories. I have not, however, forced my material into the preconceived categories of those disciplines. The record sources of London and literary remains have ample information and opinions of their own. I will be looking at the differences of experience for young people in a distant past, as well as at similarities to the present. I do not anticipate that I can eliminate all biases, but I bring to this study considerable knowledge of late medieval English family life and of social history. Just as a field observer cannot leave behind his or her basic views of life while observing an alien culture, I cannot completely erase my own views, despite my knowledge of the period. I have a basic optimism about human nature that comes through. To the pessimists of the world, I suggest taking your biases into the archives as I have done and painting your own pictures in darker hues.

Sources for Studying Childhood and Youth

The literary and archival sources for this study are diverse and very rich. The brief description here is intended to introduce the reader to the major sources so that they appear as familiar faces rather than as aliens when they pop up in the text.

Late medieval England, as I have said, had a certain preoccupation with the stages of life and with the need to groom youth for adult roles. In the language of the times, youth were to become "sad [serious] and wise." In order to define the expected behavior, late medieval writers revived a considerable medical literature, stretching back to the Greeks, on the planets, seasons, and humors that governed human development. Since the savants did not keep this knowledge to themselves, it appeared in a range of literary texts that either moralistically or humorously took up the theme of the "ages of man." Some of this literature is full of platitudes such as one finds in the famous scene from *Hamlet* that contains Polonius's advice to Laertes. Other writings are very religious in their warnings. Plays, poems, books of advice, and proverbs all speak to the follies and foibles defining each age and offer suggested remedies.[20] Chronicles, the usual literary sources of historians, have little to say about children or youth unless, like Richard II, they are somehow notable.

Court record materials are remarkably rich for medieval London. When one takes into account the destruction caused by the Great Fire of London in the seventeenth century and the bombings of World War II, much has survived. Probably more was lost through later generations' failure to place value on the records and, therefore, to take care of them. London officials at the time, however, showed a remarkable interest in preserving records of their courts because they referred to them and, on occasion, used them as precedents for determining other cases. A London mayor, for instance, had the major documents of the city recorded in the *Liber Albus* (a book bound in white), so that they would be readily available. While the courts dealt with much routine business, many of the decisions reflect "executive sessions" in which the mayor and aldermen discussed the evidence and the implications of particular cases, delving into the history of the events and the precedents for guidance on how to resolve the disputes. A historian, therefore, often has much more than the bare bones of the case; the background of the parties to the dispute may be available as well as the history of the friction and ordinances that might apply. The record sources fall into basic categories. Those that derived from the activities of the civic authorities are housed in the Corporation of London Record Office, near the heart of the Old City.[21] Reading these records leaves one with the impression that the mayor and the aldermen were busy listening to citizens' complaints from morning to night. In the fourteenth and fifteenth centuries, the Husting Court (meaning a court held inside) met on Mondays and Tuesdays to hear land transactions, including the registration of wills involving bequests of land and the registration of deeds. The other branch of the Husting Court was common pleas. It was to this court that a widow seeking to recover her dower would come. The Husting Court's business became so great with the increase in population that two days were not enough to hear all the cases, so the mayor and the aldermen heard cases involving personal actions, debts, and other causes of action on other days of the week. This was the origin of the mayor's court, whose records yield much information on violations of apprenticeship and service contracts. In addition, the mayor, aldermen, and chamberlain formed a council that decided a wide variety of business matters and examined records. Their decisions are collected in the Letter Books, so named because they were catalogued according to the letters of the alphabet. The Letter Books provide the rich information on orphans that appears in this book, as well as information on age of marriage and on apprenticeship. Finally, the coroners' rolls, which recorded the proceedings of inquests into homicide, suicide, and accidental death, have contributed vivid narratives and valuable insights into incidents in individual children's and adolescents' lives as they ended in tragedy.[22]

The Guildhall Library Archive has a diverse collection of records. Many of the medieval guild records were burned in the Great Fire because they were kept in their respective guildhalls, but some of the surviving ones are in the Guildhall Library. In addition, some ecclesiastical records have been deposited there, including manuscripts of the last wills and testaments from the London Consistory Court and the Archdeaconry Court. These wills are interesting because they are often of people on the lower end of the economic scale; some were even paupers. A wealthy Londoner, in addition to dividing real estate in the Husting Court, might make a will in one of the other courts for other bequests. For the late medieval period, the proceedings of the London Consistory Court are available. They deal with issues of defamation and debt and with moral issues, such as prostitution and fornication. They provide information on the risks that servant girls ran in the households in which they served and paint a Boswellian picture of sex in London's alleys.

The Public Record Office contains the wills of London citizens whose ownership of property all over England was recorded in the Prerogative Court of Canterbury. These people, of course, tended to be quite wealthy. Some late-fifteenth-century room-by-room inventories, taken at the death of London citizens, are also preserved. They prove very valuable to anyone investigating the material environment of households of varying wealth. But the most interesting of the late-fourteenth- and fifteenth-century materials relating to London are the petitions to the Chancellor. One could petition for a special hearing by the Chancery if all other recourse in other courts had failed or if other courts would not hear the case. These petitions contain the heart-wrenching stories of both fools and unfortunates. In providing a sense of the disputes in which people found themselves, they rival the coroners' rolls. They contain a wealth of information on marriage contracts, courtship, apprenticeship and service contracts, and other social and economic contracts. Because they are written in English instead of Latin, they give the reader a sense of the way people narrated their own pathetic tales or did so with the assistance of a professional, experienced scribe.[23]

Literary and archival sources have a common failing as providers of a complete picture of society. They are better and fuller in their accounts of the activities of elite and middle-class males and are particularly weak in their accountings of the lives of the lower classes and of women in general. Seeking the female voice is often an exercise in what our literary colleagues would call listening for silences and looking for absences. Why are these voices not here? One theme of this book will be that the female voice is frequently a subtext to the main events and narrative of the social history of medieval London. There are times, however, when the female voice is very strong. Widowed mothers were favored in London law as guardians of their children and were much sought after for remarriage. In general, as already noted, female sexuality tends to move women from a subtext to a major market commodity. I have endeavored to bring women into the mainstream of this book, but I have realized that a separate book on women in London will prove to be a better way to give a more complete picture of their lives.

The Historical Context

We have moved far from pageants and parades, away from rituals that all Londoners enjoyed. So much of London life was lived in public that such ceremonies provide a good backdrop for outlining the history of London society in the late Middle Ages. The royal entries were only part of the pageantry. Mumming at Christmas, the boy bishops at St. Nicholas's Day and throughout the Christmas season, Shrove Tuesday, Easter, St. John's Eve and the Midsummer Watch, and the Lord Mayor's inauguration, to name but a few highlights, occasioned citywide celebrations. In addition, guilds celebrated their patron saints' days with parades in livery and with feasts. Individuals planned more or less elaborate funerals, weddings, and christenings. London knew how to parade, pageant, and party.

Holidays were a time of leisure, profit, advertisement of guild crafts, and establishment of social hierarchies within the city. For apprentices and schoolboys, they were days without tedious chores and endless lessons, since shops and schools were closed. For younger children, they were times of indulgence when sweets were available. Even poor children could hope for some extra tips and treats because the benefactors would be in generous moods when they paid urchins to run errands for them. The young street vendors of everything from apples to eels could hope for a good profit from the crowds who came to watch the parade. Young cut-purses saw parades as golden opportunities.

Youths who wanted to strut about in their fine clothing could do so without reprimands from their masters on a parade day. Their masters themselves were dressed almost royally in their dazzling red and white or red and black liveries, as were the mayor and aldermen. A parade day was a time of inordinate show, of feasting, of giving, of pomp and circumstance, of profit. It was also a time of drunken revelry, when fountains spouted wine and the conduits that carried the city water ran with wine, as well. Taverns were stocked with beer. It was a time when the haves made their exalted position clear to the have-nots. To wear livery, to meet the king, to feast, to be conspicuous consumers of luxury set off the elite from the craftsmen, yeomen, apprentices, servants, and poor of London. London was a very hierarchical society, and the elite had many ways of enforcing its dominant position.

Men organized these grand spectacles, but what did the pageants and parades mean to women? Women's space was the home and the quarter. Did they go to Cheapside or to St. Paul's to see the parade? Were these special occasions for them as well as for men? In the pageantry that celebrated Richard II's coronation in 1377 and the arrival of his bride in 1382, beautiful young virgins had some ceremonial roles. The women in the vending business enjoyed the profits from parades, just as the young men did; the women of the elite, surrounded by servants and dressed in their finest clothing and furs, observed the parades. Sometimes they joined their husbands in royal welcomes to London. It was they who directed the servants for the feasts, but they sat at the table among the silver plate, rather than cooking the dishes. The pageants and parades were also a time of risk for women. For the prostitutes who hoped to meet drunken revelers to ply their trade, parades offered opportunity, but for the many servant girls going about errands in the streets or even waiting on drunken masters, guests, and fellow servants, the possibility of sexual attack increased.

When Richard II was crowned in 1377, London was enjoying a period of optimism. The plague, which had been bad in 1368 and 1369, had receded. That plague had hit the young particularly hard.[24] The old king, Edward III, was finally gone, and so was that awful woman Alice Perriers, his mistress. The city government was in good order. A constitutional change approved by the "Good" Parliament of 1376 authorized the election of the Common Council by the guilds, rather than by the wards. The guilds had been playing an increasingly major role in politics, so this change was not surprising. Nicholas Brembre, a grocer, was mayor.[25] The war with France was in remission, perhaps for good. London had reason to be optimistic for the future and could afford a fine celebration.

The political realities had changed substantially when Anne of Bohemia entered London as Richard's bride in 1382. London was in the midst of a power struggle between the elite and the lesser guilds. In 1381 the Great Revolt, led by Wat Tyler, had brought a rabble of peasants from the countryside into London, and Londoners had joined with them in settling old political, economic, and social scores. Flemings had been harassed and killed. John of Gaunt's great palace, the Savoy, had been burned to the ground, along with its great wealth, and the king's chief advisers had been hunted down, even in the Tower of London, and their heads put up on

London Bridge. King Richard, a lad of sixteen, had averted further destruction by and to London citizens. Riding about on horseback in the company of Mayor Walworth, he had met with the rebels, heard their requests, and urged them to go home. Mayor Walworth had accompanied him to Smithfield for a parley with Wat Tyler. When it appeared that Tyler would not leave, Walworth had pulled him from his horse, and a squire had killed him. As the rebels had angrily approached the king's small party, Richard had taken charge, telling them that he was their leader. Walworth, meanwhile, had returned to London and brought troops. The rebels had dispersed with promises of pardon.

It was, then, as a hero that young Richard could conduct his bride through the capital in 1382. The scars of burnings were still evident, and the memories of the rebel crowds filling Cheapside, inflamed by John Ball's sermons on the lack of equality between rich and poor, were vivid. London's constitutional fights between the elites and the commoners had reached a new and serious level. The pageantry that accompanied Anne's entry into London served as a reaffirmation of order reestablished in the realm, if not in the city.[26]

The century preceding the pageants had seen a number of other parades and political upheavals. At the beginning of the fourteenth century, Edward I had brought his queen, Eleanor of Castile, back to London for burial, erecting a cross in her honor at each resting place. Charing Cross was, for Londoners, the most significant, the last and closest to their walls. Many later parades included a show at this spot. Edward II's reign had brought wars with the Scots that cost Londoners money, but the political unrest during his reign was more disruptive. Revolts against his abuses of power culminated in 1326 with the arrival of Isabella, his queen, and Roger Mortimer, her paramour, who acted in the name of young Edward, Isabella's son by Edward II. Although the couple was welcomed by London and received its support in the overthrow of Edward II, their decision to order a general release of prisoners caused problems for London. At least Edward III had proved a decent king for London. The wars with France were costly for Londoners, but the profits to the city were also great because it provided the supplies for the wars and acted as the chief center for the taxation and sale of wool (the staple) that Edward III imposed as part of his economic embargo on Flanders.

But tragic pageants were also London's lot. London was not immune from the famines of 1315 to 1317 or even from the milder one of the early 1320s. London's coroners recorded that on July 3, 1322, a multitude of poor people were waiting for a distribution of alms from a bequest by Henry de Fingrie, a fishmonger; fifty-two men, women, and children were crushed to death. Prison inmates, who were dependent on alms for their food, died of starvation and disease in great numbers during these years.[27] Spread by the bite of a flea living on the common house rat (*Ratus ratus*, a scientific name with a redundant ring), the plague of 1348 hit London, with its crowded living conditions, as only the wrath of bacterial infection can when no immunity is present. As we see in Chapter 2, Londoners made great efforts to keep the city clean, but the rat population thrived nonetheless. Once the plague—the Black Death—started, it carried off perhaps 50 percent of the population. The burial of the dead was without ceremony, except for the rude lead crosses that have been recovered from the mass graves of the plague's victims.[28]

One reads of the disruption that the plague caused for both the haves and the have-nots in 1349 and 1350. All Londoners were exposed to flea bites, so all had a more or less equal chance in the lottery of death. Among the propertied, the number of wills recorded in the Husting Court increased substantially, and telltale phrases creep in—"If she should die, then her portion to . . ." and "Wardship of the children given to my wife should she survive, if not . . ." One also reads that servants and workers suddenly saw the marvelous working of supply and demand and started charging higher wages as a consequence of the depletion in their numbers.

Influencing the relationship between master and servant was the Statute of Laborers, which attempted to control prices and wages. The king's council had responded swiftly to the increased demands of workers in 1349, approving the Ordinance of Laborers (made a statute in 1351), which tried to counter the law of supply and demand by fixing prices and labor costs at their 1347 levels. Enforcement efforts were futile and hated. For urban craftsmen, the statute meant that they were to sell goods at 1347 prices even though they might have to pay higher wages to workers. For laborers, both skilled and unskilled, it meant that they were mandated to accept the same rate of pay as that prevailing in 1347, when an overabundance of laborers had led to lower wages. In the end, few masters were prosecuted under the statute, but laborers and servants risked arrest and fines for violations.[29] The statute, as we shall see, became a way of manipulating service, with masters accusing servants not only of breaking contracts but of violating the statute.

The fear of death hung over the city from 1348 on. The plague returned with each generation, if not more frequently. It was disconcerting and worrisome; women and children retreated to country estates when possible, and businessmen left town, leaving their servants, apprentices, and business factors in charge. From the city's viewpoint, the fact that those aged twenty-five to thirty-five were more likely than older citizens to be killed by the plague meant that both the most skilled and those most likely to reproduce biologically had a greater risk of dying. As if the plague were not enough of a calamity, other diseases—including various fevers and sweating sicknesses, fluxes, tuberculosis, and smallpox—carried off large numbers. Children, of course, were very susceptible to diseases that caused diarrhea and that led to rapid dehydration and death.

Life was fragile. One could react in a number of ways: with great sorrow, with morbid curiosity about death, with humble or grandiose plans for a funeral, with grand living today for tomorrow the devil takes it all away, with extreme piety and spiritual exercises for salvation, or with membership in guilds dedicated to a communal salvation of the soul. All these alternatives required their own ceremonies and parades. Pilgrimages were popular. Pious processions of parish guilds on their patron saints' days, religious offerings, and feasts of celebration were characteristic of the period.[30] But for the most part, people got on with living, demonstrating that wonderful human capability of hoping to beat the odds.

The possibility of death, particularly for children, was uppermost in Londoners' minds and played itself out, as it often does, in gambling. Robert Duplage, a tailor in London, petitioned to the Chancellor that William Chapell, a London knight, citizen, and alderman, and he were a company "among other idle and merry sport" when William said that "he would deliver a gold ring to Robert worth no more than 13*s.* 4*d.* on the condition that he would be bound that when his wife, Joan, deceased he would live sole, unmarried and then William would never demand of him the ring." Apparently the game went on, because a second petition admitted of an additional wager of a gold ring worth 13*s.* 4*d.* The parties agreed that if any son of Robert lived to the age of twenty-eight, Robert should pay. To the first case, Robert said that the wager was made in "game and disport," and he agreed to return the ring "with due consideration" because his wife had died and he had remarried. He also lost the second bet because his son survived to the requisite age. He claimed that he was "unlettered and did not realize the bond he was sealing."[31] His was the fortune and the misfortune of having a son who lived beyond adolescence during those perilous years. Apparently, he, his tormentor, and his son survived the plague, but his first wife did not.

The depopulation of London by the plague and by other diseases had a profound influence on London's children and youth. We will see that the orphan population increased for a time in the fourteenth century, but as depopulation continued and the wealth of the survivors—both widows and children—became more and more concentrated, the remarriage of widows with children and the early marriage of orphans became matters of intense bargaining.

Depopulation both in London and in the countryside in the aftermath of the plague and other diseases created a shortage of young people. But the evidence concerning the age of entry into service and into apprentice-ship is counterintuitive. One would assume that depopulation and the availability of high wages and apprenticeships in London would act as magnets for young men and women from the countryside, encouraging them to abandon the peasant life. In fact, the opposite occurred. Age of entry into apprentice positions increased during the late fourteenth and the fifteenth centuries. So desperate was the demand for labor in the countryside that kin and parents who would have normally encouraged careers in London for younger sons and daughters kept them home to work for the family in their fields and businesses until the sons and daughters were in their late teens. The London craftsmen and merchants, on the other hand, rather enjoyed the profits to be gained by the reduced competition for the smaller markets. Wealth became concentrated in the hands of fewer and fewer people. But there was a nagging problem of a lack of cheap, skilled labor as a result of the shrinking pool of available youth. One solution, as we shall see, was to employ foreigners, particularly Flemings. But the foreigners were resented, and massacres occurred in 1381 and later. The London elites accommodated their requirements to country terms; they raised the age of entry into apprenticeships to sixteen and then to eighteen, required more education, and extended the term of apprenticeship to ten years, with two additional years as "bachelor" in the service of the master. The advantage was on their side, as well as on that of their country cousins. It was easier to train an older boy, and the longer term, with the added two years of "bachelor" work, meant that masters could be assured of skilled labor for twelve years. For the youth in question, it meant a delay in entry into adulthood.

As the fifteenth century progressed, London's society was increasingly dominated by a small group of the very wealthy. The powerful guilds—Mercers, Grocers, Drapers, Fishmongers, Goldsmiths—vied with one another for control of the positions of mayor, sheriff, and alderman. London was moving toward a government dominated by livery companies.

The fifteenth-century political upheavals put London in a precarious position. Throughout the struggles for the throne in the fifteenth century, London welcomed each successive victor in the Wars of the Roses. On the one hand, it was a disaster to give a ceremonial welcome to a contender who would become a loser in the next round of fighting; on the other hand, it was risky not to recognize the winner with a magnificent parade and gifts. London's elite preserved the city for the "wild and wanton" who would eventually become "sad and wise" with the right nurturing and training so that they could take over the city, defend its rights, and celebrate its greatness with pageants.

The overhanging houses of medieval London streets. (Drawing by Wayne M. Howell, from *Old England: A Pictorial Museum of Popular Antiquities* [London, 1845], vol. 1, p. 365)

2

The Material Environment
of London's Youth

Glowing descriptions of medieval London abound, beginning with Fitz-stephen's from the twelfth century.[1] But looking at the city through the eyes of its children and youth gives a different perspective on the city and on the material conditions within it. The London that most children knew was an intimate one that included their house or tenement rooms, their street (which was also their play area), and their parish. This microcosm must be our first vantage point as we investigate the London of young children. As the children, particularly the boys, grew, their perambulations could take them farther afield, as they went to school or began to be useful for errands. The city walls extended for 2 miles and 608 feet and enclosed only a little more than 1 square mile.[2] One has a sense of an intimate environment in which one could walk from the Tower to Ludgate in about half an hour.

Most of the young people inhabiting the city, however, did not grow up in it, and their initial view of the city was quite different from that of people who had been born there. London, like the other cities of medieval Europe, did not replace its own population as a result of the prevalence of disease, delayed marriage, and high infant mortality. It relied on recruits from the countryside for its servants and apprentices. In the view of these young people, London must have looked vast. They could enter London through one of the seven gates, gates so huge that two of them, Newgate and Ludgate, had prisons in them; the others served as dwellings. If they came from the south, they would have seen a panorama as they approached the city, with St. Paul's dominating the skyline. They would have crossed London Bridge, with its 138 shops.[3] Once in the city, they might well have found it oppressively and confusingly crowded. (In the years before the plague of 1348, London had an estimated population of between 40,000 and 60,000, or higher. After the plague, the population dropped and remained low, reaching perhaps 50,000 in 1485.[4]) Most of the young men and women who came to London were from villages of perhaps 200 people, and even if they came from York or Norwich, they would have left towns with populations of only about 12,000.

As we describe the material environment of youth in fourteenth- and fifteenth-century London, we must keep both perspectives in mind: that of the neighborhood and that of the larger metropolis. Throughout this book, we will try to see London through the eyes of its young people.

Housing

The size of young Londoners' houses or tenements and the amenities in them varied considerably, depending on the wealth of the youths' parents, guardians, or master. In the beginning of the fourteenth century, houses were arranged on plots in essentially three different configurations. The large houses of prosperous merchants had courtyards. The front of the property (perhaps 30 or 40 feet of street frontage) had a range of buildings containing shops and other rental units. The proprietor might use one of these shops, but he or she could rent out the others at considerable profit. As a visitor entered the courtyard, he or she would find the large hall and other buildings of the owner or renter directly ahead. The second configuration, typically used for narrower properties, was an L shape, with the frontage use being similar to that for larger properties, but with the hall placed at a right angle and extending back along the property line. The courtyard occupied the other part of the property. The third configuration, used for the smallest properties, included street frontage with a shop, a room behind, and a kitchen in a small courtyard; there might be no courtyard at all.

Record sources give us considerable information about living arrangements. For instance, in 1384 a lease for a group of houses on the Thames specified that the lessee would build a range of buildings along the street that would be three stories high, with the individual stories measuring 12 feet by 10 feet and reaching 7 feet in height. Behind this street frontage, he was to build a hall measuring 40 feet by 23 feet, a parlor, a kitchen, and a buttery. Underneath the structures would be cellars 7 feet high for storage of merchandise. Three-story houses, especially on the main streets, were typical in the fourteenth and fifteenth centuries.[5] Another lease for 100 years at £12 a year required the tenant to build new housing 40 feet high facing the street, with three stories measuring 12, 10, and 8 feet high, respectively. In addition, he was to build a chief dwelling place with a hall measuring 40 feet by 24 feet, a parlor, a kitchen, and a buttery. All these buildings were to be made of heart of oak (the most durable building material) and to have cellars to the depth of 12 feet.[6] Wattle and daub filled the space between the timber framing, although, by the fifteenth century, brick had come into use. For a more luxurious appearance, some houses had façades of stone.

Concern about fire, obstruction of public passages, nuisances, and the tempers of the citizens prompted the first mayor of London to issue what amounted to a building code in 1189. The walls between adjoining buildings were to be 3 feet thick and were to extend up to the gables which were to point toward the street. Aumbries (arches in the wall for larders) could be only 1 foot in depth. Roofs were to be made of slate, stone, or, later, tile, because thatching posed a fire hazard. Outside stairways and ladders were used to reach the various levels of the houses because each level could be used as a freehold or an independent tenement. To prevent disagreements between neighbors over waste water, latrines, and windows overlooking one another's property, Fitzalwyne's assize set regulations that the city enforced through the Assize of Nuisance.[7]

An apprentice arriving in London from the countryside would have been struck by the height and density of the houses. To someone used to low buildings scattered about closes in peasant villages, the London streets must have felt like canyons, with their overhanging buildings and a forest of signs spreading over them horizontally like tree branches. A contemporary poem described the "[d]yvers sygnys hih and lowe / Wher-by that men ther crafft mak knowe." Lions, eagles, griffins, and other painted animal motifs were common on signs. Taverns put out boughs of green or fresh bunches of straw. The city finally had to regulate the length of the poles supporting the signs, decreeing that they could be no more than 7 feet long.[8] To gain extra room in the upper stories, projections called penthouses started 9 feet up from street level (high enough so that a man on horseback could ride under them). The shops on the ground floor also projected into the streets when their horizontally shuttered windows were opened for business. Stalls for exposing wares could extend no more than 2½ feet into the street and were supposed to be movable.[9]

A few preserved inventories from the end of the fifteenth century permit us to form an intimate view of the halled houses, with their parlors, chambers, kitchens, butteries, shops, and storehouses. The new apprentice, passing through an entrance between the shops facing the street, would have seen his master's hall directly across the courtyard. If the apprentice had arrived at Richard Bele's house in the 1480s, he would have been ushered into the hall, which probably had a raised eating area at one end furnished with benches made comfortable with six luxurious Flemish-tapestry cushions. The walls were hung with cloth painted with designs and, as was typical in these halls, with old weaponry. Furniture was sparse, consisting of a few chairs and stools and a folding table made in London. A container for holy water hung by the door. A fireplace, burning either wood or coal, heated the room.[10] The apprentice's tour of his new surroundings would have included a look at the shop, with its axes, cleavers, knives, tubs, scales, and weights. This type of shop was typical and—be it a butcher's, baker's, or candlestick maker's—could be managed by a master and one or two apprentices. A journeyman might also work with them if demand was high enough. The buttery and the kitchen contained such luxuries as candlesticks, pewter pots, and a chafing dish. Most of the valuables in Bele's house were kept in the chief chamber (master bedroom) in chests and cupboards. The house also included a sparsely furnished room for a maid and, finally, the garret, where the apprentice might sleep and which was also sparsely furnished, with old and broken furnishings.[11]

Bele's estate was modest (amounting to 65s. 8d.) compared with that of Sir Matthew Phyllyp, who was an alderman. Phyllyp had a richly furnished and tapestried hall and a parlor for more intimate conversation. This private room contained such pleasant amenities as two cupboards for displaying plate, a bird cage, a looking glass, and a book, *The Chronicles of London*. Phyllyp had at least three chambers in addition to the chief chamber.[12] But the grandest housing for the merchant princes of London resembled palaces, such as that of the grocer Crosby, who built Crosby Hall.[13]

Many types of more modest living arrangements were available, including shops with living quarters, rented rooms (particularly garrets), and impermanent shacks erected against walls and buildings. By the time of Edward II, annual rents were 40s. or less. Parish churches rented various properties that had been left to them in pious bequests. The churchwardens' accounts for one church from the late fifteenth century indicate that annual rents varied from 8s. to £4 in that period. The houses ranged from one with eighteen rooms to some with one or two rooms.[14]

The drama of life (and death) in one of the solar or garret rooms comes through clearly in a coroners' inquest. Robert de Keng, a cordwainer, his wife, Matilda, and their two sons, William and John, had gone to bed "in a certain high solar." Matilda had fixed a lighted candle to the wall; a little before midnight, the candle fell on the bed of Robert and Matilda and set the whole house afire. Robert and William were caught immediately in the fire and perished, and Matilda and John escaped with great difficulty.[15] One can imagine the problems of being caught in a fire on the third floor, with a steep stairway or a ladder as the only exit. Straw was the normal sleeping pallet for the poor who inhabited the solars, and the floors might also be covered with straw or rushes.

Rent of a room, since the room did not contain a kitchen, usually included board as well. In the mid-fourteenth century, a landlord complained that a man and his wife had "lived at his table" for three months and owed him 34s., or about 11s. a month for room and board. An inn room in the same period could cost as little as 1$\frac{1}{2}$d. a day. In a fifteenth-century suit, a woman paid 6d. a week for room and board.[16]

As in modern cities, the homeless were also a presence. Children learned early the custom of giving alms to the poor who stood at church doors. The poor paid for these privileged positions. Margaret Kind, who occupied a bench at St. Andrew Hubbard, paid 2s. a year to the church-wardens for the privilege.[17] Alice de Goldenlant, a pauper and beggar, had a lean-to by the wall of a chapel and died of disability in this makeshift abode.[18] Squatters were also a problem, breaking into unoccupied property and staying there against the will of the owner.[19]

Such living arrangements had a number of social implications for the growing child. First, it meant that the rich, middling, and poor might all live on the same property or on the same street. From early in life, children mixed with a varied population. Second, although some children were reared in commodious surroundings akin to palaces, the majority grew up in two rooms and a kitchen, or perhaps even less space. Apprentices, family, and servants shared the space. Probably few children had rooms of their own. Thomas Cowper, a stockfishmonger whose probate is dated 1488, apparently had his children with him in the chief chamber, in which there was a little feather bed with a bolster and a cradle with an old pillow.[20]

The crowded living conditions also presented their share of tensions in which children, apprentices, and servants might well become embroiled. In 1473, the Goldsmiths' guild had a difficult time mediating a quarrel between Edward of Bowden and David Panter. Their living arrangements were partly to blame, since one disputant and his family lived above the other. Finally, the wardens of the Goldsmiths' decreed that in the future neither man should stop up the other's gutters or drains or cause his wife or servants to do so:

And because the house of the said Davy is over the shop of the said
Edward . . . and the said Davy shall not willfully of malice, he or his
servants cast or pour on his floor any water or other liquor to run or drop
down into the said Edward's shop, not make a dunning [loud noise] with
hewing wood. Nor cast down water or dust out of the window upon the
said Edward's stall.

Each was to have a key to the front door, and the door was not to be bolted
against the other household. Furthermore, the guild would install in each
dwelling a bell hanging in a convenient place so that the disputants could
summon the members of the guild if one or the other started the affray
again. If a dispute broke out again, the one injured was "to suffer and keep
silence, whatever be said or done, except bodily hurt" and to report the
incident to the warden.[21]

The closely packed housing and the shared space also reflects on the
sanitary conditions in which the children grew up and explains why so
many of them did not survive childhood. While the city ordinances regulated the placement of latrines and stipulated that their walls be lined with
stone, too often the latrines proved to be a nuisance to neighbors or were
placed too close to wells.

Children probably received their initial toilet training either in the
freedom of yards or streets or, for the more refined, on chamber pots
("jakes," as they are called in the probate inventories). Privies constituted
the second phase of toilet training. Cesspits with their privies might be
located in yards, or under houses in cellar floors. These latrines could be
terrifying to a young child because the holes revealed a dark, smelly pit.
One can imagine children sitting on the edge of the bench, worried about
falling in. Even adults occasionally fell in. Poor Richard le Rakiere, who,
according to his surname, must have made his living pushing the muck
down London streets, died by his trade. He was seated on a latrine in his
house when the planks, being rotten, gave way, and he fell in and
drowned. Some houses had privies located in or off the solars, with
wooden chutes (called pipes) connecting them to the cesspit.[22] Some of
these privies were cleansed with runoff water from roofs. Alice Wade had
an illegal arrangement in which she connected the seat of a privy in her
solar to a gutter that ran under the house of a neighbor, who was bothered
by the stench.

Londoners felt strongly that their privies should afford them privacy.
When some of their neighbors removed parts of the roof of a shared privy,
Andrew de Aubrey and his wife complained that the extremities of those
seated on the privy could now be seen, "a thing which is abominable and
altogether intolerable."[23]

Stench from privies was a continual problem. Privies had to be cleaned about every two years; "gong farmers" did the job at night. The cost of cleaning a privy in the late fifteenth century was 2*s.* a ton, and for the cleaning of one privy the churchwardens recorded a 10*s.* expense plus 16*d.* to have the muck carted off in a dung boat.[24] If one adds the dirt of poultry, pigs, dogs, and horses, as well as kitchen waste, the filth generated by London's households was considerable.

Neighborhoods: Streets, Parishes, and Wards

With living space cramped, one would expect that children and adults alike would spend time in the streets. As we discuss the activities of youth, we will find that, indeed, this was so. Playing, carousing, soliciting, pimping, working, and carrying on business deals were often done in the streets. The next most common place of public encounter was a tavern or church, of which the city boasted many. During the day, therefore, the streets were crowded. But were they clean?

For the most part, refuse from the households found its way into the streets. The wider streets had gutters running down each side that were to carry away the runoff rainwater from roofs, as well as the contents of chamberpots, kitchen refuse, and other waste. Narrower streets had only one gutter. Streets also served as an alternative to latrines, although the city provided public latrines. Richard Whittington, of storybook fame, left money for a latrine that provided two rows of sixty-four seats each, one for men and one for women. The latrines were located where they would be flushed out by the tide.[25]

In spite of municipal provisions, people found it inconvenient to climb down the ladders from upper stories to go to the latrines. We have already related in Chapter 1 the story of the servant who "rose naked from his bed and stood at a window of the solar 30 ft. high to relieve himself towards the High Street" and fell to his death.[26]

The city of London went to considerable efforts to keep its streets clean, not relying on rainwater alone to wash away the filth. Rakers regularly cleaned the streets, and the city provided carts and rented "gong boats" for removing the refuse. Londoners took an active role in city cleanliness. In 1299, two citizens reprimanded a groom of the prince for relieving himself in a lane rather than going to a public privy, which would have been "more decent."[27] For the most part, the system seems to have worked well, but in the period following the Black Death, the streets apparently did become dirtier. Although not clean by our standards, the

streets that children played in were perhaps not as filthy as modern my-
thology about medieval times would have them.[28]

While the city and its citizens tried to manage the refuse and the filth,
rats, mice, and bacteria could not be eradicated. One of the churchwardens' accounts tells of the problem of rats eating holes in prayer books
and even in the altar cloth. To try to control the rodents, the wardens paid
4d. to the rat taker for milk and "rattisbane."[29] It is no wonder that the
plague in 1348 was so devastating.

To better preserve order in its crowded streets, London had a curfew
at night and provided for the wards to patrol the streets to see that it was
enforced. Curfew was rung on the bells of St. Mary-le-Bow, All Hallows
Barking, St. Bride in Fleet Street, and St. Giles Cripplegate at perhaps nine
or ten o'clock. All city gates closed, and taverns were also to close. People
wandering on the streets were challenged by the ward patrols.[30] But some
people, apprentices and servants among them, often defied the curfew in
pursuit of revelry. Thus about midnight on February 2, 1322, a group of
fourteen revelers came up Bradstrete "singing and shouting, as they often
did at night." When a shopkeeper asked them to be quiet so he and his
neighbors could get some rest, they responded by taunting him and daring
him to come out. When he finally did, he was armed with a staff and killed
one of the revelers.[31]

People knew one another well within their street, parish, and ward.
London had 107 parish churches by the late Middle Ages. The large number of parishes indicates a preference for neighborhood worship, a place
to be baptized, married, and buried among close friends.[32] Wills and surviving churchwardens' accounts reflect the strong attachment of parishioners to their parish churches and their clergy.[33] Our investigation of youth
begins at the parish church with the baptism of the infant and ends there
with the marriage ceremony that, for many Londoners, marked the end of
adolescence.

The largest neighborhood unit was the ward. London had twenty-
four wards until 1394, when Farringdon was divided into that Within and
that Without, making the number twenty-five. The wards, the basic gov-
ernmental and peacekeeping units of London, had initially functioned like
the hundred courts under their head men or aldermen.[34] Each ward had
an alderman and other officials, including a beadle and his sergeants. It
was at this level that the daily squabbles of inhabitants and other irritants
could be brought up in the wardmoot. The alderman presided over the
moot, which, in addition to listening to charges and complaints, registered
freemen, examined hostlers and victualers, and appointed such officials as
rakers, scavengers, and ale-conners.[35] Those wards located by the city
gates also had the responsibility of protecting the gates and of regulating

traffic. All wards had a watch that enforced the curfew, pursued suspected felons, and policed the streets. Apprentices and servants wandering at night would come to know the night watch.

The surviving wardmoots indicate that neighborhoods contained a wide social mix. Aldermen lived side by side with craftsmen and prostitutes. For instance, Lymstrete reported on January 10, 1423:

> Mawde Sheppyster keeps open shop, retails and is not a freewoman; also she is a strumpet to more than one and a bawd also. Thomas Brid is a forestaller and regrater of victuals coming to the market. John Cool is a sustainer of them in his shop. Anneys Edward, Gass Furneys, Cateryn Sprynger and Julian Blyndale are regraters of poultry and wildfowl.

In addition, the prior of Wenlok had a garden that extended 3 feet into the highway and stopped the dung and water flowing in the gutter, making it hard to walk in that part of the street. In Cripplegate Without, a stewhouse, or brothel, in Grub Street was attracting a bad sort of clientele, including priests and their concubines. Not only the stews' privies but also those of grocers and goldsmiths (high-status occupations) were common nuisances.[36]

Children, therefore, grew up in an environment that provided sharp contrasts of luxury and poverty; pious morality and drunken, depraved immorality; exhortations to cleanliness and order and surroundings full of filth and noise. Providing a "sheltered" environment for children would have taken a major effort. Instead, children were instructed on the behavior that was appropriate to their place in the social hierarchy or to that position to which their parents aspired.

The Larger City: Forays Outside the Neighborhood

London had two major centers that drew youth outside their own neighborhoods. St. Paul's Cathedral was the center of much of London life. Since it dominated the London skyline, it was an obvious place for people to meet. It played a prominent role for those conducting business deals, partly because there were taverns nearby and partly because the altars provided a convenient place for swearing to contracts. The Folkmoot for London citizens was also located near St. Paul's. On major feast days and days of celebration, the citizens came in procession to the cathedral to hear Mass. Disputes among the guilds over the most prestigious locations in processions and in St. Paul's were heated enough to cause major fights. The Mercers, for instance, took great exception to the upstart Grocers taking the Mercers' place in St. Paul's on Halloween; finally, the mayor had to arbitrate the dispute.[37]

The other focus of general civic business was Cheapside, a wide market street, and the nearby Guildhall. Children went to St. Paul's for religious processions and to Cheapside and the Guildhall for the mayor's show and for various political processions, such as the entrance of a new king or queen into London.[38]

The Guildhall, the seat of London's government, also entered into the lives of youths when they enrolled their apprenticeship. Enrolling required that the apprentice and the master go together with the apprenticeship contract to the mayor. When a London citizen with minor children died, his orphans became wards of the mayor and might appear in person to have their goods and persons assigned to guardians. When an apprentice became a citizen or an orphan came of age, he or she again went to the Guildhall to receive the symbols of his or her maturity. The mayor and the aldermen held their many courts at the Guildhall, so youths suing or being sued would appear there as well.

Other features of the city with which apprentices and servants would be familiar were the various districts in which specialized shops were located. West Cheap was the center for traders in luxury goods, such as those found in goldsmiths' shops. East Cheap was also a market center, with chandlers and other services. The quern at St. Paul's was the major corn market. Names such as Bread Street, Milk Street, the Poultry, Wood Street, Friday Street, Ironmonger Lane, Fish Market, and the Stocks Market (source of dried and fresh fish) all indicate the location of major markets for various goods. Because the slaughter of animals gave rise to problems of waste disposal, the butchers were segregated to the Shambles, located initially near Newgate but eventually moved to Smithfield.[39] Since medieval artisans and traders tended to live in or behind the shops in which they practiced their trade, the street names also indicated a concentration of residents working in particular crafts and trades.

By the fifteenth century, artisans and traders also had their own guildhalls in or close to their districts, so that they had a common meeting place and perhaps also some almshouses for elderly members. Apprentices and journeymen knew these halls well because they took their oaths in them before the guild wardens and because disputes with their masters came to the wardens for arbitration before they went to the mayor.

Pursuit of pleasure took the young people not only to the local taverns, but also across the river to Southwark for bear baiting and prostitution. For some of the young women we will meet, the taverns and stews of London and Southwark led to a life of prostitution instead of the honest service positions they undoubtedly sought when they first arrived from the countryside. Smithfield, the horse and cattle market, was also a center for horse racing, to which youths came to watch, bet, and act as jockies. Judicial punishments might lead them to go to Tyburn to witness the hanging of felons or to the Tun on Cornhill to watch the pillorying of false traders or the shaving of prostitutes' heads. To be sure that no one missed such events of public humiliation, musicians played rough music as the miscreants were paraded through the streets.[40] The meeting of Parliament in Westminster drew crowds of young people looking for diversion. The Tower of London provided a constant parade of political prisoners (including the king of France), nobles and courtiers, soldiers, judges, and high church officials.

The Thames and London Bridge were places of both work and pleasure. Many youths worked at the wharves or on London Bridge. In the fifteenth century, the mayors began to take a barge upriver to receive their office from the king, and their fine and colorful boat processions drew crowds. Of course, there was also the diversion of viewing traitors' heads on poles at the entrance to London Bridge.

Monasteries and hospitals played a large role in some London youths' lives. For sons and daughters of wealthy citizens who aspired to a religious life, they were appropriate establishments with which to affiliate. They were close to town and well endowed by London citizens; one almost surely had a relative among the monks and nuns. For the poor, including children, they were a source of alms. Large, extramural monasteries and hospitals—such as Clerkenwell Nunnery, Charter House, and St. Bartholomew's Priory and Hospital, northwest of Aldgate—drew considerable patronage. In addition, a few of the more urban-oriented orders established themselves in the city proper during the thirteenth century. The Franciscan (Gray) friars, Whitefriars (Carmelites), and Augustinian (Austin) friars all acquired property within the city for chapels, cloisters, and other monastic buildings. The Franciscan establishment was very grand and became the preferred burial place of the nobility and of wealthy Londoners in the thirteenth century. The Blackfriars (Dominicans) acquired the site of Castle Baynard and built such a large monastery that they had to tear down the city wall on the west to accommodate it.

The crowded conditions within the walls did not preclude large gardens, nor did they drive Londoners to create extensive suburbs. The roads leading into London had bars, and because some development occurred near the bars, five of the city's wards—Farringdon Without, Aldersgate, Cripplegate, Bishopsgate, and Portsoken—were outside the walls. To the west of the city, the presence of royal government in Westminster encouraged both business and residences. Bishops and nobles built their palaces along the Strand, and today the Savoy still lends its medieval name to grandeur. The presence of the Inns of Court, Fleet Prison, and the seat of royal justice fostered considerable residential development in the Holborn and Temple sections outside the walls. The presence of the Inns of Court also attracted a number of apprentice clerks, who, lacking the supervision common to other apprentices, frequently caused riots in the city. But the ring of suburban development was shallow, and city inhabitants, with their children and apprentices, often went to the country outside the walls for recreation.[41]

The Material Standard of Living

We now move from the larger outside world back into the homes that young people occupied with their families or surrogates for them (masters and guardians). This section provides a context for the more specific discussion in subsequent chapters of the provisions for children and youth.

Obviously, the degree of comfort in a home varied considerably with the wealth of the proprietor. It also varied with the time in which the home's occupants lived. In general, the quality of the houses, diets, and dress of all groups improved during the course of the fourteenth and fifteenth centuries. As terrifying as the plague was to London's population, the market response to depopulation was to increase wages for survivors and thereby encourage more investment in food, housing, and luxury goods. Thus youth coming of age in late-fourteenth- or fifteenth-century London could look forward to a much better provisioned environment than could those growing up in the early fourteenth century.

A 1332 subsidy roll gives us some idea of the relative wealth of the different wards in London and the distribution of trades in which wealth resided. Roughly speaking, the three wards on the river in east London contained the largest concentration of the wealthy mercantile class. These included vintners, fishmongers, and other long-distance traders who needed access to the quays. The shopkeepers along the Cheap to their rear formed a prosperous center, with the goldsmiths heading their ranks. To the west, workers in the trades involving butchering, tanning, and so on inhabited wards of moderate wealth. The poor tended to be on the northern and eastern fringes of the city.

To be subject to tax in 1332, a man had to have more than 10s. of movable wealth, so taxpayers came from only the well-to-do class of citizens. Considerable status differences existed within this group. Only 16 citizens had property worth more than £60; 172 had property worth between £15 and £60; and 141 had property worth between £7 10s. and £15. Members of the wealthiest group are referred to as "merchants of England"—that is, those engaged in long-distance trading. The next two groups contained some merchants, but also had a considerable number of shopkeepers, including fishmongers, goldsmiths, skinners, and practitioners of various crafts related to leatherworking. The 253 people paying on goods valued at from £3 15s. to £7 10s., the 502 with possessions valued at between £1 and £3 15s., and the 543 with possessions worth from 10s. to £1 also included butchers, ironmongers, plumbers, and other crafts people. The lower two groups also included a number of victualers and brewers.[42]

Much of the untaxed population must have had wealth below the 10s. limit, but was not poverty-stricken. In addition, for every adult male citizen, there were perhaps three Londoners who were not freemen. They were not necessarily poor people, although many of them were probably servants, street vendors, and laborers. A writ refers to them as *mediocris populi,* or people of middle condition, in the city.[43]

The number of very poor is hard to assess and probably varied with conditions. For instance, in the famines of the early fourteenth century, people seeking charity probably flocked to the city. It was during one of the famine years, 1318, that Robert de Lincoln left a bequest of 1d. for each of 2,000 poor people.[44]

Wills and the few extant probate inventories help us to form some picture of the living conditions that a child or youth might experience as a member of these different economic groups. Since the more descriptive of these documents come largely from the late fourteenth and fifteenth centuries, they help to show the change that had taken place as a result of depopulation.

The poor are, of course, the most difficult to describe. While it is easy to think of them as single, old, and decrepit and as strangers to their community, in fact, we shall meet some in the course of this book who were well integrated into their parish and their guild and who managed to raise children to adulthood. Some glimpse of their economic and social position comes from wills. As part of their attempt to provide all Christians with an opportunity to make a will, the London ecclesiastical courts recorded those of a few people that they labeled as beggars. One such woman, called simply Alice, was a beggar. Her estate, which she asked the chaplain to administer, included a bequest of 29s. to the parish church, 6s. 8d. to be distributed to paupers. Hers was the largest estate of any of the paupers. If we recall Margaret Kind, who paid 2s. a year to beg at the parish church, we can see that begging had some rewards. Another woman, the widow of a minstrel, was described as a pauper. She left the residue of her estate to another minstrel and asked to be buried next to her husband.[45] Of the seven women and eight men who were listed as paupers, most seem to have had some tie to a parish and even to have some living kin, whether spouse, children, or siblings. Two of the men had practiced a trade; one was a carpenter and the other, a goldsmith. One widow had a house and garden (in dower) but an estate worth only 14s. 4d., and another had kept the amenity of one silver spoon.[46] These examples come from the late fourteenth and early fifteenth centuries, when the standard of living, even for the poor, had improved considerably compared with the conditions evident from the earlier tax records.

Laborers and servants also had very modest estates, but missed the label of pauper because they had an assured living with room and board. Many of those in low-paid occupations made simple wills that left the residue to a wife or an executor; the value of the estate was not given. A laborer left the residue of his estate to his wife, but also gave his parents 40s. and a surgeon and his wife, 6s. 8d.[47] The estates of most people in this group consisted of movable goods, such as clothing, bedding, perhaps some kitchen equipment, and maybe silver spoons or a fine girdle, or belt. People might also bequeath the residue of a lease on a tenement. Although many of the testators in this group were not married, a few had wives and children.

Craftsmen appear in great numbers in all the will collections, but their estates often were not recorded beyond mentioning the residue and specific bequests. All the testastors appearing in the Husting Court wills had real property, although some were simply craftsmen. A twice-widowed lighterman and shipwright left his married daughter a house, and his son, a boat, a tenement, and a house.[48] A 1495 probate of the will of Richard Leman, a tailor, revealed goods worth £115 in his house. The house included a hall, a parlor, two butteries, a kitchen and bake house, three chambers (including one for a maid), a counting house, a garden by the waterside, and a white boat. His was a modest establishment, but his trade gave him access to rather fine fabrics. Red silk hangings in the hall and stained ones in the parlor and tapestry cushions stuffed with flock stood in contrast to the few tables, one chair, and some stools. His cupboards contained not silver, but pewter and latten objects that amounted to only 66s. in value. He indulged in green silk hangings in the master chamber, along with feather beds and bolsters. Despite his being a tailor, his clothing was rather ordinary and came to only 8s. 6d. in value.[49]

Wealthy citizens such as Sir Matthew Phyllyp, mentioned earlier in this chapter, had considerably more furniture and bedding, as well as chests and cupboards to display their plate. Phyllyp's clothing included numerous gowns and cloaks lined with a variety of furs. Henry Barton, a skinner whose will dates from 1436, had jugs, basins, platters, cups, and crosses, all of gold and silver.[50] Salt cellars provided an opportunity to display considerable wealth, and some appear in the records described in elaborate detail. The alderman Stephen Forster pledged a silver-gilt one in 1448 that weighed twelve pounds troy. The base was embattled, and within these mock battlements was a hedge in silver gilt enclosing a landscape dotted with silver sheep. A shepherd and shepherdess in white silver were pictured driving a wolf away from the sheep. Also part of the scene were a bloodhound and a bear. The bowl of the salt cellar rose out of this relief work and was itself chased like bark. The cover, attached by a silver chain, repeated the theme of the base and included seven silver-gilt banners with coats of arms.[51] A child growing up in such a household, surrounded by luxury and beautiful objects, must have imbibed a strong sense of social privilege. Girls knew that a part of this plate was reserved for their dowry and would grace their own tables when they were married. Indeed, wealthy families had a tendency to establish themselves as country gentry within a few generations.[52]

The inventories indicate colorful dress for inhabitants of London: violets, greens, scarlet, crimson, russet, red, murrey, blues, and mixed colors describe outer garments, gowns, hats, and hoods. Linings were of wool fleece or of various furs, depending on the wealth and status of the owner. Doublets were a bit more subdued, often tawny or black. Bright colors were not necessarily the preserve of the upper classes. A thriving trade in frippery (secondhand clothes, shoes, and furniture) took place in evening markets at Cornhill and Cheapside. Because the city tried to force merchants of past finery to sell only during daylight hours, we can form some idea of the nature of those selling and buying. The sellers seem to have been small-scale merchants who came under suspicion partly because they obviously could defraud their customers better in poor light and partly because they were suspected of buying stolen property.[53] Londoners of the lower orders, then, might be seen in faded and frayed secondhand garments.

Clothes given in alms, however, were almost always subdued in color, because they were given to paupers who took part in funeral processions. Henry Barton ordered gowns and hoods of the best Welsh gray cloth for paupers.[54] Thus it seems that only paupers, the clergy, and perhaps widows routinely wore dark-colored clothing, in contrast to the rest of the population. Of the dress of youth, we will say more later.

Diet was as varied as were living accommodations and clothing. Part of the conspicuous consumption of wealthy Londoners was grand feasts. Guild banquets were affairs of many courses, mostly protein of various sorts, and quantities of ale and wine.[55] Even the weekly expenses of running a large household seem overwhelming. Robert Basset, an alderman, had his house supplied with beer at a rate of seven barrels a week, paying from 3s. to 1s. 8d. a barrel, depending on the quality of the beer.[56] Laborers demanded meals along with their wages, so that three carpenters and two plumbers lunched on a shoulder and brisket of mutton, bread, and ale for working on a church porch. The churchwardens would have found payment in ale perfectly normal, for they went out to a tavern every time they hired a priest, sexton, or bell ringer.[57] Food and drink were part of the enjoyment of life.

The government of London continually tried to regulate the quantity, quality, price, and distribution of basic victuals so that no one would make an undue profit and all would have access to the necessities of life. An assize regulating bread and ale guaranteed the quality of these items, and by the end of the fourteenth century, the mayor even introduced a farthing (1/4d.) loaf of bread and measure of ale so that the poor would have ready access to these necessities of life. The city had installed conduits for water so that all citizens could have water, even if they did not have wells. The prices of meat, poultry, eggs, fish, shellfish, cheese, candles, and charcoal were also regulated.[58]

Provisions were available either at markets or from local vendors and hucksters, so much of the daily shopping could be done in the neighborhood. The cries of London street vendors were legendary even then. Cooks and their knaves cried, "Hote pies, hote! Gode gris [pigs] and gees, gowe dyne, gowe!" And taverners cried, "White wyn of Oseye [Alsace] and red wyne of Gascoigne, / Of the Ryne and the Rochel [Rochelle] the doste to defye."[59]

We will cite many cases that give a sense of this active street market because vending was one of the occupations available to youth. William Routh, a fruiterer, said that he was walking along the street with a basket of fruit when he was called into the house of John Douning outside Cripplegate. He went in at the residents' request, but they wanted to pay him 1d. less than he could afford to accept for his fruit. When he tried to leave the house, they dumped out his fruit and kept his basket and cloak, thus inhibiting his chances of earning a living.[60]

Remembering that London streets and neighborhoods contained a mix of people from very different circumstances, we can end the discussion of the material environment with the annual celebration of Midsummer Eve (St. John's Day). The wealthier inhabitants set out tables in the streets to feed their neighbors. Bonfires burned in the street, carefully watched to avoid disaster. All houses were decked out with flowers, boughs of leaves, and branches of herbs, and some houses also hung lanterns. All men of the wards turned out in bright harness for the Midsummer Watch and formed a procession, led by the giants Gog and Magog, through the city.[61] Young children must have been awed by the giants, and one can imagine the fun had by the apprentices and servants who found the occasion one for drink and possible riot.

The birth of a child, with attendant midwives. (Drawing by Wayne M. Howell, from British Museum, Cotton MS. Julius, E4)

3

Birth and Baptism: Membership in a Social and Spiritual Network

Following the tradition of the ancients, Venerable Bede equated childhood with the season of spring, the element of air, the humor of blood, and the qualities of moistness and heat. These categories corresponded to children's behavior: "merry, delightful, tenderhearted, and much given to laughter and talk." Later medieval commentators continued the tradition, adding the years at which transition occurred; for the *puericia vel infantia*, this condition of the seasons, elements, humors, and qualities prevails through the fourteenth year.[1] Medieval preachers saw the period as one of delightful innocence: "The property of a young child is that he cannot be maliciously disposed." Even a child who is chastised will show no rancor, but will respond with hugs and kisses if offered a flower or a red apple. The child is generous to other children, to "houndys and to cattys."[2] Nothing bleak appears in the descriptions; there is no hint of indifference to a child's birth and no question about the desirability of having such an infantile presence among adults.

It is well to keep in mind the preachers' and savants' pleasant picture of childhood because modern historians, perhaps having too much black choler themselves, seem intent on looking at the dark side of medieval childhood. As we observed in Chapter 1, medieval children, as biological creatures, had the same basic needs as modern ones to be fed, to be kept clean and warm, and to be held, rocked, and given affection. Since children's biological development, including increases in both motor skills and psychological maturity, has not changed over the centuries, we can expect to see many parallels in the process of growing up then and now. The process of socializing children, including encouraging them to walk, speak, and play, will also seem familiar. In some respects, the modern preoccupation with the developmental process is an extension of the scientific approach of Bede and the ancients, providing a descriptive framework for separating biologically observable behavior differences between childhood and adolescence.

While these elementary aspects of child development provide a sense of continuity for the human experience, the cultural differences in attitudes toward this first stage of life become apparent as we look at children in medieval London. Growing up in fourteenth- and fifteenth-century London could not have been the same experience as growing up in modern London.

Birth and Baptism

Practices associated with normal births in medieval Europe are shrouded in secrecy, not because the births were hidden at the time, but because they were a woman's ritual and women did not pass on information about them in writing. Indeed, we can be quite sure that the event of a birth was well known within the immediate community. Living close together, the neighbors would hear the cries of a woman in labor and would observe the midwife and female friends gathering around. But what occurred in the birthing chamber was not known to the men listening outside, and so it was not recorded. The learned clerical treatises on gynecology contain no descriptions of normal births, only abnormal ones. Male doctors never attended a normal birth, so they knew nothing about them. They were called in only when surgery was needed.[3] Folkloric sources make it clear that men were excluded from the birthing process. At most, they assisted by some symbolic action of release, such as shooting an arrow into the air or opening a box lid. Christianity gave them the option of offering prayers and gifts to saints to ensure a safe delivery.[4]

We must leave the worried father (should he be home) in another room opening boxes and fidgeting with his rosary and enter the birthing chamber. A description of his child's entry into the world must be pieced together from later sources and from bits of information in various records. A midwife with more then ten and perhaps as many as thirty years' experience would certainly be present. She would probably have a couple

of assistants who were learning the skills of the art. In addition, the prospective mother might have female friends or kin in the chamber. She
would give birth probably in a semicrouched position. A medieval English
treatise depicts a woman in labor pulling on a cord fixed to a beam above
the bed. The expectation was that, in a normal birth, the child would
appear, head first, within twenty pangs or shortly thereafter.[5] Of course,
all might not go well, and no doubt many women suffered from difficult
births such as Margery Kempe complains of in her autobiography.[6]

The midwife and her assistants tied the umbilical cord, aided the child
in its first breath, and then washed it in warm water, using oil, salt, or rose
petals. This first administration of postnatal care evoked a powerful, sentimental image among medieval people, if one can judge from the popular
Middle English carol "Cherry Tree." In it, the Christ child is depicted as so
poor that he is washed only in water, rather than in wine or milk. One
imagines that London children born into the higher classes were given the
most luxurious bathing that custom dictated, whereas the children of the
poor made do with warm water for their first bath. All were swaddled,
probably in linen strips.[7]

The evidence presented so far suggests a warm atmosphere in the
birthing chamber. The room was warm because a fire heated water for
bathing the infant and the mother. A strong, sweet scent of olive oil, herbs,
wine for the midwife, and perhaps rose water pervaded the room. The
whole ritual was conducted by a venerable midwife, with female friends
bringing solicitude and joy. However comfortable the setting could be
made, the normal pain and the extreme risks from an abnormal birth
made the occasion an anxious one. Among our folkloric beliefs is the
conviction that men outlived women in the Middle Ages because women
routinely died in childbirth, but the large number of widows in our records
belies this common belief. In Florence in the fifteenth century, there were
14.4 maternal deaths for every 1,000 births.[8] The conditions of birth were
probably freer of disease with a midwife attending at home than in the
lying-in hospitals of the early nineteenth century.

Not all women had the comforts of a well-equipped chamber with a
fireplace to heat the room, but even so, hot water could be brought up to a
tenement room from a kitchen below. One can assume that some children
came into the world in even less favorable circumstances, since St. Bartholomew's Hospital had endowments to provide a lying-in hospital for
women bearing children out of wedlock. Sir Richard Whittington endowed eight beds for this purpose in St. Thomas's Hospital. With characteristic concern, he stipulated that the women's identities be kept secret so
that the women might ultimately marry without stigma.[9]

Although the majority of births passed without mishap, many complications could occur for both mother and child.[10] A poem on the periods of a man's life sums up the risk well:

> How mankinde dooth bigynne
>   is wondir for to scryue so;
> In game he is bigoten in synne,
>   the child is the modris deedli foo;
> Ot thei be fulli partide on tweyne,
>   In perelle of deeth be bothe two.[11]

The dangers of the situation were an integral part of medieval culture: begotten in sin, the baby became the mother's deadly foe in birth.

The Church was very concerned about the possibility that a child might die unbaptized and in a state of original sin. For this reason, manuals such as John Myrc's *Instructions for a Parish Priest* overcame the prejudice against a sacerdotal role for women and authorized midwives to baptize infants who would not live until a priest or a layman could arrive. Myrc went so far as to instruct that if the mother had died in childbirth, the midwife was to cut her open, extract the baby from the womb, and baptize it. She was to keep clean water available for this eventuality and was to repeat the simple phrase "I baptize you in the name of the Father, the Son, and the Holy Ghost." Myrc, of course, permitted the midwife to perform the baptism only if a man could not be called on to do it. In a London church court case, a pimp was said to have baptized the child of a prostitute.[12]

The other possibility was that the child was not wanted and would be drowned or suffocated, rather than bathed and swaddled. In the rush to label all unpleasant practices as "medieval," popular opinion and many historians have conjured up visions of unwanted children being abandoned in great numbers. No record sources, including London's, show such a widespread slaughter of innocents.[13] Although few ecclesiastical court records are preserved for London, a series from the late fifteenth and the early sixteenth century reveals allegations of fewer than one infanticide case a year, none of which ended in conviction. In one case, three women, presumably a midwife and her assistants, took the child to the Thames with the connivance of the mother. The record does not indicate if the child was alive. In a more touching case, Agnes Lewes became pregnant while a prostitute. She delivered her child at the home of Alice Fort, a woman charged with pimping for Agnes. The charge reads that Alice killed the baby, but made a likeness of it out of swaddling clothes and displayed it to the mother. Here the sad tale ends without any hint as to the motivation. Alice denied the charges, and no further consideration of the case appears.[14] A coroner's inquest for 1315 records the death of a child, a quarter of a year old, who was found in a ditch by the Tower. But there is only a vague description of a woman with a kerchief placing her there.[15] Societal attitudes certainly opposed infanticide; a slander charge in the church courts was "that sche schuld [did] sley her owen childe."[16] While willful slaying of newborns does not appear, attitudes toward bastards and female children did sometimes produce neglect that ultimately led to the children's deaths. These problems are discussed in Chapter 4.

Since even infants found dead in suspicious circumstances bore Christian names, we may suppose that most children born in either humble or luxurious surroundings survived at least long enough to go through their first rite of passage, baptism. What ceremonials surrounded this threshold experience of crossing from the state of the unnamed to that of the named? Baptism made possible the transition from the state of original sin of Adam and Eve; it was a cleansing ritual and an exorcism that named and welcomed the new Christian into the fellowship and community. Since a child was baptized as a newborn, the ceremony was more meaningful for adults than for children.[17] The mother had no role because the Church honored, although it did not require, the Jewish custom of banning women from holy places for six weeks after giving birth. The midwife or the godmother stood in her stead.

As soon as the child was born, the father assembled the godparents: two females and a male for a girl and two males and a female for a boy. The godmother or the midwife carried the baby to the church door, where the priest met the baptismal party. This part of the ceremony was the exorcism. The priest inquired about the sex of the child and whether it had been baptized yet. He blessed the child, put salt in its mouth to symbolize the reception of wisdom, and drove out any demons lurking in the child. The Church envisioned a primarily spiritual role for the godparents—they were to teach the Pater Noster, Ave Maria, and Credo—and for this reason the priest tested their own knowledge of the prayers as part of the baptismal ceremony.[18]

The party then moved inside to the baptismal font, where the priest anointed, immersed, and named the infant. The godparents raised the newly named Christian from the font and wrapped it in a christening robe. This gown or crysom was white and could be made elaborate with embroidery of pearls.[19] On the other hand, it might be borrowed from the parish church or from a friend, to be returned after the ceremony. From the font, the party moved to the altar for the profession of faith, with the godparents answering for the infant. Returning to the parents' house, the celebrants offered gifts and feasted in honor of the new child.

From the infant's viewpoint, baptism was probably not a comfortable event. The ceremonies outside the church door and at the font and the trip home could leave the infant chilled. The salt was hardly pleasant, and the water in the font could be terribly cold in winter. One presumes that most babies cried through much of the ceremony.

Although the child could not understand it, the baptism ceremony was truly a crossing from one state to another. Many consequences for the child's life derived from this social and religious occasion. The name that the child was given would identify it for the rest of its life, even if it failed to survive the baptismal ordeal by more than a few hours. Its birth order and sex would influence its relationship with its family. Its first social network outside the family was established with the godparents and perhaps a nurse. The relationship of the child to its godparents and that of the godparents to one another and to the child's parents would form part of the child's life. The broader network included the parish in which the baptism occurred. Baptism was the beginning of the development of an individual's social network.

The name that a child bore held more layers of identity than is common for modern London children. The first name was still a "Christian name"; that is, it was often a saint's name and one conferred at the baptismal font. Priests' instruction manuals indicate that the principal godparent, the one who raised the child from the font, gave his or her name to the child. Existing English baptismal records go back only to the sixteenth century, so our knowledge of naming practices for medieval urban children remains conjectural. In London, for instance, only wills tell us about the names of godparents and godchildren. From 1352 to 1500, only 23 godchildren are mentioned by 17 (out of 1,258) testators recording their wills in the Husting Court. Thirteen of the godchildren have the same name as their godparents. Typical of these cases is that of the widow Christina Malyng, who named her goddaughter, Christina, daughter of Ralph Bakelowe, as her chief beneficiary.[20] In late-fifteenth-century York, more direct evidence survives. Because York was so close to the scenes of hostilities between the Scots and the English, the city required tradesmen suspected of being Scottish to prove that they were English before they could engage in business. The obvious way to prove English birth was to produce a baptismal record that included the names of the godparents, thus indicating that the person was of English rather than Scottish birth. Of these testimonials, 65 percent of the godsons had the same name as their godfathers.[21]

We might suppose, however, that some families had favorite names or wanted to name their children after either the father or the mother. They could easily arrange a perpetuation of names by selecting a like-named godparent or by ignoring the custom of using the godparent's name.[22] A precise assessment of family sentiment about naming is hard to determine. Records on citizens' orphans assigned as wards, provide some measure of the frequency with which children and parents bore the same name. From 1300 to 1350, 29 percent of the sons and 26 percent of the daughters had the same name as their same-sex parent. From 1440 to 1450, 34 percent of the sons had the same name as their fathers. The tendency toward concentration of names within a family also increases in wills as the fifteenth century progresses. All these figures, however, are unreliable. A child bearing the father's or mother's first name might predecease the parents, so that the evidence underreports the true frequency of shared names. The overlap is highest for the most common names, such as John, Thomas, and William, and could, therefore, be coincidental.[23] One does, however, find families that seemed to have attachments to particular names. For instance, Philip Gentyl I had two sons, named Philip II and Philip III; when Walter Colrede died in 1420, his wife apparently named the child in her womb after him.[24] Perhaps London families were rather like modern ones, with some preferring perpetuation of family Christian names and others liking the sound of new or even exotic names.

Londoners drew on a much larger, more imaginative pool of names than did those living in the countryside. For men, John was by far the most common name, but William, Thomas, Richard, Stephen, Robert, Roger, Nicholas, Simon, and Walter were also popular. Foreigners from Italy, France, and the Low Countries contributed names such as Geoffrey, Alan, Bartholomew, Arnold, and Alexander. For women, the names Johanna (Joan), Isabella, Alice, Matilda, and Agnes predominated, but again more exotic names, such as Nichola, Idonea, Roesia, Emota, Olive, and Petronille, appeared. Monarchs' names apparently did not influence the naming of children. Edward was not particularly common, even though it was the name of the monarch for most of the fourteenth century. Philippa, the popular wife of Edward III, did not seem to inspire a spate of little Philippas. By the end of the fifteenth century, biblical names, such as Simon, David, and Sarah, seem to have become more common.[25]

The incidence of two sons bearing the same name has led some historians to assume that, with high infant mortality, parents tried to preserve favorite family Christian names by doubling up names in hopes that at least one son would survive to adulthood.[26] The strong popularity of some names, as well as the custom of the godparent giving the name, argues against such sentimentality in naming. Two sons, for instance, could easily have godfathers named John. In the records, the sons are distinguished by age as "major" and "minor," just as fathers and sons are distinguished by "senior" and "junior."

The baptismal name was only the first identity a child had. Throughout a person's life, the Christian name, together with the father's or mother's name, became an identification that clarified the legal status of an individual and was used in the records when the person was still young and in certain legal situations, such as an inheritance, a wardship, or an apprenticeship. Thus one finds names such as "Thomas Aillesby, son of the late John Aillesby, senior," recorded in an apprenticeship dispute. Depending on whether the mother or the father was the responsible party, either parent's name might appear. Such naming seldom played the role it did in Welsh names, in which Robert *ap* Robert *ap* David might be a significant part of the name. One did not forget parental names, as they were essential for legal identity.

A surname formed a third part of the child's naming. Many of the surnames indicated the immigrant quality of London's population and identified the county, city, or village of origin. The great majority of these surnames reflect an East Midlands or West Midlands origin.[27] Place surnames were usually expressed with "de" as in Thomas de Lenne or Maud de Milham. By the second half of the fourteenth century, many of these names had lost their "de" designation and had become last names. Surnames were far from stable even into the fifteenth century, so that the appearance of an alias is not infrequent in London records. An apprentice or a servant moving into London might take his master's surname.[28] A person might also become identified with a craft and adopt a name such as Fuller, Draper, or Webber. Such a surname could change if a son took up a craft different from that of his father.

Birth gave the infant an immediate set of social networks. Kinship, both by blood and by affinity, is the most obvious network. The immediate nuclear family included parents and, perhaps, siblings. We can form some idea, even if an incomplete one, of the most common number of siblings by reviewing the wardship entries that appear in the Letter Books. From 1309 to 1348 (the preplague years), the average number of children per family was 1.79; from 1349 to 1398, the average number was 1.66. During the first plague decade (1349–1358), there were 1.5 siblings per family. Family size began to increase between 1409 and 1418, averaging 1.98 children; during the period from 1399 to 1448, the average number of siblings recorded in wardship cases was 2.0. During the second half of the fifteenth century, population continued to expand, with 2.2 children per family.[29]

The evidence for this measurement is, of course, incomplete because these are truncated families; perhaps one parent (usually the father) died prematurely and left minor children, so that a complete fertility cycle is not represented. The children may have had older half-brothers and half-sisters, and their mother might have remarried and produced younger half-siblings. Furthermore, the increase in the number of children per family in the second half of the fifteenth century probably represents greater longevity for the parents, rather than for the children of the family, as we discuss in Chapter 6. Thus the parents more nearly completed their reproductive cycle before dying.

A child's network of kin, therefore, might have included half-brothers and -sisters, and the child might very well have been raised by a stepfather or stepmother. As we shall see when we look at wardship, the child's kinship ties could have extended to aunts, uncles, and grandparents from both the mother's and the father's families. These kin might act as either guardians or benefactors. Some might still be in the town or village from which the parents had migrated, in which case the child would see them infrequently.

Godparents formed a spiritual kinship network. According to the Church, godparents were not to be drawn from those who had a tie of either blood or marriage with the child's parents. They were not to be uncles, cousins, grandparents, wives of uncles, or even people who might enter the family through marriage in the future. The Church believed that the spiritual bond of being co-parents created a close enough tie to prohibit marriage. The parents, therefore, had to take care in selecting godparents, keeping in mind future plans for marriages as well as the child's welfare. Most likely, godparents were friends, neighbors, fellow guildsmen, employers, or secular clergy. Again, the York citizenship records give some hint. Of the seventeen certificates of English birth, only one is for a child with a godfather and godmother having the same surname as the godson. The parental strategy appears to have been to have at least one godparent, usually the one naming the infant, of a higher social status than the parent.[30]

In establishing a network of co-parents outside that of a kinship based on blood, what expectations could the parents or the child have about the functions that it would perform?[31] The Church presumed that godparents would take on some nurturing role in addition to the spiritual role, so that one might expect to find godparents acting as guardians of orphaned godchildren. William Trippelowe, an armorer who died in 1390, stipulated in his will that his executors (including his widow) provide his goddaughter, Elizabeth, with a living until she married.[32] He is probably not the only godparent to have acted as guardian, but the records often do not specify any relationship. Other hints of a close or nurturing relationship survive. In 1456, an unmarried silkwoman left Agnes Fremley, her godmother, a small bequest.[33]

With testamentary evidence being our sole source of information, a close relationship between godparents and their godchildren is difficult to document. Only 3 percent of the testators appearing in the Archdeaconry

Court from 1393 to 1409 left bequests to their godchildren, and a mere 1 percent did so in the Husting Court wills filed between 1357 and 1500.[34] Typically, those leaving such bequests were older people and those who had no children or close kin. For these testators, the pressures of providing for family did not exist, and they could afford to disperse bequests to more distant contacts. No doubt these bequests also indicated a warm personal relationship between godparents and godchildren. Six of the testators in the Husting Court were widows, and one was a clerk; the other ten were married men without children. In the Archdeaconry Court, two widows, one single woman, two clerks, and two older men mentioned godchildren. The bequests were usually not large. One woman did leave a third part of the proceeds from selling a tavern, and Christiana Reynewell, the widow of an alderman, left two goddaughters 20 marks for their dowries, but only the customary 6s. 8d. to other goddaughters and 20s. to yet another. John Northwich, who was a schoolmaster at St. Laurence College, gave three of his "spiritual children" 20s. each. They may even have been his students as well. Items of silver, such as spoons, and clothing and household goods were also common gifts.[35]

One might assume that godchildren would provide a ready source of adoptable children for childless couples, but neither English secular nor ecclesiastical law provided for adoption.[36] Occasionally (in half a dozen wills), a godchild was named chief heir. Roger Elmesley was a servant to a wax chandler and had no wife or children. He selected Robert Sharp, his godson, to become heir to his property.[37] Some wills refer to "adopted sons" (*filiolo*). For instance, John de Enefeud, a goldbeater whose will was enrolled in 1308 and 1309, states: "To John, son of Robert de Gloucestre, goldsmith, his adopted son, certain rents in the parish of St. Giles without Cripplegate." In other cases, the term "adopted" seems to refer only to godchildren.[38] Sylvia Thrupp, a historian of the London merchant class, could find only one family that provided sure evidence of adoption.[39]

Prescriptive literature and folklore are as silent on a special relationship between godparent and godchild as are the record sources.[40] Sadly, no fairy godmothers appear to inspire hope of easy access to wealth, happiness or upward mobility. Equally absent is any evidence of a close relationship between parents and co-parents. In modern Latin America and southern Europe, these bonds may be as important as or more so than the tie of godparent to godchild, but we know that in England the relationship may have been significant only because we have preserved the word "gossip"—derived from *gosse* (co-father) and *gossep* (co-mother)—as a form of familiar address and, later, as a derogatory label. The baptismal network may have been a close one, but our sources are silent on the matter.

In addition to kin, the child's social network might also have included unrelated people who would have been part of a prosperous household, including perhaps a nurse, servants, apprentices, and journeymen. Neighbors, parishioners, and members of the father's guild were all potential parts of the child's network as well. The quality of the child's relationships to these people, as well as to more immediate kin, will be discussed in Chapter 4. In the first days of the child's life, the mother, perhaps a nurse, and the spiritual kin were predominant.

Some of the flavor of the child's first social networks comes out in Thomas Seint John's suit for his inheritance. His father's executors claimed that he was only nineteen, but Thomas called on the spiritual and social ties of his infancy and childhood to prove that he was of age. His godmother said that he would be twenty-two years old on July 25; his first schoolmaster said that he knew Thomas was twenty-one; the husband of his nurse said that he had turned twenty-one last July 25; an apprentice of his father remembered that Thomas had been six when he became an apprentice; the current chaplain of the parish church said that Thomas had been born before he became chaplain twenty years ago; and finally a neighbor, a carpenter, remembered Thomas playing with his brother eighteen years earlier.[41]

"Thomas Seint John Imagined"

Thomas Seint John was born into comfortable surroundings on July 25, 1418.[42] His mother gave birth in the master chamber of his father's house, a room hung with cloth painted with scenes from the Bible. Although the furniture was sparse, the room had a large bed, a cradle, and a smaller bed. A variety of chests, a clothes press, candleholders, and a small joined table furnished the room. A holy-water container hung on the wall. Midwife Alice had attended the birth. Thomas was washed in warm rose water near the fireplace and wrapped in swaddling clothes before being put in the cradle. His birth was attended by some anxiety because his mother was in ill health and could not nurse him. Because of her large network of patients, the midwife knew of a reliable wet nurse, who was immediately contacted.

Meanwhile, his nervous father contacted two guild brothers, his good friends Thomas Sampson and John Wolfey, to act as godfathers and sent to the aged parish priest to let him know about the birth and the need to baptize the baby quickly in case a nurse could not be found. A friend of Thomas's mother who was at the birth acted as godmother and carried the baby to the parish church door. Crying the whole time from hunger, salt in the mouth, and general discomfort, the newborn urinated on his god-father when Thomas Sampson lifted him from the font. Fortunately, his godfather had a sense of humor and commented that those who bore the name Thomas were ever doubters, at least since St. Thomas the Doubter.

After a short ceremonial walk from the church with young Thomas, who was dressed in a beautiful crysom gown with seed pearls embroidered on it, the party arrived home to find a nurse waiting for young Thomas and a maid waiting with water and sponge to clean the violet gown of godfather Thomas Sampson. Comfort restored, the godparents presented gifts of a silver spoon, a silver porriger, and a rattle with a piece of coral on it for both good luck and for teething. The maid and manservant had arranged the feast in the hall while the party was at church so that wine, game pies, roasts, bread, and sweet date pudding were ready laid. For the infant Thomas, the discomfort of his first hours of life were now over, and he was returned to the master chamber and the cradle alongside his mother's bed. His nurse gave him his first milk. He was to spend hours in the cradle, lying swaddled and warm but sometimes restless and cranky with frustration from trying to move his limbs.

Both the house and the neighborhood were crowded. Thomas's fa-ther's apprentices took an interest in the baby and carried him around after working hours. By the time Thomas was three years old, he was playing in the street with a neighbor boy whose older brother was appren-ticed as a carpenter. Thomas was particularly close to one apprentice who joined the household when Thomas was six years old. The apprentice was only fourteen himself and had come from Yorkshire. Homesick, he found comfort in entertaining young Thomas.

Thomas was generally a well-cared-for child. His father was wealthy enough to afford good food and clothing, as well as an education for his son. His nurse and her family and the neighbors all paid attention to his needs and interests. His godparents gave him beautiful bright clothing, toys, and a little chest of his own in which to put his things. He had his own little chair in the hall and a small bed with a feather coverlet and bolster in the master chamber. He had the unrivaled affection of his parents. Although his mother bore two more babies, both girls, they did not survive beyond their first two years.

Meanwhile, his education was seriously discussed. His godfather vis-ited him often and asked him to recite his prayers, correcting him when he faltered over the Latin words. A young, new parish priest replaced the old one, who had died when Thomas was two years old. The priest had been educated at Oxford and thought that Thomas and the other children of the parish should get an education. He argued that education would be necessary if Thomas were to advance in a profession; more and more guilds were requiring that apprentices be able to write and keep accounts.

By the time his father died when Thomas was eleven years old, the boy was already in the charge of his first schoolmaster, learning to write Latin with a stylus on wax tablets. His mother, who had received the house as her dower, remarried quickly. She and his stepfather retained the wardship of Thomas. He did not live at home for many more years; when he was fourteen, his mother arranged for him to become an apprentice to his godfather. From Thomas's point of view, this was a welcome change because now he had a half-brother who had taken his place in the household.

When Thomas had to prove that he was of age, all his friends from the first days and years of his life were still available to give him support and help. He was able to prove that he was twenty-one and thus could inherit his father's wealth and finally be of age. The community of friends, neighbors, and fellow Christians had been his support.

A boy rides a hobbyhorse. (Drawing by Wayne M. Howell, from Pieter Bruegel, *Kinderspiele* [Kunsthistorisches Museum, Vienna])

4

The Fragile Years of Childhood

Once baptized, the child had crossed the threshold from a state of limbo, as Dante described the circle of hell in which the unbaptized resided, and moved into the struggle for survival within the network of family and community. Evidence about these first years of life is hard to find in historical records, and most of what we know presents a grim picture overshadowed by high rates of mortality. The chief records for studying childhood in London are the wardship cases that appear in the Letter Books. Thus we know the most about those children who lost at least one parent, usually the father. This sort of source, combined with wills and coroners' inquests, points toward childhood experiences dominated by the Grim Reaper. Considering the filth of London streets and the marginal cleanliness of even the best houses, survival was not assured. Demographers estimate that infant mortality was 30 to 50 percent in the premodern world. Since we do not have parish registers for the Middle Ages, we cannot arrive at an accurate estimate of the number of children who died. But London's practice of providing mayoral supervision for citizens' orphans does give some information on the mortality of the better-fed class.

A childhood in which the specter of mortality predominated, however, cannot be entirely accurate. The young have little concept of the meaning of death, even when parents try to instill one. The first years of life also had carefree moments, games, and nurturing. The theme of neighborhood and parish that dominates any description of medieval London and is apparent in the ritual of baptism emphasizes the nurturing children received, both in the family and in the community networks that they began to establish at their baptism. The information, although sparse, shows a lively neighborhood concern for the welfare of children. Thomas Seint John's story is not a unique one, nor would it have applied only to the comfortably well off.

Survivors and Nonsurvivors of Childhood

Much of what one would want to know about the early years from birth through seven or eight remains as elusive as the information on natural childbirth. The nursing of young Londoners is perhaps the most obscure aspect of all. Thomas Seint John had a nurse who was living in the country when he was twenty-one. Does this imply that London middle-class babies, like Florentine ones, were sent to the country to be wet-nursed?[1] We know about the nursing arrangements common in Florence from the *ricordanze*, diaries that men kept to note daily events and business deals. If London men kept similar diaries, the journals have not survived. Since the hiring of a wet nurse was a contractual arrangement, we might expect to find cases involving broken contracts in the mayor's court. But nurses are not mentioned. Nor are they mentioned in the petitions to the Chancellor, where, again, one might find evidence of broken contracts. Finally, one might expect that wills would provide evidence of nurses, that testators would remember fondly their "milk mothers" with bequests or prayers. The sparse references to nurses that do occur, however, could just as well apply to those nursing a person through a last illness.[2]

As in the case of midwives, the records are silent on this very important aspect of women's lives. It is hard to imagine, given the example of royalty and the nobility, that wealthy citizens' wives would not imitate their betters by putting their children to a wet nurse. They would have the same motivations—vanity and the wish to avoid the encumbrance of nursing—as their social superiors. Indeed, a variety of scenarios may account for Thomas Seint John's being put to a wet nurse. If wet nursing was common in London, we cannot trace the children or nurses either in the countryside or in the merchant houses.

The image of Mary nursing the infant Jesus was a very strong one and may have influenced women to nurse their own babies. Folk songs present an earthy picture of Mary suckling Jesus:

As she him took all in her lap.
He took that maiden by the pap.
And took thereof a right good nap [grip].
And sucked his fill of that licour.[3]

Mothers of lower social rank must have nursed their own children, and possibly most other London mothers did as well, since records to the contrary are rare. Nursing might last from one to two years and sometimes more.[4] Our ideas about nursing practices in London, however, remain purely speculative.

The early nursing and nurturing of children made a great deal of difference in their chances for survival. Those who were not nursed were given animal milk and bread soaked in milk. The feeding mechanisms were not sanitary; typical were feeding horns and rags with food for the child to suck. The risks of infection and malnutrition were great. Medieval childhood was fragile, and even relatively well-off citizen's children who became wards of the city did not necessarily survive.

Although 1,731 London orphans are recorded as wards in the Letter Books from 1309 to 1497, for only 631 individuals do we know the final outcome of their wardship. Of these, 199, or 32 percent, died before they came of age.[5] This figure does not represent children who may have died in infancy before they became wards, but children whose average age was between seven and ten when they became wards (see Chapter 6). It also underrepresents overall childhood mortality because the wards were relatively healthy children whose fathers had a good living as artisans or merchants and could provide a good home and adequate food for their pregnant wives and children. London also had a considerable population of wealthy aliens—French, Flemish, Italian, German—who enjoyed similar living conditions. We can assume that the children of prostitutes, laborers, hucksters, servants, and other lower-class individuals had higher mortality rates because the mothers' diets were not good and the conditions into which the children were born did not permit as high a level of care.

The risk of children dying increased during the fourteenth and fifteenth centuries. Prior to the appearance of the Black Death in 1348, 18 percent of the orphans did not survive to the end of wardship. Between 1349 and 1398, the percentage increased to 27; it exceeded 33 in the fifteenth century (Appendix, Table 1).[6] Conditions for survival of London children did not improve following the initial visitations of plague; the cause of death may have been other diseases, such as pox, sweating sickness, flux, and various fevers, all of which made the fifteenth century such a dangerous period.[7] If we had more information on the age of the children at the time of death and knew the month in which they died, it might be easier to speculate about the causes.

Whatever a child's overall chances of surviving, it appears from the wardship cases that girls were less likely to survive than boys. At the time they entered wardship, 780 (45 percent) of the orphans were female and 951 were male (55 percent). The disparity in the number of males and females over the two centuries varied greatly. From 1309 to 1348, or just before the outbreak of the plague, there were 14 percent fewer females than males on the wardship rolls. During the years of the worst plague visitations, from 1349 to 1398, the disparity was only 8 percent, but from 1399 to 1448 it reached 22 percent, dropping to only 2 percent between 1459 and 1497 (Appendix, Table 2). The underrepresentation of females decreased with the general recovery of population at the end of the fifteenth century.[8]

In normal births, 105 males are born for every 100 females, but females have a biological advantage in surviving disease, and the initial imbalance is quickly lost. In modern Europe and the United States, we would expect to find more women than men in the group under age twenty-one, so the 10 percent shortfall of girls in the London wardship records suggests a pattern of early female mortality.[9] As we point out in Chapter 6, there is no reason to assume that female children did not appear before the mayor just as often as male children did, since boys and girls inherited in equal portions.[10]

A qualitative difference in the care and nurturing of male and female children, rather than female infanticide, may explain the shortfall. Apparently, male children were given better care because they had a higher social value. Londoners could not have been immune to thinking that a female child meant an outlay of wealth for dowry at the time of marriage, whereas a male child brought in wealth when he married.[11] But the problem of high female mortality also reflects society's attitude toward women and the economic opportunities available to them. Therefore, the subject of the lower survival rate of women must become a topic for ongoing analysis.[12]

Different practices in nurturing and nursing male and female children, whether done by a wet nurse or by the mother, could occur at any juncture. A male child might be suckled longer—until age two or three, whereas girls might be weaned at one—and, therefore, not be exposed to bacterial infections that were ingested with prechewed pap and cow's milk fed from "nursing horns."[13] For older children, the difference in survival might result from mothers or nurses sitting up with sick male children and coaxing liquids to combat diseases with symptoms of fever or diarrhea, the common killers of children. But in spite of maternal solicitude, boys were more likely to be adventurous and to die in accidents than were girls.[14]

In developing countries today, some of the high female mortality can be attributed to parents who spend their limited resources on medical attention for male children, rather than for females. London parents may have made the same choice, but medical practice was so backward that a visit to a physician might have been more of a hazard than a help. Simon Linde, a stationer, sought the services of Peter Blank, a surgeon, to cure his son of a "pin and webbe" eye disease. The surgeon provided the necessary medicines only on the promise from Simon that he was to make sure that the child did not put his hands on his eyes. When the child was not cured, a malpractice suit was instituted.[15]

In addition to female children, the other large group of London children at risk of differential nurturing were bastards. Unfortunately, we have no comparable records through which to study their fate numerically. Prostitutes, female servants, and singlewomen were at risk for conceiving illegitimate children. Bastardy, therefore, must have been common. For instance, it was charged in the church court that Thomas Person impregnated a woman named Peryn. The woman stayed at a house in Holborn until the child was born. The boy was baptized at the Church of St. Sepulchre. Three days after the birth and baptism, the mother wandered away, and no one had seen her since.[16]

As such fornication cases and Whittington's will indicate, a stigma apparently was attached to women who had premarital sex and bore children out of wedlock, but it did not necessarily extend to the children themselves. London law barred bastards from inheriting the chief estate (as opposed to a life use of it), but it did not prohibit people from making other provisions for them through bequests of movable property or usage of real estate.[17] The status did not carry with it the slanderous meaning that it does today; indeed, it does not appear among the many terms of defamation that came before the London courts.[18] When it is mentioned, the term appears in connection with efforts to establish legitimacy in order to inherit property, rather than as a slander.[19]

A number of wills indicate that men not only recognized their bastard children, but also maintained familial relations with the mothers and children. The grocer John Godyn apparently had a legitimate family because he left his daughter, Amy, a house in Sopwelle and annual rents. But he had a parallel illegitimate family of two generations: "To George, son of Thomas Godyn his bastard son, he leaves certain of the above tenements in tail, after the death of Christina his wife; remainders to John, brother of the said George, and Johanna, sister of the same." He left George other property that he could pass on to his children, should he have any.[20]

Some patterns that may explain illegitimacy emerge from the wills. One is that the lives of traveling salesmen and buyers were lonely ones. People were away from home for long stretches of time and established semipermanent relationships in different locales. For instance, Thomas Gippyng (alias Lyncoln) was a draper from London who spent considerable time in Lincolnshire on business. His wife in London had died, and he included her in prayers for their souls, but he left the residue of his estate to Beatrice and Juliana, his bastard daughters, and his "beddying" to Juliana Pleydon of Lincoln, who was, perhaps, their mother.[21] Another typical case is that of a man who kept his female servant as a concubine. Roger Longe, a vintner, had two legitimate sons who were his heirs. His wife was dead, but he left a bequest of money to John, his bastard son. He left to Maud Beccote, probably his mistress, £20, clothing, and bedding toward her marriage and another 20 marks if his executors believed that she was pregnant.[22]

Some of the settlements to bastards must have been painful to the legitimate children. For instance, John Lane, a mercer, provided that Thomas, his bastard son, should have an annuity out of the inheritance he left to his legitimate daughter, Johanna.[23]

The other great source of London's bastards, of course, were the numerous servant girls who occupied an ambiguous position in their masters' houses, as we will see in Chapter 10. The master's role was perceived as part patriarch, entitling him to sleep with all the female servants in his house, and part protector of the virgins in his house. Margery Saules (or Sawles), for instance, continually pleaded with the mayor's court to get a fair share of the £20 bequest that Giles Avenell, a broderer of London, had left to her as his former servant and to their son, William. She said that the child was his "by the said Margery" and that she "has looked after the said child since the feast of St. James last past and paid for his keep 10*d.* per week and other expenses for his clothes." His keep alone totaled 31*s.* 8*d.*, but "she has not been recompensed at all. Therefore she begs that the said 20 *li.* be delivered to her on sufficient surety at the Chamber of the Guildhall in London, and she be repaid the expenses incurred on behalf of the said child since the death of the said Giles." Since Giles had been a citizen of London, Margery also requested that the mayor's court make her an official guardian. In her next plea, she said that the parson and Giles's widow were refusing to pay and that the mayor should take into consideration that her son was only two years old. Her own ambiguous position put the survival of her child in jeopardy and barred her from being guardian of the property.[24]

Some bastards thrived and made very respectable lives for themselves. The Frowyk family supported two illegitimate sons, one of whom became a mercer.[25] Thomas Albon, a woolmonger, had two bastard children, John and Elizabeth, as well as legitimate children. When John died, Elizabeth inherited his portion as well. Elizabeth made a very good marriage to Thomas Christofre, valet to the king.[26]

Even if the stigma against bastardy was not strong, an illegitimate child's chance of survival might depend on the status of his or her mother, unless the father intervened and provided a living for both the mother and the child. A woman with an illegitimate child would, as Whittington perceived, find it hard to establish a normal family environment for her child and might be forced into prostitution. The child's chances of survival, given a less desirable environment, would decrease.

How did mothers and society in general feel about the very frequent death of children? The presumption of callousness about children's death simply because infant mortality was such a frequent event does not stand up to the cultural evidence that we have. Although wills do not usually include prayers for the souls of dead children, as they do for parents, spouses, and siblings, the children were buried in the parish church. The charge was usually very low, from 4*d.* to 2*s.*, but even unknown children found dead in a parish received a proper burial at the expense of one of the wealthier members.[27] The presence of such waifs who died without known identity strikes a sad note about childhood in London.

John Wycliffe's English sermons emphasized fortitude for mothers who had lost children, and the story of Abraham and Isaac also offered an opportunity for moralizing about the need for faith and courage in the face of a child's death. A fifteenth-century version of the dance of death has a child sing:

> I am ful yong
> I was born yisterday
> Death is ful hasty
> on me to ben werke.[28]

In spite of the injunctions to bear up under the strain of losing children, one woman was said to have gone insane because of her child's death.[29]

Even the preserved lullabies are often grim reminders of the prevalent mortality. Mary is depicted comforting the infant Jesus while contemplating his death on the cross. Other children were comforted with songs of impending doom:

> Child, if bitide thou shalt thrive and thee [prosper],
> Think thou was a-fostred upon they modres knee;

Even have synde in thyn herte of tho thynges three—
Wan thou comest, whan thou art, and what shal come of thee.[30]

Like Mary, many mothers could expect to see their children die. If the children did survive, it was in a world that would require constant vigilance. The lullaby images were not of magical kingdoms, but of life's struggles and inevitable death.[31]

"A Child of the Parish"[32]

London's parishes were small because Londoners liked to worship with those who lived close to them. They came to know their neighbors well. They knew who lived in which rooms, who owned which shops, whose servants were honest and whose were not. So much of their daily routines took them into the streets that they became crowded places of business, gossip, and friendly exchanges. Neighbors came to have a loyalty to one another, becoming very protective of the young children who were about the streets of the quarter and resentful of intruders. Londoners told stories about the lengths to which the neighbors would go to protect their own. Indeed, the London coroners knew that they would be in for long, highly detailed accounts of any violent death and that the jurors would be forever correcting one another as they filled in details. The stories were told for years afterward, and so it was that Joan came to know, as soon as she could comprehend the stories, that she would have been dead if it had not been for the sacrifice of John of Harwe, a porter.

"It happened at vespers," one of the old men in the tavern would begin, "back in the days of the old king Edward, son of the first Edward, not the current Edward. If it hadn't been for John of Harwe, wench, you wouldn't be here serving me my ale. He was a good man, hired a solar room from Robert de Pelham and worked right here in St. Martin's in the Vintry. He was strong. He used to wrestle on Sundays. Said he was a champion in his village of Harwe. Probably was."

"Well, gramps, you're not the first to tell me. Not as if the life I lead here was worth his dying for. Care for another ale?"

"Later." He paused and drank. He started telling the story to a journeyman in his early thirties. "You're too young to remember, William. It was that esquire of the Earl of Arundel and another blood who was riding as if to war in the street out there. Right across from the house of widow Sorweles."

"No, gramps, my father always said it was the king's poulterer, and it happened in Billingsgate."

"That was another no-good blood who chased that poor girl into the Thames."

"Well, have it your way. You're old enough to have been there."

"I *was* there, you young upstart; I was on the coroners' jury. They was coming down the street at a gallop. Vespers. Street was crowded with people. Dark rainy night after St. Luke's Feast. Joan's mother, that was a servant here, was carrying little Joan in her arms. Damned esquire knocked them both to the ground. Joan here gave a great shriek, and she had always been the favorite baby of the neighborhood because she always laughed when we stopped to tickle her chin. You still do, don't you, wench?"

"Watch your hands, gramps. Your tankard's drained. Have another before curfew?"

"Don't mind if I do. We thought she'd got kicked in the head by the horse. John, he stepped forward as a towering presence and told them— polite-like, mind—to ride more carefully. That young hot-head of an esquire. He drew a sword and gave John a horrible cut. Right here, see? John dragged himself to his bed up in the solar, but he died. Old Benedict the priest made it up in time for confession. But because of John, Joan here grew up to be a fine lass. A real comfort to the men of the parish."

"The cheek of these earl's men, gramps. They think they own the streets and can get away with, well, murder. We laboring folk have to put up with their fine ways. There will come a time, mark my words, when the mighty shall be cast down and the meek shall inherit the earth. Where were these men in the days of our first parents? We were all equal when Adam delved and Eve span. I ask you, where were all the gentlemen then?"

"Well, William, you are getting preachy in your advanced youth. If you got yourself a wife, you wouldn't talk such nonsense. Keep your dangerous ideas to yourself, or you'll end up in the Tun."

"Both of you, drink up and get home before curfew rings, or the watch will put you both in the Tun till morning. If you stay here, you pay for lodgings as well as your beer."

The First Seven Years

London children spent their early years much as did their country cousins. We know far more about the early life experiences of peasant children than we do about those of children in London because the coroners' data on country children's accidental deaths are so rich. We know what they were doing, at what age, and who was or who was not present. That material is useful in helping us to present an overall picture of the first years of life. However, the real urban–rural contrast appears when the children became toddlers. Fewer children appear in London's coroners' inquests because there were fewer children in London and they had fewer accidents. Paradoxically, London children were probably better supervised, even though their risk of dying from disease was greater than that of their counterparts in the countryside. Child care in London may not have been organized, but the streets and houses were crowded with adults going about their business or pleasure. London parishioners and neighbors seem to have taken responsibility for intervening, as John of Harwe did. In the city, the neighbors were always there, whereas in the countryside, the family and neighbors were in the fields, often having left the children with inadequate babysitters, such as slightly older siblings or the disabled.[33]

The children's life experiences fell within the range of normal child development.[34] We may assume that urban children, like rural ones, spent the first year of their life swaddled and in a cradle. Keeping in mind that the environment was cold and damp, swaddling might have prevented chills. It was also a way of keeping an infant safe and immobile in the cradle. Risking having a baby crawl about in the filth of London or out the door onto a street was more dangerous than leaving the baby in a cradle. Although few children died of cradle fires in London, such fires were relatively common accidents for one- and two-year-olds in the countryside. Evidence from the countryside suggests that babies were not swaddled all the time and probably began to crawl about by the eighth or ninth month. In rooms, halls, or gardens, urban babies might have done the same.[35]

The baby's first few months, however, were relatively passive, with much time spent in a cradle. The mother was the primary caretaker. Matilda la Cambestere and her one-month-old daughter slept on the shop floor. They were already asleep by curfew, but Matilda had left a lighted candle on the wall. The candle fell onto the straw of the shop floor, and they suffocated and burned "before the neighbors knew anything about it."[36]

The case of one-month-old Joan, daughter of an immigrant shopkeeper, Bernard de Irlaunde, indicated another of the risks for children in London. Her parents lived in a rented shop in Queenhithe ward. An hour before vespers, her mother left her alone in a cradle, no doubt swaddled. It was a pleasant day in mid-May, and her parents left the shop door open when they went out. While they were gone, a sow entered and "mortally bit the right side" of the child's head. Pigs were strictly forbidden to wander the streets of London, but they did, to the great nuisance of the populace. "At length" her mother returned. She "snatched up the said Johanna and kept her alive until midnight."[37]

Even these tragic cases give a sense that mothers devoted time to nurturing their babies during the children's first year of life. Nursing, being bounced on the knees of adults, being washed and swaddled, and learning to crawl and to babble occupied a baby's days and nights. A baby's view of the world at large would be from a cradle or from the arms of its mother, its nurse, or other household members. As our "Child of the Parish" tale indicates, infants may also have been carried around while the mothers were out on errands. A poor mother would not have had a servant to look after her child and might have had to take it along to shop and even to work. Margaret, the wife of John Hilton, worked as a brewer for a London baker. She brought her five-year-old child to work with her and claimed that the apprentice had beaten it so severely that it died two days later.[38]

By their second and third years, children were walking and investigating their surroundings. A couple of London coroners' inquests give us some picture of city children's play, which was not unlike that of their rural cousins. Like Thomas Seint John, three-year-old Petronilla, daughter of William de Wyntonia, played in the street outside her father's home. One day in August 1301, a groom riding a spirited horse belonging to a London clerk ran her down because he could not control the horse. Margery, three and a half, daughter of Adam Lopechaunt, was wandering outside one day in January 1339 when she entered the house of Thomas le Irysshman, perhaps seeking warmth, and fell into a vessel of hot water.[39] These cases do not give as complete a picture as the rural coroners' inquests do. The latter clearly show a pattern in which boys followed their fathers outdoors and little girls imitated their mothers' work and had most of their accidents in the house. The early identification of toddlers with the division of labor by sex in their homes no doubt also occurred in London.[40]

The toddler years demanded supervision by parents or servants in feeding and clothing children. Those years are a time of motor development and of acquisition of language and of control of bodily function. Remembering the "jakes," streets, and latrines of London, one can well imagine the process of toilet training. No doubt, the street served for many. Chamber pots were available for the more well-to-do and for those who lived in solars with their children and could not consider taking them down ladders or steep stairs at night. But the latrines must have held their own terrors for the initiates to toilet training.

The physical surroundings could, however, be quite comfortable for the children as they grew up. A servant to a wax chandler apparently raised his godchild, Robert Sharp, and made him chief heir. The description of his posessions sounds as though he pampered the boy: a little feather bed, a pair of small sheets, other cloth, a mazer, silver spoons, candlesticks, brass pans, a silver crucifix, and silver beads, a little painted table, a little joined stool for a child and another joined stool "to sit on when he comes of man's estate," and a little coffer to put his things in.[41] Little Robert lived well, even if he and his godfather were sharing one room in a solar.

By the child's fourth year, discipline began to play a major role in socialization. For medieval parents as well as for moralists, the maxim of childrearing was "spare the rod, and spoil the child." The presumption seemed to be that only corporal punishment could impress on a child correct behavior, moral judgment, and adequate respect for his or her elders. A five-year-old boy, for instance, was in a neighbor's house at vespers when he took a piece of wool and put it in his cap. The lady of the house, "chastising him, struck the said John with her right hand under his left ear." He cried out and Isabella, his mother, raised the hue and carried him home, where he died.[42] The jurors apparently felt that the death was a misadventure, a necessary disciplinary action that ended up killing the boy, and did not bring an indictment for homicide.

Children in their tender years were sometimes subject to outright abuse, as opposed to legitimate discipline. Alice de Salesbury, a beggar, was found guilty of taking Margaret, daughter of John Oxwyke, a grocer living in the Ropery, and carrying her away. She stripped her so that her family would not recognize her and made her beg with her. Alice was put in the pillory for an hour.[43] A girl of seven petitioned the Chancellor, saying that she had been put into prison for eight days because someone had an evil will against her mistress. A five-year-old and a seven-year-old apparently had been molested, and the younger one perhaps even raped.[44]

Other children suffered because of their poverty. When, in the famine year of 1322, fifty-two people were crushed to death around the gate of the Preaching Friars as they struggled for alms, children were among those dead. Robert Fynel and his three sons died that day. A boy of seven, described as a pauper and a mendicant, had awakened (probably from sleeping in the open) at sunrise and had gotten up to "relieve nature" when he was run over by a cart driven by a twelve-year-old.[45]

Play, rather than serious work, was still very much a part of children's lives. Indeed, a mother complained that a man had wrongfully made her seven-year-old daughter a servant, with a contract for seven years. The mayor's court agreed and returned the child to her mother "out of charity because of the youth of the infant."[46] Other children were wandering around and playing games such as walking on logs or playing ball with friends.[47]

Childhood in London was a precarious venture. But disease, rather than accidents and homicides, claimed the lives of the vast majority of those children who died. Even though female infants and probably illegitimate children died in the greatest numbers, they were not willfully destroyed. London, like other major cities, did not replace its population with children born within the city walls. The material environment, with its crowded living conditions and prevalent filth, was bound to be inhospitable to children, who played freely in streets running with raw sewage and other waste. The grim picture of childhood mortality, however, should not obscure the fact that parents, godparents, family, servants, apprentices, and neighbors all looked after the welfare of the children. Friends and family mourned and buried those who died, but they trained, played with, and materially rewarded the ones who survived. The citizens were always in the streets, intervening on behalf of the children. No wonder so few of London's children appear in accidents and homicides. Thus neighbors intervened when a boy carrying water in a tankard came opposite a shop owned by Adam de Boctone, and a cook and clerk began ill-treating him. The neighbors did not know the defenseless boy, but feared that the men would kill him. They accosted the pair and asked why they were beating the boy "so maliciously." The clerk replied that "they would beat him as they liked" in spite of the neighbors. Then the clerk bit the man who questioned him. In the fight that followed, the clerk and the cook were beaten up, and they later sued for damages. The neighbors stood firm and said that if those two had received any harm, "they had no cause to complain."[48]

A boy is disciplined in a classroom. (Drawing by Wayne M. Howell, from a hanging sign for a Basel schoolmaster [perhaps Myconius], attributed to Ambrosius Holbein [Offentliche Kunstsammlung, Basel])

5

Childrearing, Training, and Education

Socializing the young is, ultimately, the parents' or guardians' responsibility. But this has never stopped moralists from providing books and poems of advice on what it means to be a well-brought-up child or youth and on how parents can achieve this desirable end. Manuals of childrearing in the medieval period were as spiced with proverbs as is Polonius's advice to Laertes; no doubt, Shakespeare was familiar with this pervasive literature. Because London's population was continually being replenished with recruits from the countryside and because its urban elite turned over rather quickly, the market for books on deportment and on rearing children for success in an urban environment was very good. London had few established elite households where the young could learn manners. Young people who aspired to success in London, either as merchants and craftsmen or as servants, needed to know the polite behavior that would make them acceptable in wealthy households. Parents with ambitions for their children also needed to know how to instruct. Thus the socialization of children and young people into polite society occupied an important segment of medieval London culture.

An old proverb that appeared in a variety of forms at the start of childrearing books and poems was

> A child were better to be unborn
> Than to be untaught and so be lorn.[1]

Although many of these books were written for people aspiring to service in noble households, others, such as "The Young Children's Book" were specifically adapted for those who would earn a living. These books stressed injunctions against idleness: "You must eat what you get with your hands" because "a man's arms are for working as a bird's wings for flying."[2] The advice poems and manuals that are discussed in this chapter are those directed at this more general audience of social climbers, rather than those designed for noble houses. The audience addressed is explicitly young—children or babies—and some of the books are on nurturing and schooling. They bear titles familiar to the young, such as "The ABC of Aristotle," whose points are easy to memorize because they follow the alphabet.

Some of the writers do not presume a literate audience. "Symon's Lesson of Wisdom for All Manner of Children" was written in rhyme in the hope that it would be catchy enough for children to pick up orally:

> All manner of children, ye listen and hear
> A lesson of wisdom that is written clear.
> My child, I advise thee to be wise, take heed of this rhyme.[3]

The author of "The Young Children's Book" explicitly states that he does not expect a learned reader: "This book is made for young children that bide not long at school." He tries to make it simple to understand so that it can make bad children good.[4] These tracts and poems, then, are distinct from the general works on health and courtesy that are meant for an older audience.

Training belonged to the natal home or the surrogate for it. If the parents did not know what to do, the manuals would tell them.[5] Socialization included instilling moral attitudes such as honoring father, mother, and master; encouraging courteous behavior in general; and teaching principles of clean and healthful living. These rudimentary traits were felt to lay the groundwork for a child's future success in schooling, apprenticeship, service, career, and marriage. Without them, no child could hope to thrive in society:

> All that have young people, good manners set them to learn;
> To their elders with gentle conditions let do nor say no harm.
>
> If they do ill, wise men may report their parents soon;
> How should they teach other good, belike themselves can none.

A good father maketh good children, if wisdom be them within,
Such as of custom use it in youth, in age they will begin.

He that lacketh good manners is little set by;
Without virtue or good conditions, a man is not worth a fly.[6]

For the most part, training manuals were directed to the male children of the family, but in one poem for females, "How the Good Wife Taught Her Daughter," the mother's responsibility is clear: "Lack of the mother's teaching / Makes the daughter of evil living."[7]

One case shows the length to which a London mother might go to teach her son a lesson. Richard Claidich, a scrivener, borrowed £8 2s. 6d. from a grocer. Since he did not repay it, he was thrown into prison. His mother, Adeline Claidich, arranged for two men to pay the debt, and Richard entered into an obligation to them for the amount. Adeline quietly repaid them, but asked them to keep the obligation. Eight days before she died, she pardoned her son for the mistake. He then tried to get back the obligation, and the men told him that Adeline had asked them to keep it in order "to kepe therby the said Richard under lawe and drede."[8]

Adeline was not the only parent who resorted to such measures to keep a son in line. John, son and heir of Thomas Grene, petitioned the Lord Chancellor to be released from a bond of £20 that his father had him make with Stephen Wulf, a London fishmonger, when he was "of tender age" and becoming an apprentice in "Davys Inn." His father did so "to the entent that if your said oratour [John] did demeaned or gedyd himself otherwise than well, that the said Stephen Wulf should have caused your said oratour to have been arrestyd uppon the said obligation and leyd in the Counter [a prison] in London, tyll such tyme and season as your said suppliant wuld have refourmed hym self to better governance." Since both older men were dead, John wanted release from the obligation.[9]

Other parents controlled their children's training from the grave. Adam Nayller left inheritances that were to be used by his wife to see that Richard, their son, "be advanced becomingly." Richard died in the plague only four years later. Another father left his son £10 to be given to him only if the executors thought he was "willing to make good use of the same." William Wylewan, a goldbeater, left his son, John, tools of the trade, with instructions to his executor (his wife) to deliver them to the son a year after the father's death "with condition that he be tendable and well and truly serve his mother for the whole year after my decease."[10]

In spite of neighborhood concern for the welfare of their parish children, Londoners assumed that the parents would take responsibility for their offspring's behavior. Simon and Catherine le Coteler were warned that they must not harbor or maintain their sons, who had been "ill-treating neighbors," and so were fined when the boys continued to do so.[11]

The first injunction for those teaching children was to beat them to ensure their obedience. Children were to accept the beatings as delivered in their best interest:

> And as the wise man saith in his book,
> Of proverbs and wisdoms who will look:
> "As a sharp spur maketh a horse to move,
> Under a man that should war prove,
> Right so a yard may make a child
> To learn well his lesson and to be mild."
> Lo! children, here may ye all hear and see,
> How all children chastised should be.
> And therefore, childer, look ye do well,
> And no hard beating shall you befall.[12]

Beatings were regarded as more effective than scolding, and cursing children (suggesting that the devil take their souls) was strongly forbidden by the Church.[13] The "Good Wife" told her daughter to take a "smart rod" and beat her children until they cried for mercy and knew their guilt. Her conclusion has a modern ring ("Dear child by this lore / they will love thee ever more"), akin to our joke about mothers who say, "Some day you will thank me for this."

The Daily Routine

Children were to arise, as did their elders, "betimes"—that is, at "six of the clock at the farthest." Only seven hours of sleep were recommended for children, although adults were advised to sleep for eight or nine hours:

> Seven hours for a child is temperate and good,
> If more, it offendeth and hurteth the blood.[14]

All manuals urge some devotion or prayers upon arising. Then the children were to sponge and brush the clothing intended for the day's wearing, clean their shoes, comb their hair, and wash both hands and face. Nails were to be pared if they needed it, and teeth were to be cleaned by washing or by scrubbing with an ivory or a wooden stick. Children were advised to take care to dress neatly and according to the social rank to which they belonged, with the collar at the neck, with no seams split, and with the girdle fastened about the waist. Prudent youth were to have a clean napkin that they could use "for cleaning the nose of all filthiness." They were to make their bed if they had one or to fold up the bedding neatly if they slept in the hall or on the shop floor.[15]

Children were not to be allowed to choose their own clothing because they would want clothing of fantastic cut and color, "their foolishness is beyond measure" and parents who indulged them were no better. Instead, children were to be clothed modestly and decently, according to their social rank, in good, sturdy, clean clothing. Clothing in disrepair was to be mended, and worn shoes replaced.[16]

Diet likewise concerned the moralists. In a society in which beer and wine were the common drinks at meals, moralists realized that a child might succumb to drunkenness early in life. A child was not to start a meal with drink and was not to have drink after eating hot broth or milk. Parents were advised to allow a child only two or three drinks of wine or beer during a meal because those beverages deformed their minds and caused an unreasonable diet. Parents were also told to teach their children to eat in moderation and to wait to be fed.[17]

Expectations set by the mayor and the chamberlain for those caring for city orphans seemed to reflect the moderate course set out in the books of advice. Guardians were to find food, linen and woolen clothing, shoes, and other necessities. In the case of an orphan, John, son of William Hanyngtone, these necessities included a furred gown and matching tunic, four pairs of linens, shoes, a bed, and 1*d.* a week for room and board. Records for expenses were carefully kept, either by a tally stick or in written records, so that the officials could be sure that the money remaining was given over to the orphan when she or he reached the age of majority. Gilbert de la Marche, a potter, had guardianship of the property of William, son of Sara la Feyte, but John de Linlee acted as the infant's guardian and provided nourishment, for which the potter gave him 40*s.* by tally.

The amounts spent on children's upkeep varied greatly. In 1376, the cost of keeping John, son of John Gartone, was committed to John Bas, a draper, whose daughter the boy had married at the tender age of nine. When the young wife died, her husband was still a minor, and the father-in-law rendered account for expenses that amounted to 2*s.* a week. The care of an invalid daughter of a cordwainer for six and a half years in the 1380s cost about 12*s.* a year, or about 3½*d.* a week. Obviously, she lived less well than the draper's daughter. Other guardians reported paying amounts of £1 a year, 6*d.* a week, ½ mark a year, and 66*s.* 8*d.* annually, to a high of £7 19*s.* 3*d.* for a five-year-old goldsmith's daughter over a two-year period.[18] The social status of the orphan, rather than his or her sex, seemed to determine the amount spent, so that, in accordance with the advice books, the children were maintained according to their station.

After rising and washing, now soberly and cleanly clothed, the children made their first public appearance of the day. On proceeding to the hall, they were expected to greet their parents or master—young men, by removing their caps—showing respect and humility. Breakfast consisted of good meat and drink, consumed after grace had been said.[19] The drink might have been milk, but was equally likely to have been "small beer," a low-alcohol beer made from a second brewing.

The morning routine varied with the age and plans for the children. Boys might go to school in the morning, or they might play in the streets. Apprentices, of course, worked in the shops. Moralists recommended Mass each morning, and, no doubt, youths did attend Mass on some mornings. Deportment in church was to be attentive and reverent. Talking with others (even the clergy), looking about, and laughing were, of course, in bad taste.[20]

Appearances were to be kept up in the street as well. "Symon's Lesson of Wisdom for All Manner of Children" not only gave the usual counsel to young boys to keep their heads up, doff their caps to their betters, and greet people courteously, but elaborated on the bad things that boys might do instead. The author no doubt had observed that boys were likely to throw sticks and stones at dogs, horses, and hogs and to imitate the behavior of women and men behind their backs. They were warned not to fight, swear, get their clothing dirty, or lose their books, caps, and gloves.[21]

The moralist was concerned not only about demeanor in the streets, but about the potential for accidents:

> Look thou keep thee from fire and water.
> Be ware and wise how thou look
> Over any brink, well, or brook.
> And when thou standest at any schate [fence]
> Be ware and wise that thou catch no stake;
> For many child without dread,
> Through evil heed is deceived or dead.[22]

Symon had a tender worry about the accidents that happened to children. Perhaps he had served on coroners' juries and knew about accidents firsthand. Thomas, son of Alice de Westwyk, was only six when he was walking alone at dusk and fell into a tub of scalding water. On a June evening, Robert, son of Ralph de Leyre, went to Fishwharf to bathe, but he drowned. The same fate occurred to a sixteen year old who was bathing in a ditch. Water claimed the lives of nine-year-old Mary, daughter of Agnes de Billingesgate, who went to get water from the Thames in an earthen pot, and of another girl who fell in while filling water jugs.[23] As we have seen, house fires also claimed the lives of children.

Although young boys were told to look people in the eye in the streets and to greet them courteously, the "Good Wife" taught her daughter to keep her eyes cast down:

> And when thou goest on thy way, go thou not too fast,
> Brandish not thy head, nor with thy shoulders cast,
> Have not too many words, from swearing keep aloof,
> For all such manners come to an evil proof.

On the whole, it was better to remain at home:

> Dwell at home, daughter, and love thy work much,
> And so thou shalt, my lief child, wax the sooner rich.

Women seemed to obey the injunction to stay in their homes; 50 percent of their accidental deaths occurred in houses or adjoining buildings, with the other 50 percent occurring in the streets, in bodies of water, and in churches. Only 20 percent of men's accidental deaths were in the home; 16 percent occurred in shops, and 60 percent in public spaces. The young girls, however, sometimes felt cooped up at home. Eleven-year-old Juliana, daughter of John Turgeys, was so desirous of seeing what was going on in the High Street that she stood in an open window in a solar and fell out trying to get a better view.[24]

Many exciting events occurred in homes, of course. Alice, daugher of John de Markeby, was at home after curfew when her father got drunk and began leaping about the house until a knife that he had on his girdle wounded him in the leg.[25]

The main meal was a midday dinner. If the courtesy books are correct, this was a meal taken with considerable ritual. But we must assume that such was not the case in all London households. The polished young man, however, was instructed to enter the hall, and say "God be here," and speak courteously to those present. Many houses had a holy-water strop by the entrance, and the guests were to dip their fingers in and cross themselves when they entered.

As described in the inventories referred to in Chapter 2, the better houses had basins and jugs for washing the hands before eating, along with a quantity of towels, napkins, tablecloths, pitchers, bowls, and magnificent salt cellars. Missing from the list of goods found in the pantry or buttery were plates, forks, and knives other than those used for carving. The guests, both men and women, always had their own knives on their girdles (thus explaining the tragedy of John de Markeby). People ate with their fingers; for that reason, washing the hands and keeping the nails clean were important aspects of good table manners. Rather than using a plate, four-day-old bread or a rough bread was carved into a trencher from which to eat. The trenchers were collected at the end of the meal and given to the poor, with the sauces of the rich man's table soaked into the bread. Soups were served in bowls, and the host was expected to provide spoons. Silver spoons were prized items and a common gift to a godchild, so that even relatively modest houses might have them. Failing silver, wooden or horn spoons sufficed.

The young male social climber was expected to stand and chat respectfully with his elders until the host indicated the seats for his guests, according to their degree. It was impolite to dispute the designated seating arrangement. The host sat in front of the salt cellar and placed the most respected guests by him. Those of lesser degree, including most youths, sat below the salt.

Diners ate in pairs, sharing the beer or wine cup and the meat. Thus the moralists instructed the young to "be fellowly and share with him that sits by you." As a practical matter, they also advised wiping the edge of the cup with a napkin after drinking, wiping knives on the trencher rather than on the tablecloth, dipping only a clean knife into the salt cellar, and putting meat scraps in a voider rather than back on the serving dish. Contrary to our perception of diners in the Middle Ages, the refined did not throw their bones to dogs. As the author of "The Young Children's Book" says: "Make neither the cat nor the dog your fellow at the table." And, of course, diners were admonished not to "make a noise as you sup as do boys" or scratch themselves lest people think they had fleas or pick their noses or let a pearl form on the end of the nose or run their hands through their hair lest people think they had lice. "Whether you spit near or far, hold your hand before your mouth to hide it." Guests were to praise the meal, sit up straight, talk courteously, and have a good time without laughing too loud.[26]

But did society really expect this sort of behavior? A case against an apprentice indicates that only a few code words were necessary to paint a picture of disreputable behavior. Maud Fattyng claimed that her apprentice "beat her, her daughter, and her household, despised his food, tore his linen clothes," and owed her money. It took a jury to confirm that he was not such a boor as to beat his mistress, complain about his food, or destroy his clothing, but he had to pay the money back.[27]

We may assume, however, because the moralists dwelt so long on behavior at the table, that ordinary eating was not as refined as they portray it. Most youths would not have been raised in the usual course of their lives to behave correctly at such a meal. The city had many taverns and places to buy prepared food, so many Londoners must have had a pint of beer and a meat pie on the go. Most families would have shared a one-pot meal, accompanied by bread and beer. And, too, there were all those paupers munching on stale trenchers in the streets.

Dinner, especially if it had been the elaborate repast that the moralists describe, might be followed by a postprandial nap for the diners. Servants, of course, had more than enough work to clear up from the dinner. Most artisans returned to their shops to take advantage of the daylight hours. Schoolboys probably returned to school; girls worked on embroidery or other needlework or helped with the household chores.

On Sundays and feast days, excursions outside the walls might while away the holiday. The court records give us some idea of these outings. On a Sunday in August 1337, "Walter de Mordone and his whole family were playing in the fields after dinner."[28]

The evening meal was a light one and was usually followed by leisure activities. London law prohibited evening work, so evenings could be devoted to visiting and entertainment. While the moralists would have had the youth safely at home and early to bed, the evenings sometimes turned into riot. As we have seen, even the drinking at home could get rowdy. Londoners were more at risk in their leisure than they were at work. Only 33 percent of men's accidental deaths and 8 percent of women's occurred in daylight, whereas 67 percent of men's and 92 percent of women's accidental deaths occurred in the evening or at night. Only 10 percent of male homicidal deaths (and no female ones) occurred during the day, but 90 percent of male homicidal deaths occurred in the evening or at night. As we shall see, drinking, gaming, and visiting harlots occupied the time of unruly youth. These activities could lead to violence and homicide or careless accidents caused by drunkenness.

One young woman spent a terrifying evening in the tavern of her guardians, Gilbert de Mordone, a stockfishmonger, and his wife. Walter de Benygtone came with seventeen companions to the brewhouse with stones in their hoods, swords, knives, and other weapons. They drank four gallons of beer while they lay in wait to "seize and carry off" Emma, daughter of the late Robert Pourte, who was Gilbert's ward. Gilbert's wife realized that there would be trouble and, together with the brewer, "prayed" Walter and his companions to leave. They refused, saying that they would stay and spend their money there since it was a public house. Gilbert's wife "seeing their folly returned to her chamber taking the said Emma with her." Walter and his companions were so angered by this maneuver that they attacked the brewer and the other people of the house, one of whom fled into the High Street when he was hit by stones to raise the hue and cry. Walter was right behind him, with a knife in one hand and a dagger in the other. A crowd gathered and asked Walter to surrender. When he would not, someone grabbed a staff and bashed him over the head.[29]

For other children, as we have seen, evening was a time for begging and for seeking a warm, dry place to sleep. Not all young people had the luxury of sleeping in a bed with thoughts of rising early to brush their clothes and make up their beds.

Games and Play

London adults knew that children must and would play. As far back as the twelfth century, Fitzstephen observed the games of children with fondness. We may think these games bloodthirsty and unfit for children: on Shrove Tuesday, schoolboys brought fighting cocks to their masters, and they all watched the cock fights. They also played ball in the London fields, with the scholars of each school having a team. London adult males went out on horseback to recall the days of their youth.[30] Many of the games were unorganized, with the children taking the opportunities that lay in their parish to create diversions. They played ball and tag, ran races, played hoops, and imitated adult ceremonies such as royal entries, Masses, marriages, and the giants Gog and Magog. Again, Symon proves to be the moralist with some of the shrewdest observations!

> Child, climb not over house nor wall,
> For no fruit, birds nor ball.
> Child, over men's houses no stones fling,
> Nor at glass windows no stones sling.
>
> . . .
>
> And child, when thou goest to play,
> Look thou come home by light of day.[31]

His lessons were very perceptive, as the coroners' inquests confirm. John atte Noke fell to his death when he climbed out a window to retrieve a ball that had landed in the gutter when he was playing. Seven-year-old Robert, son of John de St. Botulph, was playing with two other boys on pieces of timber when a piece fell on him and broke his right leg. Richard, son of John de Wrotham, would have done well to heed Symon's advice about getting home in daylight, for he went to a wharf on the Thames at vespers in October, fell in the river, and drowned. Six-year-old Philip, son of John de Turneye, was walking by a ditch after sunset and slipped and fell in.[32]

Although it was unlikely that children of this age would use weapons in their bird hunts, their stone throwing could be as destructive as the games that older youth played. The city proclaimed in 1327 "against shooting pigeons and other birds perched on St. Paul's or on the houses of citizens, with stone bows and arbalests, because the missiles frequently break the windows and wound passers-by."[33]

Children also participated in games of the "sad and wise," such as horse racing. Being of light build, lads of twelve or thereabouts acted as jockeys to put horses through their paces at Smithfield. In York, two Londoners set a wager about which of two horses would arrive at a cross called "grymstone cross," standing midway between York and Hull. A child was to ride each horse—one starting at Hull and the other at York—always keeping to the right of way. But the man starting off one of the horses put his hands on it and sent it off to the fallow, thus throwing the child rider and breaking the rules of the race. The child was not hurt, but the wager was lost.[34] In general, the boys must have enjoyed such opportunities to ride a swift horse. In the countryside, they seem to have delighted in watering the plow horses after a day's work in the fields.

The urban environment of many cities, including London, provided a number of parades and pageants, as we have observed, that involved children and certainly entertained them. In addition, some celebrations were reserved for children. The most notable was that of the boy bishops, whose festivities coincided with the Christmas season, beginning on St. Nicholas's Day (December 6) and ending on Holy Innocents (December 28) or the Feast of St. William (in honor of the boy said to have been murdered by the Jews of Norwich [January 7]). St. Nicholas's association with young scholars goes back to a legend about two young boys on their way to Athens to study. Their father had instructed them to visit Bishop Nicholas in Myra, but they decided to see to the arrival of their goods and rest for a visit the next day. The landlord, seeing their wealth, killed them and cut them into little pieces to sell as pickled pork. Bishop Nicholas (later a saint) had a vision about the disaster and hurried to the inn. He reprimanded the innkeeper and sought his forgiveness from heaven. His wish was granted, and the pieces of the boys emerged from the brine tub and reassembled. The bishop then sent the boys off, amid great rejoicing, to their studies in Athens.

The oddity of the boy-bishop celebration was that it disassembled the bishop, rather than the boys. The best or most favored scholar was elected from the school to impersonate the bishop as *Episcopus Puerorum*. The rest of the boys formed his dean and prebends. The boys took over the church or cathedral for the services and the sermon, ousting the real bishop. It was one of those medieval, world-turned-topsy-turvy events. The boys, whose life seemed all discipline, were given a taste of the power to discipline. They also got to travel in style with their "clergy," stopping at parish homes and religious houses to ask for alms and offerings. They progressed with fine ceremonial copes, rings, and crosses. Like any bishop, they expected a gracious meal and gifts. They sat with the host above the salt and discussed matters of papal dispensations and finer points of philosophy. A sample of their wisdom is preserved in a few of their sermons.[35] What insufferable young twits these boys must have been for a fortnight at Christmas! At least it gave them a chance to taste the power they might someday have and to let off some of the aggressions that had built up under severe discipline during the year. The boys could be rather cute as well. London parishes were reluctant to see the celebration abolished during the Reformation and restored it under Mary Tudor.

"A Schoolboy Who Aspired to Be *Episcopus Puerorum*"

Richard, son of John le Mazon, was eight years old and felt that he had been harassed from birth. His parents were very desirous for him to have a future that involved more than stonecutting and building, his father's trade. While his friends, who lived on London Bridge, as he did, ran around the streets playing, he had to do his lessons. His friends' parents allowed their sons to have hot pretzels and beer for lunch, but his mother insisted that the family sit down to a proper dinner. His parents had a proverb for everything he was supposed to do. When he did not do something correctly, his father or mother spanked him. His father always said on these occasions that to spare the rod was to spoil the child, and his mother always said, "Someday you will thank me for this." Richard was not so sure.

His morning began at six o'clock. In winter, he grumbled at the maid who came to wake him and burrowed deep in his feather bed. She would plead with him that they would both get in trouble if he did not get up. She was right, of course; so when she left, he got up. But this morning was a sunny day in July, and tomorrow was the Feast of St. Mary Magdalen, so he would not have to go to school. He washed quickly in the warm water the maid had brought, being sure that his teeth and ears were clean, for his parents were sure to inspect. He put on his clothes—the somber ones his parents thought appropriate, not the bright scarlet-lined cloak he fancied. Still, if he became boy bishop, he would get to wear a rich cope and a fine ring. He made his bed and descended from his small sleeping chamber into the hall. He greeted his parents and said his prayers with them. After breakfast, the fuss of getting him ready for school began. Since neither of his parents could read, they regarded school as an almost sacred activity. His father said that the preparation of his school satchel with wax tablets, stylus, and grammar book was like "the soldier preparing himself to the field, [who] leaves not at home his sword and his shield."[36] The proverb wore thin when repeated every morning.

He made the morning trip to school in the company of his mother. They stopped at church for the morning Mass, and then he went on to school while she shopped for dinner. She always kissed him goodbye (to his immense embarrassment, in front of hucksters who always commented in rude terms) and exhorted him to be good.

His progress to school was a combination of looking at the shops and running fast to make it to school on time. He was bound to be reverent to his schoolmaster; if he were not, he was sure to get a whipping. But today he would behave, because tomorrow he was free. All the boys were in a holiday mood, determined just to get through the day. The drudgery of Latin exercises wore down their spirits, but no one felt the sting of the willow twigs, so it was a good morning.

Returning home for his dinner, he entered the hall, crossed himself with the holy water by the door, and took off his cap. His father and the apprentices were assembled for lunch. Richard took his place at the table and said the Latin grace for his father. Several other masons were there in anticipation of the holiday on the morrow. After the meat was served, his father allowed him to have a glass of wine and asked him what he had learned that day in school. He repeated some of the Latin and made his father very proud in front of his guests. They, of course, all praised his learning, saying that he would probably become a bishop.[37] His father said that surely he would be the boy bishop in the next year or two and would be around asking for some pence for alms come Christmas next year or the year after. The proud father allowed him another glass of wine and sent him off to school, with the usual inquiry about his sword and satchel. It made his father feel learned in front of his friends to quote the proverb.

Since his elders would sit longer than usual at the table, he was free to play. His fond mother gave her usual admonitions to go gravely back to school and return immediately, without stopping to play with the rowdy children of the neighborhood. She reminded him that he was not to get his new school clothes soiled.

With a suppressed yell, he escaped into the bright midday sun to join his friends in street games. The game of the day was to hang by the hands from a beam that protruded from the side of London Bridge. Richard was feeling brave from the wine and the praise at lunch and felt that he could do just about anything. As future boy bishop, he would be a real tyrant about demanding a glass of wine and cakes. But when he swung himself out on the beam, he felt his hands slipping. As Richard plummeted toward the river, he prayed to St. Nicholas to save him, promising that he would always obey his parents. His satchel pulled him down, and Father Thames claimed another victim.[38]

Schooling

Schooling became increasingly important in the late fourteenth and fifteenth centuries, with many guilds requiring functional literacy before an apprentice could be enrolled. By 1478, the Goldsmiths forbade members to take apprentices "wtout he canne writte and Rede." The Skinners had a similar rule by the 1490s, and the Ironmongers required their apprentices to write their names when they registered. So severe were the requirements that Thomas Bodyn complained about his master, saying that he had become an apprentice at age fourteen with the promise that in his twelve years of apprenticeship he would have schooling at his own expense in the first year and a half to learn grammar and in the second half-year to learn to write. But his master, a haberdasher, set him to work immediately. Another young man said that his master was to pay for his schooling with a priest, but instead had set him to degrading tasks, such as carrying water and working in the priest's kitchen.[39] Perhaps 40 percent of lay male Londoners could read Latin, and 50 percent or more probably read English and perhaps French.[40] Moralists reflected the increased societal demand for schooling and informed the young and their teachers how they were to behave at school. Private citizens and London institutions also responded to the growing need for schools by establishing schools or leaving money to support students.[41]

Schools to teach Latin were in the control of the bishop of London. The original three schools grew to six in the fifteenth century. Many of the graduates went on to Oxford or Cambridge and later sought careers in the Church, the law, or the government. Many private individuals, smaller establishments, and churches also offered elementary education.[42]

One parish church, for instance, had a choir school, which was conducted in a separate chamber in 1523 and for which the church hired the organist John Norfolke to teach. The school had one or two forms and a desk. Some of the children were sent at the expense of the parishioners, who paid for clothing, boots, and board, in addition to tuition. But the school also made money by renting the services of the choir for 3s. 4d. to private parties who wanted it to perform at wakes or at Christmas. The children also earned 1d. per performance, and this fee amounted to enough in wages for at least one choir boy to borrow against his earnings. He died before he could pay back the advance.[43]

The curriculum included perhaps some Latin, but certainly provided literacy in English and training in keeping accounts. A manual for commercial French published around 1415 advertised that a twelve-year-old boy at William Kyngesmill's hostel had learned to read, write, cast accounts, and speak French in only three months and was ready for a London apprenticeship.[44]

The presence of so many schools for elementary and commercial literacy gave rise to a considerable book trade in primers. In the late fifteenth century, James Ravenell of London, a stationer, said that he had for years bought primers from a Dutchman named Frederick Egemonde and had made an agreement to buy unbound primers from him worth 16*s.* at a trade fair.[45]

Some of the wills of fifteenth-century merchants indicate a long-term commitment to their children's education. The 5 to 10 marks provided in wills would have permitted a term of education starting when the child was seven or eight and continuing to age fifteen or sixteen. In that time, the child would have gotten a good grasp of writing English, French, and Latin, as well as of doing accounts. As early as 1312, Nicholas Picot, an alderman, wanted his sons, Nicholas and John, to study and attend school until they could write Latin poetry. Although many of these young people could find education in London while living at home, some were sent to country boarding schools along with the gentry sons. Some of these young men went on to university, but many entered apprenticeships at the age of sixteen.[46]

Some parents felt that a foreign education would benefit their sons. Christine and John Herford arranged with Mark Storzi to have their son, Thomas, accompany Storzi to Pisa. He was to provide the boy with meat and drink while he was in school there. When Storzi presented the bill, the mother refused to pay.[47]

Girls of the better class may also have received some education. A chandler's orphaned daughter, for instance, attended school from age eight to thirteen at a cost of 25*s.* for school fees. Other evidence indicates an education of four or five years for girls. They learned English and perhaps French as well as accounting, but probably not much Latin. Their education might have been at grammar schools along with the boys, but at least one schoolmistress is mentioned in a bequest, so they may have had separate schooling.[48] Since London law permitted women to trade on their own and widows to carry on their husbands' businesses, parents had to prepare their daughters for this eventuality. One can imagine that an educated young woman would be more desirable as a marriage partner.

Moralists, of course, could not rely on youths to know automatically how to conduct themselves in school and wrote at length about their expected behavior. Perhaps some of the moralists were schoolmasters and wrote in self-interest.

The schoolboy was to pack up a satchel of his books, along with writing implements: pen, parchment or paper or wax tablets, and stylus. On the way to school, he was to greet his betters reverently, and he was to arrive expeditiously at the school. The master, of course, was to be greeted, hat in hand, with reverence and fellow schoolmates with tokens of love. Then the student was to go straight to his appointed seat, undo his satchel, and apply himself to the lesson with industry and love of learning. During classes, the ideal student did not let his mind wander, answered the schoolmaster expeditiously, and was not disputatious with fellow students.

Returning from school, students were exhorted to be orderly, rather than "running in heaps as a swarm of bees."

> Not using, but refusing,   such foolish toys,
> As commonly are used   in these days of boys,
> As whooping and hallooing,   as in hunting the fox,
> That men it hearing   deride them with mocks.

And if the student applied himself as Cato recommended of old, then he could aspire to respect from his elders and advancement in society, for even a man born to a lower status could hope to achieve a higher position through education.[49]

In a poem from about 1500, a schoolboy wrote that he would gladly become a clerk, but learning was such strange work because the birch twigs were so sharp. He particularly hated to go to school on Monday mornings and usually arrived late:

> My master lokith as he were madde;
> "where hast thou be, thow sory ladde?"
> "Milked dukkis, my moder badde":
>
>   . . .
>
> My master pepered my ars with well good speed:
> hit was worse than fynkll sede;
> he wold not leve till it did blede.
> Myche sorow haue he for his dede!

This sad adventure is followed by several verses in which the student imagines his teacher as a hare and all his books as hounds. The student himself is a jolly hunter who blows his horn and releases a brace of greyhound-books to kill the teacher-hare.[50]

A fond London father, a goldsmith, had a priest who was teaching his son imprisoned because of damages the priest caused by beating the boy. The priest claimed that he had not done the boy any hurt, but had "chastised the child as a child ought to be for his learning."[51] How the schoolboys must have rejoiced when an Oxford master, out early one morning to collect willow twigs for a switch to beat them, slipped and fell into the river and drowned.[52]

Moral Behavior and Its Goals

The goal set by teachers for youth was for them to become "sad and wise"—that is, sober and restrained, as adults were supposed to be. To be "wanton and wild" was characteristic of youth. The ideal child was "meek and fair to look upon, very eager for learning and with a great desire to all goodness." "Obedience learn in youth, in age it will avoid vice," people believed.[53]

Because the parents were to be the primary teachers of virtue, the first injunction to children was to honor father and mother:

> And child, worship thy father and thy mother;
> Look that thou grieve neither one nor other,
> But ever, among them thou shalt kneel down,
> And ask their blessing and benison.[54]

The same obedience was to extend to a master, who was also to be treated with respect: "An thy master speak to thee, take thy cap in hand."[55]

Many testators did show their reverence for their parents by including prayers for them along with those for themselves or by arranging burial near them. Alice Brudenell, a silkwoman, showed unusual filial piety in having prayers said for her father, Thomas Pygot, her grandfather John, and her great-grandfather Nicholas.[56]

Children though, might repay their parents and stepparents with lawsuits and beatings, rather than with respect and thanks. Thomas Grey, a grocer, complained that his son counseled another man to have Thomas imprisoned. Another son beat his father and led a gang that terrorized the Smithfield neighborhood.[57]

In addition to teaching respect for their parents and masters, one of the main goals of the guides was to inculcate in the young an understanding of and a reverence for hierarchy and authority. In a society in which feudal hierarchy was very much a part of royal government and in which sumptuary legislation regulated what each estate could eat and wear, and in a city in which fine social distinctions regulated daily interactions as well as government, it behooved a youth aspiring to either maintain his parents' social position or achieve a better one to learn the rules.[58] Thus books of advice tell those seeking household service positions how the upper estate should be treated and what the seating arrangement should be:

The Mayor of London, a baron, a mitered abbot, the three chief justices, the Speaker of Parliament—all these estates are great and honorable, and they may sit together in chamber or hall, two or three at a mess, if it so please them; but in your office you must try to please everyman.[59]

Such information was also useful to those who succeeded in improving their social position, for they would know who was above them and who below.

At least one of the guides was directed to urban youth and contained advice on how to behave in business: "Use no swearing of falsehood in buying or selling, else shall you be shamed at the last. Get your money honestly, and keep out of debt and sin. Be eager to please and so live in peace and quiet."[60] These values were reinforced in the guild regulations when the youth finished apprenticeship and took his oath as a master.

The advocacy of general truthfulness in all dealings and avoidance of gossip was shrewd advice. As one writer put it: "[B]e not full of tales; beware what you say, for your own tongue may be your foe. If you say aught, take good heed where and to whom, for a word spoken to-day may be repented seven years after."[61] Such practical advice included speaking no ill of neighbors and making no promises that would be hard to keep.

Londoners had many occasions to see the plight of the poor, and moralists took the traditional Christian line that one should not scorn the poor. Apparently, Londoners imbibed this lesson, for they were generous in bequests to the poor in their wills.

Above all, youth was to accept the conservative, Christian values of the society and to give the impression of stability. As the "Wise Man" said to his son: "If you be well at ease, and sit warm among your neighbours, do not get new-fangled ideas, or be hasty to change or flit [move]; for if ye do, ye lack wit and are unstable, and men will speak of it and say: 'This fool can bide nowhere!'"[62]

The strongest teacher of morals, then, was the opinion of others. As we shall see in Chapter 11, those youth who did not follow the moral injunctions and adopt manners of the "sad and wise" would continue as adolescents and not move into the ranks of adults. That the elders had the power to deny access to adult status was a strong argument to learn approved behavior in youth.

Most educational programs have rather limited success, and many students never learned the behavior required in polite society. Most of the apprentices and servants came from the countryside and may or may not have had the recommended training before they arrived in the city. For many Londoners as well, fine manners and even cleanliness were not always necessary. But when we try to find out what the life of a less privileged youth was like, the evidence is more difficult to come by.

The books of manners actually tell us much about ordinary behavior because they are full of advice about how well-raised youths are to differentiate themselves from the multitude in the streets. We can assume that less favored children were loud and boisterous, played games in the street, and drank too much beer, frequented taverns, tore their clothes, and spoke disrespectfully to people.

John de Shaffeld, described as a "strange boy" (*garcio extraneus*), certainly fell into this category. At curfew, he entered a brewhouse and "privily took away a woman's hood worth 9*d.*" When the brewer followed him to recover the hood, the boy took out a knife and struck him near the navel.[63]

But even some of the youth from what should have been privileged families failed to live by the rules. For instance, William, son of Henry atte Rowe, a goldsmith, was standing near the top of St. Vedast Lane near the Cheap and "made water into a certain urinal [and] cast the urine into the shoe of an unknown young man, and because the latter complained, the said William struck him with his fist." A man standing near by, no doubt a "sad and wise" adult, upbraided him for his actions, but William became furious and grabbed a staff, bashing his adviser on the forehead so that he died.[64] So much for the many injunctions to be respectful to one's elders, control anger, and be courteous in address to people in the street![65]

One could, however, get into considerable trouble for not obeying the codes of conduct. Thomas Gold, an apprentice to a draper, claimed that he was "going within the city in the peace of God and the king" when he was "shouldered by two Spaniards to whom he had given no occasion." The Spaniards claimed in the wardmoot that he had shouldered them, and they had him put into prison.[66]

With schooling complete and manners and moral behavior instilled, the well-raised child was ready for the next stage of life—adolescence. Parents who aspired to marry their daughters well or to place their sons in apprenticeship or service took the task of rearing their offspring very seriously. The spoiled, unruly child would not prosper in medieval London because the next stage of his or her life would be passed in a home other than the natal one. No one would take on the care of a child who was "unboxom" (disobedient), but "[w]ise child is Father's bliss."[67] The paragon of virtue was like little William in "The Merchant and His Son":

In tyme of age he wente to schole, that curtes ys and hende,
He cowde hys gramer wonder wele: hys felows cowde hym not amende;
He was bothe meke and mylde, as a gode chylde owyth to bee;
When he was comen to hys age, a godely man was hee.[68]

The instruction of a young girl. (Drawing by Wayne M. Howell, from a hanging sign for a Basel schoolmaster [perhaps Myconius], attributed to Ambrosius Holbein [Offentliche Kunstsammlung, Basel])

6

Orphans and Their Upbringing

Reading through approximately 2,000 wardship cases in London's Letter Books is enough to make a historian skeptical about Philippe Ariès's claim that children were not valued. London's mayor, aldermen, and chamberlain were busy men with their own businesses, as well as official duties, but they paid careful attention to the welfare of citizens' orphans who were in their charge. London's laws were remarkably caring. Orphanhood was common in the cities of medieval Europe, but London's approach was particularly protective of orphans' lives and fortunes. Life was tenuous for parents as well as for children. Many of London's children grew up in families with at least one stepparent, and some lost both parents and were reared by family friends or even by complete strangers. Female-headed households were not uncommon, nor were those with stepparents as well as stepsiblings. In this respect, these London children have much in common with modern American children who grow up with stepparents or with one parent (albeit because of a high divorce rate rather than because of high mortality).[1] London's laws granted medieval orphans more protection than our own courts give today's children. They determined who would raise them, monitored the fortunes of the youth, and required that people who undertook to administer their estates have sureties who would also guarantee the return of the estate with their own money; they also investigated and rectified unscrupulous or neglectful treatment of the children.

The orphans who form the basis of this study of childrearing are not those who are most familiar historically: the children of the poor and destitute who were put into orphanages. They were not foundlings. Some may have been bastards, but they had inheritances. Only rarely were these orphans the object of charity. They are also unlike our classic view of orphans in that they often had one parent, usually a mother, alive. In our terms, they were only semiorphans.[2]

The tender treatment of citizens' orphans had a curious social effect that will be discussed in this chapter. London, unlike Florence and Flanders, did not develop strong patrilines. Londoners' horizontal ties through their guilds were very powerful, but the city had no predominant families to resemble the Medicis of Florence and the Van Artveldts of Ghent.

When William Caxton returned to London after thirty years in Flanders, he was struck by the absence of long lineages among the merchant elite. In his prologue to *Caton*, he observed:

> I see that the children that ben borne within the sayd cyte// encreace/and prouffyte not lyke theyr faders and olders/but for the moost parte after that they ben comen to theyr parfight yeres of discrecion/and rypenes of age/ how wel that theyr fathers have lefte to them grete quantite of goodes/ yet scarcely amonge ten two thryve/I have sene and knowen in londes in dyuerse cytees/that of one name and lyngage successyuely have endured prosperously many heyres/ye a v or vi honderd yere/ and somme a thousand.[3]

London children, although they might have been left very wealthy by their fathers, did not often succeed in carrying on the family name or fortune. Only two in ten families in London managed to perpetuate themselves, whereas on the Continent family lineages lasted for generations. Caxton concluded that the moral fiber of young Londoners was not strong enough and that if they would only read and imbibe the principles to be found in the life of Cato, the problem would be solved.

The great historian of London, Sylvia Thrupp, also took up Caxton's observation and pointed to both the high mortality rate among children, which brought many lines to a premature end, and the propensity of London families that had done well to seek to establish themselves in the country as gentry rather than continue to be part of the merchant elite.[4]

Her conclusions are sound. But London's laws, which generously provided for widows and their orphaned children, tended to reinforce horizontal ties rather than the vertical, patrilineal ones found in Florence and among the clans in Flemish towns.[5] The dower and the court's inclination to award guardianship to the mother and her kin ensured maximal survival of the children of the truncated family by guaranteeing that they would have adequate property and continuity of care from one parent. A side effect of the court's action was to encourage widows to remarry and to take both their dowers and their children's inheritances into another household.

Laws on Orphans and Guardians

Because of diligent mayoral oversight, the court records relating to orphans provide us with the best insight we can get into the upbringing of children in fourteenth- and fifteenth-century London. An orphan, by the city's definition, was a child who had lost the parent, usually the father, who was a freeman (citizen) of London. One could become "free of the city" by being born in the city, by buying the rights of citizenship (known as redemption), or by qualifying through completion of an apprenticeship. By far the vast majority of citizens were those who had gone through apprenticeships, so that the data represent artisans as well as members of the merchant class, both those who were rich and those who had not prospered. Noncitizens' orphans, be they wealthy or poor, foreign or English, did not enjoy the mayor's protection. In the late Middle Ages, about one-third of the adult males in London were freemen, and it is from this group that the wards came.[6]

London law stipulated that a testator's property be divided into three parts. One-third was for the testator to dispose of for the good of his soul, one-third went to his children or his heirs, and one-third went to his wife as dower for her life use. This last part reverted to the heirs on the widow's death, even if she had remarried. She could, however, take the dower with her into another marriage. Unless the testator modified these provisions by a will, all children, both boys and girls, received equal shares of the inheritance. For instance, in settling a wardship case for the orphans of Simon Godard and his wife, both deceased, a silk cope valued at £30 and £10 in cash, along with papers showing debts owed to Simon, were delivered to the chamberlain. The cope was given by the king to the bishop of Worcester for his consecration. The mayor and the community reimbursed the estate for its value. One married daughter received one-quarter of the estate, another daughter now of age received her quarter, and one-half was kept aside for two minor boys.[7]

In establishing their laws about orphans, London citizens seem to have had a tender concern both about their children and about what would happen to their inheritance:[8]

> A testator may bequeath guardianship of his son and his chattels to anyone he thinks fit: such guardians being bound to apply the proceeds of his inheritance to the use and advantage of such child until he comes of age. If arrangements are not made then the child is given to the side of the family from which his inheritance does not derive. If from the father, then the mother or nearest kinsman on the mother's side. If from the mother, then the nearest kinsman on the father's side.[9]

They required their mayor, aldermen, and chamberlain to protect their orphans—both their bodies and their inheritances. They also expressed doubts about the motives of their fellow men when confronted with the person and the estate of a vulnerable child.[10]

The law thus stipulated that no one who could profit from the death of the child could serve as guardian. In one case, when a mother and her second husband claimed the wardship of her daughter, Jakemina, the court said that by city law, wardship of minors "ought not to be in the hands of a kinsman to whom the inheritance could descend." Since Jakemina had all her inheritance from her mother and none from her father, her wardship remained with her paternal aunt, the prioress of Kelingburne.[11]

The city had a special Common Pleader or Sergeant (usually the youngest attorney in the mayor's court), who took an inventory of each child's inheritance. The mayor and the chamberlain could then assign the wardship of the orphan or orphans to either those designated in the citizen's will or those selected by the mayor and the chamberlain. The court had a good idea about the wishes and wealth of the dead citizen and so could make an informed choice of guardian. It took its charge seriously and required the guardians to find sureties to guarantee that they would protect the child and the property to be delivered when the child came of age. The court also enforced these provisions, as we shall see. By the early fifteenth century, the city required the guardians to post bond for the children's wealth.[12]

In undertaking the protection of orphans, the city and its citizens wanted to ensure each child's survival and material advantage. In addition to favoring the mother as guardian, the mayor's court controlled the ward's marriage and even his or her apprenticeship, thus ensuring that the child could not be married or placed below his or her rank or for the benefit of the guardian.[13] A typical entry concerned Alice, daughter of William de Thele, whose guardianship was granted to John de Gildeford provided he would "maintain, threat and instruct Alice as he ought, would not let her suffer disparagement [loss of social status] nor marry without consent of the Mayor and Aldermen and of her parents [friends]." When the child came of age, the estate would be returned along with "2*s*. in the pound according to the custom," as "mesne profit."[14]

To ensure that all surviving children and their goods were accounted for, it seems to have been customary to have the children physically appear before the mayor in the Guildhall. At least John de .London, a barber, willed that "his said children be brought before the Mayor and Sheriffs of London for the time being at the Guildhall, so that the portion of each child may, with the assent of the said Mayor and Sheriffs, be delivered to some honest and sufficient person to keep in trust for them."[15]

The laws protecting children were strong, and we shall see that they were generally enforced. But the reader is surely growing skeptical. Does this not put considerable control in the hands of the mayor and city officials? Were they honest? If these children were as wealthy as Caxton says and their guardianship was so desirable, would not the mayor be importuned (perhaps with money) to be granted the wardship of a rich orphan? The incentives to marry a widow and to take in her children, were certainly very attractive. The new husband would have the use of his new wife's dower (one-third of the estate) for the rest of her life and the use of the children's portion (one-third) until they came of age. With such attractive commodities on the market, London's laws had to be explicit to protect these luscious little plums.

The Age and Condition of Orphans

Before moving on to the potential abuses of guardianship, we need to know who these young innocents were that London was so eager to protect. Knowledge of their ages at the time of entering orphanhood, their wealth, the number of siblings, and the patterns of remarriage of their mothers helps us to form a social, if not a psychological, picture of their condition.

While the ages of the children entering into wardship are not always given, age is noted often enough to allow us to form some idea of the average ages at which the children had lost a parent, usually the father. During the fourteenth century, the average age of the orphans was seven to ten years; the children were on average younger during the first half of the century (Appendix, Table 3). The children, therefore, would be wards for eleven to fourteen years before they reached the age of majority. Put another way, the guardians would have the use of their property for that period of time. Since they were so young, most orphans were residing at home when their fathers died, rather than being in service or in an apprenticeship.

We can form a better picture of the stage in a child's development at which the bereavement occurred by looking at the percentage of children in various age groups. Sixty percent of the orphans in the preplague years and 57 percent in the postplague years of the fourteenth century were at the vulnerable age of nine or under when their fathers died. In the preplague period, 20 percent of the wards were infants or toddlers, but in the postplague period from 1350 to 1389, only 6 percent were (Appendix, Table 4). In spite of the low number of toddlers, fertility increased after the plague. In the first half of the fourteenth century, 15 percent of the children were between four and six when they became wards. This figure increased to 20 percent in the second half of the century. Twenty-five percent of the wards were between seven and nine in the first half of the century; this figure increased to 31 percent for the years from 1350 to 1389.

The majority of orphans, therefore, were still in the early developmental stages of life when they suffered their bereavement. How much difference this fact made in their training and outlook is hard to assess. The coroners' inquests involving very young children suggest maternal involvement; either the children are recorded as being in the company of their mother or the mother is noted as the finder of the body. Children were probably more reliant on a mother's presence than on a father's, so his death may not have been as important as the mother's would have been. The merchant fathers, in any case, were often absent for long periods of time. As we have seen, the child was connected from birth to a large network of people not related by blood. Servants and apprentices and perhaps even a journeyman lived in the household. Neighbors were always visiting, so the child would not feel deprived of male direction or company. The stepfather might even already know the child and might well not be a stranger. And, just as for children of divorced families today, the commonness of the experience might have made it easier to accept.

Whatever psychological trauma the death of the father might have caused, most of the children were, as Caxton observed, materially well provided for. Their property included real estate, such as taverns, messuages, houses, and tenements. In addition, a certain amount of their inheritance included cash, plate, clothing, and household goods.[16] Although the total value of the inheritances cannot be measured, that of the cash endowments can be calculated. The value of cash settlements was only £80 before 1348, but rose steadily in the period following the onset of plague to reach a high of £901 by the years 1429 to 1468 (Appendix, Table 5). The change is partly due to the care in recording the orphans' property during the later part of the fourteenth century.[17] Better recording, of course, meant that the guardians would be less able to cheat their wards when they returned the property.

The effects of widespread death in postplague London also influenced the fortunes of orphans. Those who survived became the heirs to greater concentrations of wealth because the law required that the survivors share the portion of any co-heirs who died. The number of siblings in these orphan families indicates that the pool of surviving children who could inherit contracted with the outbreak of the Black Death, as we observed in Chapter 4. Although fertility increased so did mortailty. As heirs of their siblings, the survivors constituted a very wealthy group of children.

The Guardians

London's wealthy young survivors were very desirable commodities. Anyone taking their wardship would have the use of their property for an average of a dozen years. Control of a wardship, therefore, could be a major financial advantage. Since no one who could benefit from a particular orphan's death was eligible for guardianship, the child's survival was in the best interest of the guardian. If the child died, his or her property reverted to the estate and thus moved outside the guardian's control unless he or she retained guardianship of a sibling. Thus the law encouraged a guardian to take a selfish interest in the orphan's survival.

The citizens seem to have had confidence in their law and in the mayor as its primary administrator. In the late medieval Husting wills, only 210 men designated guardians for their children.[18] Their overwhelming preference (55 percent) was for the mother to assume this role. After her, the testator looked to friends (27 percent), kin (8 percent),[19] executors (6 percent), and, finally, apprentices, servants, and churchmen.[20]

The mayor followed similar patterns when he selected guardians for the citizen's orphans. The mother was the favored guardian; from 30 to 57 percent of the individual children were in the care of their mothers, either alone or with a stepfather. The period covered by the lower percentage included 1350 to 1388, when a number of the mothers must have died in the new visitations of the plague (Appendix, Table 6). The father alone as guardian does not appear until the end of the fourteenth century, which suggests that the number of London heiresses had increased.[21]

On the whole, the mayor and aldermen seem to have made an attempt to keep the children with kin. Until the onset of the plague, 61 percent of children were placed with kin. The percentage fell to 36 percent in the worst of the plague years and only gradually recovered to 54 percent by the middle of the fifteenth century. Since some of the people in the nonkin category might have been distant kin or kin on the mother's side, the actual percentage of orphans who went into the household of relations must have been even higher.

The presence of so many stepfathers (17 percent in 1309–1348, increasing to a high of 34 percent in 1389–1428) indicates the workings of one of London's most lucrative marriage markets. Widows with minor children were very desirable and remarried quickly, sometimes when they were still pregnant with a child by their late husband. Canon law did not require a period of mourning before remarriage.[22] Between 1309 and 1458, 57 percent of the 212 widows who appeared before the Court of Orphans had already remarried. The proportion is very high, considering that in sixteenth-century England only about one-third of widows remarried.[23] Furthermore, the tendency for widows to remarry increased in the late fourteenth and fifteenth centuries. From 1309 to 1388, only 36 percent of widows remarried, but from 1389 to 1458, 73 percent remarried. A comparison of the growth in the size of orphans' inheritances (Appendix, Table 5) with the increasing incidence of remarriage of widows suggests that London men were not insensitive to the considerable charms of manipulating the dower of the widow, along with the inheritance of the minor children until they came of age. When widows remarried, they tended to marry men in the same trade or guild as their former husbands. Although widows with only one child were more likely to remarry than were widows with more than one child, the number of children did not make a substantial difference in remarriage.[24]

An example makes the figures clear. A fifteenth-century London grocer married a widow with six children. Her dower was £764, and her children, of course, had an equal amount as inheritance. In other words, the grocer gained the use of £1,528 until the children reached the age of majority and retained the use of his wife's dower for as long as she lived.[25]

London citizens came to rely increasingly on guild brothers or masters to act as surrogates for themselves in rearing their orphans. A small percentage of the selected guardians were masters to children already apprenticed, but the dependence on guild brothers indicates that strong emotional bonds of trust and friendship had developed among the members of guilds. The horizontal ties of London society, therefore, were not only underscored by the remarriage of widows, but also reinforced by the granting of wardship to guild brothers. This sort of tie is apparent in the case of William de Lewes, who requested that Thomas de Frowyk, a fellow goldsmith, become the guardian to Edmund and John, aged twelve and eight. Thomas was to hold the deeds that granted William's wife a house and tenement for life with entail to her sons. Two other goldsmiths stood surety for the arrangement.[26]

Although maternal kin were favored over paternal kin, they did not enjoy a significant privilege. Testators could use their wills to empower kin to take an active role in rearing children. For instance, Nicholas de Halweford entrusted the money for his three sons to his brother, although his wife was to rear them. He also gave his brother and sister-in-law 10 marks to take two daughters, Margaret and Matilda, into an apprenticeship. Matilda had an additional 5 marks toward her marriage.[27]

When little fortune and no immediate relatives could be associated with the orphan, the chamberlain took responsibility. Thus in 1320, when "Walter, son of Richard the cook, a vagrant orphan," came into the hands of the chamberlain, that official appeared with the child before the mayor. The child's goods, such as they were, and his rearing were assigned to Andrew Horn, the chamberlain. If a child was truly destitute, the chamberlain might charge the city for expenses of custody.[28] No citizen's child, therefore, should have been without a home.

Our consideration of children who were raised by one parent has not included a discussion of that large group of semiorphans whose fathers were still alive but whose mothers had died. Most of these fathers controlled the family wealth and so did not appear in the Court of Orphans. If the remarriage of widows was common, it was even more common for widowers to remarry, and many of these orphans grew up with a stepmother in the house.[29]

"Alison, the Bastard Heiress"[30]

Margaret had told herself when her master, John Rayner, died that at least she was set for some years. Yes, she had been mistress as well as servant to Rayner, cornmonger and citizen of London, but she bore him an illegitimate daughter, Alison, whom he adored. When he died, he left Alison 110 marks, mazers, two pieces of silver with covers, one "note" with foot and cover of silver gilt, and eighteen silver spoons. All these goods were delivered into the hands of the mayor and chamberlain, as was proper, for the child was a citizen's orphan. John had assured Margaret that the mayor usually granted the mother wardship. Margaret would have a bequest, in addition to the use of Alison's considerable inheritance until the girl was sixteen or more. With that bequest, Alison's inheritance, and the house he was leaving jointly to them, Margaret could make an honorable marriage.

But gossip in London spread as fast as fire in a thatched roof, and "one John Bryan, fishmonger, came before [the mayor] and begged to have the goods and chattels delivered into his wardship until the majority of Alison together with her body." He was awarded guardianship upon presenting sufficient surety to answer for her at her full age for goods and chattels according to the custom of the city—that is, 12*d.* for every pound sterling. The mayor explained to the furious Margaret that she was only Rayner's former concubine, not his widow; she could not claim guardianship of her own child because no one would stand surety for repayment. Rayner's paltry bequest to her of 40*s.* 4*d.* could not attract a husband of the right station to gain the wardship.

The household into which Alison was born was a prosperous one located near St. Paul's, where her father traded in grains at the corn market. She slept in the master chamber over the great hall, sharing the room with her mother and father. The household contained both male and female servants, along with two apprentices. When visitors dined at the house, her mother did not sit at the table with the guests, as other mothers did, but waited on them as a servant might. Alison was only six years old when her father died, too young to realize that her mother was really only John's concubine and not his legitimate wife. Her father was an amiable old man who had spent more time playing with her than most fathers in the neighborhood devoted to their daughters. She was very sad and frightened when he died, although her mother assured her that she would be all right.

Within a week of her father's death, Alison's life changed dramatically. She and her mother went to live with a complete stranger, John Bryan, the fishmonger, and his wife and two children. They moved from the comfortable house smelling of grain near St. Paul's into a house on the other side of the city that always smelled of stale fish. Although she was treated as a member of the Bryans' household, her mother became a servant in the house. Alison slept with her mother in the "maid's chamber," a room sparsely furnished with a straw pallet for her mother and a little feather bed for her. But this arrangement lasted only a month. As soon as the executors could sell the house and pay Margaret her small bequest, Bryan dismissed her from service. With a little more than 40*s.*, Margaret rented a room nearby and kept an eye on Alison, but she had to work as a huckster to supplement her money. Alison played with Bryan's children and began learning needlework and some reading and writing. She took her meals in the great hall with the Bryans, their visitors, and Richard Fraunceys, the apprentice. She continued to dress as well as she always had, but she ate more fish than she cared to.

As Alison was growing up to be a very pretty twelve-year-old, the Bryans' fortunes began to falter. Margaret, who sold beer as a regrator in the street, had heard all the neighborhood gossip about the Bryans' problems. She was worried that the Bryans would absorb the 110 marks that

John Rayner had left for Alison's apprenticeship as a silkworker. It was time for Alison to begin the apprenticeship. Margaret warned Alison about the financial straits of the Bryans and told her that they were borrowing money. She also told the girl to be wary of any change in her treatment and to report such changes to Margaret immediately.

Mistress Bryan greeted Alison heartily one day as she had her breakfast in the hall. She said that they were going to go to the Cheap to look for a gold ring for her, and then they were going to have a new holiday dress made. Alison was suspicious. It was a hot summer, and Bryan's business always suffered when fish spoiled in the heat. The smell of fish that had gone off permeated the neighborhood. Margaret was also nervous about this unseasonable generosity and had a suspicion about the Bryans' plans.

When the ring and dress were ready, Mistress Bryan announced a party for August 20. Richard Fraunceys's family was coming for dinner, and they would have a roast of beef, rather than the usual fish. The parish priest, a frequent visitor, was also invited.

The dinner was a luxurious one, with wine, meat, and a pudding for dessert. After the meal, the adults talked seriously to Alison about her future and about how good a match Richard would be as a husband. Alison had come to like Richard, who had always acted like a sympathetic big brother, willing to listen to her troubles. However, Alison said that she could not marry without first talking to her mother and that her father had wanted her to be apprenticed to a silkwoman before she married. But the Bryans insisted that they were not really discussing a marriage; they just wanted her to agree that she would be happy to marry Richard. In any case, the marriage would not take place for some years yet. Richard was still an apprentice and could not marry, and she was too young to be married. It would be five more years before they could talk of marriage. She agreed that she would like to marry Richard, and Richard presented her with the gold ring, which was so pretty that she happily wore it to bed that night.

The next morning, when she told her mother, there was a terrible row in the street between Margaret and the Bryans. The Bryans claimed that Margaret cared only because it meant that she would not get the profits from marrying off her daughter and that, in any case, she had no right to any such profits. Margaret accused the Bryans of contracting a marriage for Alison illegally. As official guardians, they did not have the right to make espousals for Alison. She was as good as married now in the eyes of the Church. She accused them of making the arrangement to get Alison's inheritance to pay off debts they owed to Richard Fraunceys. Yes, Richard's family had cooperated, 110 marks was a good dowry, but what had Alison gotten in exchange by way of dower? No promises at all, since she had no friends present at the espousals.

Margaret took the case directly to the mayor's court, but the Bryans had moved quicker, and the mayor and the chamberlain said the marriage was registered in the Letter Books. Since Alison would suffer no disparagement in the proposed marriage, they granted permission, and Bryan paid a 20*s*. fee. A citizen's concubine could only rage.

Abuses of Wards and Orphans

The case of Alison, the bastard heiress, alerts us to the possibility that the value of orphans' property could lead to abuses of the system. Fierce fights for wardship could ensue, and, because a wardship could be sold, plans for a child's optimal rearing could take second place to the value of the child's inheritance. To the extent that an orphan was a valuable market commodity, his or her well-being was at risk. Potential abuses included misuse of the orphan's inheritance, failure to produce the funds or goods when the orphan came of age, marriage of the ward without the mayor's permission, and insufficient care in rearing the ward. The Letter Book evidence indicates that only 5 percent of the 495 orphanage cases (with a case being the children in one family) from 1309 to 1428 suffered an abuse of wardship. Most of these complaints involved diversion of funds, rather than arranging marriages without permission. Although the incidence of abuses of wardship was certainly higher than this figure suggests, by far the majority of children in wardship did not experience misappropriations.

Detection of abuses rested with the "next friends" of the orphan or with city officials. In other words, someone other than the guardian had to keep watch over the welfare of the children and their estates. Alison had ineffective help from her mother, but others could rely on uncles, neighbors, and family friends.[31] Again, it was those early childhood networks that continued to oversee the welfare of London's children. They had to go to the chamberlain and the mayor to complain. Sometimes the chamberlain acted on his own, as Richard Odyham did in bringing a bill relating to the two daughters of John de Heylesdon, a mercer. "By virtue of his office, he forced a reclamation" of the £400 not paid to them.[32] Other times, the orphans had to wait until they came of age and then go to court themselves to recover their goods.

The most obvious abuse involved retaining or wasting the inheritance. In 1352, the "next of friends" to the five children of William de Hanampstede accused William, Jr., his son and executor, and guardian of the young children, of concealing £240. The court forced him to make payments to them in £40 and £50 installments. If the original guardian was dead, the wardship payment had to come out of the guardian's estate.[33]

Standing surety for a guardian was a real liability. When the daughters of John le Long complained through their mother's brother that their guardian had wasted their inheritance, the guardian fled because he could not afford to pay the £22 12s. 3d. that he owed the girls. His two sureties paid up, and the uncle was made guardian. The sureties' function can be seen in the case of Walter, son of Adam Glendon, who had been left £80. The guardian died, leaving insufficient funds to cover the wardship trust. The three sureties who were in London, including the executor of one of the sureties, had to pay the full amount owed to Walter. The fourth had no goods in the city that could be detained, but when he returned to London the others brought suit against him and forced him to pay his share.[34]

When the children had to wait until they had reached the age of majority to complain about abuse of inheritance, they often asked for the property belonging to siblings who had died when they were minors as well as their own property. Thus the daughter of John Hudde and her husband claimed the estate of her brother, John, who had been a child in his mother's womb when their father died; John had subsequently died.[35]

Guardians were full of excuses. John Gubbe died in 1309 and left a minor son, Richard. In 1316, Richard complained to the mayor that, even though he was of age, he could not recover his property from his guardian. The guardian, a kinsman, acknowledged that he had received £88 20d., but claimed he had spent £45 20d. on repairs to the property that Richard had inherited and further funds for the boy's maintenance. Finally, he had had to fight off an action of dower that Richard's mother brought against the estate. Although he confessed that there was still a balance due of £43, he was unable to pay. He was sent to prison, leaving Richard to pursue other avenues to get the property back.[36]

Another way to make money out of the wards was to arrange advantageous marriages for them. The mayor and the chamberlain were supposed to contol the marriage of wards to be sure that their estate was paid and that they were not married to the disparagement of their social status. Nonetheless, marriages of such well-endowed children were profitable because suitors would pay the guardian considerable money to secure the marriage. One may assume that Margaret had hoped to make a bit of money marrying off Alison.

The arrangements made by the greedy might involve marrying the mother of the minor. Agnes, widow of John Laurence, and her new husband, Simon de Burgh, were appointed guardians of little Agnes, who was eight months old. The couple contrived to marry Agnes, who had property worth 40 marks, to Thomas, son of Simon, who was eleven years old. The banns had already been read and the wedding garments purchased (little Agnes's dress must have been a glorified christening gown) when the "next friends" intervened and Agnes was removed from her mother's custody.[37] In a similar case, the marriage actually occurred. The guardian had married the widowed mother of an orphan and had then married off the little girl, even though he had covenanted with the mayor not to marry her off. He was put into prison and fined the amount her marriage was worth, £44.[38]

Nicholas, son of John de Mockyng, a fishmonger, had many complaints against his guardian, John Wroth, also a fishmonger. He claimed that his guardian had misappropriated property bequeathed to him by his father and mother and had married him to Margery, daughter of John Malewyne. Malewyne had given a considerable sum to arrange the marriage, but Nicholas had not received any of it. His guardian said that he was ready to render account to the auditors for £100, along with plate, glass and silver cups, ewers, and spoons. He also said that he made the marriage without disparagement to Nicholas. Nicholas, however, did not appear to be of full age, even though he brought the complaint to the mayor himself, nor did he appear capable of taking care of himself. He was put in the guardianship of his father-in-law. His problems were not over, however, and four years later, when he was past sixteen, he was abducted from his father-in-law's house. The next year, the mayor judged "Nicholas capable of managing his affairs," and he was given his property. After this eventful childhood, he died the next year.[39]

Walter Cote had a similar story to tell. He claimed that Roger de Evere, his guardian, "by promises and smooth words" persuaded him to demise his houses and rents for a term of years and to betroth himself to Roger's daughter, Alice. Roger then "bound his hands behind him and beat him until he made a charter of feoffment" and eventually forced him to quitclaim the property. Roger later enfeoffed the property to Walter and Alice, which guaranteed her rights in the property even if the couple did not have children.[40] Had the property been awarded as dower, which was normal, she would have had only a life interest in it.

Forced marriages such as these created problems because church law made divorce difficult. But because these marriages were forced and done without consent of at least one party, divorce was possible.[41]

Finally, the guardians might not carry out the terms of the testator's will in regard to the child or might in other ways neglect his or her upbringing and care. John, son of William Hanyngtone, had continual problems with his guardian, Lawrence de Hanyngton, a skinner. The mayor intervened and insisted that John be decently maintained, spelling out that Lawrence was to provide for him yearly while he was at school "a furred gown, a coat of 'Alemayne' with tunic to match, 4 pairs linen clothes, sufficient shoes, a decent bed, and every week 1*d.* for commons and lodging." Lawrence did not abide by this, and three years later John asked for the £8 Lawrence owed him. He won, but because he was still of "tender age," he was asked if he had a "friend" who could keep the money for him. He named the man who had married his mother.[42]

Some of the most abusive cases described in the London court rolls did not involve London citizens, and in these cases the mayor and the aldermen were powerless to do anything. These sad tales serve as a reminder that our sources tell only about those orphans who could find ready protectors in the city. The son of Richard atte Halle was bequeathed a considerable country estate, and as a consequence his wardship and the rights to his marriage were sold several times. When, at last, the boy was taken into the hands of the city, the mayor and the aldermen reluctantly concluded that because the boy's father was not a freeman of London and the boy had been born outside London, they could do nothing.[43]

Our folkloric tradition about orphans strongly implies that it is the wicked stepmother, and sometimes the stepfather, who abuses the interests of the children of the first marriage.[44] Our evidence so far indicates that either stepparent could abuse the relationship, but we have reason to believe that Londoners' decency or at least London's laws generally protected the children of citizens.

When a marriage or property was misappropriated, the child's mother as well as the stepfather was often implicated. In a long case involving the children of Robert le Convers (alias le Orfevre), the mayor and the aldermen decided that Robert's two boys, seven and three years old, should be placed with Nicholas Farndone. Their mother, Roesia, was already remarried to David de Cotesbroke and was given custody of a one-year-old girl, Katherine. Costesbroke died three years later. He had not rendered account for Katherine's inheritance, and £50 was attached from his estate to cover it. Roesia married a third time and absconded. The men who had stood surety for Katherine's estate found various silver cups belonging to young Katherine and succeeded in making up the inheritance. At the age of thirteen, Katherine married, and her husband collected her inheritance.[45]

Stepmothers were less likely to appear in the records as abusers of children's property rights, largely because they had few controls over the inheritance. If they were abusive and mean-spirited toward their stepchildren, this fact would not appear in the court records that are our only source. The city undertook to protect the property of the children and to carry out the wishes of testators, but monitoring families for evidence of the Cinderella syndrome was beyond their legal competence. We know far less about the actions of new wives of surviving fathers than we do about remarried mothers and stepfathers, since these women did not figure in the Court of Orphans.

A few cases suggest the existence of the classic strife between stepmothers and stepchildren, which, of course, was by no means one-sided. John Hammes petitioned against his father's widow, saying that she had arranged a forgery to try to convert the properties that he inherited from his father into an inheritance for herself and had attempted to force him to sign the forgery.[46]

The other side of the coin is represented by the death of Alice, wife of Robert de Portesmouthe. She lived with her husband and stepson in a solar. She and her husband argued, and the stepson hit her with his hand. She tried to leave the solar, but as she stood at the top of the stairs, her husband took a "wombedstaf" and hit her in the neck so that she fell down the stairs and broke her neck. The son was not charged with murder, but the father was. Their meager estate came to 15s. 5d. It appears that Alice was more abused than abuser.[47]

Resentment against stepmothers and remarried mothers probably had less to do with their treatment of stepchildren than with rivalries caused by the perceived threat to the position of the children of the first husband. While stepsiblings could not influence inheritance, they could displace the children of the first husband in the mother's affection and family ambitions. The dower, which gave the widow one-third of the husband's property for life, also caused resentment. An adult child could see a stepfather enjoying the use of property that would eventually come to him or her on the death of the mother. The law did not provide for a percentage of profit in dower property in the same way that the laws governing wardship did. If the stepfather was frittering away dower or letting tenements run down, tensions were sure to result, and the only recourse was to sue. Furthermore, dower delayed the child's full inheritance of the paternal estate and therefore caused hard feelings between orphan and stepparent.

Disruptions of Wardship

The loss of a father, and sometimes a mother as well, was disruptive for the young children who became wards of the city. But added to this bereavement were the problems of adapting to a stepparent and perhaps also to stepbrothers and -sisters, of moving out of the natal home in some cases, and of experiencing the breakup of the family as siblings were placed with various guardians. The Storteford family provides a good example and a good lesson. London was small enough that even though the family was split up, the members remained in intimate contact. The children lost their father, John, in 1298. His wife, Laura, was still alive, but the children did not stay with her at the principal dwelling. Instead, John, the eldest, was granted to John de Canterbury, an alderman. Gilbert, Adam, Cecilia, Margery, and "Nargery" (a nickname because of two daughters with the same name) were granted to Gilbert de la Marche (possibly the maternal grandfather). By 1301, Gilbert de la Marche was dead. Twelve-year-old Gilbert and four-year-old Nargery were given to John Lucas, a stockfishmonger. Three-year-old Adam and nine-year-old Margery were given to John le Botoner, Jr. Nargery claimed her inheritance from John Lucas when she was nineteen years old. Gilbert lived to age thirty-two, and when he died he left bequests to his mother; his sisters Cecilia and Margery; a Thomas de la Marche, who was called an uncle; and a brother, Walter. Adam is mentioned as deceased.[48] Thus although the children were reared in various households, they seem to have maintained close contacts throughout their lives.

As with the cases of abuse of wardship, it is important to know from the start that the incidence of siblings being separated was low. Of the 495 families of orphans coming before the mayor in the Letter Books from 1309 to 1428, only 54, or 11 percent, were dispersed to various guardians. Some of these cases, as in the case of the Storteford family, may represent a child like John, who was old enough to go into a home where he would eventually be apprenticed. Children over eight or nine years of age could be useful in a household and thus could be sent to friends, neighbors, and fellow guild members, but the younger children were more likely to remain with their mother. While the figure derived from wardship cases in the Letter Books certainly is distorted by underreporting, it is a valuable corrective to any assumption that medieval civic officials were unconcerned about the welfare of children and the family unit.

Separation of siblings and other disruptions could occur for a number of other reasons besides the death of a father. These include the death of a guardian, the sale of a guardianship and the inability of the guardian to maintain the child in accordance with the terms of the inheritance. In these cases, the guardian would bring the child back to the court and render account. Again, the Letter Book evidence from 1309 to 1428 shows surprisingly little change of guardianship. Of the 495 cases, only 37, or 8 percent, required a move to a different guardian.

The mayor and the chamberlain seem to have taken particular care when a change of guardianship had to be arranged, especially if the previous guardianship had been abusive. Older children were asked to name a "next friend" to take care of them or their money. When Christina, seven-year-old daughter and heiress of Geoffrey of Hundesdeche, was committed to two men, the mayor asked them to return her six months later. The mayor then put her in the care of Christina de Evre, perhaps a godmother, given the coincidence of name, until a suitable guardian could be found. After that, she was placed with her mother and her mother's new husband.[49]

A more common reason for a change in guardianship was that the children reached a stage of life in which they took up a religious vocation or entered into apprenticeship. Only seven girls and two boys among the wards entered monasteries. But sixty-two boys and nine girls entered into apprenticeships. A few of the children married at tender ages and went to live with their new in-laws. Gilbert, son of Alan de Breuncestre, was put into wardship in 1319 with nonkin, even though his mother was still alive. In 1324, when his mother died, he had already married the daughter of Richard Godfrei, called le Joinour, and was put in Richard's custody until he came of age. The next year, Richard died, and Gilbert and his young wife remained in the custody of Richard's widow. Gilbert lived with his wife until 1348. In another case, marriage between minors had already taken place, and the father willed that the children remain with the father-in-law.[50]

To balance the picture of instability presented by abuses and dispersals of wards, we end our discussion with an example of an amicable relationship. John de Guldeford was married twice, but had no surviving children of his own. After many pious bequests and dower provision for his second wife, he left bequests to the son of his first wife and his son (John's stepgrandson), Thomas. Thomas had a foster brother, Gervase, who had apparently delighted the old man, who also left him and his son bequests. In this family, the emotional bonds seem to have been close even though the household contained children with a variety of relationships to the family head, and the good will passed into the second generation.[51]

Caxton's Puzzle Revisited

We must return to the puzzle that Caxton posed over the absence of strong patrilines in London and the influence that wardship and the remarriage of widows might have had on this development. The very generous dower of one-third of the husband's estate for life use and the provision that the widow could take it into another marriage made London widows particularly attractive marriage partners. Added to this generous provision was the tendency of both written law and practice to favor the mother or the mother and her new husband as guardians for orphaned children. The new husband, therefore, had the use of two-thirds of the first husband's property. Few London citizens restricted the remarriage of their wives. Instead, both they and their guild brothers exerted some pressure on the widows to remarry and to do so within the guild or within the social status of the first husband. In thirty-seven cases from the fifteenth century, thirty-four widows chose husbands from the merchant class, twenty-two of whom were from the same company as the former husbands. Between

1360 and 1500, the mayor and the aldermen arranged the marriage of sixty-three orphan daughters of merchant-class families, fifty-three of whom married into the same class. By the sixteenth century, the pressure on widows to marry within their husbands' company was more formalized.[52] Preference for perpetuating the guild interest is also seen in the increasing number of guild brothers who served as guardians for orphans. The advantage that Londoners perceived in this arrangement was that it kept the wealth within one guild and one social class.

Londoners, therefore, tended to create strong horizontal bonds, to the disadvantage of patrilineal ties. The widow's right to life use of one-third of the patrimony deprived the patrilineal line of this property until the dowager died. Furthermore, the wardship laws, which excluded anyone who could directly inherit the orphan's estate, tended to favor the mother or the matrilineal kin and prohibited the patrilineal kin from taking charge of heirs. Guild loyalties furthered the horizontal ties.

The social structure that evolved in London was markedly different from what an observer such as Caxton saw on the Continent. In Florence, the dower had been abandoned before the fourteenth century. Women entered marriage only through the dowry and were, therefore, dependent on their husbands' families or their natal families for support when they were widowed. Although in theory women could take their dowry with them when their husbands died, in practice they were manipulated by the husbands and their families to leave the dowry in their patriline. Children also had to remain in their fathers' houses, and belonged to the fathers' lineages. Florentine women seldom remarried and frequently had to return to their natal home, abandoning their children to their husbands' families.[53] Florentine society, therefore, was characterized by strong patrilineages. In Ghent, widows also had a generous dower that they could take into another marriage with them, but the control of orphans and their inheritances went to the fathers' side. Thus clans remained strong in Ghent.[54]

London's laws of dower and wardship were very effective for ensuring the survival of citizens' children. London widows were well enough provided for that they could raise their children alone or remarry without disadvantaging the survival of their children and their inheritances. A by-product of these laws was the development of strong horizontal lines of social structure. Londoners probably did not feel the absence of strong patrilineal lines, which Caxton had come to believe were essential signs of higher culture. London was not an aristocratic city, but one of merchants and traders. To the extent that Londoners wanted to imitate noble ideas of lineage, they preferred, as Thrupp has pointed out, to do so on a country estate where such a social model seemed more appropriate.

Boys, one of them wearing a school satchel, turn somersaults on a rail. (Drawing by Wayne M. Howell, from Pieter Bruegel, *Kinderspiele* [Kunsthistorisches Museum, Vienna])

7

Life on the Threshold of Adolescence

The Western tradition of recognizing the change from childhood to puberty is one with deep roots. In the ancient physicians' and philosophers' division of life into four stages, adolescence was conceived of as hot and dry, as are summer and fire, and its humor was red choler. Youths, according to Bede, are "lean (even though they eat heartily), swift-footed, bold, irritable, and active." Those who divided the life cycle into six stages according to the planets envisioned youth as Venus, which "implants an impulse toward the embrace of love."[1] The folkloric traditions, as well, included good descriptions of the transition period. "The Mirror of the Periods of Man's Life" is primarily a vehicle for moralizing, but it also divides life into stages according to years and qualities. In the fourteenth year (puberty), "knowliche of manhode he wynnes," and throughout his early twenties the youth is a battleground for the struggle between the seven virtues and the seven sins. Reason dictates an education at Oxford or at the law, but lust has other ideas:

> Quod lust, "harp and giterne there may ye leere,
> And pickid staff and blucklere, there-with to plawe,
> At tauerne to make women myrie cheere,
> And wilde felaws to-gider draw."

Music, drink, mock fights, and wild companions vie with obedience, reason, and those other attributes that are to make one "sad and wise."[2]

Establishing a definition for the adolescent years in late medieval England is a complex problem. Certainly, the current preference of early modernists to regard the life stage as definable only by youth culture and juvenile societies of misrule limits discussion to a very narrow manifestation of adolescence and completely ignores gender differences. But the very apparent preoccupation of books of advice, city ordinances, royal decrees, and even the language of court cases indicates a growing preoccupation with potential problems that riotous young men could cause in a city. As the adult population postponed both the symbols and the reality of adult life to later ages, the problems of dealing with this liminal group of young men became more intense. The late medieval period may be a transitional one for conceptualizing behavior characteristic of male adolescence. Conceptions of female adolescence, however, were less well formed and perhaps changed less.

Enough has been said in previous chapters about the gender differences in rearing male and female children to raise questions about the general applicability of either the medieval learned or the folkloric description of adolescence to females. Although Venus also guided women's lives in this stage of development, was red choler the humor that dominated their lives? When studying this step across the threshold from childhood to adolescence, we must consider a number of questions. To return to Arnold Van Gennep's distinctions, we must ask the extent to which this transition reflects biological development and the extent to which it is a cultural construct.[3] In more direct words, what role did sexuality play in defining adolescence in medieval London? Was sexuality the same for young women as for young men? With Victor Turner's ritual moments in mind, we must inquire if medieval society had ceremonies to separate the neophyte from his or her former state and to move him or her into the new life stage.[4] Keeping in mind the binary oppositions Turner proposed for differentiating the adolescent from the adult, we must wonder if teenage women went through any transitional ceremonies and how women marked changes of status.

Leaving aside, for the time being, the formal aspects of apprentice and service contracts (see Chapters 8 and 10), we look here at the markers for separation from childhood and entrance into adolescence. As Glen Elder Jr., has said, the entrance into adolescence is more difficult to discern than the exit from it. We need to look at the behavior that characterized the childhood experience and compare it with that of the adolescent. A distinctive change of surroundings and activities, rather than simply new labels, plays a role in formulating a definition of adolescence.[5]

Social Puberty and Biological Puberty

If biological change is taken as the dividing line between childhood and adolescence, then physical changes in the body serve as markers for the transition from one stage to the other. The most obvious of these is the onset of menses in women and of semen emissions in men. But we also know of puberty from a number of secondary sexual characteristics: the appearance of body hair, the development of breasts in women and facial hair in men, the appearance of skin blemishes, rapid growth, change of voice, and increasing motor control and judgment. Like the medieval poets, we also associate adolescence with a rowdy expansion of behavioral horizons, or "misbehavior," to use the adult world's view. The period of biological and behavioral changes from childhood to adolescence does not necessarily correspond to social practices. As we shall see, society in the late Middle Ages extended the period of social childhood for males well into biological puberty and proportionately raised the age of exit from adolescence well into biological adulthood. The female experience was somewhat different from the male experience in London society, but still did not follow biological puberty exactly. While Londoners tended not to marry off their daughters at biological puberty, they did link their definitions of adolescence and coming of age for females more closely to biology than they did for males. Similarly, the adolescent experience within different status groups varied. The transition to a service position might begin sooner than the move into an apprenticeship, but the exit from service might be delayed even longer.

Medieval records are remarkably quiet about biological puberty, but before concluding that it did not matter in the definition of adolescence, we must remember that the records are equally silent about childbirth. Some rituals were particularly female and may not appear in the records simply because women had no ready need or means to keep an account. The little historical information we have on the subject (not more than a dozen references to actual women) places the age of menarche at between twelve and fifteen.[6]

Medical discussions of the four stages of life do include the particular biology of women. Phlegm was considered characteristic of women as well as of children: "Blood comes to demand its dues from about fifteen years to about thirty." Following this authority, women did not experience a transition to the red choler that adolescent males did, but remained moist with the humor of blood. Their element remained air until it switched to earth when they became adults. The whole scheme for their biology failed to fit the model for males.[7]

A variety of explanations for the medieval silence on the subject of the onset of menstruation is possible. Menstruation was one of those aspects of women that made them "unclean" in the eyes of theologians and of other men, so that women might choose not to call attention to the matter.[8] It is also possible that the first menses was not highly significant for women. Margery Kempe, for all her straightforward talk in her autobiography, did not feel the need to record menstruation.[9] Since medieval medical experts and women did not know about fertility cycles, they had no reason to keep a tally of their menstrual periods in relation to conception. Finally, menstruation, as we shall see, had little to do with the actual ages at which women married or with other rituals for women.

For men, as well, no ceremonies surrounded physical puberty. Monastic sources recognized the problems that biological puberty could cause among the novices and took precautions to keep them in separate beds, with a candle burning and a senior monk in the dormitory. But such foresight hardly constituted a rite of passage. For lay youth, manuals of advice and apprenticeship contracts cautioned against sexual activity, rather than encouraging fathers to see that their sons became experienced at the local brothel.

The legal demarcations for transition from childhood, although set close to the age of physical puberty, were fixed and did not vary with the actual biological phenomenon. Furthermore, both lay and ecclesiastical law skipped over an adolescent period. Criminal law directed that a boy aged twelve or over be in a tithing group. Both male and female children aged twelve were held responsible as adults for their criminal acts because they presumably had developed the ability to know and to comprehend the wrongfulness of their felonious deeds. Criminal law thus incorporated a sharp break from childhood, thrusting youth into adult responsibilities early. Medieval criminal law had no juvenile justice provisions. The poll tax of the late fourteenth century, however, made youth taxable only at age fourteen. But legal demarcations were somewhat contradictory, the age of inheritance was twenty-one for both males and females. Young women could inherit at marriage if they were at least sixteen. Canon law considered girls mature enough to marry at age twelve and boys at age fourteen. Thus, presumably, the Church was willing to move youth quickly into marriages, implying adult status. But, as we have seen and shall explore further, couples marrying at this age were still in the control of one of the parents and did not gain control of their inheritances.

Medical treatises and poems on the ages of man offer various ages for the transition. Ptolemy, who was widely quoted in the Middle Ages, put the age of entrance into adolescence for men at fourteen. In vernacular literature, such as the morality play *Mundus et Infans*, fourteen was also the age of entry into the character Lust and Liking. The author of *Ratis Raving* put the beginning of the sanguine period at fifteen.[10] But a different authority claimed that youth did not start until twenty-five, thus giving each of the four seasons the same time span.[11]

For many of London's youth, males more than females, the transition from childhood to adolescence was marked by entry into a service or an apprenticeship contract. In the early fourteenth century, fourteen was the usual age of entry into apprenticeship; a city ordinance specified thirteen as the minimum age. An earlier placement for orphans might be desirable, so that an apprenticeship by age eleven was possible in some cases. But the age of entry crept up to fifteen or sixteen, even for orphans, by the end of the fourteenth century, depending on the circumstances and on the educational requirements of the apprenticeship.[12]

During the course of the fifteenth century, the age of entry into apprenticeship increased to at least sixteen, but delay until age eighteen was more common. This change is a dramatic argument for the dominance of social over biological puberty in medieval London. The new arrangement prolonged childhood well into the period of biological puberty. The reasons for this increase were several. Many of the elite London guilds, such as the Mercers, Goldsmiths, and Ironmongers, began to require that their apprentices have an education before entering into their apprenticeships.[13] Thus young people spent longer in grammar schools than had apprentices in the fourteenth century. A variety of economic factors arising out of the depopulation that resulted from the plague and other diseases also delayed the entry of youth into the adolescent stage. (These factors, along with a discussion of the delayed age of exit from adolescence, appear in subsequent chapters.)

Although little evidence survives, what does remain suggests that females entered into service and apprenticeship contracts earlier than males. For instance, John Ermyne, a mariner, said his daughter was ten when she entered into an apprenticeship contract in 1393, and an orphan became an apprentice at age eleven in 1358.[14] Katherine Lightfoot's father, however, complained that his daughter had entered into an apprenticeship contract with a carpenter's family against her will and his. The carpenter claimed that she was fourteen and free and willing to enter into the contract. Her father said that she was really much younger, and when he produced her in court, the mayor agreed "after an examination and numerous other proofs" that she was not fourteen and must be released from her contract.[15]

Without an obligation to educate their daughters, families may have been willing to part with them earlier and may have welcomed the opportunity to place a female child outside the home, where someone else would be responsible for feeding her. Young women might also have entered apprenticeship contracts as threadmakers and silkworkers at an early age in order to finish their training and enter into the marriage market by the time they were in their mid- to late teens. Such a move would give them an early start on making good matches, with some useful supplemental skills and a bit of money laid by.

The age of entry into university and legal training seems also to have risen to the late teens in the late fourteenth century. Among the city orphans, some young men, such as Robert, son of John Hoke, wanted to attend Oxford at age eighteen but did not have the money. Robert requested, and received, 20s. to pay for his expenses out of his patrimony. As a minor in his late teens, John Wodehous asked for an advance of 20 marks to pay for his legal education in London.[16] These young men were following the dictates of "conscience" rather than "lust" in pursuing careers at law and university.

Positions as servants, however, could begin as young as seven, but older children were preferred since they were more useful and responsible. The evidence for contracts involving younger children comes from complaints by parents that the children were too young to work. For instance, Juliana Chamberlain complained against William Clerk that he wrongfully detained Ellen, her daughter, from the age of seven years to be his servant for seven years. Ellen was released to her mother.[17] On the whole, however, entry into service positions probably did begin at a younger age because parents did not have to pay any money to a master by way of a bond to procure an unskilled service position and because the child needed no prior education. The urban poor and country youth seeking such positions needed to move into the work force early in their lives and so may not have reached biological puberty when they crossed the threshold into adolescence.

Adolescent Games

Since ages are so seldom given in medieval records, the evidence on age-based distinctions between childhood and adolescence can prove frustratingly meager. Behavioral differences, particularly in the types of games played, can often reveal more about the changes that occur between childhood and adolescence and, later, between adolescence and adulthood. Adolescents moved away from the games of childhood and began to experiment with wrestling, sword play, and archery, which were adult male games. In addition, they began to frequent taverns and to learn such games as dice and checkers.

The medieval morality play *Mundus et Infans* captures the difference between the innocent pranks of the child and the "love-longing" of youth. On the whole, the author seems to delight in the antics of the smart little Wanton, a child who grows from seven to fourteen during the play. Wanton tells all his secret games with relish. He can spin a top, but he has also found that he can use his "scroug-stick" (a whip for the top) to beat his playmates on the head. He has learned to manipulate his family, biting and kicking his brother and sister if they thwart him, but being able to pout and cry if his father or mother interferes. He can "dance and also skip, . . . play at the cherry-pit, . . . and whistle you a fit." He has learned to do all those things on the way to school that the moralist told him not to do. He steals fruit from gardens, goes after birds' eggs, and ends up feeling the whip of his master.[18] Wanton resembles the real London children from the age of seven to fourteen that we have already encountered.

When Wanton is fourteen, his name changes to Lust and Liking. Mundus tells him that the next seven years are to be all games and glee, all "love-longing in lewdness." And so he sets out in pursuit of women, revel, and riot.[19] But the playwright does not dwell on his carousing and conquests. For that, we must turn to the record sources.

London provided vast temptations, which apprenticeship contracts tried to counteract. Apprentices agreed in their contracts and oaths that they would live in their masters' household and not stay out at night and that they would not dice or game, visit theaters or taverns, or consort with prostitutes. They would not spend their masters' money on fine clothes. How well the masters knew of the potential problems![20] In the poem "How the Good Wife Taught Her Daughter," the mother warns her daughter about taverns, saying that she should not spend the money she gets from selling her cloth in taverns. And should she go to a place "where good ale is aloft," whether she be serving or drinking it, she should not get drunk, "for it falleth to thy shame."[21]

For all these sworn agreements and good advice, we find that three apprentices, Henry Pykard, Walter Waldeshef, and Roger Fynch, were charged in 1339 with being "addicted to playing knuckle-bones" at night and leading other apprentices into gambling habits. People in one ward found that Richard de Pelham was "a good man and true," but his son, Richard, was a "rorer."[22]

The tavern was certainly a temptation for male youth and a place where they could learn the bad habits of adult men. The tavern scenes must often have been wild. Moralists were right to warn against frequenting such places. For instance, two men were having a quiet game of checkers on a bench when three men brought in a woman and laid her over the checkerboard. The checker players reprimanded the intruders, but one of the rowdies in return attacked a checker player, stripping him of his clothes down to the girdle. When the ruffian found a dagger on the girdle, he chased the man to a room upstairs. Having lost his quarry, the assailant then followed the other player, who had escaped into the street, and killed him.[23]

It was hard enough to control apprentices in London, but the situation was even worse when the older ones were abroad on their masters' business. The Mercers, in order "to avoid evil among the youth of the fellowship" when they were in Flanders, established six English houses there to be run by men of good reputation. The apprentices could eat only at these houses or face fines. They were to have only four groats' worth of English beer (not the strong Continental beers) and no wine. They were not to play cards or other games for money and were not to dance, revel, or sit up past nine o'clock in the evening.[24]

The elders were not always innocent, and sometimes they led their apprentices and servants in rowdy games. The prior of Friars Minor complained in the mayor's court that Richard Haltham and his friends entered their close and played at Paulme there, breaking the windows and disturbing the monks in their devotions. Richard's apprentices also stopped up the lead pipes of their conduit, causing 100 marks' worth of damage. One can imagine the havoc caused by these young rowdies—broken windows, loud voices, and the final insult of cutting off the water needed to flush out latrines and wash hands.[25]

The antics of youth became so obnoxious on occasion that the king had to intervene, as he did on behalf of the king's council, threatening to imprison "any child, or other person" who played "at bars or at other games not befitting, such as taking off the hoods of people, or laying hands upon them, or in any other way causing hindrance, whereby each person may not peaceably follow his business" at Westminster Palace during sessions of Parliament.[26]

A characteristic of adolescent games is that they are preparation for adult games and sport. Organized tournaments, for instance, were for adults, but adolescent males began to train for ritualized or real fighting. The city fathers were against such training because it belonged more properly to the nobility and because it would simply lead to a disruption of civic order if urban youth learned the use of swords. Thus they indicted Master Roger le Skirmisour (his name being an indication of his trade) for keeping a fencing school "and for enticing thither the sons of respectable persons so as to waste and spend the property of their fathers and mothers upon bad practices; the result being that they themselves become bad men."[27]

Indeed, not too many years later, two young men, including the son of a Gloucestershire knight, dueled in front of the Broken Seld, a tavern in the Cheap. Wounded in the belly, head, and arm, the young victim made his way to the church of St. Peter de Wodestret and died "sounding the bells."[28]

Wrestling was another game that youths played at, but that became a more serious, competitive sport for adult males. Youths did not have the physical strength or body weight to do more than experiment with this popular sport. Two servants who were left behind to guard their master's house "engaged in a friendly game" of wrestling with each other. One young man fell over the other, and the knife on his belt entered the other's belly. They continued to live together amicably in the house, but the young man died within three weeks.[29] London men had organized matches with one another and also with neighboring Westminster. The sport, which was very popular with spectators, also enriched the winners.[30]

The fields outside the city walls, especially Moorfields, were places in Fitzstephen's time and onward for races, javelin throwing, mock battles, archery practice, and ball games.[31] The king and London officials disapproved of some of the pastimes. Proclamations forbade "hokkying on hokkedayes and the levying of money for games called fote-ball and cokthresshying," handball, stone throwing, skittles, and dice.[32] Archery was the sport the king wished to have pursued so that he would have a supply of soldiers for his wars. One curmudgeon, who seems to have shared these views, put "hidden engines of iron" in one of the playing fields (probably modern Lincoln's Inn Fields) to maim the apprentices of the king's court. He got a pardon, but in the disorders of 1381, the mob trashed his house and pulled him out of a church where he had taken refuge.[33]

Other times the youth simply hung around watching men's games. William Py, for instance, complained that on a Tuesday in Witsuntide, he and other men were shooting at targets at Mile End outside Fleet Street. William Ardene, an apprentice, was watching the shooting when "out of folly he ran to the prick" just as Py was shooting and was wounded in the leg. Py was now angry because he had agreed to pay compensation for lost work time to William's master. He had already paid 10s. and now was being sued even though the accident was clearly William's fault for being in the way of the men's games.[34]

Youths, of course, were drawn to the popular entertainments of bear baiting and other sports of cruelty to animals in Southwark, as well as to horse racing in Smithfield and to the numerous processions, parades, and pageants that punctuated the calendar of London's year.[35]

Of course, none of these fine activities could be performed in the sober gowns that the masters advocated.[36] The late fourteenth and fifteenth centuries were notable for lavish and extreme dress. Women began by showing a bit of neck in the late fourteenth century and progressed to showing considerably more in the fifteenth century. Young men wore hose with very short jackets over them, thereby revealing much leg. Head-dresses for both men and women were wild. The government tried to regulate dress through sumptuary legislation, and the moralists were out-raged that even maids decorated their gowns with fur, which dragged in the dirt and harbored fleas. Servants wore sleeves so long that they dipped in the soup.[37]

A passage in a play sums up youth's idea of dress. The character says that when he speaks to a pretty tapister in town, he has a fine shirt of cloth of Rennes with sleeves that hang down, and his hose and doublet are always in line. To show more of his fine body, he leaves off a stomacher in the summer. He even boasts of shaving in order to give a youthful appear-ance.[38]

Apprentices were chastised for wearing fashionable dress that imi-tated that of the gentry. To avoid embarrassment to the guild when their apprentices were abroad, the Mercers required their apprentices and ser-vants to wear capes, partellettes of silk, furred gowns, and double-turned cappies shoes and slippers when going to the Mart.[39]

Moralists also complained of the low-cut dresses and furs that young women wore. Concerning leisure activities for maidens, they advised: "Go not to the wrestling or shooting at the cock / As it were a strumpet or a giggelot [giggler]."[40] If respectable young women did not go to watch the games, many others did but they risked the title of harlot. Women did not appear in the young men's games except as spectators unless they were harlots. One presumes that respectable young women had their games, but they were played within the household and do not appear in court records that are our chief source of information.

"Joan Rawlyns of Alderham"

Joan Rawlyns's trip to London from Alderham in Hartfordshire had been an arduous one, and not entirely pleasant. John Barton, a tailor, had been engaged to conduct her, but he was just the sort of person that her mother had always warned her about. He tried to get her eye, but she kept hers cast down. She did not trust him. He said that a beautiful young woman such as herself could become a fine lady in London with very little work. With a tailor's appreciation for clothing, he described—with too-familiar touching—where the neckline of her bodice would come and how her slender waist would sport a girdle of silk and silver. Other girls from the village who had gone to London had worked hard to come home with enough money for a dowry so that they could marry. She and Robin had agreed to marry, and she was determined to get a good dowry to set up their household. She was not looking for an opportunity to become a fine lady; she could never hold a candle to her dear mistress, Lady Willesdon. At the inns along the way, she sat near respectable older woman so she could avoid talking with Barton. The good Lady Willesdon, whom she had served as a scullery maid since she was only eight years old, had offered to help her find more lucrative service in London so that she could marry. John Barton had brought my Lady some fine clothing from London, and she had seized upon the opportunity of promoting Joan's career through him. She had paid Joan's way to London and given Barton some more money to find her "good and honest service." Joan had no other option but to "put her trust in him."

For all the difficulties of the journey and her suspicions of Barton, Joan found her first glimpse of London's steeples and walls thrilling. They stopped at a waterman's house where Barton asked her to wait while he went across the river to Southwark to make arrangements with her future employer. So Barton was planning exactly what she had most feared. She had seen enough of him on the road and had heard enough cautions about the brothels in Southwark from her friends who had returned from service in London. As soon as he left, she "begged the waterman's wife on her knees that she should be delivered and conveyed to the city." The waterman's wife had seen too many of these cases and was impressed with Joan's courteous address and obvious distress. She arranged for the mayor and the aldermen to interview Joan.

Having been used to the county dignitaries at Lady Willesdon's house, she was equal to the interview and told her story in a straightforward manner, even though John Barton was there denying it all. What she did not know was that he had done this before and had previous charges against him. The mayor and the aldermen had him imprisoned in Newgate and then arranged that he "be paraded about town holding a horse's tail and having a paper on his head" explaining his crime. This proclamation was to be read at various places so that young women and others would know about him. He was then put into a pillory so that all could know his face and his crime. Finally, he was denied entry into the city ever again.

As for Joan, she had impressed the court very favorably with both her beauty and her presence of mind. One of the elderly gentlemen at the court hobbled up after the trial and said that he and his wife would be very happy to take her into their service and that anyone who had served Lady Willesdon would certainly be well recommended in their household. Joan, still suspicious (and who would not be after the experience she had just had?), suggested that if she were to serve his wife, she had best meet her before making a commitment. After all, it was the lady of the house who should hire the domestic servants.

Joan was delighted with the frail old matriarch who greeted her in the hall of a substantial merchant's home. She was an older version of Joan's former lady. Joan gladly accepted a three-year contract to work for the old couple. She would get word back to Robin through a trader going to Alderham that she had a good position at good wages, and she would also send a message to her lady, thanking her for her pains. No need to tell her about the terrible Barton. He would be in disgrace in London for years to come. After dinner on Joan's first day in service, her aging, wine-bemused master detained her at the table and told her that his wife was getting on in years, well-you-know-how-it-is; that he was as young as ever if-she-knew-how-that-was; that she could be a very fine lady of the house in a gown with a neckline down to there if she was a good girl and made him happy (as she should know how, since all country girls did); and that should his wife die, well, who knew what her status might be? Joan knew she would have to keep two jumps ahead of him! But perhaps that would not be too difficult, considering his gout.[41]

Sexual Initiation

For anthropologists, rituals surrounding sexual initiation are one of the major indicators of crossing the threshold from childhood to adolescence. Medieval England must once again disappoint those seeking rituals involving physical markers indicating the onset of adolescence. Medieval moralists, however, were convinced that "lust-longing" dominated the adolescent experience. Their chief concern was to protect both sexes from the risks of this powerful impulse. In their fear that biological urges might take over, moralists were full of advice on situations to avoid. In all other matters, moralists were mostly interested in young males, but in the matter of sexuality women ceased to be a subtext and became the main subject. The record sources, which give so little information on female apprenticeship and other matters involving women, are replete with cases involving female sexuality.

Cautionary tales abound. The "Good Wife" cautions her daughter not to speak to men in the streets, "lest he by his villainy should tempt thy heart."[42] Others speak of "proud young men and maidens" who go to church and the market to make eyes at each other and then meet to "talk light love and sly." A young man takes a girl to a tavern and buys her a drink to win her favors. She goes with him and "thinketh no shame" even if she risks a beating from her father and mother. But then she finds out how fickle men are, for "when her body showeth that childing is nigh," her boyfriend is nowhere to be found.[43]

It would do medieval society an injustice to assume that only the voices of the moralists were heard in the land. Chaucer's pilgrims relished sexual innuendo, and so did the population at large. Among the preserved popular poetry is one poem that contains slang recognizable to a modern teenager. A young woman comments of her priestly lover, Sir John, that he is quite willing to pay for his pleasure and puts his offering in her "box.":

> [S]er Iohn ys taken In my mouse-trappe
> ffayne would I hauve men bothe night and day.
> he gropith so nysleye a-bout my lap
> I have no powre to sa[y him nay].[44]

The flippant verse may well have been written by a sexually experienced clerk—certainly not by a young woman.

The moralists preached that both females and males should remain virgins until they married. Medieval romantics, like modern ones, felt that young love should be painfully wonderful, with much sighing, singing of praises, and longing for consummation. The reality was that for males who entered apprenticeship or service, the age of entry into adulthood and, therefore, the status of married man were increasingly delayed during the course of the late Middle Ages. Under the circumstances, they were likely to find sexual outlet with prostitutes. Females who entered service, on the other hand, were likely to experience unwanted sexual initiation in the arms of their masters or by being sold by their mistresses. Only those females of the better classes, who were married relatively early, expected to find sexual initiation only on marriage.

Leaving aside discussion of the special vulnerability of female servants for later (see Chapter 10), we can note that the records are replete with stories of both voluntary and forced sexual initiation of young women. The parents of Elizabeth Mappulton complained that a Spaniard, Francis Derbyet, has come to their house for more than a year and "there craftily has moved and stirred their daughter to go with him." He has "persuaded her to be of vicious living of her body contrary to the laws of God and to the utter destruction of her body." He makes her go with him to various parts of the city. She has complained to her parents about it, but the only way they can control the situation is to keep her in the house. If they do that, they cannot get any benefit from her labor by sending her on errands. Derbyet has threatened to have them imprisoned if they deprive him of their daughter.[45] In other words, the parents depend on the economic contribution of their daughter to the household, and her lover is depriving them of that. He will not marry her and thereby give them an honorable solution. Throughout their petition to the Chancellor, they refer to their daughter as a "maiden," so presumably they equated that status with being unmarried rather than with virginity. Sexual initiation did not change her status from adolescent to adult; only marriage could do that.

When the deflowering was forced and the girl had parents or friends to argue her case, she was likely to get compensation. For instance, Robert Trenender, a brazier, and his wife complained that Philip Rychard had deflowered their daughter. They took the matter to arbitration, and Philip bound himself by £100 to abide by the arbitration. He agreed that he would give their daughter, Agnes, a pipe and a half of woad or £20 as compensation and agreed not to "vex" the family again. The idea behind the settlement was that Agnes would have enough funds to give her a good dowry and make it possible for her to contract an honorable marriage.[46] Another man who had criminally assaulted a girl younger than fourteen years old was to pay £40 to the chamberlain, who would keep it until the victim either arrived at full age or married. The man was stripped of his citizenship and denied access to the city.[47] The punishment was severe, again showing the concern of the city government for at least the respectable young women of the city.

Family and friends, of course, could also be the ones who forced the girls into sexual initiation. A girl, simply called Margaret, lived in lodgings with her mother, who sold her to a man called Roy Em, who deflowered her. Afterward, on the counsel of an old woman, her mother sold her to a certain Lombard, who fornicated with Margaret at the lodgings. Alison Bostone was condemned to stand at the pillory for three market days for an hour, being brought there from prison with "pypys" or other "opyn Minstralsy" for having hired out her innocent young apprentice for immoral purposes.[48] Actual cases of incest, however, were rarely reported.[49]

Even priests, or, some might say, especially priests, could not be trusted with young girls. It was said of a curate, Sir Geoffrey, that

> after he had shryvyn yong women at Ester in the vestry and asayled them, then he wolde commen with theme and kysse and put his handis under theyr clothis and comen with theme to haue poynted with them, wher he and they myght mete to do syne with theme and specially with Johan the servaunt of Agnes Nele.[50]

Prostitutes, pimps, and keepers of bawdy houses were continually on the prowl for girls to sell to their customers. Elizabeth Thebyn confessed that she was a prostitute and had lately taken to walking the streets of the city dressed in priest's clothing, "to the rebuke and reproach of the order of the priesthood." She and another woman procured a thirteen-year-old girl for a man who "committed the foul and detestable sin of lechery" with her. The cases of forced prostitution of vulnerable young teenage girls can be multiplied in the record sources, but the repetition of such sad cases becomes depressing.[51]

For many of the young women from the country who came to London hoping to find a service position, selling their bodies was the fastest way to make money. There was little that the city fathers could do except punish those who victimized them. They had no way to provide safe havens for these young women. For instance, when Emma, daughter of William le Wirdrawere of York, was found in the streets after curfew on the night of November 11, 1320, with only a bundle of clothes, the authorities could do nothing other than put her into the Tun for the night.[52]

For young men, the opportunities for sexual initiation in London were numerous. The cases that came into the ecclesiastical courts involving fornication, pimping, and prostitution, as well as slander alleging these actions, make London appear very much as it did in Boswell's London journals. While the city fathers wanted to keep prostitution in Southwark and Cokeslane, in fact it was practiced fairly casually in inns, in people's houses, in rented rooms, and even in the street. Sexual encounters occurred in fields outside the walls, "behind a mud wall," "in the angle of Broadstreet," and in lanes.[53] In addition, there were adulterous wives and perhaps the unwilling or willing servant girls. What distinguishes the experience of the male from that of the female, however, is that no young men appear in the records as being forced into sexual encounters. Homosexuality does not appear in the records.[54]

In a story worthy of Chaucer's miller, Richard, son of John le Mareschall of Smithfield, was charged with abducting the wife of Stephen of Hereford. The neighbors were full of gossip about it. Richard had been seeing this woman for some time. When Stephen was away at Winchester Fair, Richard was at his house all the time, and the neighbors and friends of Stephen determined to put a halt to it. They searched the house for Richard, but could not find him. Finally, they directed the adulterous wife to open a chest closed with iron, and therein they found Richard. Richard left London for Waltham and did not see the wife again. When she learned that her husband was returning, she left home with some goods. Finally, she got the ecclesiastical court to force Stephen into a reconciliation with her.[55]

Richard was certainly not the only young man to have found a married woman for his sexual gratification; adultery was a common charge in the church court. Often the woman was a member of the same household as the young man. For instance, a master's son was accused of begetting offspring with a woman living in the household, and Richard Goldsmith was accused of fornicating with a woman living in his master's house.[56]

Depending on the pimp and the prostitute, casual sex could be procured for as little as 4*d.* or a sheaf of wheat. But Thomas Philipp, an apothecary, complained that his apprentice, John Nondy, left his house every night, leaving the door open, so that he could consort with a concubine. The young man confessed to having spent £20 of his master's money on her.[57]

Some young men seem to have entered into semiestablished relationships with concubines. Walter de Anne and Alan de Hacford, for instance, were described as sharing a concubine. Alan conspired with the concubine to kill Walter.[58]

I have come across no cases of gang rape, such as the attacks that characterized sexual initiation for some of the young men of Dijon. In this medieval French city, young men went about in rowdy groups of from two to fifteen, breaking down the doors of their victim's house and either raping her there or taking her to the house of an accomplice.[59] As we shall see, London youth did riot, but they apparently did not seek their sexual initiation through this means. Gang rape is an unusual crime and one suspects that the historian is taking the rare and turning it into a typical ritual of sexual initiation. In Dijon, as in London and all other urban centers of Europe, prostitutes were readily and cheaply available.

Not to leave a sense that only the sordid characterized the sexual initiation of youth, we present the story of Anthony Pontisbury, which speaks to real romance in sexual relations. He explained that he had been bound as an apprentice at "a tender age" seven years earlier for a term of nine years. He had agreed, as was usual with such contracts, not to marry during his term. He broke that contract and married but defended himself, saying that the prohibition on marriage was "contrary to the laws of God and causeth much fornication and adultery to be within the said city." His observation was certainly astute. He went on to explain, "[H]aving an inward love to a young woman dwelling in the said city and the young woman having the same unto him, intending that both to love under the laws of God . . . he has lately married and taken to wife the said young woman." His master had him arrested for trespass and put into prison.[60]

Riot and Misrule

London records are as deficient in information on the carnivalesque youth abbeys of misrule as they are on rituals of sexual initiation.[61] London society was certainly no stranger to riot and "rough music." The two, however, were not combined. The city routinely employed minstrels to accompany people to the pillory with pots, pans, and drums. City ordinances also insisted on symbolic clothing, such as particolored hoods for whores and special clothes for the condemned and the hangman. While London officials feared riots, skirmishes, disorderly conduct, and disrespectful behavior, they did not have to contend with organized youth bands. The laconic court cases of riot must not be overinterpreted as having a full-blown youth culture behind them. Much of the frustration that led to riot centered on deprivation of adult status rather than a desire to prolong or glorify youth.

London tried to accommodate the need for a youthful release by making such holidays as St. John's Eve (Midsummer Eve) a time for general celebration, feasting, and bonfires, as well as the evening during which the mayor, the aldermen, and the respectable men of the ward paraded in the principal streets carrying torches. This was the famous Midsummer Watch. At Christmas as well, London permitted all sorts of sporting events. But the city ordinances indicate a fear that the festivities might turn to riot. They forbade, for instance, the wearing of masks in the streets. This rule, which was reissued several times, implies that carnival was a part of the events and had led to troubles in the past. Taverns were to close early on holidays to discourage drunken brawling.[62] The traditional inversions of the "boy bishops" were, as we have seen, carried out by the parish churches of London and appear to have been regulated. The destruction of brothels associated with Shrove Tuesday in the early modern period does not appear in the medieval court records.[63]

The "sad and wise" were continually bothered by the misbehavior of adolescents, particularly apprentices. The wardens of the Mercers' guild lamented to the membership that "they have lately known and herd that divers mennys apprentices have greatly mysordered theymself as well in spendyng grete Summes of mony of theyre Maisters goods in Riott as wel uppon harlotes as at dyce, cardes and other unthryfty games as in their apparell," to the great hurt of all. They needed some ordinances to deal with the problem.[64] A few years later, on May Day 1517, a general riot among apprentices occurred, and the Mercers and others heard from the king that they must do something about the "wild, undiscrete Parsones named to be menes apprentices and menes servauntes of this Citie."[65]

City fathers had good reason to fear riots among the apprentices, as well as among other inhabitants of the city. The revolt in London in 1381 involved a number of servants. Trade fights led guild members to take to arms and attack one another. When adults began a fight, their servants and apprentices automatically joined in, so that a crowd of 500 or more could assemble quickly and deaths often resulted. If the riots became serious, the king could threaten to take away the city's charter, and sometimes he did. It was not, therefore, mere moralizing that led the guilds and the city fathers to take a keen interest in suppressing riots.[66]

The most unruly group of apprentices were those of the Bench—that is, those young men who were studying common law at the Inns of Court.[67] These youths were in their late teens or early twenties and lived just outside the city gates in the Holborn and Fleet area. Unlike the apprentices associated with merchant and craft guilds, they did not live in the master's house and so were not directly supervised. Instead, they lived in rooms, often with their own servants, and learned case law by studying with jurists and attending court. Their living arrangements permitted them to congregate with one another easily at taverns or in the streets. Together with their servants, they contributed substantially to violent crime in the city.

Their affrays were often committed in small groups. For instance, Richard de Kerdif and John Barri, an Irishman, and John de Worcester are described as apprentices of the King's Bench and "common evil doers" who lay in wait at night and robbed passersby of their purses and girdles.[68]

The more typical crime was less organized and more in keeping with the activities of youth bands, especially on or near days of celebration, such as St. Martin's Day (November 11) and the Feast of St. John (June 29). Four apprentices of the Bench (one each from Somerset, Cumberland, Northampton, and Essex) assaulted two men (probably also apprentices of the Bench) in the High Street, wounding them with swords and staffs. But these roving groups of apprentices were not always instigators. A Fleet Street taverner, who had obviously acquired the loyalty of his apprentice clientele, was attacked in a premeditated assault in his tavern. He raised the hue and cry, and John de Glemham and a number of apprentices of the Bench came to his rescue, but Glemham was killed by one of the co-conspirators.[69]

By far the worst riot of the apprentices of the Bench was on June 11, 1326. Around sunset, a great number of apprentices from York and Norfolk (or northern and southern apprentices of the law, according to the chronicle account) came running out of Aldersgate with swords drawn and in hot dispute. The bells were rung to signal a riot, and a crowd assembled. A group of servants joined in the general melee, and one of them shot into the crowd, killing an innocent bystander.[70]

The apprentices of the Bench were as close as London came to having distinctive youth groups with a youth culture. They had independent wealth, housing that was not in the control of a master and his family, and a habit of partying together from their university days. Living together in one area, they could be a menace to the peace. London had no university, so escaped the problems that plagued Paris and other cities with a large student population.

Some of the guilds also seem to have had a concentration of rioters, both young and old. The Fishmongers were involved in a major riot with the Goldsmiths in 1339. A year later, a group of young apprentices and journeymen took part in a riot in which they wounded a man and in general were described as "rebellious against their mistery." This was apparently just part of the life phase of being "wanton and wild" for John Fressh, one of the rioters, who went on to become Lord Mayor.[71]

Two of the most serious riots were far from carnivalesque in their origins and outcome. Apprentices as well as masters felt the wealth and the grasp on London's markets of foreign competitors, particularly Lombards (Italians) and Germans (a lumping together of those from the Low Countries and German towns). In 1456, a major riot occurred between Mercers' guild apprentices and Lombards. A young man had taken the dagger of a Lombard and had broken it in two. He was immediately arraigned before the mayor at the Guildhall and committed to the sheriff's custody. On his way home to dinner, the mayor was held up in the Cheap by a crowd of Mercers' guild apprentices and other people, who demanded that the youth be released. The mayor gave in, but this only encouraged the crowd, which later in the day attacked the Lombards in their homes and took goods. Some rioters were arrested and put into Newgate, but when the king's justices proposed to try them, the crowd threatened to ring the Common Bell, the signal for arming the city. Although some of the offenders were eventually hanged, the situation was so unstable that the king and queen left London for a time.

In 1493, the Mercers' guild apprentices rose against the German traders and collected a mob of servants, apprentices, and children. The merchants had prior warning and shut their gates in the Steelyard, the part of the city assigned to the Hanseatic merchants. The chronicler reporting the event was at pains to point out that no householders were involved in the attack, only apprentices, servants, and journeymen.[72]

Many young men, either alone, or in groups, were indicted for being "common ill-doers," "nightwalkers," and "common beaters,"[73] but the indictments do not indicate a ritualized adolescent riot. They are simply reminders of the perennial correlation between being young and male and engaging in aggressive and potentially criminal behavior. Grown men were also indicted for this sort of behavior, so it is not necessarily a type of juvenile delinquency.

It is the absence of a fully developed youth culture for both males and females that is perhaps the chief difference between adolescence then and now. Even the early modern period may have known more of organized youth gangs, entertainments, and dress than was prevalent in the Middle Ages. But a youth culture is only one aspect of describing adolescence; many of the other indicators were present and well known to adult observers.

Moralists despaired of youths' behavior. Some were of the opinion that young people turned out so badly because they were not adequately beaten. Others opined that youth's rebelliousness was the result of too much beating and that young people became callous because of it. Still others felt that the home environment was so poisonous that young people lacked role models for how honorable people ought to behave.[74] How could they be expected to behave better than their elders? The laws, customs, ceremonies, and contracts that marked the transition from childhood to adolescence likewise show a keen understanding of the disruptions that occur during adolescence. If adults seem as perplexed as modern moralists, psychologists, and parents about this stage of life, it is because they were fully cognizant that it existed and that it was different from childhood and adulthood. Medieval moralists came up with the same explanations that we moderns use because of the similarity between behavior then and now among adolescents and the expectations of those who had to deal with them.

Thomas Hoccleve, while employed in the office of the Privy Seal, wrote amusingly of the conflict he felt personally in behaving like a youth when he knew perfectly well what adulthood required. He knew, and his friends told him, that he would never get ahead if he went on as he was. But he says that "wilful youthe" will not obey: he is a glutton, he is tempted by taverns, Venus always can catch him in her snares, and he likes a good fight.[75]

8

Entering into Apprenticeship

Apprenticeship marked a decisive break from the status of child. In this formative life stage, which could occupy almost a quarter of their lives,[1] young people learned not only a craft but the characteristics of the role they would eventually play as adults. Apprentices moved out of their natal home into that of their master, becoming part of his familial environment. They slept in the shop or the house, shared meals with the family and other apprentices, received their clothing from their master, and endured his discipline. Their lives also changed in that they began to form an identity with their masters' guilds and with the city of London, of which they would become citizens when they completed apprenticeship. Daily activities also altered radically from the routine of school or household, for apprentices spent most of their day in the shop learning their craft. The gradual learning of a trade or craft was regarded as an initiation into its mysteries, and, indeed, an alternative name for the guild was a "mistery." Entering apprenticeship at fourteen to eighteen years old, youths spent seven to ten or more years in this stage between childhood and adulthood.

Apprenticeship is a complex subject, little addressed in the historical literature. Economic historians have been interested in the role of apprentices in medieval production of goods, but have had little interest in the

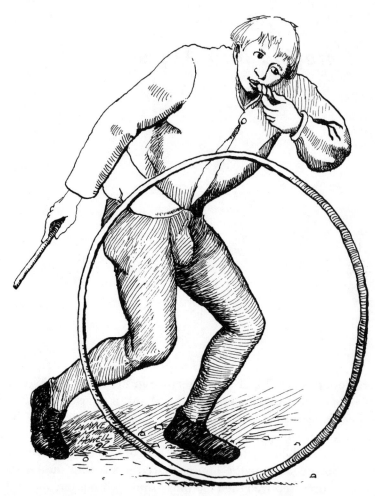

A youth plays with a hoop. (Drawing by Wayne M. Howell, from Pieter Bruegel, *Kinderspiele* [Kunsthistorisches Museum, Vienna])

experience of apprenticeship.[2] The relationship of apprentice and master, a fascinating aspect of medieval and early modern social life, has failed to impinge on the consciousness of historians writing about families and family surrogates or on the life cycle.[3] Being an apprentice was an uprooting experience for the youth and a difficult exercise in teaching and discipline for the masters. It meant that the master's family would have young, nonkinspersons in their household for all their working lives. For both apprentices and masters, the living arrangement was a potentially uncomfortable mix of familial and professional roles. With such close living and such potential for deep emotional conflict and attachment, it is not surprising that archival sources record both terrible abuse and close friendships within the apprenticeship arrangements. Furthermore, the experience of male and female apprentices was so different that the female experience must be treated separately.

Selection of an apprentice, considering the intimate living arrangements, was done with care. A master wanted an apprentice who had already learned the ways of urban politeness and who was of moral character. After all, the apprentice was a potential guild brother, son-in-law, and even successor to the master's wife and business should the master die. Because of the closeness of the relationship, the most satisfactory way to find an apprentice was through mutual friends and connections. Londoners tended to keep up contacts with their families in the country, with their home villages, and with the gentry in the county in which they had bought their estates. These networks of mutual acquaintance made the selection of an apprentice less risky. The apprentice was in a sense "guaranteed" or "certified" by family and friends.

The establishment of an apprenticeship contract was a matter of regulation, custom, and social bonds. Both the city and the guilds examined the apprentice and regulated the contract. All was finally sealed with ceremonial rites of passage to impress on both youth and master the gravity of the bond.

Not all young men and women in London entered into an apprenticeship. Indeed, the majority of apprentices came from the counties, rather than from the city itself. Apprenticeship was a privileged position because it offered the potential for upward mobility, wealth, and security. Although in the early fourteenth century most men became citizens of London through redemption (purchasing citizenship), increasingly apprenticeship was the common way of becoming a citizen.[4] Youth who could not afford to become apprentices went into service, which is the subject of Chapter 10.

Establishment of Apprenticeship

Family and friends—those indispensable figures in the life of the successful child and youth—helped young people secure apprenticeship positions. Selection of a master depended entirely on the connections and the
networks cultivated by the sponsor of the would-be apprentice. The youth
might have no inclination to become a pouchmaker, for instance, but
could end up making pouches because the only connection his parents had
was with a practitioner of that craft. What role, if any, the youth had in
selecting the type of trade he or she would be apprenticed to does not
appear in the record. Obviously, to become an apprentice in one of the
more prestigious guilds, such as Goldsmiths, Mercers, and Grocers, required good social connections and considerable wealth. In the sixteenth
century, one of the best indicators of one's chances of garnering an apprenticeship in one of these great companies was to have a father who was
already a member. But Caxton's observation about the paucity of London
lineages holds up in the apprenticeship arrangements. In the Mercers'
guild between 1391 and 1464, only 15 percent of the 1,047 members had
fathers in the guild. In any case, the succession continued for only one or
two generations.[5]

The social status of the family also determined the types of contracts it
could make. Thus gentlemen's and yeomen's sons were more likely to
enter prestigious guilds than were the sons of husbandmen.[6] Not only did
parents seek to find apprenticeships for their sons, they also sought positions in the houses of guildsmen who held the high social rank conveyed by
wearing the guild livery. Contacts made in such a person's household
would further future business and marriage possibilities.

Sponsors of young women had few choices. Young women were usually apprenticed to makers of silk thread, to dressmakers, or to embroi-
derers. Theirs would be a trade that they could take into a marriage.
Ambitious parents sought the same advantages as they did for their boys,
placing the girls in a socially prestigious household to advance their training and marriage opportunities.

Sometimes a father, perceiving that his death was near, tried to arrange his children's apprenticeship through a will. Thus John de Toten-
hale, a fripper (dealer in old clothes), arranged for John Robynet, also a
fripper, to be both his executor and his son's master. His younger son was
also to be apprenticed to a fripper. Another solution was to assign a guardian who would eventually become the master when the youth reached an
appropriate age.[7]

In other cases, the widow and the stepfather or guardians made the arrangements. Thus in 1334, a stepmother and her stepdaughter came before the mayor and asked him to release 10½ marks for an apprenticeship. A mercer and his wife who were guardians of Joan Bosoun, a daughter of a goldsmith, apprenticed her to become a silkworker. And a stepfather and his wife apprenticed the wife's son to a trade.[8]

Failing immediate family, youths relied on other connections to find them a place. The urban–rural network of friends and patrons is well illustrated in the case of Ellen Semy, daughter of John Semy of Buckinghamshire. She was apprenticed by Elizabeth Thorne of Elstowe nunnery to Thomas Thorne, a salter in London, and his wife to become a coarse weaver. A young man relied on John Birchenshaw, abbot of a monastery in Chester, to place him with a tailor in London. In another case, Sir William Lucas, an "ancre recluse" at the church of All Hallows in London Wall, was sued for £10 that the plaintiff claimed was owed him because William had induced him to take a bad apprentice. Whether these people had any blood relationship to the young people or simply acted out of friendship cannot be determined.[9]

Standing as sponsor for an apprentice meant entering into financial risk. As in all other types of city contracts, bonds of surety were posted, as Sir William Lucas had done, to ensure that the terms were kept and the apprentice lived up to expectations. If the apprentice did not, then the sponsor was liable. Robert Claymond, for instance, stood surety for £40 for William Bothe when he became an apprentice. The apprentice was not enrolled with the city, as required, and left service. He came back but then left again, and Claymond was faced with paying the full amount.[10]

All aspects of apprenticeship contracts were expensive, so that money, as well as the range of the sponsor's contacts, restricted entry. Even in the thirteenth century, when crafts had just begun to regulate apprenticeship, the cost of entry was 30*s.* among the Lorimers, and the Cordwainers required that apprentices pay 40*s.* for their teaching, 2*s.* to the Commune, and 25*s.* to the poor of the guild.[11]

By the late fourteenth and fifteenth centuries, when the guilds were more organized and played a substantial role in the regulation and governing of their members, fees for apprenticeship increased even more. An apprentice to a goldsmith in the late fourteenth century could expect to pay 10 marks for seven years' training and 100*s.* for ten years' training. In addition, he had to pay 20*s.* to 40*s.* for entrance into the Goldsmiths' guild.[12] The Mercers had similar entry fees for apprentices.[13]

These fees represented only those that the guild required. In addition, either the sponsor or the candidate had to pay a varying amount to the master as an inducement to take the apprentice and to cover part of the expenses of lodging.[14] In 1275, Johanna de Frowyk, for instance, acknowledged that she owed 20s. for the apprenticeship of her son, Robert. She agreed to pay 5s. in installments, and Robert agreed to pay his master 20s. at the end of his apprenticeship or to continue to serve him without pay until that sum was made up. In another contract, a man agreed to pay 1 mark quarterly for nine years for the apprenticeship of his son.[15] By the late fourteenth century, the typical charge by the master was 4 to 5 marks.[16] An alternative arrangement was for the apprentice to put up a certain amount of money that the master could trade with but that he had to return at the end of the apprentice's term. John Hale, for instance, complained that he had made an obligation of £100 to put his son to the apprenticeship of John Percevale. When the apprenticeship was up, the young man made his accounting for expenses to Percevale, who kept the books and the money.[17]

In their charter of 1393, the Goldsmiths tried to protect apprentices and their sponsors by establishing a schedule of premiums to be paid to the master. If a ten-year contract was signed, the minimum payment to the master was £5. If a shorter term was agreed to, the premium was 10 marks. Fines of £5 could be levied on the masters for not abiding by these arrangements.[18] Premiums ranged from £2 to £6 in other guilds.[19]

Guilds may have had two classes of apprentices, those who paid premiums and those who did not. Those who did not would become neither guildsmen nor free of the city. Barely half of the apprentices enrolled with the Grocers completed their apprenticeship. This group of second-class citizens may have represented young men who aspired only to become journeymen or to return to the country with some skills.[20]

With the terms and fees agreed on, a contract between master and apprentice could be drawn up. A typical contract is that from the Merchant Tailors for 1451:

> John Harrietsham contracts with Robert Lucy to serve the said Robert as well in the craft and in all his other works and doings such as he does and shall do, from Christmas day next ensuing for the term of 7 years. He is to receive 9s. 4d. at the end of the term, and he shall work one year after the seven at wages of 20s. Robert is to find his apprentice all necessaries, food, clothing, shoes, and bed and to teach him his craft in all its particulars without concealment. During the term the apprentice is to keep his master's secrets, to do him no injury and commit no excessive waste of his goods. He is not to frequent taverns, not to commit fornication in or out of his master's house, nor make any contract of matrimony nor affiance himself without his master's permission. He is not to play at dice, tables, or checkers or any other unlawful games but is to conduct himself soberly, justly, piously, well, and honorably, and to be a faithful and good servant

according to the use and custom of London. For all his obligations Robert binds himself, his heir and his executors, his goods and chattels, present and future, wherever found.

The two parties signed, sealed, and delivered the contract to the guild.[21] Contracts could, of course, contain other clauses, such as agreements about premiums to be paid to the master or about education to be provided in addition to the teaching of the craft.

While apprenticeship contracts contain economic elements, the emphasis is on the behavior expected from both parties. The apprentice swore not to marry and not to fornicate. Included in the latter was the wise precaution that the apprentice not have sexual relations with anyone in his master's household. He was not to engage in the temptations of the city, such as drinking, gaming, and going to theaters. Especially, he was not to gossip about his master's affairs, but to remain loyal to the master's interest and not waste the master's money. The apprentice was expected to accept discipline, including corporal punishment, provided it was not too severe. He also undertook not to leave the apprenticeship to serve another master or simply to run away. If he did run away, his sponsors could be fined and he could be barred from the craft.[22]

The master, likewise, accepted a series of obligations that regulated his behavior in this quasi-familial pact. He had to provide room, board, and clothing. He could not ask his apprentices to perform tasks, such as carrying water, that were for menial servants.[23] He had to treat the youth as a younger member of his own status group. He had a duty, as did a father, to chastise his apprentice for wrongdoing, but he could not be abusive. Above all, he was to instruct the apprentice in his trade or craft without concealing trade secrets that would hinder the apprentice from becoming a master.

The length of the term varied greatly both for individual contracts and with conditions before and after the plague. The city of London established seven years as the minimum term in the early fourteenth century, but did not fix an upward limit.[24] A transcript of the chamberlain's register from 1309 to 1312 gives a good picture of the variations in length of term for that period. While seven years was the minimum and also the usual term of apprenticeship, almost one-third of apprentices served for a longer period. Of the 536 apprentices recorded, 12 percent served for eight years, 4 percent for nine years, 9 percent for ten years, and 5 percent for between eleven and sixteen years.[25] The age of entry during this pre-plague period was around fourteen.

The plague of 1348 and the subsequent visitations made apprentices more difficult to acquire. The depopulation was severe, and parents in the country tried to keep their sons at home to compensate for the greatly reduced labor force.[26] The low rural population also increased opportunities to purchase or rent land and made alternatives to a career in trade more attractive. Peasant youth could also earn sufficient wages to support a family without accepting the long-delayed adulthood that apprenticeship required. The steep costs of entry were another hindrance to apprenticeship. If a youth persisted in pursuing an apprenticeship, he might have to work longer as an agricultural servant to earn the necessary money and to meet the new requirements of literacy. The young men who were the chief source of apprentices—the husbandmen—therefore felt a pull to remain at home.

Some crafts, such as the Fursters, showed a reluctance to take apprentices. The city of London accused them of taking no apprentices in order to restrict the number of people practicing the trade and thereby to raise prices. In their defense, the Fursters claimed that the pestilence had made it difficult to attract apprentices and that "they [guild members] were feeble from a life of labor" and could not have trained them in any case.[27]

Other guilds responded by lengthening the term of the apprentice contract to ten years. By making the apprentices serve longer, masters were able to guarantee a reliable source of skilled labor in the last years of the apprenticeship at a very low cost to themselves. The Goldsmiths by 1393 had already mandated that the term be ten years, but they agreed to reduce it for an extra fee or for sons of Goldsmiths. By their own records, however, the average term was 10.6 years.[28] The trend toward longer terms was established by the first half of the fifteenth century, when only 41 percent of apprenticeship contracts were for eight years and 59 percent were for a longer period.[29] Guild ordinances and scattered references to contract violations indicate that the average length of a term was ten years in the fifteenth and sixteenth centuries.[30]

The apprentice did not necessarily enter a household teeming with other apprentices and journeymen. The establishments were generally small, and the guild often limited the number of apprentices that a master could have. As a precondition, the master had to be a citizen of London. The Mercers stipulated that the master had to demonstrate a need for an apprentice, and then the wardens would give him a license to have one or more apprentices as he needed. Fewer than half the Mercers enrolled from 1391 to 1464 had apprentices.[31] Thus not everyone competent to practice a trade actually engaged in training. The number of apprentices that a citizen could have was also limited by the guilds in the interest of maintaining trade standards. The Fishmongers in the late thirteenth century limited their masters to two or three apprentices, according to their ability to support them.[32]

Even without such regulation, the number of apprentices depended on a household's ability to assimilate them. Between 1349 to 1410, 457 master goldsmiths took in approximately 1,120 apprentices. During the course of their active years as masters, 50 percent had only one apprentice, 19 percent had two, 10 percent had three, 7 percent took four, and 14 percent took five or more.[33] Most drapers in the fifteenth century took only one apprentice at a time, but some enrolled two or three a year.[34] In the Mercers' guild, most masters had fewer than five apprentices, with only 3 percent having more than ten. Two mercers, Henry Frowyk and Ralph Verney, had more than twenty.[35]

It was the masters with large, elite establishments who took more apprentices. Goldsmiths with major commitments, such as Hugh Bryce, who had charge of the mint, enrolled twenty apprentices in twenty-eight years. His establishment had perhaps four or five apprentices at one time. A man who enrolled eight apprentices during the course of seven years or eighteen over the course of twenty-two years would have had a very full house.[36] Some overlap was desirable in the larger shops to allow a continual stream of apprentices at various levels. Guild regulations permitted such overlap.[37]

The early mortality of masters and the increased length of apprenticeship also help to explain the low number of masters who took multiple apprentices. If a master lived to age forty and had set up an independent business at twenty-eight or thirty, he would probably live through only one apprentice.[38] Figures on the Goldsmiths, of course, come from a period of high plague mortality, when life expectancy might have been lower.

The low number of apprentices in an ordinary household explains much of what we observe about the adolescent experience. With only one or two apprentices in a household, it was hard for the young men to form a strong youth culture in defiance of their masters. They were locked into a close, quasi-familial relationship with their masters, rather than forming separate youth groups. The master who took only one or two apprentices during his lifetime placed a higher premium on the relationship than if the apprentice was one of a succession of foster youth in the household. It is easy to imagine that part of the intensity of the master–apprentice relationship grew out of the master's need to mold this sole disciple into an image of himself.

Still, masters who took from five to twenty or more apprentices during their active careers trained more initiates and had proportionately more influence on the guild than those who trained only one or two. For the masters, training a number of apprentices brought prestige. But even those maintaining large households might form close relationships with their apprentices.

The potential for conflict, however, was ever-present, and both formal and informal mechanisms for release existed. Sometimes a period of a fortnight was allowed in the indenture for the parties to change their minds about the arrangement. The formal enrollment of the apprentice at London's Guildhall had to be done within a year and a day after the signing of the contract. Before that time, the apprentice and master could dissolve the contract if they both agreed.[39]

The rules governing apprenticeship also permitted the master to sell the contract either to the apprentice himself or to another master. He could also transfer the apprentice as he would other property. Thus John atte Wode, a salter, transferred all his goods and chattels, including debts, apprentices, and all other things, to his daughter and her husband.[40] Apprentices were frequently left to widows in wills on the presumption that the widows would either carry on the business or marry someone in the trade, as they frequently did. Such arrangements provided, as we shall see, a potential for abuse of the apprentice's expectations about training.

Many apprentices bought their way out of their contracts or ran away. In the sixteenth century, only 41 percent of the apprentices finished out their terms.[41] Leaving aside the high mortality of London apprentices, reasons for terminating the contract varied. Apprenticeship, as we have seen, was not absolutely necessary to become a citizen. If an apprentice felt that he had adequate training, he might want to set out on his own. Guilds, of course, preferred to keep control over former apprentices. Thus the Goldsmiths would not admit a former apprentice to membership unless his master released him or he in some way completed his apprenticeship.[42] Or the apprentice might want to acquire only sufficient knowledge of his trade to allow him to return to the county or market town of his origin to practice. Walter Hastings, for instance, served for only a year and three-quarters and then bought his way out for £8. He had considerable other wealth and left apparently owing his master money.[43] A continual complaint was that incompletely trained apprentices set up in Westminster or Southwark, where they were out of the reach of guild control. Finally, although guilds had numerous rules against the practice, some apprentices left to serve with other masters.

The personal, quasi-familial relationship, established through the intermediation of friends and acquaintances and made formal by contract, was guaranteed by both the guild and the city government. Examination of the apprentice and the contract, enrollment with the guild masters and the city chamberlain, and public ceremonies marking entry into this new life stage laid the groundwork for enforcement of the contract.

Ceremonies of Initiation

Late medieval society, being largely still an oral culture, retained a suspicion that the written word was not adequate for important matters, such as becoming an initiate into the mysteries of a craft. As a consequence, the act of entering into apprenticeship required solemn ceremonies with many witnesses in order to impress on the mind of the youth and those around him that he had taken a major step, with obligations and implications for his life for the next seven to ten or more years. One remembered obligations better when rituals reinforced them. The two powerful authorities in the apprentice's life, the guild and the city government, both had initiation rituals.[44]

After the master and the apprentice's family and friends had signed and sealed the contract, the next step was for the guild wardens to examine the apprentice. The examination included making sure of the age and good physical condition of the youth and making inquiries into his background. By 1510, the Mercers had spelled out the specifications that had to be met. The apprentice had to be sixteen years old, free of birth, tall, lithe of limb, and not disfigured in body or members. Nobody could have an apprentice who had "carried packs in the country" or was a villain's son. But the wardens despaired of accurate judgments because "daily there be presented and also admitted divers apprentices which be very little in growing or stature." Faced with an onslaught of what they perceived as runts, the wardens considered compelling the apprentices' friends to swear to the fitness of an apprentice, but decided against it.[45]

Not only were the youth to be without deformities, but increasingly the guilds required a demonstration of reading and writing ability. The Goldsmiths, for instance, required apprentices to prove their skill by writing in "a book to be dormant in the treasury of the Hall." The book came to be known as the "Dormant." The Ironmongers had an "Apprentices' Book of Oaths," which served a similar purpose. One master was fooled, or so he said, by an apprentice he had taken from Banbury. The apprentice was so skilled in engraving letters that his master thought he could read and write, but he could not.[46]

Examination and contract complete, an oath was repeated orally to the guild wardens and masters. This must have been an impressive ceremony for the fourteen- to eighteen-year-olds, many of whom had come from the country. By the end of the fourteenth century, many guilds had adopted a livery, or special clothing, of splendid color and fabric that members wore for ceremonial meetings. The oath-taking ceremony would impress on the initiate not only his own inferior position, but also the heights to which he might aspire should he reach the rank of master. The words of the oath, administered by the resplendent wardens, impressed on him the obligations he was to undertake:

> Ye shall swear to be good and trewe to our sovereign lord king and to his heirs. And well and trewly ye shall serve your master for the terms of your apprenticeshood. And ye shall be obedient unto the wardens and to all the clothing of the fellowship. In reverence the secrets of the said fellowship ye shall keep and give no information to no man but of the said fellowship. An if it fortune that ye part from the mistery ye shall not serve anyone out of the fellowship without licence of the wardens. And in all these things ye shall well and truly behave you and secretly keep this oath to your power so help you god and all saints and by that book.[47]

As in most medieval oaths, God, saints, and the gospels bound the apprentice's oath.

To underline the sacred nature of the obligation, the master might take the apprentice first to the church associated with the guild. Thus the Mercers required that every person taking an apprentice first enroll and swear him at St. Thomas Church. By 1510, the Mercers had moved the ceremony to their own hall (most guilds built halls for meetings and banqueting during the course of the fifteenth century) and provided a ceremony to remind the apprentices of their obligations. The first Monday after "clean Lent," at an assigned hour, the wardens were to read to the assembled apprentices the terms of their contracts so that they could not claim ignorance. Apprentices were to be fined 12*d.* for nonattendance.[48]

Apprenticeship in London was not only the first step toward becoming a master, but also a preliminary to London citizenship. For this reason, the city had an official role in apprenticeship. Registration with London's chamberlain could be delayed, but had to be done within a year and a day after signing the contract. Again, the occasion was an impressive one, for it was intended to show the apprentice the power of civic authority. In the early fourteenth century, the apprentice and his master met with the chamberlain, who examined the candidate and his indenture. William Bothe described the ceremony when he appealed against his master for a broken contract. He said that he and the man who was to be his surety "went before Robert Colwythe, Chamberlain of London, as was customary and the Chamberlain reviewed the articles of apprenticeship and examined William Bothe." His apprenticeship was approved and entered in the papers.[49]

The record of enrollment, which is always referred to as the "paper," was kept by ward. One apprentice said in 1442 that his contract was enrolled in "the register marked D of apprentices."[50]

Feeling the competition from foreigners after the Black Death, the Commons of London asked that one day in the month be set aside for "gildedaies" to distinguish the importance of apprenticeship examination and enrollment from all others. Apprentices should pay 60s. for the ceremony. The enrollment should be further dignified by having not only the master and apprentice appear, but also six other men who were full members of the mistery to testify to the apprentice's fitness. If the apprentice was found acceptable, then he should be received in the presence of three aldermen and the chamberlain. While designed to make it difficult for foreigners to enter into apprenticeships, the ceremony was also meant to inspire awe and perhaps fear in the hearts of the candidates.[51]

Failure to enroll an apprentice with the chamberlain was a grave offense for which fines of £20 levied against the master were not unusual. The city tried public embarrassment as well, ordaining that the names of apprentices not "entered on the paper" in the first year were to be published at the next Husting so that fines could be imposed. But both masters and apprentices had many reasons to avoid enrollment. First of all, the enrollment fees paid to both guild and city were expensive, running from £1 to £5 for apprentices and £1 for masters. High company standards made it difficult for a master to secure an apprentice and for an apprentice to meet all qualifications. In the period of low population, in particular, masters wanted to try to attract apprentices to help with the work, but did not necessarily go to the additional expense of enrolling them. The Cutlers' guild complained in 1485 that its members were employing too many apprentices and not training them adequately. Since the apprentices were not enrolled, the company could not control their workmanship. From the apprentices' viewpoint, enrollment was expensive and could limit their flexibility to leave once they had an adequate knowledge of the craft. If they did not want to become citizens of London, they had little reason to enroll. Thus a number of apprentices were never enrolled.[52]

Those youth who would not enroll or who were not enrolled could not hope to enter into the higher orders of London life. They could not aspire to be liveried guild members and wear the luxurious, colorful "cloth" of the fully initiated. They could not aspire to an independent shop, to master status, or to any of the advantages or glory of freemen. London offered only servant and laborer status to an Englishman (as opposed to a foreigner) not free of the city. The ceremonies of enrollment were a step over the threshold toward potential advancement and riches, but they guaranteed admission only to an antechamber, not full access to the advantages accorded the initiate.

Female Apprentices

Maidens' experience of entering into apprentice contracts was sufficiently different from that of young men to require separate treatment. For a woman, apprenticeship was not perceived as a stepping stone to an independent life as a citizen of London, although some women, particularly silk workers, might either remain single and practice their craft or practice as *femme sole* under London's law. London permitted married women to carry on their own businesses, contract their own debts, and settle their own legal cases.[53] As we shall see, London heiresses, whose capital was much in demand, tended to marry in their teens. These women did not need a trade to induce men to marry them. But for a woman with a modest dowry or for the bastard daughter of a citizen, the added advantage of a skill that could be practiced at home and contribute to the household economy was of considerable value in the marriage market. Because a large proportion of the arrangements for young women were predicated on a truncated apprenticeship should a marriage be the offing, women's experiences with apprenticeship and even their contracts could be quite different from that of their brothers.

As we have seen, young women found their masters or mistresses through the same type of networks of family and friends that young men used. Maidens were usually apprenticed to women, but if the mistress was married, the contract was made in the name of both husband and wife. Ann Lyde, for example, was put as an apprentice to John Coke of London, a purser, and his wife, Elizabeth. Ann was to learn the wife's trade of "schepstrie."[54] Thus the contractual relationship might go through the intermediation of the head of the family, rather than being directly with the mistress who would be doing the instruction.[55]

A maiden's age of entry into apprenticeship, as observed in Chapter 7, might be younger than a young man's, and the cost of entry could be less. For instance, Ann Lyde's friend posted a bond of only £10. Although female as well as male apprentices fell under the provisions of the city law requiring that the term be a minimum of seven years, shorter contracts seem to have been possible. Again, to take Ann Lyde's case, her contract was for only four years. When such a contract came to the attention of the court, however, the mayor was quick to enforce the law. Thus when John Catour of Reading complained that an embroiderer who was his daughter's master ill-treated her, testimony revealed that the contract was for only five years when it should have been for seven.[56] Contracts for nine and even as many as fifteen years appear for female apprentices.[57]

Maidens' contracts, unlike young men's, seem often to have included a clause permitting the apprentice to terminate the contract for a sum of money if she wished to marry. Thus Agnes Cok, who was apprenticed and duly enrolled to William and John Kaly, was allowed by her contract to leave before that time, provided that she paid 4 marks.[58]

If maidens under apprenticeship contract were to be treated the same as young men, the great mystery is why they never appear in city records as enrolled in apprenticeships or as gaining citizenship through completion of apprenticeship. The city proclamation required that every free man and women with a male or female apprentice enroll the trainee with the chamberlain within a year and a day.[59] In the one surviving chamberlain's listing of apprentices and in the guild records, the names of no young women appear. And yet masters and mistresses were fined for not enrolling their female apprentices, and families brought suit for nonenrollment.[60] Enrollment of a girl's contract was a protection for the parents and for the girl. Any abuse of the contract or of the apprentice could be brought to the mayor as a violation of a written indenture, rather than as a dispute over an oral agreement. Among his other faults, the master of John Catour's daughter had never enrolled her.

One reason for the absence of information on the enrollment of female apprentices is that London had no female guilds. Women entered the male-dominated guilds not through an apprenticeship system, but as wives or widows of guild members. The female-dominated trade was the making of silk thread, but the London women were not organized into a guild, as were the Parisian women. Brewing was another occupation in which many women participated as brewers and as innkeepers, but although they had a guild, the brewers seem not to have had a regular apprenticeship system until the sixteenth century and rarely accepted women as full members.[61] Women trained by a master in a more established guild, such as the Tailors, might become dressmakers but were not admitted into the guild.

Families might also have been unwilling to spend the large sums needed to arrange advantageous contracts for daughters. The fees, as we have seen, were high, and the better familial strategy might have been to put the money toward a dowry, rather than toward formal training in a trade. Skills at a craft such as silkwork or brewing were an inducement to marriage, but did not replace the dowry.

For whatever reasons, the experience of female apprentices was different from that of males because gender led to different expectations for male and female adults. Although the evidence for enrollment of females' contracts before the mayor and the chamberlain is scanty, enrollments must have taken place. But maidens did not undergo the elaborate ritual oath involving the guild masters and members. By becoming apprentices, however, women, like their male counterparts, did enter another phase in the progress toward adulthood. They changed households, exchanging their subservient, childhood position in the parents' house for a subservient, contractual arrangement in another person's house. For female apprentices, too, the step over the threshold was a step into the foyer of adulthood, but it was accompanied by less fanfare and less expenditure than it was for their brothers.

Profile of the Apprentice Population

An idealized portrait of the perfect apprentice appears in a fifteenth-century poem, "The Childe of Bristowe." The father of the eponymous child is a wealthy, if unscrupulous, member of the country gentry who dotes on his only son. The boy goes to school at twelve, and, when he is learned, his father determines that he should study law even if it costs the father 20 marks. But this paragon of virtue declines a legal education, saying that it would endanger his salvation and that, instead, "[h]it hath ever be myn avise / to lede my lyf by marchandise." Father and son go off to Bristol to arrange a seven-year contract with a well-known merchant: "He gaf hym gold gret plente / th child hys prentys shuld be." The merchants, both young and old, love him because he learns quickly and "he wax so curteise and bolde."[62]

The ideal accounts for at least part of the reality. Most apprentices were males, rather than females, and entered into their apprenticeship at around age fourteen during the fourteenth century and at age sixteen or older by the end of the fifteenth century. Their average level of education increased during the course of these two centuries, with most apprentices able to read and write or at least to write out their apprenticeship oaths. The masters expected them to be honest and to have learned their manners by the time they entered into the contract. Apprentices were, by preference, straight-limbed and freeborn.

By the middle of the fifteenth century, additional limitations on access to apprenticeship appear in the records. The children had to be born in England. John Payne, a glover, had taken as apprentices two brothers who were sons of an Englishman but who had been born in Flanders. He needed a special dispensation to make them free of the city.

The prohibition against the apprenticing of serfs had to be modified by the middle of the fifteenth century, when serfdom was disappearing in England. In an attempt to restrict, access to apprenticeship to the elite, the royal government passed a statute requiring that parents of prospective apprentices have land and rents producing 20s. a year. Symon Welles, one of the clerks of the king's court, brought a bill of contempt against Richard Claidich, a writer of court-hand, claiming that he had contracted with an apprentice who did not meet the terms. The defense argued and won, saying that the statute said nothing about apprentices who made their own contracts. The mayor and the aldermen then asked that the statute be struck down, and it was.[63]

Insisting on elite recruits in a time of decreased population hindered both recruits and recruiters. Needless to say, the guildsmen and the citizens would have preferred to draw potential new members from their own kind or from the country gentry. Richard Whittington, the Horatio Alger figure of the early modern tale, actually came from the gentry, not from poor peasant stock. (The cat is fictitious.)[64] But finding apprenticeship candidates was difficult, and standards were lowered simply to get the cheap, subsidized labor that apprenticeship provided. In a fifteenth-century poem dealing with the Masons, masters are warned not to recruit apprentices from among the serfs because lords have the power to come and claim them. This analysis was out of date, but the poem contains something of a lament: "By olde tyme, wryten Y fynde / That prentes shchulde be of gentyl kynde." Part of the reason for preferring apprentices drawn from the gentry was that they increased the prestige of the master and the guild.[65]

The anxiety expressed in the poem and the statute reflect the social reality. At various times, masters complained that it was so difficult to get apprentices that some masters were accepting those who had no money. Among the Skinners and Tailors, 32 percent of the apprentices had fathers who were merchants or craftsmen, 30 percent had yeomen fathers, 19 percent were husbandmen, 16 percent were from the gentry, and the other 3 percent had fathers from miscellaneous backgrounds.[66] By the middle of the sixteenth century, 47 percent of the apprentices were sons of husbandmen, 23 percent were of yeoman origin, and another 23 percent were native Londoners, with only 7 percent drawn from the gentry. By the sixteenth century, then, husbandmen formed the predominant source of recruits, whereas townsmen and yeomen had dominated in the fifteenth century.

In the more prestigious guilds, however, native Londoners, members of the gentry, and yeomen dominated the apprenticeships. In 1551 to 1553, native Londoners, for instance, accounted for one-quarter of the apprentices sworn to the Haberdashers, Skinners, and Vintners and one-third of those apprenticed to the Goldsmiths, Ironmongers, and Mercers. The vast majority of gentry sons and three-quarters of yeomen's sons joined the prestigious guilds. In fifteenth-century London, two-thirds of the apprentices who were indentured to the elite, liveried members of the Skinners came either from the gentry or from the merchant and yeoman classes. While the Masons may have been rightly concerned about attracting the best sort of apprentice, those guilds that dealt with long-distance trade or that offered opportunity for amassing considerable wealth had no trouble attracting the upper crust.[67]

Networks certainly helped to produce the pattern of elite attracting elite. Londoners apprenticed their sons to friends in their own guilds when they could, sometimes even apprenticing their sons to themselves.[68] The payment of higher premiums was also more likely among sponsors from the gentry and the yeomanry than among the husbandmen.

Although Londoners' sons enjoyed advantages in terms of finding apprenticeships, in the fourteenth through the sixteenth centuries, they formed the minority of those who were apprenticed. Of the 536 apprentices listed in the chamberlain's register from 1309 to 1312, 185, or 35 percent, were certainly from outside London; they were described as being from a specific village (for example, "John, son of William Walrond of Stuntefeld"). Another 221, or 41 percent, had surnames that indicated an origin outside London (for example, "Thomas de Bolnhurst"). The rest bore occupational surnames, and some of these apprentices were probably Londoners. In the early fourteenth century, recruits came mostly from the home counties (those surrounding London), but by the fifteenth century, London was attracting more recruits from the north and the west. In addition, a sprinkling of Welsh and Irish was always added to apprenticeship ranks.[69] From 1551 to 1553, 83 percent of the apprentices were from outside London, with half coming from northern and western counties.[70]

The vast majority of apprentices, therefore, were making a major transition in their lives when they entered into apprenticeship. They were separated by long distances from their natal families, their new surroundings in a major metropolis would be substantially different from the villages and market towns in which they had grown up, and they might well be moving into housing that represented a higher standard of living than that to which they were accustomed. No wonder so many books of courtesy, manners, and advice existed to help make the transition easier. The homes of masters served not only as places to learn a trade, but also as places to smooth the raw edges of the country bumpkin. London's apprenticeship system offered socialization as well as training.

An Italian Traveler Leads Twentieth-Century Historians Astray, or the Lasting Importance of the Natal Family and Friends

I have carefully refrained from mentioning the observations of the late medieval Italian traveler until now because he has caused so much mischief among twentieth-century historians. He has convinced them that the English did not love their children and therefore sent them off to live with other families at a tender age. His English informants, in their turn, claimed that he misunderstood their customs (should we picture him as an early anthropologist). They loved their children so much that they sent them off to other families so that they could learn better and be disciplined. Should they have undertaken such an important trust themselves, they would not have been able to beat the poor youngsters sufficiently to see that they were well raised.[71] Historians, taking the side of the anthropologist rather than the natives, have accepted the traveler's interpretation. The English did not love their children because they lost so many in childhood and therefore became callous. The best thing for parents to do was to send their children off into the great world of men and be rid of them. It is time that we listen again to the voice of the native. It speaks clearly in the field notes and is corroborated in independent evidence.

London citizens valued the apprenticeship experience for their sons. Although sons of citizens could enter a guild at a reduced fee without going through the apprenticeship, increasingly in the fifteenth century they took the more traditional route. Sir Thomas Gresham explained that "my father, Sir Richard Gresham, being a wyse man, knew [that] although I was free by his coppye it was to no purpose except I were bound prentisse to the same whereby to come by the experience and knowledge of all kinds of merchandise." Few fathers wished to have their sons serve as apprentices in their households. Only four apprentices served with their fathers among the fifteenth-century Mercers; a similar number did so among the Goldsmiths. Most parents preferred that their sons expand their social contacts and learn additional trade secrets through another master.[72]

The move of a child from the natal home to that of the master was certainly a major event in the lives of the child and the parents. In the fourteenth century in particular, the parents were sending a child of perhaps no more than fourteen a very long way from home to live with a comparative stranger. The networks that linked the potential apprentice and his master provided some assurance of good treatment for the child, but often the network was no more than a local nun who had a relative in trade in London. In other cases, children went to an uncle or a neighbor who had made good in London.

Having a child enter into an apprenticeship represented a considerable emotional and monetary investment for the parents. They perceived the arrangement not as getting rid of a child, but as establishing his future and perhaps theirs. Capital put into the contract might prosper and be returned to them in old age by a successful son or daughter. In addition, a successful apprenticeship might serve as a conduit for other children into the greater wealth that London could offer. Like prudent parents throughout history, medieval parents did not want to see their investment of emotion and capital come to naught. Children who encountered unpleasant situations or fell ill retreated to their parents for help.

When problems arose between the apprentice and the master—the subject of Chapter 9—it was the natal family or the sponsors who intervened. By the fifteenth century, when the age of entrance into apprenticeship had risen, the apprentices often were able to sue in London courts for themselves. But the fourteenth-century cases and those of London citizens reveal close supervision on the part of the natal family.

A typical case is that of the son of William de Beverlee. The father complained that his son's master mistreated the boy and drove him away, leaving him no recourse but to return to his parents (perhaps all the way to Yorkshire). The defendant, a chaucer, claimed that the apprentice had lent his master's goods to others and had not restored them or their value. The jury concluded that the apprentice had lent two pairs of shoes belonging to his master and had not restored them. The master, however, had not fed and clothed the apprentice as he ought because he could not afford to do so. The youth had run away because he was so frightened by the beating he had received for not returning the goods that he refused to stay in the house. A compromise was reached between the master and the father. The boy would return and be compensated 40d. for the lack of food and clothing, since the master could now afford to keep and instruct an apprentice. If this arrangement was not agreeable, the father was to have back the money that he had put up for the indenture.[73]

Parents often went to some lengths to ensure their rights to protect their children during apprenticeship. A father disputed an apprenticeship contract involving his son because the father was not named. A father "of right ought to have been surety for his son . . . as usage is." But many of the complaints in which the role of the natural parents came to the fore were more serious. Alice Kyng, a remarried widow, and her new husband brought a petition to the Chancellor, saying that her son was apprenticed to John Crychefeylde, a goldsmith, and that "he did diverse things to her son which should be done to no apprentice." As his "natural mother," she had gone to the chamberlain and had her son removed from the master's house, but now the master was threatening a suit against her for taking her son away. In another case, John Suthwode and his wife complained to the Chancellor that their son had been in prison across the seas for three years, but the master would do nothing to procure his release. They had gone to the master of the Mercers' guild and the mayor of London to force the master to act, but he would not. One mother outright accused her son's master of having killed him.[74] Other kin also looked out for the welfare of relations. One young man whose contract had been sold twice went to the house of his sister and brother-in-law for refuge.[75]

One father told a harrowing tale about the treatment of his son and himself at the hands of a master. John Bartlet had apprenticed his ten-year-old son to a glover, John Parker, for a term of ten years. Parker sold the term to a tailor for 4s. to earn needed money. The tailor, in turn, sold the contract to a weaver, Robert Hobbok, for 3s. 4d. In this household, the apprentice was so badly looked after and ill-fed during the winter that he almost lost the use of his limbs and his body was covered with vermin. So severely was he beaten by his master's servants that he could not help himself. When John Bartlet went to see how his son was doing, the servants attacked him.[76]

When apprentices fell ill during their terms, they often went to their parents' house or were taken there by their masters. John, son of Luke de Ware, had been at St. Botolph's Fair with his master and had returned to London, where he traded in goods from the master's shop. But John fell ill, and his master had him taken to his father's house. He then sued for the profit from those goods. John's father took in his ailing son and stood surety for him.[77]

Parents not only remained in contact with their apprenticed children, but claimed rights above and beyond the contractual rights of the master and apprentice. When occasion demanded, they argued that the natural parent had a higher claim in the law than the surrogate. Apprenticeship did not sever the power of this bond. When the system worked at its best (and, as we shall see, it often did), the apprentice's family and master were in agreement over the best interest of the youth.[78]

"William Bothe, Mercers' Apprentice"

William Bothe, Jr., had good London connections through his father, although the old man had retired to the country and established himself as a gentleman in Sussex. Still, the old man kept his ties with the Mercers' guild, and when his second son needed some honorable prospects in life, the obvious solution was to put him as an apprentice to one of the distinguished guild brothers. William Hill was a liveried Mercer, who proudly wore the lavish, colorful livery of the company. In 1461, he and a select few had donned green riding gowns over a doublet of the guild colors and sleeves of black satin or damask; they also wore black hats with "typpettes" of black damask to ride on horseback as resplendent Mercers to meet Edward IV at his entrance to London. It was traditional for these elite dealers in cloth to exhibit their wares on such an occasion, but the news of it reinforced old Bothe's plan to apprentice young William to Hill. A man who rode out to the king had good connections that could further the boy's career.[79]

Although the old man had no qualms about getting his son accepted as an apprentice in the guild through which his family had risen, he realized that he was getting on in years and must plan carefully. He could negotiate a good situation for William, but he could not ensure that he would be alive when the young man completed his apprenticeship. William was already sixteen and would need at least another year of school in London before he could start his apprenticeship. He needed a younger man, who could oversee any problems that might arise, to stand surety with him. Robert Claymond was wealthy enough to afford the expense. He was a stepbrother, a product of his mother's second marriage to Claymond, Sr. As an uncle to William, he would be an appropriate sponsor. The old man had his suspicions that young William needed a steady, guiding hand. The boy showed a certain disdain for following a trade— thought he was above it. He wanted to be a soldier and a courtier. But that was no sure life. He would be a mercer, whether he liked it or not. The old man could die in peace, having placed his son with the distinguished William Hill with his stepbrother, Robert Claymond, as sponsor.

He had worked out the apprenticeship contract himself. There were the usual provisions. The boy was apprenticed for ten years. Within a year and a day, he would be enrolled before the mayor in the "papers." The time-honored formula went into the contract: the master would feed, clothe, house, and train the boy in the craft of the mercery, allowing him into the secrets of the trade gradually and seeing that he was enrolled as a freeman of the city at the end of his apprenticeship. Of course, the boy would not be expected to do any servile labor during the period of apprenticeship, such as carrying water like a common house servant. But Hill had a full complement of house servants, so that was not a real worry, as it might have been with some of the poorer guild brothers. Bothe also put in the usual clauses about the sort of behavior his son would maintain. William might be a problem, so it was best to have him swear in a written contract to behave. The expectations were spelled out: sober dress, no theater, and no gambling. The old man pondered. If anything, young William was a cross between the knight's squire and one of the more disreputable sorts out of old Chaucer's stories. Could he really guarantee that William would not try to sleep with his master's wife, daughter, or maidservant? He seemed not to have learned that commandment about not coveting a man's maidservant. He had had trouble enough in his own household; William's lechery was one of the reasons old Bothe wanted to get him out. At least, in London, prostitutes were readily available. Of course, William would have to forswear them in his contract as well.

Second sons were a necessary evil. Good insurance on inheritance, but a pain to live with and place, should the first son be healthy and produce a fine crop of grandsons. William Hill, the potential master for young Bothe, knew all about the risks. He and the old man had kept up contacts, hunting together in Sussex and visiting together in London. Still, Hill had beaten sense into worse young dandies than William Bothe, and he could not be the financial loser. Old Bothe was willing to put up a considerable premium to cover the liabilities of his second son, and Claymond, the sponsor, who stood as surety, was a wealthy man who was was willing to sign a £40 bond for the contract and for young Bothe's good behavior. The deal might be a headache, but it would not be a financial loss for an old guild brother to take on the son of his ailing old friend.

The covenant was signed, and Hill had his money and the bonds, should the arrangement fail. It was time for the final formalities. No one anticipated any problems at this stage. William Bothe was a tall, handsome young man. He had completed his education in London and had no problem writing his oath in "The Book of Apprentices." He knew how to handle himself before the guild masters and was not awed by their ceremonial behavior or their fine clothes—after all, he was rather like old Chaucer's squire and knew how to handle himself in such situations. He had all the bearing that the Mercers expected from someone who might become a warden of the company or even an alderman or a mayor. He went through that ceremony with much poise, the truth was that he enjoyed ceremonies.

The next ceremony, before the mayor and the chamberlain, could wait for a year and a day. This would give the master and the apprentice (with his family and friends) time to assess how well the arrangement had worked out before it became irrevocably registered with the city in the "papers." At the enrollment, William Bothe impressed the city officials with his education, wit, and good bearing. Robert Claymond was there as well to act as surety for the contract and to offer his bond for young Bothe's fulfillment of the contract. Robert Colwythe was chamberlain, and it was he who reviewed the articles of apprenticeship and examined the youth.

Several years later and with much bitterness all around, one of the few things that all parties agreed about was that Robert Colwythe was the chamberlain who had examined William Bothe when he became William Hill's apprentice. They all agreed that the contract had been enrolled. But William had left his master's service. Bothe had been an irritant all along. When he lived in the household, he had flirted with Hill's new young wife. He had diverted some of Hill's cloth to have fine clothing made for himself. When William had enough training, Hill was glad to get him out of the house and over to Flanders. The Mercers' safe houses in Bruges might correct his deficiency of "sad and wise" behavior. He would have to live by English regulations and drink only English beer. But young Bothe's behavior had not improved, and he had responded to Hill's reprimands and the Mercers' guild fines by running away.

Bothe's father had died in the first few years of the young man's service, and then his older brother had died. Now William was principal heir and free at last. He could return to Sussex as a country gentleman and never have to deal with cloth again. He failed to realize the binding nature of the apprenticeship contract, his oath, and his enrollment in the "papers." His uncle Claymond pointed out that he was liable for £40 and would sue young William if he had to pay it.

William's first response was subterfuge. He returned to London and tried to convince the wardens of the Mercers' guild that William Hill had mistreated him, had kept money that his father had left him, and had forced him out of his service so that he had no recourse but to run away. The masters would not hear his plea, and so he tried a piteous petition to the Lord Chancellor, hoping to force Hill to take him back.

William Hill knew that this petition would get nowhere and that he would get his compensation from Claymond. Young Bothe finally began to see the enormity of the problems he faced. He might be heir to a modest country estate, but he would have this contract and debt hanging over his head. He could not return to London to see to his tenements there without being imprisoned, and he would not be able to make a marriage in London because of his broken contract.

Sitting in his hall in Sussex and pondering his future, he received a slim parchment from Master Hill, a poem entitled "The Childe of Bristowe," with a note saying that he remembered how much William's father had liked poetry and that he would take young William back if he heeded the poem's lesson. At first, Bothe read with some disgust about how this ideal young man rejected the law in favor of a merchant career. He had to laugh at that. But the verses about the father's condemnation to hell because he had squeezed the wealth out of his tenants and debtors in the country made him think about his own position. How else would he get his wealth if he did not become a merchant? He thought the young apprentice a fool for selling his patrimony at a low price to his master so that he could pay off his father's debts to save his soul. But then he read that the master had cautioned the young man not to impoverish himself, but the apprentice had responded that it was better to sell cheap to a master he trusted than to any other man. As he read the final passages, when the apprentice's father had been saved and all the poor young man had to sell was his body into bondage, Bothe's eyes were full of tears. For all the religiosity of the poem, the end was materialistic enough. The master praised the self-sacrifice of the apprentice and made him his heir because he had no children of his own.[80]

Hill was certainly a good master, as young Bothe could now see. Bothe also realized that he had really been a bad apprentice and difficult to rule. Although he could buy out his uncle's bond for the apprentice contract from his inheritance, he might end up like the father of the Bristol apprentice. Hill was not without children, of course. Indeed, young William remembered with great fondness young Joan, Hill's daughter by his first marriage. Hill had no other children as yet, not from that young wife William used to tease. The easiest solution to his problems seemed to be to return in contrition to the Mercers, pay his fines, and hope Hill would forgive him.[81]

A fishmonger and his customers. (Drawing by Wayne M. Howell, from British Library, MS. Facs. 183/6)

9

Relationships Between Masters and Apprentices

The story of Walter Prata, a thoroughly disreputable apprentice, gives a clear picture of the division of labor in a medium-size shop and of the relationship between the master and his apprentices. Walter was apprenticed in 1400 to John Lincoln, a liveried goldsmith. Being, perhaps, fourteen at the time, Walter was the youngest apprentice in the establishment. The two others, Henry Goldsmith and William Fannt, completed their apprenticeship a year after Walter joined the household but continued to work in Lincoln's shop as bachelors. Lincoln took in another apprentice as well, John Lannden, so that the business consisted of himself, two experienced workers, and two apprentices. The two apprentices lived with the master, as did Fannt, who occupied a separate chamber. They all took their meals together.

Following breakfast, the apprentices lowered the shop-board that formed a counter. The goods were actually displayed in a cupboard behind the counter, its latticework doors permitting viewing of the objects in a locked display case. Items were brought out to the counter for a customer to inspect, or the customer might bring in plate or jewelry to be repaired. Lincoln waited on the customers while the apprentices and "young men" (bachelors) worked in the back. The goldsmith's shop had a furnace, a melting hearth, anvils, and work tables. Tools of the trade, such as balances, hammers, and tongs, were hung on the walls. Goldsmithing could be a noisy, hot business. The men working together had to rely on one another to avoid accidents. The working atmosphere, as we shall see, could vary considerably. Masters could be ill-tempered and abusive, or they could be conscientious, resorting to corporal punishment only as perceived necessary for serious infractions. Apprentices such as Walter Prata could also poison a shop's atmosphere.

While young in age, Prata was a precocious cheat. If a customer brought in silver to be weighed on the balances and turned into a new object, Prata knew how to steal a three- or four-pennyweight in the weighing process. His master sent him off to get change for a gold noble, and he shortchanged his master by 7*d.* silver. When he went to a goldbeater on an errand to deliver silver gilt, he returned short of silver. While the others were at dinner, he would excuse himself and go to the melting hearth to find grains of gold and silver that had fallen into the ash. These thefts were all performed in the course of his work as an apprentice, but he soon branched beyond petty larceny. He went to a jeweler on London Bridge and claimed that he was borrowing a silver cup for his master. He sold the cup and kept the profits. As his skill developed, he made duplicate keys to his master's display chest and to Fannt's chamber and chest. On one occasion, he stole three ounces of gold from Fannt's chest and did not confess to the theft for three days while Fannt and the others turned the shop upside down looking for the gold. He stole chemicals (sal ammoniac and saltpeter) and offered a man 10*s.* to show him how to use them. His ultimate goal, he finally confessed to the wardens of the Goldsmiths, was to steal his master's gold and silver and go to Flanders with John Sasse, a Fleming. The account concludes that "in this wise he made much dis-ease among the men." The guild expelled him with no possibility of gaining readmission.[1]

When the relationship between master and apprentice soured, as it did between Lincoln and Prata, one or both parties could be at fault. The problem might lie in a breach of the contract, in the unreliability of the apprentice, or in the excessive cruelty of the master. But the numerous cases that we will investigate in which the arrangement did not turn out well will be balanced by a consideration of those in which very close relationships developed. One must always remember that court cases tend to present a negative picture, focusing as they do on contracts gone awry. They cannot be taken as the typical experience. The combination of fostering and training inherent in apprenticeship encouraged a full range of emotional responses, from hatred to familial intimacy.

Faults of Masters

The position of master was one of considerable power and, as such, was open to abuse. Although the apprentice's natal family and sponsors, as well as the guilds and the city officials, oversaw the contractual arrangements and had power of intervention, apprentices were in a very vulnerable position. They might have come from a faraway county where their family could not hear about their troubles, or they might be too young to protest ill treatment. In any case, the master–apprentice relationship was that of a powerful superior and a very dependent inferior. Physical abuse was only one of the threats a master could use. His ultimate weapon was to withhold admission into the freedom of the city. Apprentices often put up with considerable hardship before complaining either directly to the city or to their family and friends. Sometimes they acted only after they became mature enough to feel adequately knowledgeable and confident to lodge a complaint. By that time, many years of abuse might have occurred.

A common complaint was that the master was not teaching the apprentice his trade. For instance, John Malmayn of Jerking complained that his master, John Coggeshale, a haberdasher, had agreed to a ten-year apprenticeship contract with him, but after four years he had learned only to make points and had been clothed only in a russet gown and an old "paltokes." He said the only work he had "was to carry a child in the streets." After four years of babysitting, he finally protested and was transferred to another master. Another young man complained that he had been indentured for seven years and was duly enrolled at the Guildhall. He "loyally" performed his term, but his master had not taught him to be a pouchmaker. Instead, the master had put him to unsuitable work, "to wit foder fosser and caller clogges," at his country place in Kent. He also did not keep him in clothing, food, or drink.[2]

A variety of circumstances might force a master to neglect proper instruction. Some of them were beyond the master's control, but in some cases the master was thoroughly disreputable. The death of a master sometimes brought about an uneasy transition in which the apprentice was abandoned entirely. John Crane, for instance, had been apprenticed to a bowyer for twelve years, but when his master died, he passed as part of the estate to the widow. The widow left the city, leaving John behind. When Geoffrey Prany's master died, the widow, who inherited the contract, married a man who did not keep a shop, so that Geoffrey could not continue in the pinner's trade. The solution to such cases was either to transfer the apprentice or to discharge him if he preferred.[3]

Some apprentices were simply abandoned. A master might take his craft to another city and not maintain his residence in London; he might switch crafts or become a debtor and a felon. John, son of John Lucas, late citizen and common clerk of London, for instance, complained that he had been apprenticed to a goldsmith, but the man had left London long ago. The goldsmith's wife did not know where he was, and so the boy was transferred. The master might also change his craft, although this was rare. But John, son of John Blythe, contracted to be trained as a saddler by a master who later switched his craft and became a painter.[4] Some disreputable masters became fugitives in the sanctuary of St. Martin-le-Grand because of debt or felony. In such cases, apprentices sometimes found it difficult to move their apprenticeship until the trial was completed or debts paid. As one young man so aptly described his delemma: his master was arrested in Calais, his shop was closed, his wife could not provide for the apprentice, and he was wasting his time "treading the streets."[5]

Basic guile on the master's part sometimes underlay the failure to teach the craft. Richard Nasshe, a waxchandler, had "craftily and subtly enticed a child in the custody of the Master of St. Thomas of Acon and brought him up from a tender age and caused the child to be bonded to indenture contrary to the mind of his father." The mayor's court ruled that the child would have no good instruction from Nasshe and that, because the child was "expert in his playn song and prikked" and because the Master of St. Thomas was a parish clerk, the child would do better under the parish clerk's care because he would set the child out with other children to hire for their singing. Another man agreed to an indenture to train a youth as a goldsmith and then put him to work in the Smithfield Fairs as a cordwainer.[6]

The selling of an indenture could be a brutal reminder of the precarious position in which an apprentice was placed. In some respects, he was the master's chattel because his contract could legally be sold. John Bakton of Norfolk said that his master, a mercer, did not keep a shop and so could not instruct him. Furthermore, the master was going abroad and proposed to take John with him, so that the apprentice would not receive any instruction. The master countered, claiming that the apprentice was his chattel to dispose of as he wished. He then proposed to sell the contract to another. The youth protested that by the customs of London, his contract could not be sold without his agreement. The mayor's court held that the contractual agreement of apprenticeship stipulated that the master must instruct the apprentice and maintain a residence in London for that purpose. The apprentice must also consent to any change. John Bakton was released from the contract and allowed to change masters. In Chapter 8, we presented the case of an apprentice whose contract was sold to different masters for decreasing amounts so that the young man moved from one trade to another. Another young man got caught in a difficult bind when the balance of his contract was sold for 60s. after his first master died. He worked out the remaining three years of his apprenticeship, but could not become free of the city because the man who bought the contract never paid the 60s. to the dead master's estate.[7]

Other apprentices ended up in limbo after their masters dismissed them without cause. Some of the apprentices had served for several years, in one case ten years, and were then evicted. When questioned by the mayor's court or the mistery, masters either refused to state any reasons or made up stories about huge damages that the apprentice's misconduct had caused. When pressed, John Hatfeld, a grocer, first refused to discuss why he had dismissed his apprentice and then said that the apprentice had caused him to lose 1,000 marks. What often lay behind these cases were arguments over money. In at least one case, after an apprentice had entered into a contract, the master asked for more money to continue the arrangement. When the apprentice protested, the master dismissed him.[8]

As we have seen, apprentices sometimes came into contractual arrangements with money of their own that was to be held in trust by the master. The agreement was similar to a wardship arrangement, and, indeed, some of the cases of abuse arose out of wardship. The master was to have the use of the money for the period of the contract and then return it, along with the stipulated increase. Thus the two orphaned sons of Robert Chaber were put into apprenticeship with a hurer who had trust over the rents left to the apprentices and who, in addition, was to pay them 20s. a year from their father's estate. The master owed the apprentices £6 and still held the houses. Other apprentices said that they had substantial sums of money or goods held in trust for them, but the masters refused to give up the property at the completion of the term.[9] Some masters retained the funds because they did not have the money to return to them at the time or because they perceived that the apprentices actually owed them money.

Physical abuse is, to our minds, the worst sort of harm that an apprentice might suffer, but to an apprentice the loss of capital might have been more important. The loss of money could mean the difference between remaining a journeyman for life and becoming a master. In medieval culture, corporal punishment was integral to childrearing, education, and the apprentice relationship. Cases of extreme brutality, however, were intolerable, as were actions that impinged on the honor of the apprentice. In such cases, the guilds and the city intervened on behalf of the apprentice if the abuse came to their attention.

One of the most common complaints involving physical abuse was the master's failure to feed and clothe the apprentice. Since agreement to provide such necessities was part of all contracts, city and guild officials acted quickly to remedy the cases brought to them. Robert Chandeler and his wife apprenticed their daughter to a capper and his wife. When the masters were later unable to find food and clothing for the girl, the parents insisted that she be returned, and the court upheld them. Similar cases appear for young men. As we saw in Chapter 8, sometimes the conditions were so horrible that the young person faced starvation and permanent impairment of limbs.[10]

A typical apprenticeship contract specified that the apprentice not be required to do demeaning work reserved for servants. The wardens of the Goldsmiths fined John Trentemos for having his apprentice draw a cart about "to the slander of the mystery" and forcing him on the threat of beating to go to Smithfield to ride horses for 1*d.* each. The master was fined 3*s.* 4*d.* Two apprentices complained to the Mercers' wardens that their master forced them to carry wood and coal and to draw water; another apprentice had to carry ale or face a beating. But none fared so badly as Thomas Bunny, whose contract was sold to Joan Hunt, who kept stews in Southwark. She set him to "all manner of grievous work," including carrying water in tynes. He fell while carrying the water for the stews and suffered permanent injury. Furthermore, she incited her paramour, Bernard, to beat and ill-treat him; when he fell sick, she ejected him. After he recovered somewhat, she wanted him to come back, but would not make amends. Fortunately, the mayor's court believed him and released him from his contract.[11]

Severe beatings and wounding with weapons was the sad lot of some apprentices. Oliver Randy was apprenticed to Elizabeth Jones, who had a fletcher's trade. She married Richard Coke, who was a skinner by trade and knew nothing about arrowmaking. Oliver complained that he ran the shop with journeymen and got no training. Complaining did no good, for his new master had several times "come at 11 or 12 o'clock at night, dragged him from his bed, and beaten him." Furthermore, the man beat his wife and his servants, so that the servants quit.[12] Edmund Pellet had an even sorrier tale to tell. He was apprenticed to a fishmonger "at a tender age," but his contract was illegally sold to a person not related to the fishmonger business. The wife of this new master continually beat him without any cause, and the master put a sharp metal through his thumb. Another apprentice complained of being beaten with a staff; when he resisted, his master had him imprisoned.

When an apprentice died of wounds, the master was under immediate suspicion. Thus the Goldsmiths' wardens warned John Hall de Petyt, after one of his apprentices died in prison and another complained that Hall's wife had beaten him so that he ran away, that he would have no other apprentices if incidents like these occurred in the future. The family of one apprentice had the master arrested for the death of their son, who died of head wounds, because they did not believe the master's story of a fall down the stairs. Young women also complained about being beaten with sticks and knives.[13]

For female apprentices, physical violence sometimes took the form of rape or prostitution. We have already seen that one woman was subjected to pillory and "rough music" for having "let to hire for immoral purposes her innocent young apprentice."[14] Although I have not yet found a case of a master seducing or raping a female apprentice, in all likelihood, such incidents must have happened. As we shall see, they seem to have been an all-too-frequent occurrence with female servants. Apprentices, however, were in a less vulnerable position than were servants. They entered the household with a contractual arrangement that was supervised by parents, friends, and city officials. Their social status was usually on a par with that of the master and mistress, and, therefore, they expected to be treated as daughters of the household. On the other hand, female apprentices were probably reluctant to report sexual abuse to the mayor's court, believing that they had even less access to that public forum than their male counterparts. They also risked future marriage prospects by making their compromised status known. Charges involving fornication, bearing bastard children, and pimping for female apprentices do not appear in the church court, whereas they do for female servants.

The master's legal position was always superior to that of his apprentice, since he knew the system and had ready access to it. Masters sometimes used this knowledge to punish their apprentices. William Morton had brought a bill against Robert de Eye, a cutler, for drawing up an apprenticeship contract that contained a punitive clause requiring Morton to pay £40 if he broke the contract. Morton refused to sign, saying that his father would never have agreed to that sum. The mayor found Morton's argument valid and removed the clause, with an injunction to the master to take Morton as an apprentice and to treat him well. The master, the father, and another sponsor swore on the gospels to abide by the agreement. Rather than taking the apprentice home, the master took him to the sheriff's prison on Milk Street and kept him there without provision for his food. The mayor responded by canceling the indentures. Other masters claimed that apprentices owed them money for waste during apprenticeship and forced them to sign bonds in order to be made free of the city. When the bonds came due, they had the apprentices arrested and thrown into prison.[15]

Some masters proved negligent or shrewd, failing to enroll an apprentice within the year and a day or refusing to make an apprentice free of the city after the term of the contract was successfully completed. Such action was in clear violation of both the apprenticeship contracts and the rules of the city, but unscrupulous masters found the cheap labor a valuable asset and well worth the risk. If a master did not enroll the apprentice or make him or her free of the city, he might possibly eke out a few more years of wage-free or minimum-wage service. He could always use the legal subterfuge that the apprentice had been lazy, negligent, or wasteful and, therefore, owed him the extra service.

The complaints involving nonenrollment were numerous and usually came at the end of the term when the apprentices and their families expected the young people to be made free of the city. In 1426, eight bills of complaint of nonenrollment came into the mayor's court; in 1442 and 1443, ten bills, a few of which involved female apprentices. The excuses were as one would expect. One master claimed that he had not enrolled his apprentice because the latter had not paid for the enrollment according to the covenant between them. The apprentice was able to show that by law he had to pay 20*s.* for his teaching and sustenance only and not for the enrollment. Another master claimed that his apprentice, Richard atte Brugge, was a "piker and a pulfrour" and not fit for the mistery, so that he was doing the tapicers a favor by not making him free of the city. He lost. One master required his apprentice to agree to make a bond paying the master £3 13*s.* 4*d.* to make him free of the city. Either this bond was intended to cover damages suffered by the master or it was outright extortion. In any case, the apprentice said that although he had paid £1 13*s.* 4*d.* and was not made free of the city, still, contrary to agreement, his former master wanted the balance immediately. In the final analysis, an unscrupulous master could trump up charges against an apprentice and have a considerable legal advantage over him.[16]

Faced with contractual relationships and intimate, surrogate family arrangements gone awry, the guild wardens and the mayor and aldermen tried a variety of ways to resolve the disputes. After gathering evidence from neighbors, guild members, family, and sponsors, they could decide that the situation was hopeless and that the arrangement should be dissolved. The apprentice and his sponsors were then free either to arrange another apprenticeship contract or to abandon the training completely. As we have seen, the mayor and the guilds preferred a compromise, with all parties agreeing and swearing that they would abide by the mediated stipulations. Such arrangements often must have worked, but not always. Oliver Randy, whom we met earlier in this chapter, had gotten the city and the Fletchers' guild to agree that he had received inadequate training and that he had been beaten. The officials tried to patch up an agreement satisfactory to all parties, requiring Richard Coke to give Oliver good training and to treat him well. The deal did not work out, and finally the Fletchers' wardens agreed that Randy should be released from his apprenticeship on payment of 26s. 8d. to Coke. Coke, however, had impaneled a jury of skinners (rather than fletchers) and was suing for £40 in damages. Oliver Randy said he was a "young, poor child" and would be ruined because he could not pay.[17]

Rebellious Apprentices

The general term used for apprentices who misbehaved, ran away, or otherwise broke their contracts was "rebellious," and an ordinance in 1326 urged that "the good men of the City, who have their apprentices, hired men or servants, working with their hands or trading," should inform the mayor and other officers of the city about any problems so that the offenders could be punished "as a warning to others."[18] Being well aware of the potential abuses of apprenticeship and the risks of having bad examples become precedents, officials moved quickly to discipline unruly youth. They were particularly concerned in 1316 because Isabella and Mortimer had released prisoners when they took over the city. The city fathers knew well that a bad apple could rot the barrel and wanted to establish controls before a riot could erupt. The extreme concern of city and guild officials about apprentice riots seems to have led to stern enough measures that apprentices did not often organize for mass actions. Apprentices' rebelliousness seemed more directed toward foreign competitors and individual masters than toward the general circumstances of apprenticeship.

Apprentices, like masters, had reasons to resist enrollment of their contracts at the Guildhall. Some may have felt that they could do better, particularly after the plague, with a flexible arrangement that would permit them to learn the trade and then work as wage laborers. Apprentices such as John, son of William of Acton (in Suffolk), and John Passu of Twekesbury (in Gloucester) refused to be enrolled and were imprisoned.[19]

Other apprentices ran away from their masters. The reasons, when given, varied greatly. Some apprentices were clearly abused and fled service in fear. The poor young man whose master put a sharp metal piece through his thumb finally fled in order to become a priest.[20] Another young man might also have been seeking a religious profession, for he fled to Westminster Abbey, whose abbot would not give him up. The master claimed to the mayor that the apprentice had "maliciously left his service . . . whereby a dangerous example is set for other apprentices in the said city in time to come unless a remedy should be provided."[21] Some of the apprentices, however, seem to have sought a more glamorous sort of service. A master complained that his apprentice, who was of a "forward and unthrifty disposition" and who was "lewd and simple in demeaning," had left his service and was now attending on John Drykland, a groom of the King's Chamber. Another apprentice who left service ended up in the household of the Duchess of Holland and Seland and was at the Savoy Palace.[22]

Apprentices also left service when they perceived that they could do very well for themselves by setting up trade in another city, by going to trade fairs, or even by trading abroad on their own. Robert Arnold, for instance, felt it necessary to repudiate his apprentice publicly before the mayor because the apprentice had been trading in diverse places in England and overseas in the master's name and to his loss.[23]

The masters often knew where their apprentices had gone and requested the mayor to write to the authorities of other towns to try to get the apprentices back. For instance, John, son of Richard Haldone of Hackney, had become an apprentice to John de Pateneye for ten years, and his indentures were recorded with the city on Christmas 1345. The master died, and his widow held the balance of the contract. She remarried, and the apprentice withdrew from service. She had information, however, that he was in Bristol and wanted to get him back.[24] Although some of these youths must simply have gone home, in other cases some detective work was necessary to discover their whereabouts. Richard Skinner commissioned John Chapman to find out where his apprentice had gone. The cost of searching for an apprentice who ran away to Cambridge was 38s.[25]

With the severe reduction in the number of skilled workers in London in the century and a half following the Black Death, apprentices and journeymen were much in demand. A discontented apprentice could easily find a position with another master. Such an arrangement was, of course, illegal. Both the laws surrounding the apprenticeship contract and the Statute of Laborers, passed in 1351 and reissued periodically, forbade taking another person's apprentice or servant. Nonetheless, apprentices either sought other positions or were enticed away. Thomas Corset had agreed to an eight-year term, but had served only three and a half years when he ran away to Exeter to take service with another man. His old master pursued him to Exeter and tried to take him back by force when the new master refused to release him. Thomas de Hexham in Newcastle seems to have run a regular conduit of saddlers' apprentices from London into his business, having enticed away two saddlers.[26] The new masters gave various excuses. One said that the apprentice was starving and the original master refused to take him back, so he had no other choice. But most of the masters stated that they did not know that the youth had an unexpired apprenticeship contract.[27]

Apprentices committed crimes and misdemeanors against masters and mistresses, although their record pales next to that of masters against apprentices. Being on the weak side of the power relationship, the apprentices had fewer opportunities for harassing their masters. But a few complaints did come before the various authorities. Warin Fatting, an apprentice of Matilda Fatting, maimed an index finger on his mistress's right hand. He was pardoned and paid her 35s. in recompense. The fullest account, however, is that of Edward Bowden, who violently and suddenly beat his mistress. He reviled her and tried to strangle her. The Goldsmiths were outraged and called "worshipful men" to decide what to do about Bowden. They concluded that he would only get worse if they sent him to prison. Instead, they had him stripped and beaten in the kitchen of the Goldsmiths' Hall until his blood flowed. The idea was to make it clear to the apprentice that his blood would flow, as had that of his mistress. Twenty years earlier, the Goldsmiths had dealt with an attempted murder of a master by an apprentice.[28]

More common than physical abuse were the theft of money or goods and the abuse of the position of apprentice to begin trading before the apprenticeship was complete. Masters were so concerned about apprentices taking their goods and selling them in order to spend the proceeds on riotous living and fancy clothing that they inserted clauses into apprenticeship contracts that forbade the practice. Of course, apprentices continued these activities anyway, and the Pouchmakers were moved to complain to the mayor that foreigners seduced apprentices and servants into brewhouses at night and encouraged them to hand over the goods of the Pouchmakers.[29] John de Eston, while still an apprentice, engaged in trade, pretending that he was free of the city.[30]

The seductive influence of foreigners was not necessary for apprentices to steal their masters' property. Thomas Philipp, an apothecary, complained that William Nondy, son of John de Sabricheford, had entered into an apprenticeship with him in 1390 and had agreed "to serve him loyally, not to damage him or waste his goods nor depart from his service by day or by night." But two years later, between Easter and St. John Baptist, William eloigned goods worth £20: wax, ginger, pepper, saffron, mace, cloves, galy-gal, and so on. He absented himself at night and left the shop door open, leaving Philipp at risk of further property loss from theft.[31]

So far we have emphasized the dependent nature of apprenticeship, but some of the cases of theft and fraud indicate that apprentices often moved into positions of considerable responsibility as they entered the last phases of their apprenticeship. They were sent to trade fairs and to the Continent with considerable money that the masters felt confident they would handle responsibly; the masters trusted them to return reasonable accounts and profit. Masters quite understandably expected that the apprentices should, at this stage of their careers, be moving toward the status of master and, therefore, toward a more colleagial relationship. Robert Ballard, for instance, lent money to Edward Hill five or six months before Hill came into his inheritance. He wanted collateral for the loan, but Edward said that he did not have it, but would pay when he was of full age. He did not do so, and Ballard then tried to collect £33 6s. 7d.[32]

Apprentices could be even more devious. John Orwell was a goldsmith and an engraver of coins for the king at the Tower of London. He had an apprentice, Thomas Withyale, who had a bequest of £100 in the Court of Orphans, and John helped him get access to this money a year and a half before he was of full age. Not grateful for his master's help, Thomas stole the patent that specified John's position as engraver to the king. Thomas threatened to sell it for £200 to a third party; then the dispreputable blackmailer agreed to enter into the patent himself for 8 marks a year. He had not paid.[33]

In a raw and more dramatic case, Thomas Horsman, a vintner, complained that John Colman, son of the late Reginald Colman, had become his apprentice on June 24, 1384, with the agreement that he would do no damage to his master beyond 12d. a year. On September 15, Horsman had sent the youth with an older apprentice, Nicholas Leykman, on a buying mission with other merchants to Bordeaux. He entrusted Nicholas with 205 marks in gold to trade. John was to go along and observe and learn "as apprentices are bound to do according to the custom of the city." The money was put into a strongbox. The apprentices had gotten no farther than Plymouth when John broke open the box while the other apprentices were on shore. He carried off £200. When examined separately, both apprentices confirmed that John had been the thief but that Nicholas had received £40 of the take. John was put into prison while arrangements were made for recovery of the money. His debt was so high that his sponsors could not cover it. On February 1, 1385, John was returned to prison for default of payment. Finally, on September 23, the boy was so sick that his master prayed for his release and bailed him. Somewhat recovered, he was returned to prison five days later. By December 15, he was again so sick that his master relented and bailed him again.[34] This combination of trust, harsh punishment, and relenting, humane treatment was typical of the London masters' ideas of the best way of dealing with recalcitrant apprentices.

Faced with rebellious apprentices, masters were often vindictive, but the official line of guild wardens and city officials was, as in the case of masters, to arrange a compromise. While imprisonment for running away, failing to enroll, behaving badly, and incurring debts was a common enough initial step,[35] masters basically wanted the service out of their apprentices and usually agreed to reasonable compromises. In the case of debt, for instance, a schedule of repayment, either by the apprentice's sponsor or by the apprentice himself, could be arranged.[36]

The reconciliation between master and apprentice might also involve a ceremony of submission on the part of the guilty apprentice. Thus when Elizabeth Peynton admitted that she had brought a false bill against her master, "the said Elizabeth on her bended knees and with raised hands humbly begged pardon of the said John for her offenses wickedly perpetrated against him." John Everard, a nephew of his master, Alan Everard, had gone deeply into debt and had not rendered accounts to his master for the sums. The master was willing to accept a confession from his apprentice and nephew and to accept restitution for only those sums confessed. In return and "as a sign of obedience and respect . . . the apprentice was to contribute 40s. towards a horse and hold the stirrup when his master mounted."[37] Such ceremonies of humiliation restored the proper power relationship between master and apprentice.

The whole of the reconciliation process can be seen in the case of Thomas Ryvers, an apprentice to Thomas Shelley, a mercer. Thomas was enrolled and sworn as an apprentice, but he withdrew from service and sought sanctuary in Westminster Abbey. The Mercers' wardens responded by ruling that no one from the fellowship could eat or drink with him, communicate with him by writing or speaking, buy and sell with him, or offer him lodging on pain of a £5 fine. This virtual excommunication from the Mercers brought results. A servant from the king came before the mayor on Ryvers's behalf. The king proposed that the apprentice should apologize on bended knee before the mayor, aldermen, and guild wardens for his angry words. The messenger also had a list of the debts owed to Ryvers that indicated that he had been ill treated. His father owed him £30, an uncle owed him £20, and various other people owed him for wares, wine, and other goods, but his master kept his reckoning book so that he could not collect what was owed him. The messenger, asked to swear on the gospels that these debts were real, did so. The reconciliation occurred, and Ryvers's master was to see that the debts were paid to him and his book was returned.[38] If all other means failed, of course, the indenture could be dissolved and the apprentice required not to serve anyone of the craft for the term of contract.[39]

The relationship between apprentices and masters is far from easy to reconstruct. The living and training arrangement was such that misunderstandings could easily arise. On the whole, the masters held the balance of power over their apprentices and were more often cited as abusers in the relationship than were apprentices. On the other hand, many apprentices who misbehaved suffered corporal punishment at the hands of their masters, and because this was deemed justifiable action, no case ever appeared in court. While a thoroughly bad master might be at fault, an apprentice might also be completely vicious and unreliable. In many of the recorded cases, both master and apprentice contributed to the bad situation. It is helpful to reconstruct a case in which the ambiguity of blame comes to the fore.

"William Raynold and Thomas Appleford, Apprentices, Versus Richard Berne, Mercer and Master"

William Raynold and Thomas Appleford were in their late teens when they became apprentices to Richard Berne. Placement with Berne was certainly an honor and a step toward becoming major dealers on the international cloth market. Berne not only wore the Mercers' livery, but had been warden in 1518 and 1519 and a member of the assembly for most of the years since then. He had played an active role in the guild, being one of the wealthy members who could be relied on to pay subsidies as the Crown demanded.[40] By 1523, however, when William and Thomas were in his shop, age was beginning to take its toll on Berne. In fact, in 1524, after his struggles with his unruly apprentices, he petitioned the Mercers' Court that he be excused from going to assemblies. His brethren agreed that he was getting too old and feeble.[41] He could no longer control his shop and his apprentices in the way he had done before.

William and Thomas formed a close friendship. Their pranks began innocently enough. William would mimic Richard, and Thomas took the role of Richard's wife. William would bumble around the shop looking high and low for something, while Thomas took a distaff in imitation of Mistress Berne and nagged and beat him with it. In the end, they had a real Punch and Judy show, just like the puppets. At first, they played their little show only for each other, but as they perfected their game, their desire for a broader audience overcame their better judgment. They played it for the journeymen and the household servants to great guffaws. Indiscretion overcoming them, they slipped off to a tavern at night and gave a performance there. When Berne and his wife heard about this, they were outraged and took turns with the willow branches beating the two apprentices. The two young men were sternly warned that any further antics of that sort and any further trips to the tavern would land them in prison.

In truth, however, Richard Berne was getting senile, and his business was, as a consequence, suffering. Mistress Berne tried to make ends meet by skimping on the household economy. She was forced to dismiss the ordinary servants who did the dirty work of the house, in order to retain the better servants and thereby keep up appearances. But who was to get the wood and the water for the household? William and Thomas were two strapping young men, so she ordered them to carry wood and coal from a strawhouse that Berne owned on Thames Street. She also had them draw and carry water. The two youth protested that their apprenticeship contracts explicitly forbade them to carry wood or water or to do other such base work. Her reply was to take a staff and beat them. The pinch of funds meant that the Bernes could no longer provide the standard clothing that the Mercers required for apprentices. Mistress Berne bought their clothes from a dealer in used clothing and bought shoes with cheap soles, rather than the double-soled ones that the Mercers specified. William and Thomas began to spend their own money on their shoes. The quality of the food also began to decline. Poverty only made Mistress Berne more ill-tempered, so that the cuffs and shoves became a daily part of the shop routine.

Meanwhile, a year had slipped by, and neither William nor Thomas felt that he had learned anything about the mercery business. Their families and friends made frequent trips to the city, and William and Thomas would slip out at night, sometimes leaving the door unbarred, in order to see them. Other times, they simply told Richard that their families had arrived unexpectedly and that they were taking the day off. They began to take days off even if no family and friends were in town; the visits were such a convenient excuse to get away from Mistress Berne. They felt justified in taking many holidays because they were not learning anything. But finally their friends became suspicious and asked them what their prospects were for going to Bruges in the next year to learn trading first-hand on the Continent, as was typical for Mercers' apprentices. They confessed that even Berne had not traded on the Continent since they had been in the shop and that, as far as they knew, he kept no factor in Flanders.

With urging from their friends, they finally requested that the Mercers' wardens investigate their situation. The wardens examined the apprentices and listened to their complaints. The young men were shabbily dressed, and their shoes had holes in them. Furthermore, the wardens knew that they had been dressed in this fashion for more than a year, and they had been seen carrying coal and wood. The wardens dismissed the two young men and examined Berne separately. He made no attempt to defend himself, but said that he would abide by the decision of the court.

The wardens ordered him to provide the regulation clothing and double-soled shoes, to cease requiring the apprentices to carry coal and wood, and to see that they were instructed in the craft. Mistress Berne was no longer to beat or otherwise correct the two youths. For their part, the apprentices had to agree to inform their master and mistress in advance when friends were visiting and where they were lodging. The wardens then required a reconciliation in which the apprentices asked forgiveness and Berne promised to take them home and treat them well.[42]

It was a somewhat glum party that returned to Richard's house. The apprentices had won their argument, but they were unlikely to get better instruction from old Berne. They would get better treatment, but would Berne have the money to provide the clothing? Mistress Berne would have to hold her punches, but she probably would not sweeten her temper. The wardens had said nothing about her scolding. What future could they expect with the Mercers in any case? Everyone knew they were not well trained, and the court case would make masters suspicious that they were rebellious. Their chances of becoming journeymen at the end of their term were limited. The young men talked over their plight and decided that it would be best to leave. One would go to Bristol and the other to Newcastle to see if they could find better employment outside the Mercers. Berne was unlikely to be able to have them traced; he would probably forget who they were by the end of the month.

Friendship Between Masters and Apprentices

While the apprentice–master relationship was fertile ground for conflict, the intimacy of contact within the household also produced close bonds between masters and apprentices. We have seen that leisure activities could involve the whole complement of apprentices and master, as well as members of the family. But the best record of the existence of good relationships comes from the remembrance of apprentices in wills.

Wills tell much about the close bonds between the parties. Three percent of the 3,330 men registering wills in the Husting Court left their apprentices bequests (Appendix, Table 7). Money (28 percent) and goods (32 percent) were the typical bequests. John Claydish, a pewterer in London, left one apprentice 13s. 4d. and a more junior apprentice, 10s. Both apprentices were going to continue in the service of his son. A goldbeater, William Wylewan, left his best mold and all other molds to his apprentice. His son inherited the shop and his other instruments. In other cases, apprentices received the shop (7 percent) and tenements (9 percent). Some men remembered all their apprentices, thus indicating generally good relationships within the shop and household structure.[43] Sometimes the relationship became so close that the apprentice was made chief heir to the master.[44]

Even a master with a family of his own might make a substantial bequest to an apprentice. Thus William de Madeford left his apprentice leasehold interest in tenements, even though he also had children to whom he left bequests. As we have seen in Chapter 6, some masters even came to feel that their apprentices were the people they could most trust to look after their children's fortunes. Thus John Stable, a mercer, left his wife in charge of his children, with half of certain sums of money to support them, while the other half of the money went to the apprentices to use for their trouble in overseeing the children's bequest.[45]

For senior apprentices, one of the most valuable bequests was release from the last year or two of apprenticeship (18 percent). This spared the apprentice the trauma of switching masters and permitted him to either work for wages or set up his own business.[46]

With the intimate familial environment, one might also expect that marriages could result from the relationship built on trust and acquaintance. Thomas Wood, who had two daughters, married one to a former apprentice, who went on to have a distinguished career in the Goldsmiths' guild. Harry ap Richard claimed that he had been apprentice to William Griffith, late tailor of London, who had released him from his indenture of apprenticeship. He had agreed with William's widow to marry her and take over the business, but, he complained, she broke the contract and married someone else.[47]

The filial relationship might also be carried to the grave. Thomas Gauder, a pouchmaker, died young, leaving a wife but no children. He left his brother and nephew his inheritance and made a number of civic bequests. At the end of his life, his chief desire was to be buried in the same tomb as William Gauder, his late master. Richard Wycombe also valued the closeness of his relationship with his former master and his current apprentices; he provided for prayers for his master's soul and gave each of his current apprentices 10s. each.[48]

Apprenticeship, with all its tensions, was a major way of assimilating the large number of country and market-town youth who would provide the city's skilled labor force and become its citizens and its elite. It was the training ground not only for workers in crafts and trade, but also for those who would lend continuity to the social and political ethos of London. Since the population of London did not replace itself by father-to-son succession, the role of apprenticeship as a fostering arrangement was of paramount importance for the survival of the city. Like the marriage of widows to other craftsmen who belonged to the same guild as the deceased husband, the ties created by apprenticeship were horizontal ones, extending across crafts and status groups, rather than the vertical ties of a patrilineage.

A maid fixes her mistress's hair. (Drawing by Wayne M. Howell, from the Lutterel Psalter, British Library MS. 42130 f.63)

10

Servants

Servants were ubiquitous in medieval London, as in all the large cities of Europe. The title included a range of unskilled and skilled workers who either lived in their master's house and received compensation in the form of room and board and wages or worked only for wages and lived in rented rooms. The age range was from seven to seventy, with the majority being in their teens or early twenties.

Service, like apprenticeship, was a phase in the life cycle that moved the adolescent from the natal home to that of a master. It was a threshold period in which the young people learned skills, accumulated capital, and dreamed of moving on to adult, nondependent roles. If the youth were journeymen who had completed their apprenticeships, they were working for a master, usually the same one who had trained them, until they could become "householders" and masters themselves. If they were scullery maids, they might hope to accumulate enough wages for a dowry toward marriage. If they were country-born, they might have come to London to earn some cash that they could take back to their village and use to start their own households and families. Servants with some education and good business sense might hope to move into the position of factor to a master and handle his trading and finances. The period of service, like apprenticeship, was a way of extending adolescence. But for some servants, a menial position would be their lot for their short lives. They would not experience the markers of adulthood: marriage, independent business, or at least a private, rented room. For them, the title of "girl" or "boy" would apply regardless of age, and their status would fall short of full adulthood.

While the category of servant was broad and included people of widely varying ages and statuses, this chapter concentrates on the experience of the younger, rather than career, servants. The young people who moved into service positions usually came from less well-to-do families than did apprentices, and servants far outnumbered apprentices. If, in the early fourteenth century, more than 500 apprentices were enrolled, perhaps three times or more that number, including women as well as men, became servants.[1] Because our concern is with service as a life stage, we will look at those who became servants, the compensation for service, living arrangements, and, above all, the relationship between masters and servants.

In many ways, the experience of servants paralleled that of apprentices. Service created a quasi-familial relationship within urban households. Major differences between a service position and an apprenticeship existed, however. In most cases, for instance, servants did not aspire to mastership in a guild or to citizenship in the city. While the apprenticeship contract spelled out the behavior expected of both parties in addition to the material benefits to be provided, the service contracts, as we shall see, did not. Apprenticeship was an elite training and service position; securing a place required payment of a premium. Entering service, in contrast, usually did not. Several layers of authorities oversaw the apprenticeship contracts, including the city, the guild, and the apprentice's family and friends. Although servants and their families and friends could appeal to the city or the Chancery for redress, service positions were less carefully monitored.

One might assume that abuses of servants were rampant and that, given that the chief sources we have are court records, all a historian would ever see would be one sad case after another. But medieval service had another side to it. When the relationship between master and servant worked well, the very dependence of master and servant on each other led to amazing displays of loyalty. Servants frequently took their masters' names and, when called on to do so, risked life and limb for their masters. Sometimes masters or mistresses became very dependent on their servants, defending them in court and rewarding them in wills.

A house, as we have seen, might have only one apprentice, but many servants. Anyone who could afford a servant had one, and it was a matter of prestige to have as many as possible. Londoners of note, both men and women, went about their public business in the company of a servant or two.[2] Servants were expected to get along not only with the master and mistress, but also with one another. Familial bonding, therefore, extended into quasi-sibling relations as well as into the quasi-parental relationship. The household was referred to in records as *familia* or *menie,* but only innkeepers received the official title of *paterfamilias* or *materfamilias* in the records.[3] Those appearing in the records in the position of servant were called either *serviens* or the more intimate *famulus* or *famula.*[4] Service was a complex emotional experience for all involved and, therefore, one deserving of detailed discussion.[5]

Formation of the Service Contract

Because of the close living arrangements and the potential for emotional bonding, employers wanted assurances as to the character of potential servants. Much the same network that produced apprentices also produced servants. Kin were the most reliable source. Younger sons and daughters of brothers and sisters, country cousins, and other relations all appear in the records as servants. A servant position was good for such relations because they could learn something of service and business, make a good marriage through the uncle's contacts, and perhaps even end up as the heirs of the city uncle.[6] Various kinds of networks—the ties of masters and mistresses to the village of origin, trade contacts with the hinterland, contacts among the clergy, and even friendships with successfully placed servants—helped those seeking service positions. In the case of Joan Rawlyns, which we looked at in detail in Chapter 7, her mistress in the country had a business contact with a trader from London. Since Joan seems to have had a good sense of how the London legal system worked, she had probably heard about employment there from other villagers who had returned from service.

The networks of placement sometimes appear in court cases related to service. For instance, John Frank was a servant of Richard Kysser. During the height of the plague, realizing that he was about to die, John Frank provided for his nephew, John, and placed him in the guardianship and service of his master.[7] Parents in London placed their children directly into service. Once one child was placed, others might follow into service in the same household. In other cases, the wardship arrangements could place a youth into a service contract and make the master guardian. The placement could also be done through acts of charity. Sir John Persy, a priest from Canterbury, said that a female servant, a stranger to the country, came to him poor and destitute and asked his aid in finding a post. He inquired around and found someone who contracted to give her meat and shelter in exchange for work.[8]

Recommending a servant was serious business, because it might make the recommender personally liable for the servant's conduct. Sir John, for instance, ended up facing a suit under the Statute of Laborers from someone who claimed to be the former master of the young woman. John Twigge, a haberdasher of London, brought Agnes Copley to serve Wolfram Cook, a physician of London, on March 3, 1483. She served for three weeks and then left service. Cook later hired her back without Twigge's knowledge, and she robbed him. Twigge argued that he had not provided the reference for Agnes's reemployment and was not liable.[9]

Servants, of course, sought their own positions as well. Robert Mascall, a maltman of Aldenham, said that Joan Smyth had come to his house in Aldenham "in poor and simple array and almost perished for default of sustenance." She assured Robert that she "was clearly discharged of all manner of bonds to any man's service" and prayed "on God's mercy" to help her. He claimed that "having pity and out of alms more than any other reason he took her in." No one came forward in the six weeks he spent in finding out if she was at liberty, and so she worked for him for three years in exchange for meat, board, and wages. A skilled servant, such as John Hay, a writer, could find work easily. Even foreigners, such as Robert Rowes, a caper from Normandy, could find service readily, even though he did not speak English.[10]

As population continued to decrease following the initial assault of the plague, the demand for labor grew. Enticing and outright raiding and stealing of servants became means of recruitment. Juliana Chamberlain claimed that William Clerk, living at Holborn Ridge, a suburb of London, took and wrongfully detained her daughter, Ellen, from the age of seven. Clerk claimed that Ellen had agreed to be his servant for a term of seven years. The mayor's court found his story unlikely and returned her to her mother. Agnes Wombe and John de Sloghteford were attached to answer a charge of having enticed away the female servant of Thomas de Shene "by flattering speeches."[11] A girdler enticed a cutler's servant into the churchyard of St. Dunstan-in-the-East, saying that nothing would happen to him, but the servant was imprisoned for three days when he would not change masters. The cutlery trade was apparently short of skilled labor, for one cutler went to the trouble of getting the city to agree to qualify a foreign worker as a journeyman. When he succeeded, the guild masters employed the foreigner themselves. Cases of enticement and kidnapping were numerous, and almost all were prosecuted either under the Statute of Laborers or by original masters for damages for loss of service.[12] Guilds, of course, passed ordinances in an effort to eliminate the enticing away of servants and apprentices.[13]

Another recruitment method was to hire the eager Flemings who were fleeing the political and economic disruptions occasioned by the Hundred Years' War. One goldsmith was reprimanded for using a Dutch boy to cook and fetch water, which was lawful; however, the boy was also working in the goldsmith's shop, although he was not trained to be a goldsmith. A London brewer hired a Dutch worker for a year to help with his trade. The worker delivered beer to customers and developed a network of satisfied people. After a year, he set up shop next to his former master and took away part of his trade.[14] It is no wonder that the Flemings were so resented that they were attacked during the revolt of 1381.

The contractual arrangements covering servants left ample room for confusion, and the extreme need for labor made abuse of contracts very tempting. Although apprenticeship contracts survive, I have come across no service contracts. Their terms are known primarily through Chancery petitions and court cases that adjudicated complaints of violations. For a live-in servant, a contract included room, board, and wages. For instance, William Pyebaker hired Simon Belde on a short-term contract for eight weeks, providing him with board and necessaries, which came to 14*s*. The rate of pay depended on the skills of the servant. A baker could ask for 40*s*. a year on a four-year contract in the fifteenth century.[15] The writer John Hay described himself as a "young man" who had contracted with a parish clerk of Southwark for a year. He claimed that he gave sufficient notice, but the clerk claimed he owed another year of service under a contract that called for wages of 26*s*. 8*d*. This sum included meat, drink, and bed—not much for a skilled worker. William, a petitioner who described himself as a "poor young man" who knew nobody in London, made a contract to serve for 6*d*. a week. When his master hired someone equally skilled at 10*d*., William left. For having broken the contract, his master wanted him to bring him 4*d*. a week.[16] Young girls made even less. One man sued for the return of his daughter with three years' wages, which came to only 12*s*., or 4*s*. a year.[17]

The hours of labor varied from summer to winter. In the Cutlers' guild, as in most trades, the hours were long in the summer; between Lady Day and Michaelmas, they were from 4:00 A.M. to 8:00 P.M. In the winter, they were from 6:00 A.M. to 6:00 P.M. The city limited the hours because it did not want the products produced in the dark or in the uncertainty of lamplight.[18] The wages varied according to the season as well. Dauber's assistants received 2*d*. a day from Michaelmas to Easter and 3*d*. from Easter to Michaelmas.[19]

The working hours seem very long, but they were broken by a noon meal for day laborers, such as daubers and carpenters, and included both breakfast and an evening meal for live-in servants. The records from a London church specify the food for which the carpenters working on the church porch in 1428 and 1429 contracted, in addition to their wages. While setting up the porch, they were to get two shoulders of mutton worth 6*d.*, bread worth 2*d.*, and two gallons of ale worth 4*d.* The noon meal for five carpenters and two plumbers was a shoulder and brisket of mutton worth 4*d.*, bread worth 1*d.*, and ale worth 2*d.* The celebratory meal for completion was a rib of beef worth 3*d.* and bread and ale worth 2*d.*[20]

The length of the contract varied. Contracts could run for a year at a time, for three years, or for five years, or they could run only from week to week, as long as the arrangement was mutually satisfactory. William Gregory of London hired Alice Shevington for a three-year contract at 16*s.* a year. She, however, claimed to have "cunning in curing sore eyes" and practiced this art on the side. The master felt cheated of her services. To prevent breaches in fulfilling contracts, employers sometimes required servants to post a bond. For instance, John Cornu, a saddler, complained that John Thompson made him post a bond for 5 marks until his five-year term was up. Thompson violated the terms of the contract, but insisted on keeping the money.[21]

The work that servants engaged in varied greatly. The journeymen or bachelors who had completed their apprenticeships were engaged in the highest levels of craft or trading, as were some of the skilled foreigners. Some of the female servants were also involved in skilled work, such as finishing precious metal products, silkworking, sewing, and weaving. Also of high status among servants were the higher-ranking household servants who waited on the master and mistress, kept their accounts, and in general met the requirements of the advice manuals. At the other end of the skill scale were those who carried water, coal, and firewood, cleaned the house and shop, and performed other menial tasks. In between were servants, men and women, who worked in the victualing trades—brewing, baking, and selling foodstuffs, beer, and wine.[22] Because of the diversity of skills needed, those who entered the ranks of servants came from a wide range of social backgrounds.

Who Became a Servant?

London has no poll tax records that would tell us the number of men and women who occupied service positions. The poll tax records of 1377 for Worcester show that about 12.5 percent of the population over fourteen was either sons and daughters or servants, but in York, a city more comparable to London, almost one-third of the population fell into this group. In fact, there was little difference between being a child of the household and being a servant, because people in both groups were occupied with similar tasks. Of the small cities for which information remains, female servants were more common in Oxford and Worcester, but males predominated in Carlisle, York, and Northampton.[23]

The distribution of sexes in London must have favored males in the servant category. If one counts skilled laborers, foreigners, business factors, grooms, cooks, vendors, and valets, workers in these categories must have outnumbered the housemaids, nurses, cooks, victualers, and scullery girls.

The age of entry into service is hinted at in the poll tax. The taxable age was fourteen or fifteen, depending on the year of the tax. The royal government, therefore, assumed that by this age, young people would be employed and able to pay a head tax. Apparently, seven was considered too young, as the case of Ellen, daughter of Juliana Chamberlain, indicates, but young people of twelve had obviously made the transition to service positions. Joan, servant of William West, was twelve years old and already described as having a "right wanton disposition."[24]

Service was not necessarily a low-status occupation, attracting only peasants, foreigners, and an urban underclass. To be sure, such people occupied most of the lower-paid service positions, but the books of advice written for "servants" were for those who would be privileged to wait on aldermen, mayors, wealthy merchants, and the hereditary nobility. The polished manners and knowledge of the world of these servants recommended them for positions involving both virtuoso displays of carving skills and confidences about their masters' business. These young men were more likely to be drawn from the gentry, from the country relatives of prosperous citizens, from Oxford and Cambridge colleges, and from among the artisans and even the elites of London. Elite young women might go into a household for a period before marrying. A citizen's daughter, particularly an orphan, might have a period of service in another household, instead of entering into an apprenticeship. Such a fostering arrangement could teach her the finer arts of living. Joan Wylkynson, for instance, was a servant to Philip Coke, esquire, who had a country house in Essex as well as a place in the city. He owed her 33*s.* in back wages, and her new husband, John Shirreff, a goldsmith, became impatient and sued. Her service position probably enhanced, rather than detracted from, her marriageability.[25] Other servants were wealthy enough to make loans to their masters or their masters' clients, thereby indicating that they did not come from impoverished backgrounds. John Stalworth, for instance, worked for a hostler and lent his master's guests £3 worth of goods, which his master did not repay.[26]

The complaint of Isabel, servant to Walter Salman, gives a good idea of the relative wealth of an ordinary female servant before and after her service period. When she entered service, she had given into Salman's custody for safekeeping three pairs of sheets, one quilt, one mattress, one bedcover, one coverlet, one blanket, one broad cloth of 8 yards, two lambskins, and other goods and merchandise worth 47s. 10d. She contracted for seven years of service, covering the years from 1372 to 1379, probably receiving as compensation room and board and 1 mark a year, so that she was owed 7 marks. Salman refused to pay this sum or to return the goods, and Isabel sued. Her case illustrates a young woman's strategy toward marriage. She already had considerable household goods toward a dowry and would have had 7 marks in addition. Should she return to her village, such a dowry would be very attractive, but it also would be an enticement to an artisan or a journeyman in the city.[27]

Those taking up service positions, therefore, came from a wide range of backgrounds, from very humble to fairly high in the middle ranks of society. To be in service was not an insulting or necessarily a lowly position. The insult was to have been a serf—that is, to have been unfree and to have rendered service without receiving a wage for it. Such persons were not deemed suitable for apprenticeships and were also excluded from the higher-rank service positions.

Living Arrangements

Service contracts, as we have seen, often contained the provision that the servant receive room and board in addition to wages and sometimes in lieu of them. Societal expectations were such that to deny room after it had been promised was a disgrace to the master. Thus when William Rotheley denied room to his maidservant, the Goldsmiths not only fined him, but reprimanded him "because he . . . against all humanity, sent his maid out of his house and suffered her to lie out two nights so she was fain to borrow money to lie at the Pewter Pot to the dishonor of the fellowship."[28]

Some of the existing inventories of London housing mention chambers for servants with bedsteads, benches, and sometimes bedding. Servants such as Isabel might well have provided their own bedding. The servant's chamber was frequently in the solar, the space under the steep, peaked roof that was reachable either by steep outside stairs or by ladder.

The coroners' inquests tell us much about the living arrangements and the hazards they involved. On a December evening in 1321, Elena

Scot, servant of Margaret Sandwich, wanted to get embers to light a fire in her room in the solar, but she slipped on the top step of the stairs and fell backward, breaking her neck. John Toly, the drunken servant who fell to his death while relieving himself, lived in a solar 30 feet above the pavement. More skilled servants or journeymen sometimes had their chambers in a more desirable location in the house.[29]

Servants of the higher ranks, such as journeymen and factors, took their meals with the master in the hall. The household servants served the meals and probably ate in the kitchen afterward. The quality and quantity of food was sometimes roughly specified in the service contract. If the master was to provide clothing, that too was specified in the agreement, as it was for apprenticeship.

Journeymen and other servants, of course, did not always live with the master, but might make contracts for their room and board elsewhere. A typical contract for board was 16*d.* a week for a singlewoman. Lodging in an inn in 1345 could cost as little as 1½*d.* a week.[30]

Expected Relations Between Master or Mistress and Servant

The expectations for behavior on the part of both those offering service and those employing it were matters for advice literature. "John Russell's Book of Nurture," a manual on the duties of a high-class butler and carver, creates a hypothetical young man who lacks the skills of service. Russell meets him in a fittingly wild environment, a forest in the "merry season of May." The young poacher, armed with bow and arrow, has the right physical appearance—he is slender and lean. But he is in despair because he cannot find service: "I serve myself and no other man." Russell immediately asks the obvious question for any aspiring medieval youth: "Is thy governance good?" This child of nature confesses that he has tried to get a master, "but because I knew nothing good, and showed this wherever I went, every man denied me; day by day wanton [ill-bred] and not overnice, reckless, lewd and chattering like a jay, every man refused me." Fortunately, he is educable and can come in from the wilderness.[31]

The juxtaposition of wilderness and household provides an insight into the expectations of adults when they viewed their adolescents. The wilderness and the illegal hunting of the young savage stand for his disabilities in finding a position in civilized society. If he follows the advice of his adult mentor, he will no longer be an outcast but can become a respected member of society. The progression from poacher to servitor was a positive step in the view of adults concerned about the welfare of adolescents.

Since the mistress is responsible for the household servants, the "Good Wife" instructs her daughter how to deal with the servants:

> And wisely govern thy house, and serving maids and men,
> Be thou not too bitter or too debonaire with them;
> But look well what most needs to be done,
> And set thy people at it both rathely [quickly] and soon.

The mistress is to be particularly careful when her husband is away from home to maintain discipline, punishing those who do nothing while rewarding those who work hard. The mother also tells her daughter not to be above hard work but to pitch in like a "housewife" when there is much to do, both to get the tasks over sooner and to serve as an example for the servants. The "Wise Man" has less to say to his son about servants. The son is to maintain a balanced perspective and to referee fights between the mistress and the servants.[32]

Another concern expressed by the "Good Wife" is the level of trust one should have in servants and the need to treat them fairly and even generously, because they might go their way and gossip about their mistress. She urges her daughter to keep her own keys and not to be seduced by the flattery of servants into trusting them. To keep their tongues from wagging, servants should be paid on their term day, whether they are continuing or ending their contract. The mistress should also give them goods in kind, and "then they shall say well of thee, both the young and the old."[33]

The folk wisdom reflected in the advice literature was a real part of the expectations for the relationship between servant and master. We will discuss the reality of the master–servant relationship in great depth, but a few cases speak explicitly about the expected behavior between master and servant. In a complicated story, Thomas Pays of London, a carpenter, explained that he had been in the service of William Hatter of London, a mercer. Thomas was working as a carpenter on William's place, called the Woll Sak in Thames Street, when a man came and said he was from my Lord of Exeter and wanted to speak with William. Thomas went to get William. As soon as the master appeared, the man grabbed him by the breast. William called out to Thomas, "Help me for this man maketh upon me great affant, I wot not what he meaneth." Thomas grabbed the man and held him fast and said, "Thou shalt not thus fare with my master while I am here present. What manner of mistery man are you? I trow thou art no man of My Lord of Exeter as thou saidest." It was Thomas's expectation that his master, even one who retained him for a specific task, deserved his protection.[34] Another servant, acting on his master's orders, found himself sued for trespass. He argued that he was acting in obedience to his master, "according as a servant ought to do at the commanding of his master."[35]

Servants who fulfilled their part of the expected behavior anticipated some share of the master's goods, just as the "Good Wife" taught her daughter. When Isabel, Lady Bouchers, died, she left a bequest of a 40s. annuity to William Demon and his wife, May, "for their long and faithful services."[36]

The Reality of Relationships Between Master and Servant

Good servants are difficult to find, complains the employer. The servant counters that high-handed, overly demanding masters and scolding mistresses sour the service relationship. Living in close proximity could inflame disputes in the household or could lead to close bonds of loyalty. A master's poverty could engulf the servant, leading to a life of both rags and hunger. The blandishments and temptations of higher wages or higher-status employment could entice away a discontented servant. Given the power relationship of master to servant, the master could abuse the servants. On the other hand, knowing the master's most intimate secrets, the servant could make off with his master's money and, sometimes, with his wife. The service relationship was by its nature full of dangers for both parties. But there were compensations as well. For the servant, the security of having food and a roof over one's head was important, for the master or mistress, the knowledge that ordinary affairs would be taken care of was a relief. Whatever the risks, neither party felt that service was dispensable. Young people, such as the hypothetical young wild man, needed to learn skills and to earn money, and the medieval household needed extra hands for the labor-intensive housekeeping and crafts. One would not say, as does my aged mother, that servants are too much trouble to have in the house.

Presenting a balanced picture from the record remains is difficult because broken contracts and disappointed expectations come to court in the form of suits or petitions to the Chancellor, whereas the good relationships appear in testamentary bequests or incidentally in coroners' inquests. Much, both good and bad, was never recorded. The evidence often presents contradictory stories. For instance, John Langrake, a citizen and barber of London, found himself in trouble for taking pity on Joan, the servant of William West, rent gatherer to the Master of St. Thomas of Acres. She was only twelve, and even Langrake described her as "of a right wanton disposition," running away from service several times "for god knows what reason." He was returning home when he found her at eight o'clock in the evening, sitting at his neighbor's stall right next to his door. She was quaking and shivering with cold. Langrake asked her who she was, where she lived, and why she sat there. She said that she lived in Smithfield and that her mistress had beaten her and driven her out of the house. She had nowhere to go. John consulted with his wife and, with her consent, brought the girl into his shop and gave her supper with the other servants. He allowed her to sleep in the shop. The next morning, he again asked her whom she served and, receiving an answer, took her by the hand to William West's house. He turned her over to William's wife, who took her and said, "See what comes of thee for thy remiss to thy master." Langrake went away believing that he had done a good deed, but ten days later, West sent a neighbor to him complaining that he had sexually abused Joan in his shop. Langrake said that the whole time Joan was there, his wife, his *menie*, and three of his neighbors were present, and he would not pay the damages that West was claiming.[37]

Of the three narrative voices, which one is telling the true story? As governor of his *familia* or *menie*, a master was responsible not only for the welfare of his servants, but also for their behavior and their persons. A master regarded his servants as his property while they were under contract, so that damages that came to the servant were damages to the master. West was claiming damages to his property. Langrake was claiming that West was not a good governor of his household. Joan may really have been sexually abused by Langrake, as well as beaten by the mistress, or she may have been of a "wanton disposition"—too young and too adventuresome for service—and fabricated a story to cover up her running away. The case is a useful one for our purposes because it shows the level of complexity in service relationships. Not only do the parties involved have their versions, but outsiders also have opinions about these intimate relationships.

Damage to a servant was cause for a suit on the part of the master because it deprived him of services. For instance, when one of his servants was assaulted, Richard de Gloucester claimed that he was deprived of the man's service to the damage of £100.[38] In a more pathetic case, Edmund Fairstedt, who described himself as blind "by the visitation of God," complained that he had come to London from Brampton in Huntingdonshire when Master William Carlyll contrived to have Catherine Broke, his servant and keeper, arrested; now, Fairstedt said, he could not manage.[39]

All parties could agree that a master had an obligation and a right to discipline and to physically chastise his servant, but excessive punishment could bring criticism from neighbors and the city. A female servant, for instance, was able to get her master arrested and imprisoned because he had "offended by force against her and because she feared him." But a journeyman cordwainer who refused to go to Croydon with his master and made up a story about renting a room and being beaten and robbed by his master did not receive much satisfaction. The jury found that he had been punished only for recalcitrance and that he did not rent the room, but had it because he was a servant. They awarded him 6*d.* for damages to his clothes. Servants' complaints about physical punishment are rare, however, compared with those of apprentices. Probably servants expected to take much more verbal and physical correction than apprentices did, and probably they expected a less sympathetic hearing from the mayor. Masters might also have been hesitant to try corporal punishment on young men who were perhaps bigger and stronger than they were. Boys and maidservants were more likely to suffer cuffs. In one case, a quarrel ended with the master killing the servant. But this homicide, which took place in the High Street on a Saturday night, was more likely an argument brought on by drink and hot tempers than by excessive discipline.[40]

Because of their control over wages and their access to the city power structure, masters had a number of other ways of disciplining servants. When a servant who had been beaten up in a drunken quarrel and who had stayed out all night arrived at his master's house, his master paid him his wages and ordered him to leave immediately. Other masters took care of riotous and rebellious servants by having them put into prison and held until they agreed to behave better. John Southwell complained that his master had taken "great displeasure" and "maligned against" him, even commanding him to "pull off the hair of his head." When Southwell would not obey this sadistic command, saying that he thought he should be "as any other servant," his master had him put in prison for disobedience.[41]

Imprisonment and court cases usually came about because of disputes over wages and length of contract. The masters used the Statute of Laborers to control servants. The statute made it easy to argue that a servant was breaking the law in seeking higher wages. Although some cases were straightforward and were readily cleared up in the mayor's court, others came to light as petitions to the Chancellor and appear as stories of subterfuge and oppression. The statements must have had some ring of truth, and certainly the petitioners were in prison. That so many of these cases appear in the Chancery petitions may indicate that servants found in this institution their only realistic venue of complaint. But the difficulty of interpretation comes out in two conflicting narratives that appear in the cases of John Hochum of Havering-at-Bower and his mistress, Margaret Pounce. John complained in his petition that he contracted to serve Margaret as a glazier and did so well and truly. She was in his debt for 20*s.* in wages when she sued him under the Statute of Laborers and had him put in prison. Her petition claimed that he had worked for only ten weeks of the agreed-on term and then left her. She claimed to have lent him 50*s.* and maintained that he then sued out of malice for 20*s.*[42]

The threat of imprisonment was a powerful tool. A servant might extend service in the hope of placating a master to gain past wages, only to discover that nothing availed and that she or he had simply served more weeks without wages. Agnes Kyrkeby complained that she had served for six years and "well and truly did her service," but that her master refused to pay her wages even when she gave notice that she would leave. He threatened her with imprisonment to force her to stay beyond her six-year term. Another young woman worked an additional half-year beyond term under similar circumstances and was arrested anyway.[43]

Elizabeth Pycely of London, a singlewoman, complained of another subterfuge. She served Richard Fote, a draper of London, for the time she had contracted, and he owed her £4 in wages. When she said she would depart, he claimed that she owed him exactly £4 so that he did not owe her a penny. He kept her prisoner in the house for five days and had an obligation made out to him in her name. He would not let her go until she signed. When she did, he sued for £4 on the basis of her obligation.[44]

One petition to the Chancellor regarding a foreign servant, probably a slave, involved the selling of her person. Maria Moriana said that she had served Philip Syne of Venice for twenty years, taking from him only meat and drink. Philip had fallen into great poverty and could not fend for himself, his wife, or Maria except by alms of well-disposed people. Philip proposed to sell Maria for £20 to Dominic, a merchant of Genoa, but Maria was "utterly opposed" to this. Nonetheless, Philip made a bond with Dominic in Maria's name for £20. Philip told Maria that he would give her all the debts owed to him in recompense for the service she had provided if she would sign the bond at the notary's house. "She being innocent and not able to speak or understand English was easily persuaded to put her seal to the agreement." Philip then had her arrested for debt and put into prison. The only way she could get out was by selling her person to Dominic for the £20 she owed her master.[45]

In addition to the other vulnerabilities that female servants faced, they were subject to the threat of sexual assault. One is tempted to respond that surely young boys were equally vulnerable, but homosexuality does not appear in the records.[46] The relationship between the male head of the *familia* or *menie* and his female servants was an ambiguous one. While the master was bound by his patriarchal position to protect women servants and to see that they were not damaged, his complete power over them and his belief that he owned them could lead to an assumption of sexual license. After all, biblical and folkloric traditions upheld this role for a master among his maidservants. Unlike an apprentice, whose contract precluded such sexual use and whose situation was under the watchful eye of both friends and the city, the servant did not enjoy protection against such abuse.

Masters did seek sexual solace in their servants, sometimes through contractual arrangements. Thomasine Bonaventure was born to poor parents in Cornwall about 1450. While she was tending the sheep one day, Thomas Bumsby, a London mercer who traded in Cornwall, saw her and was struck by her beauty and good manners. He asked her to come to London as his servant. She was a clever young woman who told him that he would have to speak with her parents. Her parents required him to produce witnesses as to his character and made him contract to endow her if he died. They were apparently aware that the arrangement was for more than household service. In any case, his wife died several years later, and Thomas married Thomasine. He died two years later, and because they had no children, she got half of his estate as dower. As a wealthy and beautiful young widow, she had many suitors and finally married Henry Galle. When he died, she was about thirty years old and again without children, so she got half of Galle's estate as jointure. She then married John Percival, a merchant tailor and, later, mayor of London. When he died in 1507, she was so wealthy that she was prey for one of Henry VII's money-raising schemes. He pardoned her for a trumped-up offense in exchange for a payment of £1,000.[47]

Most young servant women, however, did not have the sensible parents, the beauty, or the good luck of Thomasine Bonaventure. For them, the situation was tenuous. Although they might receive extra compensation, they might also be turned out by the master's wife as wanton and find that their marriage prospects were ruined. It was very easy to be marginalized, particularly if the young woman became pregnant.

We have explored in depth the sad story of Margaret, mother of the bastard heiress Alison. Margaret had been a servant to John Rayner and had enjoyed a long-lasting relationship with him that produced their daughter. The daughter was well endowed, but Margaret got a rather modest settlement and could not be guardian of her own daughter.[48] Other men recognized their bastard children and their servant mothers in wills as well, but this was not a common occurrence.

A female servant's sexuality could be exploited by the master and mistress for profit rather than for their own sexual gratification. Joan Norman, a singlewoman of London, said that she was a victim of a plot between her former master and John Haliday, a London hostler. Her former master accused her of breaking into his chest and stealing 40s. She said that she had trusted her master and had given a girdle worth 40s. to him for indemnity. He had her arrested and put into prison. She said that she was "inwardly poor" and had no property but the girdle and could live only by her own hard work. Begging her former master had done no good; she had "sought him in the name of the Virgin Mary, protector of all women to be her good master." But he was willing to let Haliday pay the 40s. in exchange for Joan, "to have his way with her."[49] Mistresses, as we have seen, sold their female servants as prostitutes. Although not an uncommon charge in the church courts, selling servants into prostitution was certainly not approved behavior: Alice Broke was brought to the court on charges of defaming Joan Hiche, "saying that she would make any servant she hath a harlot."[50]

Masters exploited servants by using them to carry out illegal actions. The servants then took the blame for felony or breach of rules, while the master got off with his reputation intact. For instance, men who were selling good grain with putrid had their male and female servants display the grain for sale on the pavement, using the good grain to cover up the bad by selling it in bushel lots. Other masters instructed their servants to violate the Assize of Nuisance by breaking walls or placing filth in the streets. Still others required their servants to perpetrate acts of violence or commit thefts. Henry Wylyot and his servant lay in wait in a shop in the Cheap until William Pycok crossed the road. The servant, "in obedience to his master's orders," struck William on the head with a stick. Some of these servants were, in reality, simply hired thugs.[51] A medieval Fagan had his servant pick purses in the lodgings where he stayed.[52]

Not only the desperation of the abused servant, but the raw hatred of servants for their masters comes out in the records. William Elwold, an aggrieved London baker, told the Chancellor of a bitter domestic scene. He had returned from a pilgrimage on the Sunday after the feast of St. James. It was night, and his wife and servants had waited up for him. He was tired and "commanded his wife to set his servants to supper and he departed to his bed." Among the servants was one John Baker, who had of Elwold 20d. weekly, as well as meat, drink, and lodging. At supper, John used unfitting language in reference to his master, "despising him with so high a voice that your besecher lying in his bed heard every word that John said." William's wife rebuked John for his language, "saying that it was unfitting for him to have such language by his master that gave him drink and wages." John would not listen and continued his abuse until William rose from his bed, rebuked John, and told him that he should eat his supper and let his master be in peace or he would chastise him. John rose from the table and assaulted William. The other servants restrained him. But John left his service and took an action of trespass, even managing to put together a friendly jury that found that William owed John 100s. in damages.[53]

Masters, of course, had many legitimate reasons to lose all patience with their servants. Michael Armuier, for instance, hired John Raulyn as his servant to buy, sell, and deliver armor. He was to deliver leg harnesses to two men, one of small stature and one of large, and collect 40s. from each. With pedantic repetition, Armuier instructed Raulyn to deliver the small harness to the small man and the large harness to the large man. But instead, Raulyn delivered the large one to the small man and tried to deliver the small one to the large man. The large man refused the harness, and the servant kept it. The master sued the servant, and they eventually reached an agreement. Another incompetent let a lighted candle fall on the reeds that covered a floor, setting a fire that destroyed the documents relating to the election of a bishop and a bull of Clement VI. His clerical master was in Rome for a Jubilee when this fiasco was discovered.[54]

Thefts and other deceptions were among the greatest risks that masters faced from having servants about the house. Both male and female servants could be untrustworthy, but sometimes the female servants knew more about the locked chests and had greater access to the keys. The "Good Wife" had warned her daughter about this danger. John of Hilton, a pewterer and citizen, complained that his servant Agnes had represented herself as unmarried. While he was away at St. Ives's Fair, she broke open his chest and stole goods that she took back to her husband in Dublin. Another brazen servant duped a priest from Warmyngton, in Cambridgeshire. Elizabeth Grey was a servant of Thomas Walkot. She took goods from him and left them on deposit with the priest. She saw the priest on a trip to London and asked him to bring the goods the next time they met. This he did, and Elizabeth ran away from service, taking the goods with her. A customer of a shearman left an old gown worth 28s. to be sheared, but a servant stole it and departed. Other valuables, such as a gray hunting dog, disappeared from a master's house. Servants certainly were not necessarily trustworthy when a quick profit might be turned.[55]

Servants also ran away, taking with them their masters' property. They sometimes claimed that the goods were due them as back wages, but probably the servants were not always truthful.[56] Again, the masters had the more powerful weapons on their side. Letters from the mayor and the corporation of London were sent all over the country requesting the return of servants who, the masters complained, had violated the Statute of Laborers by leaving their terms early. The servants, of course, said that they were visiting sick relatives in the country and were "good men and loyal," not "evil of disposition." In some cases, the local authorities wrote back confirming this assessment. One master sought the restoration of clothes, silver spoons, a mazer, and other goods worth £10, of which Margaret de Marcherne, his servant, had robbed him. She had been found in

Oxford, but Oxford officials had received a letter from Gloucester testifying to her good behavior, so they had let her go. Now the master urged the mayor to write to Gloucester to get his goods back.[57]

As part of the role of the head of a *familia,* masters also faced the problem of maintaining an acceptable standard of public behavior on the part of their servants. Apprentices were under contractual agreement and could be brought into line with material threats if physical chastisement did not work. Servants might not feel the same sort of obligations or indebtedness. Servants, more than others in the London population, engaged in political riots, having rather less to lose than apprentices or householders. They played a prominent role in the revolt of 1381 and in other disturbances. If servants rioted, it was considered in part the fault of their masters for not holding them in check. A merchant of London, Ralph March, whose servants had run riot in one of the attacks on foreigners, had been required to post a bond with the chamberlain. He was accused of having failed to subject his servants to "good rule and sad demeaning" and so was personally liable for them.[58]

To balance the picture of disorder and abuse, the records also speak of devotion, shared amusements, and an atmosphere of familial affection between masters and servants. The social distance between master and servant, as mentioned, was not necessarily great, since the service position might simply be a life phase. There might be little hindrance to friendships, and some masters elicited real devotion. As the "Good Wife" instructed, satisfied servants give good service. Margery, wife of William of Kent, had certainly earned the devotion of a servant. She and her husband were quarreling at dusk in the solar. Hearing the fight, their servant, Stephen Flemyng, was moved to anger and mounted the stairs with a knife in his hand. William seized a staff and hit him on the head. Stephen died after midnight, and William fled.[59]

Devoted servants risked their lives and committed homicide to protect their lord's property. Sometimes the property was minor, as in the case of two servants who rushed out to defend their master's little dog, which was sleeping on the doorstep when two work men stumbled over it and it complained.[60] But Thomas de St. Alban, servant of Richard de Rothinge, a carpenter, risked his life while protecting his master's property. John Fuatard and his mistress climbed over Richard's garden wall at night, entered his close, and broke into his house. They stole various items, including an axe and a knife. Thomas heard them and raised the hue, pursuing them into the garden. He and John fought, while the mistress escaped. At length, Thomas saw the knife at his feet and seized it, striking John five times. Again, Thomas raised the hue and cry and "remained on the spot" until the coroner arrived.[61] While most people who killed someone fled, Thomas was so sure of his justification that he waited to be arrested. Other servants stood by their masters and fought along with them in the sometimes vicious trade fights in the streets of London.[62]

Devoted service did not go unrewarded, if the master or mistress followed the precepts of the "Good Wife." Even the guild rules made provision for "any good serving man of the trade who has behaved himself well and loyally towards his master . . . should he fall sick or be unable to maintain himself, shall be found by the good folks of the trade until he shall have recovered."[63] Of those recording their wills in the Husting Court, ninety, or 2.4 percent, of the testators left bequests to their servants. The bequests were usually made in the form of money or household goods and clothing. Some were annuities of from 20*s.* to 40*s.* One man, a widower, left his shops to his female servant. She may well have been a mistress. Another man made his cook his chief heir, with provision that he keep his chantry. Because some of these servants were also relatives, the bequests kept wealth within the family. Servants sometimes reciprocated. One servant of tender conscience left his master 20 marks for "peculations he committed against him in the shop over by the Cat and Fiddle."[64]

"Servant Murders Master"[65]

The neighbors talked about the murder for weeks. Homicides were not that common in London—even misadventures were not a daily occurrence—so the discovery of a decomposed, decapitated body in the coal-storage area of the tavern was news.[66] The head was nowhere to be found, so that identifying the body required a reconstruction of the events. Clothing and the recollection of events at the tavern led to the conclusion that it was that of Symon de Wynton. The body had been found just after Easter in 1276. The jurors put the date of death on the Eve of St. Nicholas, December 6, 1275. The neighbors, as usual, had been watching the comings and goings at the tavern in Ironmonger Lane. They had patronized it to buy wine for their dinners or to eat a meal and play a game of dice. It was not the best sort of tavern, not because the wine was bad, but because the proprietor was. What a disagreeable, quarrelsome host! And who knew what businesses he was running on the side. His house was near enough to the Jewry that many suspected he was a fence for stolen goods. He might be a Jew himself, with a name like Symon. He had been brought to the wardmoot for running a bawdy house. That business had come to an end when his wife moved out and ceased acting as the local pimp for the peasant girls who were looking for service positions. She had enticed them to the tavern with promises of "honorable positions" and then had sold them to foreigners. Without prostitution, the tavern had settled down, becoming a somewhat quieter rendezvous for gamblers.

When Symon disappeared, the neighbors were not surprised. Rumors that the business was not going well had been circulating for some time. Local residents had made inquiries, of course. The servant, known to them as Roger of Westminster, had offered the plausible explanation that his master had gone to Westminster to collect debts owed to him there. For three days, he had set out the bench of the tavern and sold wine, always offering the same explanation. On the third evening, at twilight, the neighbors saw him "departing by the outer door, locking it with a key, and carrying off with him a silver cup, a robe, and some bedclothes," all of which belonged to Symon. "Afterwards he returned, and threw the key into the house of Hamon Cook, a near neighbor, telling him that he was going to see Symon." He said that he would be back. That was the last they saw of him.

Both Symon and Roger, if that was his name, were a bad sort. Roger had been working at the tavern for only a fortnight, but he and his master quarreled bitterly. Symon always had trouble with his help, so there was nothing suspicious in yet another round of bickering. If they had both gone off without leaving a trace, it was probably because the business had failed. To confirm the neighbors' suspicions, on December 31 John Doget, a taverner, had come with Gilbert de Colecestere to recover a debt that Symon owed him for wine. The neighbors came out and watched as he tried the door. Finally, they told him that Hamon Cook had the key, but that no one had been about the place since early December. Doget opened the door and found one full tun of wine and one half full that belonged to him. He called porters to come and take away the wine and made seizin of some small tables, cloths, gallons, and wooden potels to the value of 2s. against the debt that Symon owed him. He locked the door and took the key away with him.

The house remained empty until finally the owner, Robert le Surigien of Friday Street, decided to rent the tavern again. On the Thursday before Palm Sunday, he came to the house and broke open the door, since he had no key, and rented the space to Michael le Oynter. Michael came alone on Saturday in Easter week "to examine all the offices belonging thereto, and see which of them required to be cleansed of filth and dust." It was he who found the body in the narrow coal-storage space and called the officials.

Roger had actually known Symon for some time, way back when Symon had lived in Winchester and had kept a tavern there. Roger, whose real name was Robert Hood, had found Symon's tavern convenient. He had hired on as a servant, cleaning out the tavern, setting out the wine, and serving the beer, all the while keeping his ears open for news of who was traveling on the king's highway. When a wealthy merchant or churchman was expected, he tipped off the local bandits and got part of the loot. The worst part of the arrangement was Symon. He was about as bad a master as anyone could have. He boxed Robert's ears; had not Robert had an alternative source of income, he surely would have starved on the board he was given. When Robert did not starve, Symon caught on and wanted a cut of the profits. The arrangement worked well because Symon could also fence stolen goods. But Symon squealed to the sheriff to save his own neck, and Hood had gone to jail. It was only because he was just sixteen and a minor thief that he was acquitted, but he spent six miserable months in jail waiting for trial with little to eat and people dying of jail fever around him. Symon, meanwhile, had thought it wisest to sell out and move to London.

Hood tracked him down to settle the score. He appeared at Symon's tavern in Ironmonger Lane and proposed that they let bygones be bygones. London was a city of opportunity; they would simply set up a bigger and better operation. He would work for Symon as a servant, using Roger of Westminster as his alias, while they planned their business. As usual, they argued—recriminations, fights over dividing the profits, and the usual cuffs. But Robert was older, stronger, and meaner now and gave back what he got. His plan was simple, but clever. He would encourage Symon to drink too much, not a very difficult task, and, when Symon was asleep, he would kill him. It would have to be quiet, because the neighbors were the busybody sort that everyone in London seemed to be. Robert had found a place to dispose of the body "in a certain secret spot, a dark and narrow place" not 2 feet wide, between two walls in the same house. No need to take the body outside; no worry about smells. He would set up shop as usual and tell the nosy neighbors that Symon had gone to Westminster to collect some debts.

Arguing as usual, the men went off to bed in the same room. Symon was soon in a drunken snore. Robert took his knife and, with thoughts of paying his master back for all the beatings, cut his throat with so much vigor that the head came off. Robert had not intended this, and the torrent of blood caused further complications in getting rid of the bedding. Still, this might be a nice refinement. He could dispose of the head separately, making the body harder to identify. All went smoothly when he put out the tavern bench and told the neighbors that Symon was in Westminster trying to collect debts. They seemed to have no suspicions—Symon's bad reputation had some advantages. At twilight on the third day, he made something of a show of carrying off the silver cup and Symon's best robe. He told the neighbors that he had to pawn the goods to pay his master's debts. The neighbors were so interested in his brazen appropriation that they did not notice the bloody bedding and the head concealed under the robe. The cup and robe were to sell in the Jewry; the rest went into the Thames at high tide. The risky part was returning to the scene of the crime to tell the neighbors that he was going to look for Symon. He wanted to allay suspicion, to give himself time to escape. Rather than stopping to chat with Hamon, he tossed him the key, saying that he would be back. But even if they eventually used the key to enter the tavern (and what busybody Londoner would not?), he would be long gone. He knew where his future career would take him and headed for Sherwood Forest.

Leisure and Relationships with Other Servants

Servants developed relationships not only with their masters and mistresses, but also with one another. Then, too, there were the temptations of London. Since many of the servants were young and inexperienced, they could get into trouble in their master's household or in the town. The problem of standing *in loco parentis* to one to three or more adolescents caused masters no end of problems.

First, there was the matter of relationships within the household itself. At best, the servants got along in a familial way as siblings, with the older ones adopting a parental attitude toward the younger ones. But, of course, this did not always work. A woman who worked as an alemaker for a baker's household brought her five-year-old son to work with her. When the apprentice disciplined the child and he died two days later, the mother brought charges against the apprentice. In another case, the senior servant, clerk to the master, accused the junior servant of taking a strongbox belonging to the master. The junior denied it, but the senior servant hit him with a big stick. Meanwhile, the master was upstairs in his chamber with his shoes off, getting ready for bed, when he heard the fight and the thud, so he could not prevent the death.[67]

Masters also had a problem monitoring the sexuality of the household staff. Apprenticeship contracts clearly stated that the apprentice was not to have sexual relations with anyone in the household, and the master's control over the youth's future enforced this clause. But servants were less beholden, and a master and mistress would have to be alert day and night to monitor the activities of their servants.

The sexuality of female servants was more at stake than that of males. Piers Godard, a text writer, took his responsibilities for his servant seriously and complained that William Ridmington, a servant of Laurence Wylkynson, a vintner, came to the house of Piers "against his love and his leave" and there ravished and defiled Joan Hunter, his servant, for three days while he and his wife were at Mass or otherwise busy. To add insult to injury, William took Piers by the sleeve while he was on his way to Mass and told him about his triumphs.[68] William knew well that he could taunt Piers for being unable to defend the honor of his position as head of his *familia*. Another rake who entered the master's house against his will made his servant pregnant. The master took care of the servant girl until the child was born, and then she absconded with her seducer, taking goods to the value of £20, or so the master said.[69] According to the church courts, Thomas Chelley made a practice of corrupting female servants in his neighborhood, but his accusers said that he gave one servant £40 and another 20 marks toward their marriages. Other people were simply accused of enticing away female servants in order to sell them into prostitution.[70]

Male servants were more likely to be initiating sexual adventures with a prostitute when they ran into trouble. A groom was looking for Emma de Brakkele, a harlot, to lie with her. He did not find her, but found another woman instead. They argued, and he took a knife and killed her. In another case, the servants were arguing over a courtesan, and one of them died of knife wounds in the ensuing fight.[71]

Servants' evenings on the town could easily turn to riot and assault. But they also accounted for many smaller affrays that ended in wounds or property damage. The genesis of a rather ordinary brawl unfolds in a court case. A group of servants and adolescent sons of citizens had been out on the town. Among their antics was filling an empty cask with stones and setting it rolling down Grace Church Street to London Bridge, "to the terror of the neighborhood." They then assaulted the night watch on the stroke of midnight by St. Paul's bells and, in the process, wounded one of the watchmen. The hue and cry was raised "with horn and voice," and the neighboring wards came to help suppress the riot.[72]

Servants' play could also be of an innocent nature. Friendly wrestling matches, ball games, and gambling with other servants or with masters were common.[73]

Journeymen

Journeymen were a special group of servants—day laborers who had completed their apprenticeships and had passed the guild skill test for mastery of the craft, but either were too poor to become masters or were required to work for several more years as wage laborers for their masters. This group created more disciplinary problems than any other. As "young men," "bachelors," or "lowys," journeymen could not move out of their masters' houses, set up their own businesses, marry without their masters' permission, or work on their own for wage labor. Their wages ranged from 20*s.* to 30*s.* a year, in addition to room and board. The journeymen were thus older—in the late fifteenth century, they were usually in their mid- to late twenties—and more restive and rebellious. With the shortage of skilled labor, they were eager to seek work and wages away from their masters. They were also prone to organize against their masters to force higher wages; on more than one occasion, they were involved in serious riots. These young men, kept in an adolescent stage beyond what seemed to them a reasonable age, were considered a dangerous group by London's adult establishment.[74]

These more mature servants have been described as people "in a period of probation and of subordination" who were "outside the ranks of the fully privileged."[75] Being older, more sophisticated, less beholden to masters, and more eager than younger servants and apprentices to make the transition to the adult world, they were inclined to take, rather than ask for, privileges. They gambled, visited whores, and corrupted servant girls and even wives of masters. One aggrieved master accused his journeyman of running off with his wife and £200 of goods.[76] Journeymen posed another threat as well. They could migrate to the suburbs of London, particularly Westminster and Southwark, and set up their own shops beyond the control of the London guild masters and in competition with them.[77]

While individual acts of rebellion are recorded, the real threat was organized resistance. Complaints from the journeymen to the Cordwainers came as early as 1303, when they told the mayor and the aldermen that the masters were trying to lower their pay by giving them wages in a debased coinage. They lost and were told to work faithfully for their masters and the people and to pay a fine for false claim.[78] The struggles became far more serious with the depopulation caused by the Black Death, the imposition of the Statute of Laborers, and the high demand for skilled labor. In 1349, the Bakers' journeymen were accused of a conspiracy to charge double or triple for their labor, and the Cordwainers' journeymen followed suit. By 1366, the Fullers were having problems. The Goldsmiths faced a revolt in 1398. In 1411, the Merchant Tailors cited "incessant reports that certain servants and apprentices of the tailors of the city called 'yeomen tailors' live by themselves or alone in companies and take and inhabit diverse dwelling places in the said city against license or will of their superiors." But the will of the superiors could be oppressive. In 1441, the Bakers' yeomen and servants complained that they were not allowed to go home to their wives at night without paying 10*d.* to the master.[79]

Admonitions against rebellious journeymen could be gentle, as in the case of two servants working in wood for saddles who did not return to their work: "neither the great folk of the land nor the common people can be served" to the detriment of the "commonweal."[80] On the whole, however, more serious measures resulted. The Merchant Tailors' yeomen and servants were considered "young and unstable people" and were not allowed to congregate. The mayor and the aldermen arrested and imprisoned the Goldsmiths' rebellious journeymen with the threat that the ringleaders would have to pay £10 each if they started the revolt again. In 1445, seven journeymen shearmen appeared in the mayor's court and "were given to understand that they were of dissolute character." They had to swear on the gospels to be of good behavior, to obey their masters, and not to wander at night or frequent suspicious places, such as that of that dissolute woman "Blanchapulton."[81]

The revolts, however, signaled a more profound change in the structure of London's guilds and society. In the fourteenth and early fifteenth centuries, journeymen had contracted with their masters for annual compensation for a year or more after completing their apprenticeships, continuing to live in their masters' houses, before setting up their own shops and households. But as the opportunities to establish shops of their own decreased with the decrease in consumer demand resulting from population loss and with the increasingly tight control of the existing shops and trade, "young men" and "bachelors" began to marry and establish at least separate households from their employers. Many of these journeymen would never be able to enter the ranks of the liveried masters—those who had full membership in the guilds and who wore the distinctive cloth of the guild. But they were not really servants in the same sense as a domestic servant was because they had already taken a step toward adult status by establishing a household and a family. By the mid-fifteenth century, guild books showed that perhaps 50 percent of the guild membership was not in livery. Some guilds divided their ranks into two: those with livery and those without. Others had three ranks: those with livery, households, and shops; those who had guild membership and households but did not have the livery; and journeymen.

The solution to regulating these various levels of guild membership was to create an intermediate category between the fully liveried guild members and the servile journeyman. Whereas the rebels of the fourteenth and early fifteenth centuries had tried to set up their own guilds, with separate feasts and rules of behavior, as bargaining units against the main guild, the mid-fifteenth century saw a co-opting of these organizational efforts by the liveried guild members, as guilds established Yeoman, or Bachelor, Companies attached to the parent organization. The subordinate company was controlled by the liveried elite, but was made up of householders (as opposed to unmarried journeymen). They might have their own ceremonies and their own accounts and treasury, but they did not have an independent political agenda.[82]

The extension of power into a recognized and organized yeomanry was yet another way for the guild elite to exercise control over the restive journeymen. It did not eliminate riot and dissent, but it was a clever stratagem for diverting discontent. An example from the Mercers' Court illustrates how the system worked. The Mercers' Bachelor Company was a recognized ceremonial unit in its own right, with a livery, a barge for festivals, and its own feasts. But small traders and shopkeepers of the mercery did not have the option of not belonging. When Thomas Kitson refused to wear the Bachelors' livery and go with other members of the company to the mayor's feasts, the company fined him £4, which he refused to pay. The Mercers sent him to prison until "he had better advised himself." He did so overnight and joined the procession.[83]

The journeymen's and yeomen's subordinate guilds form a useful bridge for looking at the markers of exit from adolescence and that final step over the threshold into the adult world. The efforts to extend the adolescent years far beyond the usual course of puberty and physical maturation led to conflicts and, eventually, to the establishment of yet another intermediate category between childhood and adulthood. Those in service might work for a limited number of years until they moved on, achieving markers of adulthood such as marriage, the establishment of a household or a business, and the beginning of a family. But there were also those who would remain in a state of limbo. Either they did not experience the ceremonies that marked transition to adulthood and remained in service all their lives, or, like the yeoman, they made the transition, only to be denied full access to ultimate social and political power. In medieval London, both entrance and exit from the adolescent state were carefully controlled.

11

On Becoming Sad and Wise

We must go back to a question we asked at the beginning of this book and wonder once again if people in the Middle Ages marked the "coming of age" and, if so, how they did it. The phrase that was used repeatedly to describe reaching the age of discretion was to become "sad and wise," but usually this phrase was voiced as a desirable goal or as a reprimand to someone who had not managed yet to achieve this fine state. Did anyone say, by way of great approval, "You are now sad and wise, so you can be an adult?" Could the learned books of medicine and the satiric songs on the failings of all the ages of man serve as guides to establishing when childhood and youth had been left behind and sufficient sadness and wiseness had been achieved for an individual to be considered an adult? And the insistent whisper of the subtext asks if women also had to become sad and wise, or if they were simply to remain silent. As usual, the learned and poetical theorists had an instructive view, but those who stood guard at the portals of entry into adulthood controlled the reality of coming of age.

The doorkeepers imposed many barriers to stepping over the threshold into adulthood. In London, so much was at stake for both the youth and the gatekeeper. The youth faced the perpetual struggle against adults to be independent: to move into a life in which the paternal inheritance was finally delivered; to have a marriage arranged in which dower and

Flirtations that lead to a marriage contract. (Drawing by Wayne M. Howell, from British Library, Royal MS. 15 E. iii, f. 269)

dowry were set up so that legal protections established a separate, independent household; to finish both apprenticeship and the period of "bachelor"; to become a citizen of London or, better yet, a liveried guild member; or simply to appear sufficiently mature to the civic authorities that one could be counted "sad and wise" enough to be on one's own. For the masters, selfish interests in keeping their apprentices and journeymen in their service and at a cheap rate of pay made them reluctant to allow these young men out of their service. They also had an anxiety about being sure that their apprentices were well trained and mature enough to go out into the world and be a credit to the masters' reputation. If the relationship had been a close one, simply relinquishing the emotional bond could be as wrenching for a master as it was for a natural parent. Thus the struggle between youth and the self-designated gatekeepers to adulthood became a perpetual struggle that occupied youth, their mentors, and the courts.

Age of Exit from Adolescence

The age of exit from adolescence depended on a number of variables, with physical maturity being only one and not necessarily the most important. Gender, wealth, social status, occupation, length of apprenticeship, general conditions of plague and disease, and individual variations all had some influence on the move into adulthood.

Learned texts explain that as adolescents moved into maturity, they became colder and dryer. The qualities of maturity were dry and cold, the humor was black choler, the element was earth, and the season was autumn. The mature were "solid, serious, settled in their ways and gileful." Authorities who relied on the Pythagorean division of life into four stages placed maturity at the age of forty, but later writers put the age of entry at between twenty-five and thirty. The medical description of the four stages in the life cycle became popular in fourteenth- and fifteenth-century England in poems, moral tales, and prescriptions for living and even as centerpiece ornaments for four-course banquets.[1]

The literature on the seven ages of man offers more refinements. Thus in Ptolemy's astrological scheme, the mature years from twenty-two to forty-one are dominated by the sun, which "implants in the soul at length the mastery and direction of its actions, desire for substance, glory, and position and a change from playful, ingenuous error to seriousness, decorum, and ambition."[2] In the Middle English poem "The Mirror of the Periods of Man's Life," the picture of adulthood is not such a pleasant one. Music, drink, mock fights, and wild companions of adolescence give way to pride, anger, gluttony, wrestling, and lechery as a man passes into adulthood at twenty-five. At forty and at fifty years, conscience begins to counsel him and health becomes a worry, but it is only at sixty that he thinks of mending his ways.[3] The author of the early-fifteenth-century *Ratis Raving* puts the beginning of adulthood and reason at thirty and regards this period as the prime of life.[4] None of the learned literature suggests an early entry into adulthood for males, and most of the literature ignores females entirely.

Legal prescriptions, as we have seen, had their own puzzles and ambiguities, speaking more about exit from childhood protections than about entry into adult privilege. Criminal law, canon law, and taxation set twelve to fourteen as the age of entrance into legal liabilities. Men were not eligible to be called up for the king's army until the age of sixteen. The period of eligibility lasted to sixty, perhaps indicating that the king liked a mature army. London's inheritance laws put the age of majority at twenty-one for males and for unmarried females. Married females had to be at least sixteen to eighteen, with a husband who was twenty-one or older, before they could inherit.[5]

The laws, however, did not necessarily indicate practice. It would seem that the inheritance laws at least would be straightforward, but in fact they were open to interpretation. Although the vast majority of the cases read that a youth, having obtained "full age," could inherit, some questioned either the age or the suitability of the individual to inherit. Sometimes the problem was simply one of proving that the heir was indeed twenty-one, as he claimed. To do this, he might, as Thomas Seint John did, call on his original network of nurse, neighbor, priest, and spiritual kin to attest to his age. Other times, the mayor, chamberlain, and aldermen judged with their own eyes the probable age of the heir. Thus in one case, the mayor "adjudged by examination" that a young man was able of body and awarded him his inheritance, even though he was only nineteen. Emota, daughter of Robert Foundour, was "judged capable" at eighteen and given her inheritance. Extenuating circumstances, such as the death of a master, might encourage early inheritance. When John Cornwalle died, his apprentice had four more years of his contract left. The widow was not planning to carry on the business. An agreement was reached that allowed the apprentice to inherit and to set up his own shop. The "good men" who knew the youth from London Bridge, where he lived, testified that he had the character and the ability to manage his own affairs.

The mayor and the aldermen, however, might decide that a youth did not have the character to manage his own affairs. In the case of an idiot, such as Celia, daughter of Geoffrey Parker, a guardian would continue to administer her estate because "she could not live on her own." She would remain a perpetual child.[6] William, son of John Drew, a grocer, on the other hand, came of age in 1420, but the mayor and the aldermen said that it appeared "that he was not as yet of discretion to have the whole [estate] entrusted to him. When he appeared to have better control over himself," he could have the remainder. A year later, he got it.[7]

The age of inheritance for men kept creeping up during the fifteenth century. Thus among orphans, the age of inheritance began to rise to over twenty-one, with twenty-four becoming an alternative age of majority. Throughout the fourteenth century, the median age at which young males could inherit was twenty and a half years, but in the fifteenth century, it went up to twenty-five and a half years. For instance, Robert, son of Robert Richard, was told that he could not inherit until he was twenty-four and had completed his apprenticeship. George, son and heir of William Coumbys, got his inheritance when he "attained the age of twenty-four."[8] Of the 217 orphans who lived to maturity and who can be traced through the Letter Books, 70 terminated their wardship by reaching the age of inheritance, whatever that age might be. Twenty-nine percent inherited upon finishing apprenticeship, and 1 percent went into the Church and inherited then.

The lengthening of the term of apprenticeship and the "bachelor" system delayed entry into adulthood, thus paralleling the rising age of majority. In the fourteenth century, if a young man entered apprenticeship at fourteen, he would be twenty-one when he completed the seven-year contract. But even in the early fourteenth century, about one-quarter of the apprentices served longer than the standard seven years, thus delaying their entry into adulthood. By the fifteenth century, the age of entry had risen to between sixteen and eighteen, and the term of apprenticeship had been made longer. In 1403, the Goldsmiths fixed the term of apprenticeship at ten years, but they reduced it to seven years with the payment of 10 marks. In fact, the average length of time served was 10.6 years. Other guilds had similar rules.[9] Apprentices were delayed in their exit from the adolescent state and were not able to marry or become masters and citizens until their apprenticeships were completed. Furthermore, in the fifteenth century, some guilds required an apprentice to serve his master for an additional one to three years after the end of his apprenticeship term before he could become eligible for citizenship.[10] The delay of entry into adulthood was quite deliberate. The Grocers' guild in 1490 made apprenticeships ten years long and specified that no one should come out of apprenticeship until he was twenty-five or twenty-six.[11]

The three-tiered system of guild membership, as we observed in Chapter 10, gave masters continued control over yeomen's behavior.

When Robert Careswell wanted to become a shopholder, the Mercers said that he could be sworn and entered only when "he sadly dispose him and mannerly both in his arreye and also in cutting of his here, and not go like a gallant or man of court." Robert agreed to the terms.[12]

Since women were not registered with the guilds, as their brothers and cousins were, and since their terms usually started earlier and ended sooner, the marker of their exit from adolescence was more often marriage than inheritance or entry into a profession.

Women were so seldom mentioned in the "ages of man" literature that it is a relief to find at least one analysis of the seasons of life that uses women in its description. Spring is "like a young girl adorned and resplendent before the onlookers"; in summer, "the earth becomes like a bride laden with riches and having many lovers"; autumn is "like the mature matron who has passed the years of her youth"; and winter is "like a decrepit old woman to whom death draws near."[13] This description is a classic case of "What's wrong with this picture?" It is drawn from a male perspective, of course, but a comparison with descriptions of manhood is instructive. Women, in this scheme, have no innocent period of play and blunder in childhood, but are silent objects of visual observation that presumes an audience of consumers. When they move into the period of what would be adolescent irresponsibility and sexuality for males, maidens become the object of acquisition, with some hint that there are many consumers. Whereas men are pictured as reaching the prime of their lives in autumn, women are on the decline—matrons with no qualities other than being past youth. In old age, at last, there is some equality; perhaps the woman even comes off a bit better. She is not depicted as becoming cantankerous and avaricious, but is simply a useless object awaiting death.

Women's role is passive throughout the description. Women's value is sexual; when a woman's reproductive and entertainment capacities pass, life simply lingers on. No mention is made of childbearing or rearing or of the potentially puissant roles that a matron or widow may play in family affairs. The woman is an object of lust and of possession (all the better if property is attached).

As with the male prescriptive literature, we must question the validity of this picture for real women. We have already found that young girls in medieval London were not adorned for public viewing and delight, but stayed close to their homes and streets. Upon reaching the age of sexual desirability, women took on public roles and appearances on the basis of their social status and fortune. Many spent a period of time as apprentices or servants, thus moving from one household to another. Some, particularly heiresses, married immediately and also moved to other households. Some young women became street vendors, hucksters, or tapisters and thus had public roles. Only a few went on public display as prostitutes. Women in public were certainly objects of observation and seen as desirable commodities of lascivious consumption. For that reason, the "Good Wife" instructed her daughter to avoid eye contact and advised her not to frequent places where she might be at risk. We have seen the parents' anger when a ribald Spaniard deprived them of their daughter's services for errands.

The bridal image for summer is correct in that the object for most young women was marriage. Not all of London's young women married, but the majority were reared with that objective in mind. The question of whether or not marriage was the end of life, as this single tract suggests, must remain a question for another book.

Reality is, as usual, difficult to establish for women because of the paucity of records. But the wardship cases do provide some guidance on the standards for coming of age for London women. Inheritance and marriage were bound together strongly in London law, so that the age of marriage is an important indicator of when a woman entered adulthood. Wardship cases involving both the elite and the artisanal class give some hints about age of marriage. Although the number of cases (seventeen) is limited, the clear cluster is around age nineteen.[14] We know that Margery Kempe, a resident of Lynn, married at twenty,[15] so London data seem to be in accord with her experience. Since, on the whole, London men did not marry until they had completed apprenticeship and established their own shops, in the fifteenth century the age disparity between men and women of the artisanal and merchant classes marrying for the first time could be as great as ten years.

The female orphans studied, of course, were the daughters of citizens, and thus they usually had property that they would inherit at marriage. The value of orphans' inheritances, as we have seen in Chapter 6, increased over the course of the fourteenth and fifteenth centuries, so that these girls were very desirable marriage partners. For this reason, they may have married at a younger age than nonorphans. They also marked their exit from adolescence through marriage. Of the 193 female orphans for whom there is evidence for termination of wardship (other than death), 159, or 82 percent, married.[16] None of the men were described as having received their inheritance upon marriage.

The process for claiming an orphan's inheritance required the husband and wife to appear before the mayor and the chamberlain in order for the husband to claim his wife's inheritance. Husbands with very young wives could not claim the inheritance. Thus Dionisia, daughter of John de Hatfield, was fourteen and a half years old and already married to a draper, but she was told that she could not inherit until she was sixteen.[17]

Young women with wealthy parents still alive married even earlier. Among the merchant class, marriage occurred for girls at age seventeen or younger.[18] The bride received the bulk of her claim to family property through a dowry at the time of her marriage and would have no need of a prolonged apprenticeship or period of service. The age of marriage among the upper strata of Londoners, therefore, probably resembled that of the nobility and the gentry in the countryside. Indeed, upper-class girls married members of either the elite guilds or the gentry.

Women of servant status, however, probably married somewhat later. Although they might have had some household goods with which to form a dowry, the money they earned for wages was a crucial augmentation. We might expect, therefore, that they would have been in their mid-twenties before they married. Since they married similarly situated male servants or yeoman, the age disparity between husband and wife probably was not great. Because friends and family were contributing relatively little to these marriages, the couple probably had greater freedom to select their own partners. Masters, however, often retained the right of approval and even arrangement of marriages, as we shall see.[19]

Receiving one's inheritance was, like marriage, a marker of exit from adolescence. Because women received their inheritances at marriage, they entered the adult world sooner than their brothers. Those female orphans whose age can be determined inherited, on average, at eighteen and a half years throughout the fourteenth and fifteenth centuries. Entry into a nunnery could prompt an early inheritance. Thus Alice, daughter of John Crichefeld, became a nun at Haliwell at age fifteen and a half, and her prioress went with her to claim the inheritance. Isabel, daughter of Robert Westmelne, was put into the guardianship of the prioress and could decide at fourteen whether she would be a nun or take her inheritance as a lay person.[20] Only 5 percent of the female orphans exited from adolescence by taking up a religious life. Sixteen percent of the female orphans inherited because they came of age. To indicate the variability in the age of maturation, the age range for female orphans coming of age was from fifteen to twenty-one.[21] Only 5 percent inherited by completing an apprenticeship.

Ceremonies for Coming of Age

Not only did a change of status occur with the transition to adulthood, but the society had some rituals and ceremonies that marked the step over the threshold into the adult world. Although not everyone participated in these ceremonies, the rituals were important to London life.

For those fortunate young men who entered the full adult roles of guild membership, the swearing of ceremonial oaths in the guildhall and the donning of the livery marked the rite of passage that moved the initiate out of the adolescent role and into adult power.[22] Again, females were not part of this transition. They were not registered when they became apprentices and did not join a guild when they completed their training. If they gained guild membership, it was through their husbands, not through their own induction. Their access thus came through a sexual bond, not through an acquired craft skill.

Marriage was a more universal ceremony, although at its most basic it was canonically valid for a man and woman simply to agree to be married. The Church's acceptance of free consent in marriage made it possible to contract legal marriage by this simple expedient. No ceremony, not even consummation, was necessary. We shall come across a number of such marriage arrangements and shall also see the complications that such a rudimentary but binding agreement could cause for the parties involved. Where high status and wealth were at issue, however, custom dictated gifts to the prospective bride, negotiations with the parents for a marriage contract involving dower and dowry, and a public declaration of the contract before the church doors.[23]

Although rituals associated with marriage were then, as now, more geared to the bride than the groom, the whole process was one of stylized posturing for all parties involved. The first step was identifying a potential spouse. Not surprisingly, networks of family and friends once again played a role, as they had in identifying apprentices and servants. In addition, gossip about the wealth of an orphan, the dowry provisions left to a young heiress in a will, and the elevation of a young man to the livery, as well as the sudden news about the death of a citizen and the availability of a young widow, made the rounds of streets, taverns, and dinner tables. Then there were the baser ways of finding a spouse—tricking a man or woman into sexual compromise or seductions with promises of marriage. Casual meetings at taverns, service together in a household, promises to return to a village sweetheart, service with a brother of a nubile female—all could produce marriages. With so many networks available, it is surprising to find that matchmakers also flourished. The entrées into the marriage market were so diverse that it is difficult to know where to start in this complicated game. No doubt the players considered all options.

Although love matches, in which the man and the woman allowed their emotions to dictate union regardless of property considerations, did occur, even servant couples arranging their own marriages thought of dowry and dower, as well as attraction. Attitudes toward marriage are cultural, and contemporary Western notions about how to find an appropriate marriage partner are vastly different from medieval ideas. Only the rich, such as the man who married Thomasine Bonaventure, or the poor, who could not hope to better their lot by marriage, could afford to marry without a negotiated settlement. Only the rich, the poor, and the foolish could marry for love or sexual attraction alone.

Leaving "falling in love" out of the equation, the best place to begin is with the parents, guardians, or others who had some claim to arrange a marriage. Marriage planning could begin very early. We have seen that one form of abuse of wardship was for a man with a child to marry off to look for a recently widowed mother with an orphan of the opposite sex. He would then marry the mother and arrange a marriage between his off-spring and hers, thereby acquiring the use of both the mother's inheritance and the child's until the child came of age. The arrangement was illegal because only the mayor could consent to the marriage of citizens' orphans, and it was morally and religiously repugnant because the marriages often occurred betweeen very young children who, since their parents were married, were related by a close bond of affinity that precluded marriage.

The reality and motivation of such plotting, however, come out clearly in one of the letters preserved in the mayors' papers. Geoffrey Boner

> had three daughters, to wit, Isabel, Agnes, and Alice, and that in order to marry the said Isabel befittingly, the said Geoffrey had bought the ward and marriage of one John Hockele, who had lands and tenements in London to the value of 16 marks by the year from one Thomas of London, clerk, for which he paid 40 marks and a hanape of maser worth 13s. 4d., the said Isabel being at that time 16 years of age; and that the said John and Isabel were married and the said Geoffrey and Ellen [his wife] had given them goods and chattels to the value of £9 together with rents and tenements.

Isabel, "thus advanced," then wanted to deprive her sisters of an inheritance in London, but London custom forbade her to be so grasping. As the first married sister, she could have only her usual claim to the family fortune and could make no other claim unless the first had been a partial one.[24] She had come by her grasping nature honestly, learning from her father, who had thought so far ahead in seizing an opportunity for purchasing a wardship.

Arrangement of marriage contracts was business in medieval London and it was for that reason and to avoid a misalliance for a citizen's child (marriage below one's social rank) that the mayor kept a monopoly over orphans' marriage arrangements. When John Hurlebatie married Joan, daughter of Nicholas Aghton, an alderman, without a license from the mayor, those who had aided him in defying the mayor's rights suffered severe financial punishment. The two witnesses, a merchant and a notary public, were committed to prison until they paid a fine set by the mayor. The notary public pleaded ignorance, and his fine was commuted from £20 to 20s. But the merchant, who knew and had sworn to the civic laws, was fined the full amount and put out of his citizenship. Finally, the groom paid £40, which was considered the commission on the marriage. But what of the offended Joan? Her marriage was valid. And the offended mayor? He was richer by £40.[25]

From a ward's point of view, the arranged marriage could be bewildering or irritating, depending on the age and maturity of the person involved. A fourteen-year-old girl had little recourse for complaint if her guardians and the mayor arranged her marriage. She could not easily go to the church court, which would be the most appropriate venue for complaint about a forced marriage. Abuses could also arise over the sale of the right to arrange the marriage. Again, a young woman had little recourse in this situation. John Welyngton, a young man, petitioned the Chancellor about the sale of his marriage by William Brekspere of London for £20. The rights over his marriage were sold for that amount, in addition to £24 accruing from the residue of the sale.[26]

The prices that the offended young man complained of represented market value for matchmakers. Whatever role females may have had in informal matchmaking, women are not named in the suits over bonds for arranging marriages. The type of contract is laid out in a number of cases that came before the Chancellor. For instance, Alexander Brounyng complained that John Lawley had asked him to "labor for his part in arranging a marriage with Elizabeth Rothwell, his aunt." If the marriage took place, he was to receive £40 for his "laboring." Alexander claimed that he had brought about the marriage, but John had refused to pay. Another man said that the executors of the will of William Whetenale, a London grocer, had asked him to negotiate a marriage settlement between the deceased's son and the daughter of another man. He claimed a successful contract for the agreed price of £20, but had not been paid. Expenses were involved in these third-party wooings, whether for Cyrano de Bergerac–type balcony pleas or for wining and dining the guardian of the girl. One matchmaker said that he was to get a £20 commission, but that his costs had been 26s. 8d., so that he was owed £30. In a more complicated case, a clerk arranged a marriage for £23. He seems to have been somewhat scrupulous about the usury laws and said that he only wanted the goldsmith groom to buy some plate from him. The plate, in fact, was worth only £14. Meanwhile, the bride died, but the groom had paid the full £23 and so had a shortfall.[27]

Who undertook to be a matchmaker and contract arranger? We have seen a kinsman, the mayor, anyone who could buy the rights to sell the marriage, and clergymen all take on this role. The fee seems to have been pegged, in a rough way, to the value of the estate. While £20 was the going rate, the fee could be higher if the marriage was worth more.

Although free consent meant that a person could not be compelled into marriage, charges of force sometimes appeared. One wonders how much control over marriage arrangements a minor might have had in practice. A mother who had apparently been eager for her daughter to marry a certain man swore that her daughter had not been raped or abducted, but had freely married on Christmas Eve 1436. Another ploy to force marriage was for an employer or a kinsman to claim that a male servant had seduced a female servant in the household and had promised to marry the woman or should be made to marry her. For instance, William Gerardson, who was a Dutch beer brewer, had left the employment of his former master a year earlier, but was now being exhorted by his former master to marry a woman who was a servant in the house. To force the issue, the master was suing him for £20 in damages for having corrupted the servant. The brewer had to either pay or marry her.[28]

Premarital fornication, as opposed to seduction, appears in the church court records, as in the case of William Olyner, a baker, who was accused of having fornicated with Alice "that he schulde have to his wife." In these cases, when the marriage was arranged anyway, the Church simply hastened the formal proceedings.[29]

Masters and kin could thwart marriages as well as encourage them. A prospective groom petitioned the Chancellor, saying that Elizabeth Kesten was his "well willer and lover" and he wanted to marry her, but her brother was not his "well willer" and had him put into prison, where he was fettered and held without bail. In another case, William Bumpsted, a mercer, complained that three years earlier, he had made a marriage contract with Margaret Baker, who was living in the house of Henry Bumpsted (perhaps as a ward or servant). The executors of her father's will, a clerk and a mercer, objected to the marriage and took her away from Henry's house and had William put in prison for ten weeks. The case was to go to the Archbishop of Canterbury, but the executors used their influence to get it sent to Rome. The delay would be lengthy. Now William was worried that his kinsman would be put in prison on a trumped-up debt charge.[30]

Apprenticeship contracts, of course, also interfered with marriage arrangements. Apprentices could not marry during their apprenticeships. If they did, masters could sue for trespass and breach of covenant.[31] Anthony Pontisbury, whom we met earlier, ran into this problem when he made his moving plea about marrying for love.

The Church's free-consent clause led to many misunderstandings about prior contracts for marriage. Someone from a young person's past could appear to claim that the marriage the person was about to make could not occur because of a previous marriage contract. Robert Baynet of Royston in Cambridgeshire had apprenticed as a haberdasher to John King in London. He returned to his native town and contracted for a marriage. While Robert was on a business trip to London, a servant of his former master claimed that he had made a contract to marry her while he was still an apprentice. The master backed up the servant and had Robert arrested. Robert petitioned the Chancellor from prison, saying that the matter should be handled in a spiritual court and that he did not wish to marry the servant because of the spiritual and material damage it would do to him.[32]

Regardless of who undertook the marriage arrangements, free consent meant that some courtship and wooing would be involved. The fierceness of the competition in the marriage market is revealed in the Cely letters. As the Celys' biographer observed: "Matchmaking was an enormously serious business for the parties and their relations, and a favorite sport for those less directly involved in the outcome."[33] George Cely, a mercer and stapler, competed for the hand of Margery, widow of Edmund Rygon. She was a second wife, young and childless, and had been made chief executor of Edmund's estate, with the bulk of his property at her disposal for the good of his soul. Like the Celys, Rygon had been a stapler and owned property in Calais. Here was the classic opportunity to keep the considerable wealth within the select group of Staplers. George had competition in his wooing. William Cely wrote in 1484 that a maternal relative of Margery's had arrived in Calais, apparently on a reconnaissance mission for the family, to find out what George's prospects were:

> [I]t is said here by many persons here how that ye be sure [contracted] to her. With the which, sir, I am well content and right glad thereof. And sir, all those here that knoweth you, both merchants and soldiers, commend you greatly, saying "if that gentlewoman should be worth double that she is ye were worthy to have her." And as for making of search of your dealing here, I trow there is no man that maketh any. If they do, they need go no farther than the books in the treasury, where they may find that your sales made within less than this year amounts above 2,000 *li. stg.*, where that the person that laboured for to 'a be afore you, he and his brother had not in this town this twelve months the one half of that.

George not only had to prove his business success, but also had to provide an attractive dower for the young widow Rygon and to woo her with precious gifts. Dower, of course, was real estate, and he bought more than

£485 worth at this period, along with jewels, plate, and a costly ring. Later, his sister-in-law was to claim that he spent more than his proper share of the patrimony that he had inherited with his brother, Richard, her husband. In addition, he bore the cost of the wedding feasts.[34]

Gifts were a preliminary to less prestigious marriages as well. Margaret Swan and Humfrey Charyet, an apprentice to a goldsmith, had made a marriage contract with the master's consent. "Humfrey at diverse times delivered to Margaret certain tokens," and she had given tokens to him as well. When Humfrey unfortunately died, the master wanted the tokens back, claiming that they were worth £26, whereas Margaret said that they were not above 10s. in value.[35] The tokens were usually jewelry, rings, and other such luxury items.

Much of young women's training and work had been preparation for courtship and marriage. The "Good Wife" was full of advice for her daughter on the subject of marrying. She was concerned that her daughter would get a bad reputation if she went to the wrong places or got drunk, but she was also concerned that the daughter might form a marriage without parental negotiations. She advised her daughter not to speak to a man in the street but simply to greet him and walk on, "lest he by his villainy should tempt thy heart." Likewise, she warned against taking presents: "For with gifts may men soon women overcome," even though the women be made of steel or stone. "Bound forsooth is she / That of any man takes fee." Considering all the risks, her final advice was to marry off daughters quickly:

> And look to thy daughters that none of them be lorn;
> From the very time that they are of thee born,
> Busy thyself and gather fast for their marriage
> And give them to spousing, as soon as they be of age.

Even with good advice, "maidens be fair and amiable / but in their love full unstable."[36]

The message was that daughters were to be groomed to make good marriages, to avoid the risks of unsuitable contracts, and to start accumulating a good dowry. Curiously, the "Wise Man" taught his son that in selecting a wife, he should look for one who was "meek, courteous, and prudent, even though poor." He should not put money first in his considerations.[37] Most fathers and sons, however, seemed very interested in the size of the dowry.

Daughters normally got their portion of inheritance on their marriage. The dowry was sometimes set in wills, or, if the father or mother was still alive at the time the marriage terms were being worked out, it could be negotiated. The amount, of course, depended on the wealth of the family and the number of siblings for whom provision had to be made. Robert de Convers, for instance, left property to his sons and daughters. Sibil, the eldest, was to have a thirty-year lease of a tenement in St. Dunstan. Should Sibil die, the property was to go to the younger daughter, Katherine, for her dowry. In addition, Katherine was to get a tenement after the death of her mother. The inequality of the dowries provided for multiple daughters was a feature of many wills. One man gave his eldest daughter rents by way of dowry, and the second daughter, 20 marks and feather beds, counterpanes, sheets, and towels. The third daughter received only 10 marks.[38] That dowries were ever in the minds of fathers is apparent in a bad joke that a mayor made in 1240. The king admitted him to the office, and he took his oath. The provision was that the king would restore all the honors and privileges to the mayor, but not the £40 that mayors had previously received from the city. Mayor Bat had the bad sense to quip: "Alas! my Lord, out of all this I might have found a marriage portion to give my daughter." The king accepted his resignation on the spot.[39]

Money and rents from tenements were the most common dowry items mentioned. They might come from other relatives and friends, in addition to the immediate family. Some families seemed to subscribe to a set of traditional gifts as well as money. Emma, who was twice a widow, dwelt lovingly on the heirlooms that had been her dowry and on those she had acquired. She left her daughter Christine "a piece of silver with a silver cover, 6 silver spoons and a coverlet and tester formerly belonging to your father, and a pair of sheets." Her granddaughter received a similar set of possessions: a piece of silver with a cover, six silver spoons, a white coverlet and tester, and a pair of sheets. "If she be old enough to marry, I leave her those goods my parents gave me when I married." Richard Skeet, a wealthy brewer, set his daughter's dowry at 80 marks, but also gave her a piece of silver with a silver lid, six silver spoons, a mazer bound with silver, two of his best beds with sheets, five brass pots, a napkin, and a towel.[40] In other words, some traditional pieces of silver, perhaps heirlooms, silver spoons, bedding, and some valuable kitchen equipment were all part of the traditional dowry, in addition to the money. Perhaps these valuable items were kept in a dowry chest.

So far, we have discussed only those fortunate young women who had parents, friends, and other kin who provided dowry for them. A larger group of London maidens did not have this advantage. These women, as we have seen, sought apprenticeship or service contracts as a way of accumulating skills and capital so that they could pay their own dowry. So important was a dowry in forming an honorable marriage that some Londoners, such as the brewer John Piken, left bequests of money to be distributed to "poor maidens of good name and to lame and blind persons" toward their marriages.[41]

As the gossip and gifts circulated and the parties became "well willers" toward each other, it was time for the prospective bride's family and friends to negotiate with the groom's to draw up a contract. The arrangements specified the value of the dowry and the dower and perhaps gave some indication of the living arrangements for the couple. The wife's contribution, coming largely in the form of cash and goods, helped to establish the new household and business. The dower, which the husband pledged to the wife, was her security in widowhood and was usually given in land, rents, and other real estate.[42] It guaranteed not only her support, should she outlive her husband, but also that of any children from the union. As Chapter 6 indicates, widows were usually charged with rearing the children.

The contract established a partnership marriage. While the partners might not be equal in the manipulation of the funds after marriage, their contributions toward the marriage were usually fairly equal. An example helps to understand how the formula was made:

> Sir John de Lovetot, Sr. [guardian of the bride] conveys to Robert de Bassinge marriage of Margaret, daughter and hieress of Thomas, son of Ralph de Normanville, and the guardianship of all lands and tenements coming to her on the decease of her said father and of Ralph her uncle, together with advowson of the church [in Kent] excepting dower of her mother. Robert is to pay John 200 *li*. in installments. The sum of 200 marks to be in respite, to be paid in the event of the said Margaret living beyond the term of 4 years or dying within the term and leaving issue. Robert covenants to allow his son, who is about to marry Margaret, to endow her with land worth 20*s*. a year.[43]

In this complicated case, a gentry-class girl, perhaps twelve to fourteen, married a young Londoner, probably also a minor. She was the heiress of both her father and her uncle and had claim to considerable property in Kent. The marriage contract arranged for the transfer of not only her land, but also her wardship. The groom's father paid a considerable sum for this valuable young girl. The agreement, however, gave a 200-mark respite if Margaret survived to come of age in four years or if she died in that term but had a child by Robert's son. In turn, Robert allowed his son to promise a dower of lands and tenements that would produce 20*s*. a year. When the marriage partners were so young, it was common to make an agreement about supporting them.[44]

Marriage contracts must often have been written, but London did not have a strong notarial tradition with registers of private transactions, so we know about these contracts from disputes over them rather than from examples of actual agreements.[45] Whether written or oral, the contractual process was a formal ritual. It was carried out at the house of one of the responsible parties. Present were the prospective groom, his witnesses and friends, and the bride's witnesses and friends. The presence of the bride is not specified in existing records unless she was making her own contract. Some naive grooms said they had set up the terms with "bare promises" and not with sureties who would vouch for the contract. Such a practice was obviously not desirable for any contract, let alone one for marriage.[46]

The ceremonies moved from the privacy of the home to the public arena with the reading of the banns at the church door. Several considerations dictated the reading of the banns. First, the reading was a public proclamation on three successive Sundays that two people and their fortunes were about to be united. It was a ceremony for an oral society that would "hear and remember." Second, since legal marriages could be contracted clandestinely, the public reading was a way to prevent bigamy. Other claimants could come forward to voice their objections to the proposed marriage. Not everyone, of course, had the banns read, but people with considerable property usually wished to advertise their marriages in order to bring in the public as witnesses and to inform them of a new household, new landlords, and new business.[47]

The next ritual of the marriage ceremony was also a public one, again occurring at the church door. The marriage contract was recited or read, and the couple was then married. Witnesses remembered this event and could recite the terms and date years later when the bride, now a widow, claimed her dower, as she had received it, at the church door.[48]

Ritual words solemnized the marriage. The vows have a familiar ring, but the woman's is explicit about the sexual duty of marriage:

MAN: I take the N. to be my wedded wif, to haue and to holde, fro this day forwarde, for bettere for wors, for richere for pourer in sycknesse and in hele, tyl dethe us departe, if holy chyrche it woll ordeyne, and thereto y plight the my trouthe.

WOMAN: I take the N. to my wedded housbonde, to haue and to holde, fro this day forwarde, for better for wors, for richer for pourer in sicknesse and in hele, to be bonere and boxom, in bedde and atte bord, tyl dethe us departe, if holy chyrche it wol ordeyne, and therto I plight the my trouthe.

The rings were then blessed and exchanged with the words "with this ring I thee wed and with my body I thee Honor." The priests encouraged the wedding party to step inside for a wedding Mass as a ceremonial addition, but it was not necessary for the legality of the ceremony. Of course, no ceremony at all was required for a clandestine marriage to be valid, and, no doubt, many poorer couples simply dispensed with the formalities altogether.[49]

An elaborate feast followed a wedding involving the elite. As usual, advice books have full descriptions of suggested menus to guide those who have not given such a dinner before or who could not secure a servant or cook who had.[50] Failing a private revel, the tavern would do quite well. Moralists warned that "marriages be decently celebrated, with reverence, not with laughter and ribaldry, not in taverns or at public drinkings and feastings."[51] If there was a ceremony for seeing the couple to their marriage bed and a successful consummation of the union, the London records are coy and quiet about it.

Other Experiences that Induced Sadness and Wiseness

As is usual with contracts, particularly those involving marriage, where the emotions of bride, groom, and family are all at a fever pitch, promises made at the church door could not be kept in reality. Grooms came before the courts with many a complaint that they were not given the bride's dowry. Pathetically claiming that they had agreed to the contract and had gotten married "according to holy church," they could not now collect the promised amount. One complained that the wife's mother would not give up a bequest; another that the dowry was to be paid out of a debt owed to the father and that the debtor would not pay; another that the father had died and the brother was reluctant to pay; yet another that he had been promised a share in a tavern, but the father-in-law would not give it to him. What is the use of cautioning that the groom should not have rushed into the marriage?[52] Brides were equally guilty of being blind to promises. The disputed dower cases that arose at widowhood reveal the disappointed hopes of brides. Because the necessity for claiming the dower might not arise until years after the marriage, a wife would not be aware that promised tenements and rents did not belong to her husband on the day that he endowed her with them at the church door.[53] There is nothing like a failed marriage contract to made one "sad and wise."

One of the reasons that orphans were so desirable as marriage partners was that the money and property were already in the hands of the mayor and the aldermen. If city officials did not actually hold the property, they would undertake to get it back even if they had to go to law to do so. Thus there were fewer complications in arranging such a marriage. Entry after entry in the Letter Books attest to the smooth transition of inheritances.[54] Such inheritances were not negotiable, as were dowries; one knew with certainty what they included. Although there was no room to maneuver for an increase in dower or dowry, there was also no risk of disappointment. Thus given the increasing value of orphans' inheritances in the fifteenth century and the risks of accepting a false contract in a marriage involving a nonorphan, the orphans were very desirable marriage partners indeed. The same was true of widows, for their portion was also known, even if it was for the widows' lifetime use only.[55]

Late medieval London society did not have universal ceremonies that moved all adolescents from that status to adulthood. The border between the two life stages was ragged and even disputed. While clear markers such as inheritance, marriage, entry into business, and establishment of an independent household marked a transition for many of London's youth, even these markers could be questioned. Some young people chose not to marry. They might continue in service or enter into their own businesses as single people. Single women could carry on business as a dressmaker, an embroiderer, a silkworker, a regrator, or a victualer without being married or entering a trade. A young man could enter the yeomanry of a company, set up a shop, or hire himself out as a laborer without marrying. London society accepted these people as adults, but imposed limitations on their access to full adult rights. They became second-class adults, rather than simply overgrown and aged adolescents. Some, however, through the continued dependence of being servants, remained in a semiadolescent category and carried the title of "boy" or "girl" far into their biologically mature years. Without marked transitions, their status remained ambiguous.

"John Borell, Who Tried to Live Happily Ever After as a Sad and Wise Man"[56]

John Borell was one of the most foolish among the "bachelor" wax chandlers. He was not rebellious to his master, but he was frivolous and vain. He favored the short hairstyle of the young nobles, and his tunic was so short that it showed off his finely stockinged leg and a good bit more as well. His master was in despair. John was spending his money on finery, wine, and wenches. In vain he expostulated about becoming sad and wise, about his father's ambitions for him, about the necessity of saving toward a shop and marriage. John insisted that his nights were his own. Most of all, his master was concerned about the women John entertained. No use preaching to the young man, but John could end up making some drunken declaration that one of the girls would interpret as marriage. Worst of all, he was now seeing Maud Clerk, the servant of Sir Thomas

Jeffrey. Father Jeffrey was not only a priest but also proctor of the Court of Arches, the ecclesiastical court that heard, among other matters, prior contract cases. Rumors about Father Jeffrey's extortion practices were making the rounds. He encouraged female "servants" to become intimate with up-and-coming citizens. Then when these fine young men set up shop and arranged good marriages, he threatened them with prosecution for prior contract in the Court of Arches. A young man who had set a wedding date would pay a considerable amount of money to Father Jeffrey to hush him and the woman up.

John thought that Maud was worth the risk. He had never met anyone with quite her lust for life. She dressed as well as he did, buying her finery from fripperers. She boasted of being brought up on charges of violating the sumptuary legislation because she wore fur far above her rank in society. She said that simple lamb pelts made her itchy and that she had to wear something sleeker next to her skin to keep warm. Knowing her lovely flesh, John was convinced. She loved going across the river to see the bear baiting. It excited her, and she would agree to spend a wild evening at the stews before heading home. John should have known that her service position was unusual. The girls in his master's house were not allowed to roam about and certainly would not have thought of dressing the way she did. Showed what bores they were.

But John's life changed with his father's death. In a guilty wave of filial piety, he recalled how his father had made extensive inquiries to find the right master for his younger son in London and how they had come to London together and signed the apprenticeship contract. It had cost his father a great deal of money. Now, twelve years later, he had become a London citizen, but he had let down the old man. He had not seen his father again after he came to London, but the old man had always asked friends or relatives who were going to the city to look him up with a greeting to make sure that he was treated well and was learning his trade. Now his father was dead. John had always meant to go back to visit, but he never had. With the death, he inherited a modest property in the country and enough money to set up his own shop. Just like the old man; he thought of everything. His master reminded him that unless he let his hair grow and wore more seemly clothing, he could not set up shop or be admitted to the Wax Chandlers' guild. John was ready to comply.

After a year in business, John was able to rent the chambers and solar above his shop, so that he could live comfortably and keep a servant. Being twenty-eight and established, he could now think of making a suitable marriage to a young woman with a dowry. Maud, of course, was out of the question. She was hardly suitable for his present respectable status. Besides, he had heard that she had married a fellow named Bowys. He talked to his master and kin about making a suitable match. Either a widow with a dower or a citizen's orphan with an inheritance would be desirable, but his country kin might know of a suitable young woman with an inheritance who would like to marry into the city. He hoped to accomplish his objectives without going to a matchmaker, although one quickly picked up the gossip and approached him at St. Paul's, saying that for £20 he would find John a wife. It was his master, however, who found the perfect bride. She was the nineteen-year-old daughter of his sister. The young woman was the orphan of a wax chandler and had just completed an apprenticeship in silkworking. Her fortune was not great, £40 plus some silver heirlooms and household items, but he could not offer an extensive dower either. Since her father was a wax chandler, the guild would approve of the marriage, and if the guild approved, so would the mayor. The bride could continue her silkworking after they were married and bring in extra cash to the household.

What was it that the "Wise Man" had taught his son? Riches should not be the first consideration in selecting a wife, but rather the woman's behavior and reputation. Leticia certainly had a good reputation for her skill at silkworking. But would she be interested in him? His first thought was to dig into the bottom of his chest and pull out his old courting outfits. He could tell from the look on his servant's face that the effect was not what it used to be; besides, the tunic and jacket were unaccountably tight across the middle. He directed the servant to sell them immediately. Instead, he put on what he called his "sad and wise" clothing, but took care to wear a silver girdle and a fine ring. He then stopped in Cheapside and looked at suitable tokens to take to her. The first gift should be modest, perhaps a simple silver cross, a rosary, or a ring with enamelwork, rather than jewels.

Leticia, meanwhile, had heard his praises sung by her uncle, who dwelled on what an exemplary apprentice John had been, what a good family he had come from, how nice all his kin were. He pointed out the advantages of the country property, saying that if the plague got bad, Leticia would have a place to retreat with the children. He said little about John's two years as a bachelor. She was too young at the time to have heard any rumors, and John had proved himself completely amended in his behavior. Now she was about to meet him for the first time in the hall of her uncle's house. She knew all about how she would behave—keep her eyes down, appear meek, refuse the proffered token, have a good example of her silkwork by her to work on, and observe him well. She could refuse him, although her uncle might be somewhat put out. But if he did not suit her, she would. With her skills, she could even earn a living as a single woman trader. She knew other women who did and who never married.

But she liked John. He had a bit of sparkle about him that suggested something more spirited than the average London businessman. His ring and girdle showed excellent taste. He appreciated the high quality of her silkwork and admired the coral and gold beads she was wearing. This led easily to a conversation about families and heirlooms. He described his country house as modest and comfortable. He had brought his portion of the family silver and the old weapons to London to decorate the walls of his chambers. He spoke about his plan to commission a Flemish painter to do a wall hanging of Job for his main chamber. After some wine and cakes, he left, feeling much too embarrassed to offer her the rather simple token he had bought. He should really do better for someone with her tastes.

The next meeting was an agreeable one over dinner in her uncle's hall. He presented her with a pearl ring. She accepted and gave him some costard apples tied up in a beautiful silk napkin. He left with a confidence that she was his well willer and that he and his old master could begin discussing the terms of the marriage contract. The exchange of gifts continued, and the terms were arranged and drawn up to be signed by John and his witnesses. He would get her dowry, but she would retain rights over her heirlooms, clothing, and household goods. He promised one-third of his property should he predecease her. Since she was a Londoner, her portion would be the shop and his tenement. Should they have children, the property in the country would be theirs outright, along with the shops and tenement after Leticia died.

The wedding date was set. John sent to the country to invite his friends and kin to come for the wedding at St. Paul's and the feast at his former master's house afterward. He had bought his bride a beautiful gold ring set with rubies and had his house cleaned and fresh rushes and herbs put on the floors. Then, the Wednesday before John's wedding, Sir Thomas Jeffrey appeared and said that John would have to go to the Court of Canterbury because Sir Thomas had evidence that John had a prior contract with Maud. John was furious. He went to the court, but defied it to show anything in writing to prove that he had a prior contract. He also said that it was well known that Maud had done the same thing to that fellow Bowys, saying that she had a contract with him. Maud and the priest said they did have writings, they just had not brought them. The court ordered them to produce the writings. Then, the Saturday before his wedding, the very day before it, John found Sir Thomas in St. Paul's and told him that Maud had no evidence and "in good conscience not to stand in the way of his marriage." The priest said that he would not cause any more problems if John paid him something. He suggested clothing at first, and then said that £20 would be appropriate but at least 6 marks would be necessary. John called him an extortionist and a false priest, but what was he to do? His friends were all assembled, and the expenses of postponing the wedding would be greater than paying the bribe. Since John did not have the money at hand, he wrote out two obligations to pay Father Jeffrey 40s. on two occasions. They then went to court, and the priest affirmed that Maud had no evidence so that there was no impediment to the wedding.

But that was not the end of it, as John recounted the story: "When I was in the church with my friends on the day of my wedding, Thomas came and said there was another woman who would come and stop the wedding unless she was recompensed with money. There was no such woman but his wrongful imaginings. He said he would make no more impediment if he could have my ring. And so I was married."

Married life was more wonderful than he had imagined. Leticia came with her silkwork to sit with him when he was not waiting on customers. He had much better meals with her directing the servant. And then, bed was much cozier. He found he had no desire to get up betimes. But there were his obligations and his promise to meet Sir Thomas in a week at Holy Trinity the Little, where the false priest was to be for matins. Sir Thomas pretended to be surprised to see him and asked him what was up. John said he wanted his ring back. But Sir Thomas said that John would have to pay the other woman 20s. or have his marriage annulled. He knew full well that John would not seek an annulment; all the gossip was that the couple had spent a happy week together. Sir Thomas refused to say who the woman was or where she lived. Finally, John agreed to pay if Sir Thomas would keep the whole matter secret and would treat him well over the obligations. At first, the priest demurred, but when John threatened to tell his friends, he gave him back the ring.

John had to confess to Leticia what was happening before the gossip reached her. They had their first real fight, but finally agreed on a mutual course. John was no longer to meet with Sir Thomas alone, and he was to consult with her uncle about what to do. When the first obligation was due and Sir Thomas asked for it, John went with his neighbors to pay it. Sir Thomas, however, claimed that he had given the obligations to Maud. When they went to Maud, she said that she wanted 5 nobles and 5s. to settle. John paid and asked for the obligations. She said that they were with Sir Thomas and that she would have to borrow 13s. 4d. to get them. So in all, Maud took him for 7 nobles and 5s. and never did deliver the obligations. When John threatened to sue, Thomas took the matter up in the mayor's court. John appealed to the Chancellor, and a mediation was arranged with arbiters. John and Sir Thomas put up £20 each to abide by arbitration, but Sir Thomas continued to pursue the matter in the courts and got a judgment. This was contrary to the arbitration terms, but wily old Sir Thomas said that he was innocent and that his attorney had gone to court without consulting him. John was back as a petitioner to the Chancellor to get redress and the return of the obligations.

Leticia was most unhappy with the whole affair. Her dowry had not been much, but what an insult to waste it on that vile priest and that vicious woman! If John had been sad and wise earlier, this would not have happened. And her uncle might have told her about his lapses in the past. She felt betrayed by her own kin, who should have been looking after her interests. Shouldn't a niece have precedence in protection and affection over those bonds developed during apprenticeship? Was an apprentice to be more coddled and advanced than one's own flesh and blood? But she was stuck now. She was pregnant and could not both raise the child and keep up her silk business. Her contrite uncle had promised a bequest to the child to make up for his failings to his niece. John, of course, had become sadder and wiser during the course of the whole business; he had lost the jaunty air that had made him so attractive, in Leticia's eyes. But, then, he had pursued this whole sordid business to protect Leticia from having her marriage annulled. It was not her respectable but small dowry alone that had led to the marriage or that kept John from allowing that sleazy priest to dissolve it. Who did live happily ever after on this earth? Baby Jesus had not. There was the child in her belly to think about, including setting up the network of spiritual kin and neighbors and a modest fortune to see it through should it survive and thrive. Better a stable, loving John than having the child orphaned, as she had been.

Appendix

Table 1. Number of Children Dying During Wardship

Year	Number with known outcome	Number dead	Percentage
1309–1348	44	8	18
1349–1398	224	61	27
1399–1448	159	51	32
1449–1497	204	79	39
Total	631	199	32

Source: Letter Books (1309–1497)

Table 2. Children Appearing for the First Time in London Wardship Cases, 1309–1497: Male and Female Disparities

Year	Female	Male	Total	Percentage of disparity
1309–1348	94 (43%)	126 (57%)	220	14
1349–1398	193 (46%)	230 (54%)	423	8
1399–1408	144 (39%)	227 (61%)	371	22
1449–1397	349 (49%)	368 (51%)	717	2
Total	780 (45%)	951 (55%)	1,731	10

Note: The data in this table represent all the individuals in the data set and therefore all the children alive at the time that they entered into wardship.
Source: Letter Books (1309–1497).

Table 3. Average Age of Orphans When Entering Wardship

Year	Number of individuals with age given	Average age
1309–1333	59 of 161	7.3
1334–1358	59 of 152	8.4
1359–1383	90 of 236	10.0
1384–1408	6 of 131	7.4
1409–1433	10 of 227	12.3
1434–1458	5 of 136	11.1

Note: The numbers for the late fourteenth and fifteenth centuries are so low that they cannot be taken as statistically significant.
Source: Letter Books (1309–1458).

Table 4. Number and Percent of Children at Various Ages at the Time of Wardship

Age	1300–1349		1350–1389	
	Number	Percentage	Number	Percentage
0–3	20	20	7	6
4–6	15	15	23	20
7–9	25	25	36	31
10–12	21	21	21	18
11–15	10	10	14	12
16–20	9	9	15	13
Total	100	100	116	100

Source: Adapted from Elaine Clark, "City Orphans and Custody Laws in Medieval England," *American Journal of Legal History* 34 (1990): 177.

Table 5. Average Wealth Per Family of Orphans

Year	Amount in pounds sterling
1309–1348	80
1349–1388	416
1389–1428	810
1429–1468	901
1469–1497	280

Note: The wealth is calculated for all the children of one citizen.
Source: Letter Books (1309–1491).

Table 6. Guardian's Relationship to Orphan

Guardian	1309–1348		1350–1388		1389–1428		1429–1468	
Mother alone	76	34%	59	15%	34	11%	50	23%
Mother and step-father	38	17	56	15	107	34	53	24
Father alone	0	0	0	0	3	1	13	6
Maternal kin	11	5	15	4	4	1	2	1
Paternal kin	8	4	8	2	1	0	2	1
Elder children	3	1	1	0	3	1	0	0
Guild brother or master	19	9	85	22	87	28	49	23
Nonkin or relation-ship unknown	66	30	160	42	76	24	48	22
Total	221	100%	384	100%	315	100%	217	100%

Note: At the end of the fourteenth century, the Letter Books no longer specify who has the actual charge of the child (39 cases in 1389–1428 and 102 cases in 1429–1438). The real change in procedure appears to have occurred in the period 1457 to 1468, and after that period the guardianship of the children is unclear from the record.

Source: Letter Books (1309–1468).

Table 7. Bequests to Apprentices

Bequests	Number	Percentage
Shop	7	7
Tenements	9	9
Money	29	28
Goods	33	32
Household utensils	3	3
Return from trade	2	2
Remainder of estate	2	2
Release from service	19	18
Total	104	101

Note: Rounding accounts for the total of more than 100 percent.

Source: Husting Wills.

Notes

Abbreviations

CCR	*Calendar of Coroners' Rolls of the City of London, 1300–1378*, ed. R. R. Sharpe (London, 1913).
CEMR	*Calendar of Early Mayor's Court Rolls of the City of London, 1298–1307*, ed. A. H. Thomas (London, 1924).
CLMC	*Calendar of Letters from the Mayor and Corporation of the City of London, A.D. 1350–1370*, ed. R. R. Sharpe (London, 1885).
CLRO	Corporation of London Record Office, followed by archive designation.
CPMR	*Calendar of Plea and Memoranda Rolls of the City of London, 1323–1482*, vols. 1–4, ed. A. H. Thomas; vols. 5 and 6, ed. P. E. Jones (Cambridge, 1926–1961).
Guildhall	Guildhall Library Archives, followed by record series title and archive number.
Husting Wills	*Calendar of Wills Proved and Enrolled in the Court of Husting, London, A.D. 1258–A.D. 1688*, 2 vols., ed. R. R. Sharpe (London, 1890).
Letter Book	*Calendar of Letter Books of the City of London, A–L (1275–1497)*, 11 vols. ed. R. R. Sharpe (London, 1899–1912).
Liber Albus	*Liber Albus: The White Book of the City of London*, ed. Henry Thomas Riley (London, 1861).
Memorials	*Memorials of London and London Life in the XIIIth, XIVth, and XVth Centuries*, ed. Henry Thomas Riley (London, 1869).
Mercers	*Acts of the Court of the Mercer's Company (London), 1453–1527*, ed. Laetitia Lyell and Frank D. Watney (Cambridge, 1936).
P.R.O.	Public Record Office, followed by archive designation.

Chapter 1

1. In 1382, for the arrival of Queen Anne, 140 goldsmiths wore red and black. The red party's dress was barred with silver wire and powdered with silver trefoils; on the left, they had great brooches of gold and stones, while on their heads they had hats covered with red and powdered with trefoils (Walter S. Prideaux, ed., *Memorials of the Goldsmiths' Company, Being Gleanings from Their Records* [London, 1896], p. 13).

2. Robert Withington, *English Pageantry: An Historical Outline* (Cambridge, Mass., 1918), vol. 1, pp. 129–131.

3. The case of the girl falling out the window is related in *CCR*, p. 250; the case of the drowned young woman is on p. 13. The chronicler retelling the event is made up, but his audience are people who will appear in the book.

4. Philippe Ariès, *Centuries of Childhood: A Social History of the Family*, trans. Robert Baldick (London, 1962), pp. 18–32, 411; Mary Martin McLaughlin, "Survivors and Surrogates: Children and Parents from the Ninth to the Thirteenth Centuries," in *The History of Childhood*, ed. Lloyd deMause (New York, 1974), p. 110. For a recent support of this position, see James A. Schultz, "Medieval Adolescence: The Claims of History and the Silence of German Narrative," *Speculum* 66 (1991): 519–539.

5. Lawrence Stone, *The Family, Sex, and Marriage in England, 1500–1800* (New York, 1977); Edward Shorter, *The Making of the Modern Family* (New York, 1977).

6. Shulamith Shahar, *Childhood in the Middle Ages* (London, 1990).

7. I have discussed the debate about the definition of adolescence in more depth in "Historical Descriptions and Prescriptions for Adolescence," *Journal of Family History* 17 (1992): 341–351. This is a special issue of the journal that I edited to explore the changing definition of adolescence from the thirteenth to the twentieth century. It is an argument for an evolutionary change of definition.

8. See, for instance, J. A. Burrow, *The Ages of Man: A Study in Medieval Writing and Thought* (Oxford, 1988).

9. Schultz, "Medieval Adolescence," pp. 530–531.

10. See, for instance, Nicholas Orme, *From Childhood to Chivalry: The Education of the English Kings and Aristocracy, 1066–1530* (London, 1984), and Joel T. Rosenthal, *Patriarchy and Families of Privilege in Fifteenth-Century England* (Philadelphia, 1991).

11. See, for instance, S. R. Smith, "The London Apprentices as Seventeenth-Century Adolescents," *Past and Present* 61 (1973): 149–161, or A. Yarbrough, "Apprentices as Adolescents in Sixteenth-Century Bristol," *Journal of Social History* 13 (1979): 67–81.

12. Martine Segalen, *Historical Anthropology and the Family*, trans. J. C. Whitehouse and Sarah Matthews (Cambridge, 1986), pp. 3–6, discusses the valuable interplay of anthropology, sociology, and history for the study of the family.

13. Barbara A. Hanawalt, "Childrearing Among the Lower Classes of Late Medieval England," *Journal of Interdisciplinary History* 8 (1977): 1–22; Hanawalt, *The Ties That Bound: Peasant Families in Medieval England* (New York, 1986), pp. 177–187.

14. This book was first published in 1908 in French. I have used the English translation, Arnold van Gennep, *The Rites of Passage*, trans. Monika B. Vizedom and Gabrielle L. Caffee (Chicago, 1960). Chapter 6, "Initiation Rites," contains his distinction between physical and social puberty.

15. Victor W. Turner, *The Ritual Process: Structure and Anti-Structure* (New York, 1969), pp. 94–96; van Gennep, *Rites of Passage,* p. 3, explicitly compares the liminality of adolescence to the European apprenticeship system.

16. Glen Elder, Jr., "Adolescence in the Life Cycle: An Introduction," in *Adolescence in the Life Cycle,* ed. Sigmund E. Dragastin and Glen H. Elder, Jr. (Washington, D.C., 1975), pp. 1–13. His introduction to this interdisciplinary volume provides a clear overview of the problems of defining adolescence. For a longer statement and a literature review, see Glen H. Elder, Jr., *Adolescent Socialization and Personality Development* (Chicago, 1968).

17. Elder, "Adolescence in the Life Cycle."

18. W. Scott Haine, "The Development of Leisure and the Transformation of Working-Class Adolescence, Paris 1830–1940," *Journal of Family History* 17 (1992): 451–476, has shown how different the apprentice riots were from the real youth culture that developed in the nineteenth century.

19. Turner, *Ritual Process,* pp. 106–107.

20. Alice Stopford Green, *Town Life in the Fifteenth Century* (London, 1894), vol. 2, pp. 1–23, speaks about the new consumption of books of advice in the fifteenth century.

21. There are excellent guides to these records and others related to London: P. E. Jones and R. Smith, *A Guide to the Records in the Corporation of London Records Office and the Guildhall Library Muniment Room* (London, 1950); Derek Keene and Vanessa Harding, *A Survey of Documentary Sources for Property Holding in London Before the Great Fire,* London Record Society 22 (London, 1985); B. R. Masters, "The Corporation of London Records Office: Some Sources for the Historian," *Archives* 12 (1975): 5–14.

22. Reginald R. Sharpe edited the two-volume *Calendar of Wills Proved and Enrolled in the Husting,* which I used extensively in this study. In addition, I consulted the manuscripts of these wills for such matters as provision for bastards. The dower cases from the Husting Court of Common Pleas I have read in manuscript. A. H. Thomas calendared the *Calendar of Early Mayor's Court Rolls of the City* and the *Calendar of Plea and Memoranda Rolls,* vols. 1–4. Philip E. Jones calendared volumes 5 and 6. The *Calendar of Plea and Memoranda Rolls* covers 1328 to 1482. In addition, some of the original bills for the mayor's court are preserved in manuscript. Few of the records for the lesser courts, such as the sheriff's or the wardmoots, are preserved, but those that are have been consulted in manuscript. The Letter Books were calendared by Reginald Sharpe, who also did those coroners' inquests preserved separately in the Corporation of London Record Office. I have checked the calendared Letter Books against the originals. Other London coroners' inquests are to be found in *Letter Book B;* another manuscript roll is in the Public Record Office. Full citations for all these sources are in the bibliography.

23. For the manuscript numbers of both the Guildhall and P.R.O. see the bibliography. The petitions are undated, but one can have some sense of the dates they cover by their classification: C1/4–5 (1417–1424), C1/9–12 (1432–1443), C1/26–29 (1456–1466), C1/50–67 (1475–1485), and C1/183–234 (1493–1500). Only the petitions survive, not the Chancellor's response. We do not know the outcome of these appeals.

24. John Hatcher, *Plague, Population, and the English Economy, 1348–1530* (London, 1977), is the best short summary of the dates for visitations of plague in England and its effects.

25. For London's political development during this period see Ruth Bird, *The Turbulent London of Richard II* (London, 1949).

26. The most detailed account of the political fights is ibid., although George Unwin, *The Gilds and Companies of London* (London, 1908), pp. 127–175, has an interesting account of the economic implications.

27. *CCR*, pp. 61–62.

28. The crosses are of lead and may be seen in the Museum of London.

29. Bertha Haven Putnam, *The Enforcement of the Statute of Labourers During the First Decade After the Black Death* (New York, 1908).

30. Barbara A. Hanawalt, "Keepers of the Lights: Late Medieval English Parish Gilds," *Journal of Medieval and Renaissance History* 14 (1984): 21–37; Caroline M. Barron, "The Parish Fraternities of Medieval London," in *The Church in Pre-Reformation Society: Essays in Honour of F. R. H. Du Boulay*, ed. Caroline M. Barron and Christopher Harper-Bill (Woodbridge, Eng., 1985), pp. 13–37.

31. P.R.O. C1/198/22, 23. William pretended that the first ring was worth £20 and bound John in an obligation for £22 (an interest fee). In the second wager, John signed an obligation of £20.

Chapter 2

1. The challenge for historians and novelists writing on medieval London has been to come to grips with its size, colors, smells, noise, and worldly temptations by introducing the city through the eyes of a person seeing it for the first time. George Unwin, ed., *Finance and Trade Under Edward III* (Manchester, 1918), pp. 1–6, created a knight who is visiting his cousin, a London alderman, who boastfully guides him through the city. Modern writers usually rely for their medieval tourist information on William Fitzstephen's famous description, which appears in the prologue to his life of Thomas Becket (Frank M. Stenton, *Norman London: An Essay*, rev. ed. [London, 1934], with a translation of William Fitzstephen's *Description* by H. E. Butler). For descriptions that fall between popular and scholarly, see Charles Pendrill, *London Life in the Fourteenth Century* (London, 1925; Port Washington, N.Y., 1971), and Walter Besant, *Medieval London*, vol. 1 (London, 1906). William Page, ed., *The Victoria History of London*, vol. 1 (London, 1909), is richly illustrated with maps and archaeological materials. In *London, 800–1216* (London, 1975), Christopher Brooke, assisted by Gillian Keir, provides a very valuable scholarly discussion. A very readable book incorporating archaeology is John Schofield, *The Building of London from the Conquest to the Great Fire* (London, 1984). The best short descriptions are A. H. Thomas, "Life in Medieval London," *Journal of the British Archaeological Association*, n.s., 35 (1929): 122–147, and C. L. Kingsford's essay on London in *Prejudice and Promise in Fifteenth-Century England* (Oxford, 1925), pp. 107–145.

2. Schofield, *Building of London*, pp. 66–67. The figure on the length of the walls comes from John Stow, *A Survey of London: Reprinted From the Text of 1603*, ed. C. L. Kingsford, 2nd ed., 2 vols. (Oxford, 1971).

3. For a brief and interesting account, see Schofield, *Building of London*, pp. 57–79.

4. J. C. Russell, *British Medieval Popoulation* (Albuquerque, N.M., 1948), pp. 285–287, from the 1377 poll tax a population of 35,000 and guessed that the population before the plague was nearer to 60,000. Sylvia L. Thrupp pointed out in *The Merchant Class of Medieval London, 1300–1500* (Chicago, 1948), p. 52, that

the population, using the most conservative estimate, would have been in excess of 33,000. A new, much higher estimate of perhaps 80,000 has been suggested by Derek Keene in various talks and in his pamphlet *Cheapside Before the Great Fire* (London, 1985), p. 20. His estimate is based on a reconstitution of population in Cheapside, the major trading and production area of the city; the applicability of this project for estimating the whole of the population of London has not appeared in print. One problem with extrapolating from Cheapside is that some of the square mile of London was occupied by two castles and several large ecclesiastical establishments, in addition to parish churches. For the sixteenth century, see A. L. Beier and Roger Finlay, "The Significance of the Metropolis," p. 2, and Roger Finlay and Beatrice Shearer, "Population Growth and Suburban Expansion," p. 38, in *The Making of the Metropolis: London, 1500–1700,* ed. A. L. Beier and Roger Finlay (London, 1986). These studies place the population in 1550 at 150,000.

    5. Schofield, *Building of London,* pp. 86–88.

    6. P.R.O. Ancient Deeds Catalogue, p. 210; E40/A 1779.

    7. *Liber Albus,* pp. xxix–xxxii, 319–332.

    8. H. S. Bennett, *England from Chaucer to Caxton* (New York, 1928), pp. 144–145; *Liber Albus,* p. 389. The complaint was that the poles were so long that people on horseback could not travel underneath and that the poles were destroying the houses. *CPMR,* vol. 2, p. 249, for instance, records a trespass in which a man tore down a sign of branches and leaves that identified the plaintiff's tavern. The defendant said that that part of the house belonged to him and that he would not tolerate the sign.

    9. *Liber Albus,* pp. 319–332.

    10. Schofield, *Building of London,* pp. 95–96. Fireplaces and chimneys became increasingly common in the fourteenth century, and by the fifteenth century many houses had them in rooms other than the hall and the kitchen. Coal brought from the north by boat was called "sea coal" because of the way it was transported (*Liber Albus,* p. xxxiv). Charcoal prepared in the country was carted to the city between Michaelmas and Easter and sold at 8*d.* a quarter. Sea coal was common by the reign of Edward II. Wood was also burned.

    11. P.R.O. Prob. 2/11 1483. There are thirteen probate inventories, but not all of them are complete.

    12. P.R.O. Prob. 2/8.

    13. Schofield, *Building of London,* pp. 123–126. This palace was for a time the residence of Richard III before he became king. The hall part has been moved to Chelsea and can still be seen. For the thirteenth century, see T. Hudson Turner, *Some Account of the Domestic Architecture in England From the Conquest to the End of the Thirteenth Century* (Oxford, 1851), chap. 3.

    14. *Liber Albus,* pp. xxxii–xxxix. If a renter vacated a tenement, he had to give advance notice, depending on how much rent he paid. For rents over 40*s.,* he had to give a half-year's notice. See also Henry Littlehales, ed., *The Medieval Records of a London Church,* Early English Text Society, o.s., 125–128 (London, 1905), pp. 28–29, 75–76.

    15. *CCR,* pp. 51–52 (1322).

    16. *CLMC,* pp. 47–48; *CPMR,* vol. 2, pp. 220–221 (1345); P.R.O. C1/67/38.

    17. Guildhall, Churchwardens' Accounts, St. Andrew Hubbard, 15–18 Edward VI, ms. 1279, vol. 1. Although this record is later than our period, requiring such payment was a common practice in the Middle Ages as well.

18. P.R.O. Just 2/94A, m. 2 (1315).

19. CLRO, MC1/2A/45.

20. P.R.O. Prob. 2/23, 2/143.

21. Thomas Reddaway, *The Early History of the Goldsmiths' Company, 1327–1500* (London, 1975), pp. 151–153.

22. *CCR*, pp. 167–168 (1326); Schofield, *Building of London*, p. 96; for a complete discussion, see Ernest L. Sabine, "Latrines and Cesspools of Medieval London," *Speculum* 9 (1934): 303–321.

23. Helena M. Chew and William Kellaway, eds., *London Assize of Nuisance, 1301–1431*, London Record Society 10 (London 1973), pp. 45 (1314), 79 (1333).

24. Littlehales, *Medieval Records of a London Church*, pp. xi, xli, 240.

25. Schofield, *Building of London*, p. 111; Sabine, "Latrines and Cesspools," has a full description of public latrines.

26. *CCR*, p. 142.

27. *CEMCR*, p. 40.

28. Ernest L. Sabine, "City Cleaning in Medieval London," *Speculum* 12 (1937): pp. 19–43. On the regulation of one of the most noisome industries, see Sabine, "Butchering in Mediaeval London," *Speculum* 8 (1933): 335–353.

29. Littlehales, *Medieval Records of a London Church*, pp. 243, 343, 379, 322.

30. Pendrill, *London Life in the Fourteenth Century*, p. 40.

31. *CCR*, pp. 46–48.

32. For the relationship of the ward and parish boundaries, see Brooke and Keir, *London*, pp. 122–148, 168–169.

33. The churchwardens' accounts are preserved in the Guildhall Library. They are listed in *The Churchwardens' Accounts of Parishes Within the City of London* (London, 1969). Some of them are also published: William H. Overall, ed., *The Accounts of the Churchwardens of St. Michael, Cornhill, 1456–1608* (London, 1871); William McMurray, ed., *The Records of Two City Parishes: Sts. Anne and Agnes, Aldergate and St. John Zachary, London* (London, 1925); Charles Welch, ed., *The Churchwardens' Accounts of the Parish of All Hallows, London Wall, A.D. 1455–A.D. 1536* (London, 1912).

34. Brooke and Keir, *London*, pp. 148–162. The early history of the wards makes very interesting reading.

35. Gwyn A. Williams, *Medieval London: From Commune to Capital* (London, 1963), pp. 32–33, 80.

36. *CPMR*, vol. 4, pp. 151–154.

37. *Mercers*, p. 101.

38. Robert Withington, *English Pageantry: An Historical Outline*, 2 vols. (Cambridge, Mass., 1918, 1920).

39. For a map of the layout of streets in 1200, see ibid., vol. 1, pp. 174–175; Sabine, "Butchering in Mediaeval London."

40. *Liber Albus*, pp. 32–33; *Letter Book G*, pp. 176, 283.

41. Kevin McDonnell, *Medieval London Suburbs* (London, 1978), shows how rural East London was during the late Middle Ages.

42. Margaret Curtis, "The London Lay Subsidy of 1332," in *Finance and Trade Under Edward III*, ed. George Unwin (Manchester 1918), pp. 35–56.

43. Elspeth M. Veale, "Craftsmen and the Economy of London in the Four-

teenth Century," in *Studies in London History,* ed. A. E. J. Hollaender and William Kellaway (London, 1969), pp. 136–137.

44. *Husting Wills,* vol. 1, p. 277.

45. Guildhall, Commissary Court 9171/3, 152, 302v. Both are early fifteenth century. London minstrels played on a number of occasions, including providing the rough music that led offenders to the pillory and out of the city gates.

46. Guildhall, Archdeaconry Court 9051/1, 2, 4, 6v, 8, 9v, 10v, 12, 18v, 19, 21v. All are from the 1390s.

47. Guildhall, Commissary Court 9171/6 52.

48. Guildhall, Commissary Court 9171/3, 349.

49. P.R.O. Prob. 2/98. Prob. 2/11 concerns a butcher who had an estate of £154 3s. 4d. His house was smaller, but he had plate in silver worth £8 and considerable investment in animals.

50. *Husting Wills,* vol. 2, pp. 477–478.

51. A. H. Thomas, "Sidelights on Medieval London Life," *Journal of the British Archaeological Association,* 3rd ser., 2 (1937): 111–112.

52. Thrupp, *Merchant Class of Medieval London,* pp. 103–154, has a complete description of the standards of living for the merchant class.

53. *CPMR,* vol. 1, pp. 1–2 (1323).

54. *Husting Wills,* vol. 2, p. 479.

55. For accounts of the courses and purchases for these banquets, see Guy Parsloe, ed., *Wardens' Accounts of the Worshipful Company of Founders of the City of London 1497–1681* (London, 1964), pp. 6, 26, 33.

56. P.R.O. C1/89/31.

57. Littlehales, *Medieval Records of a London Church,* pp. 71 (1428–1429), 327, 328, 331, 343.

58. Pendrill, *London Life in the Fourteenth Century,* pp. 37–40, 136, 168, 181–182; *Letter Book G,* pp. 148–151, 274, 301, 311; Thomas, "Life in Medieval London," pp. 132–133, on prices, water, and markets; *Liber Albus,* pp. 302–314, has descriptions of annual price setting and types of bread and ale.

59. Bennett, *England from Chaucer to Caxton,* p. 144.

60. P.R.O. C1/61/419.

61. Withington, *English Pageantry,* vol. 1, p. 37. Riots did break out in 1411. See also Kingsford, *Prejudice and Promise in Fifteenth-Century England,* p. 144.

Chapter 3

1. J. A. Burrow, *The Ages of Man: A Study in Medieval Writing and Thought* (Oxford, 1988), pp. 12–18.

2. G. R. Owst, *Literature and Pulpit in Medieval England* (Cambridge, 1933), p. 34.

3. Beryl Rowland, ed., *Medieval Woman's Guide to Health: The First English Gynecological Handbook* (Kent, Ohio, 1981), pp. 22–23.

4. Ibid. Men were not to read the gynecological handbook unless, in an emergency, they had to assist in a birth. Ballad literature, such as the "Leesome Brand," makes it clear that even in the wilderness women did not have men help them with childbirth, but preferred to do it alone (Francis James Child, ed., *The English and Scottish Popular Ballads* [Boston, 1883], vol. 1, no. 15). In France, the *couvade,* or "manchildbirth," in which men imitated the labor pains of women, was practiced

(Madeleine Jeay, "Sexuality and Family in Fifteenth-Century France: Are Literary Sources a Mask or a Mirror?" *Journal of Family History* 4 [1979]: 342).

5. Clarissa W. Atkinson, *The Oldest Profession: Christian Motherhood in the Middle Ages* (Ithaca, N.Y., 1991), pp. 52–57; Jeay, "Sexuality and Family in Fifteenth-Century France," p. 41. For birthing positions, see George Engelmann, *Labor Among Primitive Peoples* (St. Louis, 1883); Harold Speert, *Iconographia Gyniatrica* (Philadelphia, 1973); and Palmer Fundley, *The Story of Childbirth* (New York, 1934). On midwives and their training, see Doreen Evenden-Nagy, "Seventeenth-Century London Midwives: Their Training, Licensing, and Social Profile" (Ph.D. diss., McMaster University, 1991). On pp. 3, 125, Evenden-Nagy cites a description of childbirth in which two women lift the pelvic area at each contraction and two restrain the upper part of the laboring woman's body. See also Merry E. Wiesner, "Early Modern Midwifery: A Case Study," in *Women and Work in Preindustrial Europe*, ed. Barbara A. Hanawalt (Bloomington, Ind., 1986), pp. 94–113. That London midwives worked with two assistants can be inferred from an alleged case of infanticide in which three women presided at a birth and then drowned the child. Another source is Richard M. Wunderli, *London Church Courts and Society on the Eve of the Reformation* (Cambridge, Mass., 1981), p. 129. For a description of what to do in the case of irregular presentations, see Rowland, *Medieval Woman's Guide to Health*, introduction, chap. 10. The advice also covers what to do about sickness in mother and child. For Caesarean birth, see Renate Blumenfeld-Kosinski, *Not of Woman Born: Representations of Caesarean Birth in Medieval and Renaissance Culture* (Ithaca, N.Y., 1990).

6. Margery Kempe, *The Book of Margery Kempe*, ed. Stanford B. Meech and Hope Emily Allen, Early English Text Society, o.s., 212 (London, 1940), pp. 6, 11–15, 21, 23–24.

7. Mary Martin McLaughlin, "Survivors and Surrogates: Children and Parents from the Ninth to the Thirteenth Centuries," in *The History of Childhood*, ed. Lloyd deMause (New York, 1974), pp. 113–114. For the folkloric traditions, see Charles Wimberly, *Folklore in English and Scottish Ballads* (Chicago, 1928), pp. 371–376. In Child, *English and Scottish Popular Ballads*, vol. 1, nos. 5B and 5C speak of washing in milk and swaddling in silk.

8. David Herlihy and Christiane Klapisch-Zuber, *The Tuscans and Their Families: A Study of the Florentine Catasto of 1427* (New Haven, Conn., 1985), p. 277. About 20 percent of the married women seemed to have died in some cause related to childbearing, if not in the actual birth process.

9. Charles Pendrill, *London Life in the Fourteenth Century* (London, 1925; Port Washington, N.Y., 1977), p. 183.

10. Evenden-Nagy, "Seventeenth-Century London Midwives," p. 381, quotes some figures that show that the number of stillbirths might have been rather low—0.6 to 1.8 per 100 births. Because they had great expertise and because they were not treating diseases in general, midwives were less likely to lose their clients; they were not introducing extraneous diseases to them. The real problems for women who died of childbirth fever came when doctors spread disease by moving from a sick person to a woman in labor without washing his hands or his instruments.

11. "The Mirror of the Periods of Man's Life," in *Hymns to the Virgin and Christ, The Parliament of Devils, and Other Religious Poetry*, ed. Frederick J. Furnivall, Early English Text Society, o.s., 24 (London, 1868; New York, 1969), p. 58.

12. John Myrc, *Instructions for a Parish Priest,* ed. Edward Peacock, Early English Text Society, o.s., 209 (London, 1940), pp. 3–4. The concern of the Church for baptism echoed a more pagan tradition that if a child was not picked up and named, it could be exposed to the elements and thus probable death. See, for instance, Juha Pentikäinen, *The Nordic Dead-Child Tradition,* Folklore Fellows Communications, no. 201 (Helsinki, 1968), pp. 71–75. For the Roman tradition, see Nicole Belmont, "Levana: Or How to Raise up Children," in *Family and Society: Selections from the Annales, Economies, Sociétés, Civilisation,* ed. Robert Forster and Orest Ranum, trans. Elborg Forster and Patricia M. Ranum (Baltimore, 1976), pp. 1–3; Guildhall, Consistory Court 9064/1, 112v.

13. For a more complete discussion of the English evidence, see Barbara A. Hanawalt, *The Ties That Bound: Peasant Families in Medieval England* (New York, 1986), pp. 101–102. For information from coroners' inquest and jail delivery rolls (3 cases of infanticide out of 4,000 cases of homicide), see also Hanawalt, *Crime and Conflict in English Communities, 1300–1348* (Cambridge, Mass., 1979), pp. 154–157. For the low number of cases coming into ecclesiastical jurisdiction and the rather mild punishment for those that did, see Richard H. Helmholtz, "Infanticide in England in the Later Middle Ages," *History of Childhood Quarterly* 1 (1974–1975): 282–390.

14. Wunderli, *London Church Courts,* pp. 129–30.

15. P.R.O. Just. 2/94A, m. 2. Cases of children one, seven, and nine days old appear in coroners' inquests in 1339, but their deaths are attributed to natural causes (*CCR,* pp. 222, 254, 260).

16. Wunderli, *London Church Courts,* p. 78.

17. Joseph H. Lynch, *Godparents and Kinship in Early Medieval Europe* (Princeton, N.J., 1986), is an excellent source for a discussion of the practice of baptism and sponsorship and how it evolved. See particularly Chapters 1 and 2 for the evolution.

18. Ibid.; see Chapters 10 and 11 for a discussion of the development of the liturgy requirement that the godparents offer spiritual instruction.

19. *CPMR,* vol. 5, p. 79 (1445).

20. *Husting Wills,* vol. 2, p. 455 (1431). See also p. 175, Thomas, godson of Thomas de Felymgham, or p. 359, in which Alice, widow of Robert Lyndiwyk, recognizes two goddaughters named Alice. Mary Lodewyk specified that she was leaving a third of her estate to her goddaughter "who was named for me" (Guildhall, Commissary Court 9171/1 98).

21. *A Volume of English Miscellanies,* Surtees Society 85 (York, 1890), pp. 35–52; Michael Bennett, "Spiritual Kinship and the Baptismal Name in Traditional European Society," in *Principalities, Powers and Estates: Studies in Medieval and Early Modern Government and Society,* ed. L. O. Frappell (Adelaide, 1979), p. 8, has shown from evidence in the Inquisitions Post Mortem that 87 percent of the young men bore the name of their godfather. This sample is taken from the nobility. Louis Haas, "Social Connections Between Parents and Godparents in Late Medieval Yorkshire," *Medieval Prosopography* 10 (1989): 18, finds a similar pattern for that class in Yorkshire.

22. Haas, "Social Connections Between Parents and Godparents," p. 18, concludes that parents made a conscious effort to select godparents who had the name that they wanted the child to have. He maintains that 86 percent of the noble parents chose godparents for their name. Correct names, however, were more

important for the nobility, who were trying to establish lineages, than for Londoners.

23. These figures are taken from the Letter Books in which the wardship cases were arranged. Another source for coincidence of names for father and son are the wills enrolled in the Husting Court. The figure for the wills is quite close to that of wardship cases: 25 percent.

24. *Letter Book F,* p. 188 (1329); *Letter Book I,* p. 252. Sometimes the wills seem to indicate that families preferred some names and exchanged them from generation to generation. There is ample evidence on naming patterns in London, and further study might be able to establish a clearer picture.

25. The pool of names in the countryside was much smaller, with John not becoming popular until some fifty years after it was in London (Hanawalt, *Ties That Bound,* pp. 174–175).

26. Lawrence Stone, *Family, Sex, and Marriage in England, 1500–1800* (New York, 1977), p. 70.

27. Eilert Ekwall, *Studies on the Population of Medieval London* (Stockholm, 1956), contains an analysis of the place names appearing in the London records. He has attempted to identify the influence of immigration on London English.

28. Ibid., pp. xli, lvii.

29. Sylvia L. Thrupp, *The Merchant Class of Medieval London, 1300–1500* (Chicago, 1948), p. 200. Measuring only the average number of surviving heirs in the male line on the basis of wills of the merchant elite, Thrupp found that these men had 1.3 sons prior to the Black Death and 1 son in the plague years to 1437. Recovery to the preplague figure came after 1438. Although the data are somewhat different, the picture of decline and recovery are parallel.

30. *English Miscellanies,* pp. 35–52. In the eight cases where the social class of the godparents was listed, the York craftsmen all had at least one godparent who was a gentleman and, therefore, of a higher social class than they were. Stephen Gudeman, "Spiritual Relations and Selecting a Godparent," *Man* 10 (1975): 235, has suggested that sponsors could provide valuable social ties for youth. Haas, "Social Connections Between Parents and Godparents," pp. 9, 11, found that 15 percent of the York tenants-in-chief selected relatives, but only 8 percent had a social status higher than the father.

31. Lynch, *Godparents and Kinship in Early Medieval Europe,* p. 177, points out that in early Frankish society, should the child and the godparents survive, the relationship implied one of kinship, and the obligations that accompanied this relationship including advancement of the godchild later in life.

32. *Husting Wills,* vol. 2, p. 282.

33. Guildhall, Commissary Court 9171/5, 193.

34. Guildhall, Archdeaconry Court 9051/1; *Husting Wills,* vol. 2.

35. Guildhall, Commissary Court 9171/1 60, 87, 98, 108, 187v; Archdeaconry Court 9051/1 2v–3, 5v, 98v, 201, 203, 208. The terms for godchildren vary: "spiritual children" and *filiolo* sometimes replace "godchild."

36. Lynch, *Godparents and Kinship in Early Medieval Europe,* pp. 179–181, discusses Germanic practice, as opposed to Christian sponsorship.

37. Guildhall, Commissary Court 9171/3 431v (1435). See also *Husting Wills,* vol. 1, p. 220, in which William de Caxstone left his house to his godson William, son of William le Spicer. Jack Goody, *Development of Family and Marriage in Europe*

(Cambridge, 1983), pp. 73–75, says that godparents were supposed to take in orphans. This may be, but little concrete evidence remains.

38. *Husting Wills*, vol. 1, p. 204; Guildhall, Archdeaconry Court 9051/1 2v–3, 104.

39. Thrupp, *Merchant Class of Medieval London*, pp. 232, 339. The adoption was through marriage; that is, Nicholas de Farndon married Isabella, daughter of William Farndon, and took her name. Both men were goldsmiths. In the next generation, two sons took the surname of their mother, Farndon, and both were goldsmiths.

40. Frederick J. Furnivall, ed., *Robert [Mannyng] of Brunne's Handlyng Synne*, Early English Text Society, o.s., 119 (London, 1901), pp. 303–305, speaks of the sin of seducing a godchild but not of a positive aspect to the relationship.

41. *CPMR*, vol. 5, pp. 11–12 (1439).

42. The Seint John Family does not appear in the *Husting Wills, Letter Books*, or *CPMR*. Presumably Thomas should have been a ward of the city, but perhaps his father was not a citizen of London. It is a reminder that the net of the courts might not have been as broad as we often think. Anyone who has tried to trace a particular family or person knows how difficult it can be. The reconstructed life, therefore, rests on the accumulated sources in the chapter rather than on sources that deal specifically with him. His story is very full in itself, giving, as it does, the people who knew him in his early life and at birth.

Chapter 4

1. Christiane Klapisch-Zuber, *Women, Family, and Ritual in Renaissance Italy*, trans. Lydia Cochrane (Chicago, 1985). Klapisch-Zuber's essay "Blood Parents and Milk Parents: Wet Nursing in Florence, 1300–1530" explores the extensive use of nurses among middle-class Florentines. These nurses sometimes took the children into their own homes, rather than living with the family; one in five did so (p. 135).

2. *Husting Wills*, vol. 2, p. 48. Osbert Wynter, a poulterer, left a bequest to "Alice his nurse," but she need not have been his wet nurse, but might have been his final nurse, as in the case of Dame Alice Wyche, who left money to "two honest women nursing her in her last illness" (*CPMR*, vol. 6, p. 103). One might also expect to find women's wills that refer to a career as nurse, but neither the Commissary Court of London nor the Archdeaconry Court of London, both of which record the wills of the poorer population, has such information.

3. Frances M. M. Comper, ed., *Spiritual Songs from English MSS. of the Fourteenth to Sixteenth Centuries* (Cambridge, 1936), p. 27.

4. Shulamith Shahar, *Childhood in the Middle Ages* (London, 1990), pp. 53–76, discusses the medical and literary evidence for Europe as a whole. Mary Martin McLaughlin, "Survivors and Surrogates: Children and Parents from the Ninth to the Thirteenth Centuries," in *The History of Childhood*, ed. Lloyd deMause (New York, 1974), p. 115, assumes that most mothers outside the nobility nursed their children.

5. The age of majority in London was twenty-one for young men and for unmarried young women. Young women could inherit at that age or at sixteen to eighteen if they were married. The age of majority is discussed more fully in Chapter 11.

6. Sylvia L. Thrupp, *The Merchant Class of Medieval London, 1300–1500* (Chicago, 1948), p. 203. Using only the evidence from the aldermanic families (pros-

opographical reconstructions rather than simply the wardship accounts), she found that between 1318 and 1347, 23 percent of the male orphans died before reaching the age of twenty-one. Immediately after the plague, in the years from 1348 to 1407, 39 percent died underage. Although there is some unevenness in the pattern, on average 30 percent died before majority between 1408 and 1497. In other words, studying a more privileged group, she saw roughly the same pattern.

7. Ibid., pp. 201–202, summarizes the various chronicle accounts of diseases. David Herlihy and Christiane Klapisch-Zuber, *The Tuscans and Their Families: A Study of the Florentine Catasto of 1427* (New Haven, Conn., 1985), p. 278, find that 47 percent of the infants died each year, but the figure is not complete. The causes of death were intestinal disorders for the most part.

8. The deficiency in the number of female children is most striking in those families with only one child. From 1309 to 1349, the differential was 36 percent males to 17 percent females; from 1350 to 1390, it was 36 percent males to 26 percent females; from 1391 to 1431, it was 33 percent males to 20 percent females; and from 1432 to 1482, it was 29 percent males to 13 percent females. The differential in families of two and three children shows a slight tendency for males to predominate, but this difference disappears in families with four or more children.

9. Herlihy and Klapisch-Zuber, *Tuscans and Their Families*, pp. 131–143, find a similar shortfall of women: up to age fifteen years there were six males to every five females. Their explanation is that girls entered service sooner and were not counted.

10. The problem of early female mortality is a complicated one and will be the subject of a separate research effort. The first question to ask of the London data is whether females are underreported. London wardship laws required that all children be heirs of the father and share in the third of the property that custom allotted to them. It would have been difficult to hide children because the pledges undertook to ensure the distribution of the inheritance when the heirs reached the age of majority. The only possible reason to remove a female from the records would have been that she had married and received her portion of inheritance as dowry. Such early marriages, however, are unlikely to account for a 10 percent difference. For the large literature on early female mortality, see the review essay by Amartya Sen, "More than 100 Million Women Are Missing," *New York Review of Books,* 20 December 1990, pp. 61–66. The developed countries have a male–female ratio of 1.05, but South Asia, West Asia, and North Africa have ratios closer to the London data. Sheila Ryan Johansson, "Deferred Infanticide: Excess Female Mortality During Childhood," in *Infanticide: Comparative and Evolutionary Perspectives,* ed. Glen Hausfater and Sara Blaffer Hrdy (New York, 1984), pp. 463–485, analyzes European historical data.

11. Alan Mcfarlane, *Marriage and Love in England: Modes of Reproduction, 1300–1840* (Oxford, 1986), pp. 52–54, denies a strong preference for male children, but he has relied on sixteenth- and seventeenth-century upper-class letter writers, rather than statistics. In Florence, the selective neglect of male and female infants at a foundling hospital has been investigated (Richard Trexler, "The Foundlings of Florence, 1395–1455," *History of Childhood Quarterly* 1 [1973]: 259–284).

12. I plan to deal with the problem of women in late medieval London in a subsequent book. In an essay, "Remarriage as an Option for Urban and Rural Widows in Late Medieval England," in *Wife and Widow: The Experiences of Women*

in Medieval England, ed. Sue Sheridan Walker (Ann Arbor, 1993), pp. 141–164, I have shown that widows were in considerable demand as marriage partners. Among other reasons, they may have been sought because London had fewer marriageable females as a result of childrearing practices.

13. Klapisch-Zuber, *Women, Family, and Ritual in Renaissance Italy,* p. 139, shows that families were more likely to send female children to the countryside to be wet-nursed but to have a nurse come into the family home for the boys. The female children were weaned earlier than the male (pp. 155–158).

14. For an analysis of childhood accidents in the rural environment, see Barbara A. Hanawalt, *The Ties That Bound: Peasant Families in Late Medieval England* (New York, 1986), pp. 116–117, 179–187.

15. P.R.O. C1/187/89.

16. Guildhall, Consistory Court 9064/2 168.

17. *Letter Book K,* p. 89. A case sent to the king and his council stated that "citizens of London . . . might leave freeholds by will in the same manner as chattels." But Thomas de Petresfeld claimed that the recipient was a bastard and therefore could not inherit. Inquisition established that he was not a bastard and therefore could inherit a freehold.

18. Richard M. Wunderli, *London Church Courts and Society on the Eve of the Reformation* (Cambridge, Mass., 1981), pp. 76–80.

19. Helena M. Chew, ed., *London Possessory Assizes: A Calendar,* London Record Society 1 (London, 1965), pp. 42, 47–48.

20. *Husting Wills,* vol. 2, p. 564.

21. Ibid., pp. 412–13. For a contention of a false claim, see P.R.O. C1/229/19, in which "an evil disposed person being a bastard and a Fleming born at Bruges in Flanders, which calleth himself bastard son of John Pykering late of London, Mercer," brought a claim in his father's name against another man's estate. *CLMC,* pp. 121, 122, are cases of men who married women in Flanders. The legitimate children had to go to great lengths to prove that they were not born out of wedlock.

22. *CLMC,* p. 185 (1375). On p. 209, the testator leaves 20s. to the bastard and 20s. to servant.

23. Ibid., p. 443. See also pp. 132, 208, 424 (has wife but no children), 489 (legitimate children get £20 each but bastard daughter gets 60s.).

24. CLRO, Mayor's Court Original Bills 1/1/33, 1/1/113.

25. Thrupp, *Merchant Class of Medieval London,* p. 343.

26. *Letter Book H,* p. 387 (1392).

27. Henry Littlehales, ed., *The Medieval Records of a London Church,* Early English Text Society, o.s., 125–128 (London, 1905), pp. xliv, 78, 84, 90, 92; Guildhall, Churchwardens' Accounts, St. Andrew Hubbard, ms. 1279, vol. 1; William H. Overall, ed., *The Accounts of the Churchwardens of St. Michael, Cornhill, 1456–1608* (London, 1871), pp. 5, 10, 12, 15.

28. For quotes, see Thrupp, *Merchant Class of Medieval London,* pp. 200–201.

29. P.R.O. C1/68/4.

30. Robert D. Stevick, ed., *One Hundred Middle English Lyrics* (Indianapolis, 1964), pp. 62–67.

31. Barbara A. Hanawalt, "Conception Through Infancy in Medieval English Historical and Folklore Sources," *Folklore Forum* 13 (1981): 127–157, has further discussion of the significance of these lullabies for medieval mothers.

32. *CCR,* pp. 34–35 (1321). The elements of the homicide are faithful to the

case, including the details of her rescue and her rescuer. Joan is a made-up name; both she and her mother are described as "unknown." The street was described as being full of people, "men and women whose names were unknown and pas-sersby." The rest of the case is a composite derived from facts in the chapter or other parts of the book.

33. Hanawalt, *Ties That Bound*, pp. 180–182.

34. Shahar, *Childhood in the Middle Ages*, pp. 75–120, includes a complete discussion of the opinions of savants and literary descriptions from the Middle Ages, as well as some modern developmental psychology. Rather than repeat this material, I have based my account on archival materials, much of which appeared in my publications elsewhere.

35. Hanawalt, *Ties That Bound*, pp. 175–176. Of the fifty-eight children under the age of one who died of accidental deaths in the countryside, 33 per-cent died in fires when they were in their cradles. Cradle fires account for the deaths of 14 percent of one-year-olds and only 1 percent of two-year-olds. Un-attended babies who were not in cradles also died in house fires (21 percent). Cradle fires were common in the rural environment because cradles were placed by open hearths in the center of the cottage. Cradle fires must have been much rarer in London because of the use of chimneys and because more people were around to watch for fire. As we have seen, London was very concerned about fire hazards.

36. *CCR*, p. 12 (1337).

37. Ibid., pp. 56–57 (1322).

38. P.R.O. C1/142/18. The master took the apprentice's side and began to harass her with a suit of debt.

39. *CCR*, pp. 30, 207.

40. Hanawalt, *Ties That Bound*, pp. 157–158.

41. Guildhall, Commissary Court 9171/3 431v (1435). See also *Husting Wills*, vol. 1, p. 220, in which William de Caxstone left his house to his godson William, son of William le Spicer. Jack Goody, *Development of Family and Marriage in Europe* (Cambridge, 1983), pp. 73–75, maintains that godparents were responsbile for orphans. English records provide little evidence to support his view.

42. *CCR*, p. 83.

43. *Letter Book G*, p. 306 (1373). For allegation of taking away a child, see also P.R.O. C1/27/392.

44. P.R.O. C1/46/64, 84. In P.R.O. C1/66/233, a priest and a bachelor of law contested the plaint brought by the father of the girl for damages from the rape, saying that it was "too abominable to speak of." Guildhall, Consistory Court 90641, 55, describes an attempt at coitus with a seven-year-old. For abuse of apprentice called a child (*puer*), see CLRO, MC 1/1/48.

45. *CCR*, p. 63, 220. For another case of beggars being crushed at alms distri-bution, see P.R.O. Just 2/94A, m. 4.

46. CLRO, MC 1/1/28. See also CLRO, MC 1/1/13, in which the girl is ten years and is called "une fyle" and "enfant."

47. *CCR*, pp. 63, 191 (in this case a ball got into the gutter, and he fell when trying to retrieve it), 238.

48. *CEMCR*, p. 167 (1304–1305). This case and that of others keep the name of the child and witnesses on the street anonymous. It is not, I think, because they did not know, but because they wished to protect the victims and themselves from the necessity of presenting pledges. Only four people were usually necessary, and

as London was a populous town and witnesses were prevalent, there was no need to involve many people and their pledges.

Chapter 5

1. "Symon's Lesson of Wisdom for All Manner of Children," in *The Babees' Book: Medieval Manners for the Young,* ed. Edith Rickert (New York, 1966), p. 122.

2. "The Young Children's Book," in ibid., p. 22.

3. "Symon's Lesson of Wisdom," in ibid., p. 122.

4. "Young Children's Book," in ibid., p. 25.

5. A number of manuals of advice survive from the late fourteenth and fifteenth centuries. Their popularity in instructing the increasingly upwardly mobile society and spreading the attributes of Western civilization has received thorough treatment in Norbert Elias, *Über den Prozess der Zivilisation; wandlungen des Verhaltens in den weltlichen Oberschichten des Abendlandes,* vol. 1 (Bern, 1969).

6. "Rhodes's Book of Nurture and School of Good Manners," in *Babees' Book,* ed. Rickert, pp. 127–128.

7. "How the Good Wife Taught Her Daughter," in ibid., p. 168.

8. *CPMR,* vol. 5, p. 125 (1452).

9. P.R.O. C1/94/14 (fifteenth century).

10. *Husting Wills,* vol. 1, pp. 481, 592 (1349), 662 (1352); Guildhall, Commissary Court 9171/5, 225v.

11. *CEMCR,* pp. 110–111 (1300–1301).

12. "Rhodes's Book of Nurture," in *Babees' Book,* ed. Rickert, p. 126. A simpler statement of message appeared in "Sans Puer ad Mensam," in which the poet states: "A rod reformeth all their negligence. / In their courage no rancour doth abide. / Who spareth the rod all virtues sets aside" (p. 30).

13. Frederick J. Furnivall, ed., *Robert [Manning] of Brunne's Handlyng Synne,* Early English Text Society, o.s., 119 (London, 1901), pp. 45–46, speaks of a woman who cursed her daughter when she did not have her clothes ready after her bath. The devil obediently carried off the daughter.

14. "The Young Scholar's Paradise," in *Babees' Book,* ed. Rickert, p. 159. Frederick J. Furnivall, ed., *Early English Meals and Manners: John Russel's Boke of Nurture, etc.,* Early English Text Society, o.s., 32 (London, 1868; Detroit, 1969), pp. 128–143, quotes from a variety of manuals on healthy living for adults that recommend taking a nap, sitting up or standing, after dinner; sleeping for eight to nine hours a night; voiding of bowels in the morning after a gentle walk; cleaning teeth with an ivory; and wearing health-giving gems and gives advice about nightcaps and clothing.

15. "Young Children's Book," p. 22; "Rhodes's Book of Nurture," p. 129; and "Seager's School of Virtue," pp. 141–144, in *Babees' Book,* ed. Rickert.

16. "Young Scholar's Paradise," in ibid., pp. 172–173.

17. Ibid., pp. 173–174.

18. *Letter Book A,* p. 4 (1275); *Letter Book C,* p. 5; *Letter Book E,* p. 82 (1317); *Letter Book F,* p. 60 (1340); *Letter Book H,* pp. 52, 141, 216 (1380s).

19. "Young Children's Book," in *Babees' Book,* ed. Rickert, p. 22.

20. "Rhodes's Book of Nurture," p. 131, and "Young Scholar's Paradise," pp. 170–171, in ibid.

21. "Symon's Lesson of Wisdom," in ibid., pp. 123–125.

22. Ibid., p. 124.

23. *CCR,* pp. 59, 100, 127, 190, 194, 252–253, 258; *Memorials,* pp. 260–261.

The city passed an ordinance against bathing in the fosses or in the Thames because of the risk of drowning.

24. Figures are based on cases taken from *CCR,* P.R.O. Just 2/94A, and *Letter Book G,* pp. 256–280. There are seventy-six male accidental deaths and twenty female (*CCR,* p. 250).

25. *CCR,* p. 231.

26. "Young Children's Book," pp. 24–25; "Rhodes's Book of Nurture," pp. 132–133; and "Seager's School of Virtue," pp. 148–149, in *Babees' Book,* ed. Rickert. "John Russell's Book of Nurture," a book on the duties of various offices, has a long description of table service.

27. *CEMCR,* p. 246 (1306). She lost because of good evidence from the jurors that the apprentice "did not beat the defendant, despise his food, nor tear his clothes."

28. *CCR,* p. 196.

29. Ibid., pp. 114–116.

30. John Stow's translation of Fitzstephen's description of London in *The Survey of London* (London, 1908), pp. 84–85.

31. "Symon's Lesson of Wisdom," in *Babees' Book,* ed. Rickert, pp. 123–125.

32. *CCR,* pp. 63, 191, 201, 238–239.

33. *CMPR,* vol. 2, p. 36.

34. P.R.O. C1/67/49.

35. Edward F. Rimbault, ed., "Two Sermons Preached by the Boy Bishop at St Paul's," in *The Camden Miscellany,* Camden Society, n.s., 7 (Westminster, 1875), pp. v–xxxvi, 1–13.

36. "Seager's School of Virtue," in *Babees' Book,* ed. Rickert, p. 144.

37. "Symon's Lesson of Wisdom," in ibid., p. 125: "Learn as fast as thou may and can, / For our bishop is an old man, / And therefore thou must learn fast, / If thou wilt be bishop when he is passed."

38. *CCR,* p. 25. The facts of Richard's case are his identity and that he was eight years old and on his way to school immediately after dinner on July 19, 1301. He was crossing London Bridge on his way to school when "he hung by his hands in play from a certain beam on the side of the bridge, so that, his hands giving way, he fell into the water and was drowned." He was found on the eve of the Feast of St. Mary Magdalen, to which I have transposed his story.

39. For complaints in company records, see Sylvia L. Thrupp, *The Merchant Class of Medieval London, 1300–1500* (Chicago, 1948), p. 158; Steve Rappaport, *Worlds Within Worlds: Structures of Life in Sixteenth-Century London* (Cambridge, 1989), pp. 297–299; P.R.O. C1/19/491, C1/19/33; and Walter Prideaux, ed., *Memorials of the Goldsmiths' Company, Being Gleanings from Their Records* (London, 1896), pp. 30–31.

40. Thrupp, *Merchant Class of Medieval London,* pp. 157–158. Her figures are based on the number who acted as witnesses for ten years in Consistory Court (1467–1476). On schooling and literacy in Yorkshire for the late medieval period, see Ann Hoeppner Moran, *The Growth of English Schooling, 1340–1548* (Princeton, N.J., 1983).

41. *Husting Wills,* vol. 1, pp. 163, 177, 188, 190, 228, 269. In the Husting wills, only 2 percent of those making bequests for public uses (hospitals, roads, prisoners, poor, etc.) left money for schools and scholars.

42. A. F. Leach, *The Schools of Medieval England* (London, 1915), pp. 260–267.

43. Henry Littlehales, ed., *The Medieval Records of a London Church*, Early English Text Society, o.s., 125–128 (London, 1905), pp. xxiv–xxxv, 81, 147–48, 162, 322, 327, 405.

44. Thrupp, *Merchant Class of Medieval London*, p. 161.

45. P.R.O. C1/221/70.

46. Thrupp, *Merchant Class of Medieval London*, pp. 160–161; *Husting Wills*, vol. 1, p. 134.

47. P.R.O. C1/226/47.

48. Thrupp, *Merchant Class of Medieval London*, p. 171.

49. "Seager's School of Virtue," pp. 144–148, and "Young Scholar's Paradise," pp. 159–161, in *Babees' Book*, ed. Rickert.

50. Furnivall, *Early English Meals and Manners*, pp. 385–386.

51. P.R.O. C1/46/162.

52. H. E. Salter, ed., *Records of Medieval Oxford, Coroners' Inquests, the Walls of Oxford, etc.* (London, 1912), p. 10.

53. "How the Wise Man Taught His Son," p. 43, and "Rhodes's Book of Nurture," p. 126, in *Babees' Book*, ed. Rickert.

54. "Symon's Lesson of Wisdom," p. 123, and "Rhode's Book of Nurture," p. 128, in ibid.

55. "Rhode's Book of Nurture," in ibid., p. 132.

56. Guildhall, Commissary Court 9171/3, 38 (1440).

57. P.R.O. C1/10/313 (fifteenth century); CMCR, 1, p. 109 (1339).

58. For a discussion of the regulations governing dress by age and status, see Frances Elizabeth Baldwin, *Sumptuary Legislation and Personal Regulation in England* (Baltimore, 1926).

59. "John Russell's Book of Nurture," in *Babees' Book*, ed. Rickert, p. 71.

60. "Young Children's Book," in ibid, p. 23.

61. "How the Wise Man Taught His Son," in ibid., p. 43.

62. Ibid., p. 46.

63. *CCR*, p. 232 (1339).

64. Ibid., p. 43.

65. "Young Children's Book," in *Babees' Book*, ed. Rickert, p. 23.

66. P.R.O. C1/204/34.

67. "The Proverbs of Alfred," in *A Medieval Anthology, Being Lyrics and Other Short Poems Chiefly Religious*, ed. Mary Seger (London, 1915), p. 131.

68. "The Merchant and His Son," in *Remains of Early Popular Poetry of England*, ed. W. Carew Hazlitt (London, 1864), p. 134.

Chapter 6

1. Peter Laslett, *Family Life and Illicit Love in Earlier Generations* (Cambridge, 1977), chap. 4. He points out that one-sixth or more of American children under the age of eighteen come from families in which one parent has left because of divorce or death. In the reconstitution of a seventeenth-century village population, 32 percent of the children were orphans. By far the largest percent had lost a father, rather than a mother.

2. For a discussion of abandoned children, see John Boswell, *Kindness of Strangers: The Abandonment of Children in Western Europe from Late Antiquity to the Renaissance* (New York, 1988). This type of problem is quite distinct from the one considered in this chapter.

3. W. J. B. Crotch, ed., *The Prologues and Epilogues of William Caxton*, Early English Text Society, o.s., 176 (London, 1928), p. 77.

4. Sylvia L. Thrupp, *The Merchant Class of Medieval London, 1300–1500* (Chicago, 1948), chap. 5.

5. Christiane Klapisch-Zuber, *Women, Family, and Ritual in Renaissance Italy*, trans. Lydia Cochrane (Chicago, 1985), particularly the essay "The Griselda Complex: Dowry and Marriage Gifts in the Quatrocento," pp. 213–246; David Nicholas, *The Domestic Life of a Medieval City: Women, Children, and Families in Fourteenth Century Ghent* (Lincoln, Neb., 1985); Marianne Danneel, "Orphanhood and Marriage in Fifteenth-Century Ghent," in *Marriage and Social Mobility in the Late Middle Ages*, Studia Historica Gandensia 274, ed. W. Prevenier (Ghent, 1989), pp. 99–111.

6. In *CPMR*, vol. 2, pp. xxvii–lxiv, A. H. Thomas discusses citizenship. He concludes that fewer than one-seventh of citizens were recruited from citizen stock (p. xxx) and that for every freeman in London from 1300 to 1537, there were three adult men uninfranchised (p. lxii). In *Letter Book D*, pp. i–viii, xiv–xvi, R. R. Sharpe gives a brief discussion of citizenship and of the terms of wardship. See also Gwyn A. Williams, *Medieval London: From Commune to Capital* (London, 1963), pp. 44–49, and, for citizenship, Steve Rappaport, *Worlds Within Worlds: Structure of Life in Sixteenth-Century London* (Cambridge, 1989), pp. 23–60. On p. 53 he concludes that in the sixteenth century, about three-quarters of the adult male population or slightly more than one-fifth of the total population, were citizens.

7. *Letter Book C*, p. 205 (1307).

8. Elaine Clark, "City Orphans and Custody Laws in Medieval England," *American Journal of Legal History* 34 (1990): 168–187, has made this the major thrust of her very fine article on wardship in London and Bristol.

9. *Liber Albus*, pp. 95–96. When a man abducted and failed to register a ten-year-old girl who was a citizen's daughter, the mayor had him arrested (*Letter Book I*, p. 111 [1412]).

10. *Letter Book I*, pp. 220–221, restates the law explicitly in one case.

11. *CEMCR*, p. 77.

12. In *Letter Book D*, pp. iv, xiv, Sharpe discusses the wardship procedures. *Letter Book G*, p. 79, mentions the name of one of the Common Pleaders. For a general discussion, see Charles Carlton, *The Court of Orphans* (Leicester, 1974), chap. 1, on the medieval foundation and the rest of the book for a discussion of the Tudor–Stuart period; *Letter Book K*, p. 93. The number of years was also limited.

13. *Letter Book K*, p. 93 (1428).

14. *Letter Book C*, pp. 81, 82; *Letter Book E*, p. 121; *Letter Book G*, p. 91.

15. *Husting Wills*, vol. 1, p. 377 (1332).

16. Of the 521 orphan families (sibling groups) in which a record exists of inheritance, 49 percent were left goods and 51 percent, real estate.

17. Through 1368, only about one-third of the cases recorded the value of the inheritance. Until 1438, 40 to 50 percent of the cases register the bequest. After that, almost 100 percent of the cases record the amounts.

18. Figures from *Husting Wills*.

19. The kin included uncles or aunts of the child, grandparents, elder sons, and a nephew.

20. *Letter Book G,* p. 95 (1358), records the terms of a will in a wardship enrollment. Thomas Bedyk gave to Simon Fraunceys, a mercer, the wardship, custody, and marriage of his son Henry during his minority.

21. The father would be the logical choice of guardian if the children's inheritance came from the mother. The mortality of orphans perhaps increased the number of surviving daughters as sole heirs. The discrepancies between Clark's figures and mine represent differences in the years and the categories used. Our basic results are the same (Clark, "City Orphans and Custody Laws," p. 182).

22. Michael M. Sheehan, "The Influence of Canon Law on the Property Rights of Married Women in England," *Mediaeval Studies* 25 (1963): 121.

23. R. S. Schofield and E. A. Wrigley, "Remarriage Intervals and the Effect of Marriage Order on Fertility," in *Marriage and Remarriage in Populations of the Past,* ed. J. Dupaquier, E. Helin, P. Laslett, M. Levi-Bacci, and S. Sogner (London, 1981), pp. 212, 214. Their figures are for small towns and villages, rather than for London. See also David Herlihy and Christiane Klapisch-Zuber, *The Tuscans and Their Families: A Study of the Florentine Catasto of 1427* (New Haven, Conn., 1985), p. 217, which finds that widows seldom remarried in Florence.

24. For a complete discussion of remarriage of widows, see Barbara A. Hanawalt, "Remarriage as an Option for Urban and Rural Widows in Late Medieval England," in *Wife and Widow: The Experiences of Women in Medieval England,"* ed. Sue Sheridan Walker (Ann Arbor, 1993), pp. 141–164. Forty-five percent of widows with one child remarried, compared with 43 percent with one child who did not; 24 percent with two children remarried, compared with 18 percent who did not; 17 percent with three children married again, compared with 20 percent who did not; and 14 percent of the remarried women had four or more children, whereas 19 percent of those not remarrying had four or more children.

25. Thrupp, *Merchant Class of Medieval London,* p. 107. Another man making a similar marriage controlled £3,000 in this manner.

26. *Letter Book C,* p. 131 (1303).

27. *Letter Book E,* p. 9 (1318); *Letter Book F,* pp. 248–249 (1350), tells of an older brother who became guardian to his young sister.

28. Betty Masters, *The Chamberlain of the City of London, 1237–1987* (London, 1988), p. 11. Information is from *Letter Book E,* pp. 135, 217, in which the guardian presents his expenses for maintaining the child for eight years. See also *Letter Book G,* pp. 320–321.

29. Schofield and Wrigley, "Remarriage Intervals," pp. 212–214; Herlihy and Klapisch-Zuber, *Tuscans and Their Families,* p. 217, also find that almost all the men remarried.

30. The case is a long one in which Margaret made several involved complaints. She claimed that when John Bryan found that he could not pay his apprentice, Richard Fraunceys, the sums that he owed him, he conspired to marry him to Alison so that her 110 marks would cover the debt. These espousals, Margaret argued, were illegal because they were done without the permission of the mayor and chamberlain (CLRO, MC1/1/62). Although Margaret referred to the enrollment of John Rayner's will, it does not appear in *Husting Wills.* The other parties likewise do not appear. Fraunceys was a common name, but Richard Fraunceys does not appear. *Letter Book H,* pp. 10–12, indicates that Rayner's executors had quickly paid off Margaret's inheritance of 40s. 4d. Most likely, Bryan was eager to eliminate her influence. In 1380, five years after Alison's father had died, Bryan

came to the court and got permission for Alison's marriage, paying the chamberlain 20s. for permission. The Letter Book does not say that the marriage was to Fraunceys. Obviously, Margaret had retained some contact with her daughter, but she had no power to control her marriage.

31. See, for instance, *Letter Book G*, pp. 306, 315, in which the uncles on both the paternal and maternal sides look after the children's interests.

32. *CPMR*, vol. 3, p. 99 (1384).

33. *Letter Book G*, pp. 7, 11; *CPMR*, vol. 2, pp. 138, 227, 260, 265.

34. *Letter Book D*, pp. 180–181; *CPMR*, vol. 3, pp. 72–73 (1384); *Letter Book E*, p. 19, for another case. If the guardians would not pay, they were put into prison (*CPMR*, vol. 2, p. 37). *CEMCR*, pp. 110–111 (1301) tells of a couple who got a writ through a ruse that gave them a house belonging to a ward of the city to her damage of 10s.

35. *Letter Book H*, p. 354; see also CLRO, MC1/2/41.

36. *Letter Book C*, pp. 181, 182.

37. *Letter Book E*, p. 47 (1315).

38. *Letter Book G*, p. 163 (1363); *CPMR*, vol. 2, p. 159 (1373), reports that the fine was only 60s. In *CPMR*, vol. 2, 205–206, a girl was married at age seven. One woman who pursued her case for her younger sister accused the man of both rape and abduction. He denied the charges and said that he was the proper guardian of the girl (CLRO, Common Pleas 31, m. 12). Depending on the property, the sale of a wardship was quite lucrative. One man claimed to have sold the wardship of a little girl for £40. Since he did not receive full payment, he kept the child, and now he was being sued for damages (P.R.O. C1/86/15).

39. *Letter Book G*, pp. 38, 106; *Letter Book H*, p. 1; for the abduction of another boy at age fourteen, see Thrupp, *Merchant Class of Medieval London*, pp. 356, 342. The famous case, of course, is that of John Chaucer, father of Geoffrey,

40. *CEMCR*, pp. 203–204 (1305). Walter lost the case because he had also signed a covenant (probably not by force, since he confessed he signed it) that he would not take any action against Roger.

41. *Letter Book H*, p. 141.

42. *Letter Book E*, pp. 17–18 (1313), 26–27, 300–301. It took twenty-eight years to settle the claims against the guardians. See also *CPMR*, vol. 2, p. 175, for failure to put ward in apprenticeship.

43. *CPMR*, vol. 2, pp. 170–171. In another case, the guardian used the court to make a bond with the executors to protect the child and inheritance even though the child could not become a ward of the city (p. 169).

44. For a discussion of the tradition of steparents, see Jean-Louis Flandrin, *Families in Former Times: Kinship, Household, and Sexuality*, trans. Richard Southern (Cambridge, 1979), pp. 40–43.

45. *Letter Book D*, pp. xv–xvi (1310–1321). See other cases in *Letter Book C*, p. 197, and PRO C1/64/744.

46. *CPMR*, vol. 5, pp. 51–52.

47. *CCR*, pp. 245–246 (1339). For civil cases, see P.R.O. C1/16/307, in which the son tries to prohibit her from trading in London, although she had enough merchandise in the city before she married to cover her trade and had made a covenant with her husband about this merchandise. See also Ralph B. Pugh, ed., *Calendar of London Trailbaston Trials Under Commissions of 1305 and 1306* (London,

1975), p. 95, in which a young man is accused of beating and ill-treating his stepmother.

48. *Letter Book C,* pp. 33, 34, 92, 94. John de Storteford's will mentions John, Adam, Gilbert, Cecilia, Margery, Juliana, and Amisia (*Husting Wills,* vol. 1, pp. 134–135; Gilbert's will, p. 298).

49. *Letter Book D,* p. 181 (1309–1310).

50. *Letter Book E,* pp. 105, 198, 205; *Husting Wills,* vol. 1, pp. 508, 237.

51. *Husting Wills,* vol. 2, p. 234 (1383).

52. Thrupp, *Merchant Class of Medieval London,* p. 28; Rappaport, *Worlds Within Worlds,* pp. 40–41. For a more complete discussion of remarriage of widows, see Hanawalt, "Remarriage as an Option for Urban and Rural Widows."

53. Herlihy and Klapisch-Zuber, *Tuscans and Their Families,* p. 217; on the "cruel mother" syndrome in Florence, see Klapisch-Zuber, *Women, Family, and Ritual in Renaissance Italy,* pp. 117–131.

54. Danneel, "Orphanhood and Marriage in Fifteenth-Century Ghent," pp. 99–111; Nicholas, *Domestic Life of a Medieval City,* pp. 27–33, 76–77.

Chapter 7

1. J. A. Burrow, *The Ages of Man: A Study in Medieval Writing and Thought* (Oxford, 1988), pp. 12–37.

2. "The Mirror of the Periods of Man's Life," in *Hymns to the Virgin and Christ, The Parliament of Devils, and Other Religious Poems,* ed. Frederick J. Furnival, Early English Text Society, o.s., 24 (London, 1868; New York, 1969), p. 61.

3. Arnold van Gennep, *The Rites of Passage,* trans. Monika B. Vizedom and Gabrielle L. Caffee (1908; Chicago, 1960). Chapter 6, "Initiation Rites," contains his distinction between physical and social puberty.

4. Victor W. Turner, *The Ritual Process: Structure and Anti-Structure* (New York, 1969), pp. 94–96.

5. Glen Elder, Jr., "Adolescence in the Life Cycle: An Introduction," in *Adolescence in the Life Cycle,* ed. Sigmund E. Dragastin and Glen H. Elder, Jr. (Washington, D.C., 1975), pp. 1–13; Elder, *Adolescent Socialization and Personality Development* (Chicago, 1968).

6. Darrel Amundsen and Carol Jean Dries, "The Age of Menarche in Medieval Europe," *Human Biology* 45 (1973): 363–368. Charles T. Wood, "The Doctor's Dilemma: Sin, Salvation, and the Menstrual Cycle," *Speculum* 56 (1981): 710–727, has little to say about the age of menarche aside from suggesting that laws governing the age of marriage might indicate the onset of menses. But custom can be as powerful as, or more powerful than, biology when it comes to laws.

7. Burrow, *Ages of Man,* p. 27.

8. James A. Brundage, *Law, Sex, and Christian Society in Medieval Europe* (Chicago, 1987), pp. 53, 91–92, 156, 199, 242, 283, 451, 508.

9. Margery Kempe, *The Book of Margery Kempe,* ed. Sanford B. Meech and Hope Emily Allen, Early English Text Society, o.s., 212 (London, 1940).

10. Burrow, *Ages of Man,* pp. 37, 48–50; *Mundus et Infans,* in *Three Late Medieval Morality Plays: Mankind, Everyman, and Mundus et Infans,* ed. G. A. Lester (New York, 1981), pp. 114–117.

11. Sylvia L. Thrupp, *The Merchant Class of Medieval London, 1300–1500* (Chicago, 1948), p. 195. Keith Thomas, "Age and Authority in Early Modern England,"

Proceedings of the British Academy 52 (1976): 205–248, has a discussion of later traditions of youth and the struggles between youth and their seniors.

12. R. J. Mitchell and M. D. R. Leys, *A History of London Life* (London, 1958), pp. 46–47; George Clune, *The Medieval Gild System* (Dublin, 1943), p. 88; *Letter Book E*, p. 272; *Letter Book F*, p. 35; *Letter Book H*, pp. 165, 405.

13. Thrupp, *Merchant Class of Medieval London*, p. 193; Clune, *Medieval Gild System*, pp. 87–88. By the sixteenth century, the average age for entering an apprenticeship was between eighteen and twenty-two, with some companies forbidding enrollment of apprentices under sixteen. The reason for the late age of entry into apprenticeship was both the increased demand for literacy among apprentices and the need for their labor at home (most apprentices were drawn from husbandmens' families) (Steve Rappaport, *Worlds Within Worlds: Structures of Life in Sixteenth-Century London* [Cambridge, 1989], pp. 295–298).

14. CLRO, Mayor's Court, MC1/1/13 file 1.13; *Letter Book G*, p. 105 (1358).

15. *CPMR*, vol. 4, p. 229 (1429).

16. *Letter Book H*, p. 150 (1388). His brother, William Hoke, had become an Augustinian friar. See *Letter Book I*, p. 57 (1414); *Letter Book K*, p. 115 (1429), records an advance to go to Grey's Inn at age nineteen.

17. CLRO, Mayor's Court, MC1/1/28 files 1.28 (1380s).

18. *Mundus et Infans*, in *Three Morality Plays*, ed. Lester, pp. 115–116.

19. Ibid., pp. 117–118.

20. Clune, *Medieval Gild System*, pp. 90–92.

21. "How the Good Wife Taught Her Daughter," in *The Babees' Book: Medieval Manners for the Young*, ed. Edith Rickert (New York, 1966), pp. 34–35.

22. *CPMR*, vol. 1, p. 113; *Memorials*, p. 88 (1311).

23. *CCR*, p. 17.

24. *Mercers*, p. 724 (1526).

25. CLRO, Mayor's Court MC1/2A/21 (reign of Richard II).

26. *Memorials*, p. 268.

27. Ibid., p. 88 (*Letter Book D* [1311]).

28. *CCR*, p. 112 (1325).

29. Ibid., p. 196. For an example of men wrestling, see pp. 20–21, in which two men wrestled with each other with all their strength, and Walter broke his assailant's leg. It was an amicable match in which one lent the other a vest to wrestle in when his was torn.

30. Mitchell and Leys, *History of London Life*, p. 30, recounts a match in Westminster in 1222 that led to a riot and beating of the abbot. Several men were hanged for disturbing the peace.

31. Ibid., pp. 29–30.

32. *Letter Book I*, pp. 72, 125.

33. Ruth Bird, *The Turbulent London of Richard II* (London, 1948), p. 53.

34. P.R.O. C1/45/98.

35. Robert Withington, *English Pageantry: An Historical Outline*, 2 vols. (Cambridge, Mass., 1918); Charles Pendrill, *London Life in the Fourteenth Century* (London, 1925; Port Washington, N.Y., 1971), pp. 47–67. Peter Burke, "Popular Culture in Seventeenth-Century London," *London Journal* 3 (1977): 143–147, speaks of the older celebrations in London that continued into the seventeenth century.

36. Thrupp, *Merchant Class of Medieval London*, p. 150.

37. Frances Elizabeth Baldwin, *Sumptuary Legislation and Personal Regulation in England* (Baltimore, 1926), pp. 32–119.

38. H. S. Bennett, *England from Chaucer to Caxton* (London, 1928), p. 143. *Letter Book D*, p. xi, states that no one wearing a beard "of more notable prolyxyte or length" than that worn by other citizens should be admitted by redemption to the freedom of the city.

39. *Mercers*, p. 724.

40. "How the Good Wife Taught Her Daughter," in *Babees' Book*, ed. Rickert, p. 35.

41. *Letter Book N*, p. 92 (1517). The case is a particularly full one; the parts in quotes are in the case that appears in the letter book. Joan's placement is not in the case. As the evidence in this chapter and in Chapter 10, on servants, unfold, her story will seem more and more plausible.

42. "How the Good Wife Taught Her Daughter," in *Babees' Book*, ed. Rickert, pp. 35–36.

43. "A Little Sooth Sermon," in *A Treasure of Middle English Verse Selected and Rendered into Modern English*, ed. Margot Adamson (London, 1930), p. 6.

44. Rossell Hope Robbins, ed., *Secular Lyrics of the Fourteenth and Fifteenth Centuries* (Oxford, 1952), pp. 16–19.

45. P.R.O. C1/214/91. Some men were suspected of making a practice of deflowering virgins in their neighborhood (Guildhall, Consistory Court 9064/2 159v).

46. P.R.O. C1/45/24. Of course, the case appeared in a chancery petition because Philip did not pay up and continued to vex the family.

47. *Letter Book L*, p. 103.

48. Guildhall, Consistory Court 9064/10; *Letter Book K*, p. 17.

49. Richard Wunderli, *London Church Courts and Society on the Eve of the Reformation* (Cambridge, Mass., 1981), pp. 91–92. In the Consistory Court, the four cases were of "spiritual kin"—that is, godparents. None ended in conviction.

50. Ibid., pp. 89–90.

51. *Letter Book N*, pp. 39–40. See also *Letter Book K*, pp. 216–217, in which a maiden in the service of a neighbor was enticed into a bawdy house and debauched against her will. In *CPMR*, vol. 5, pp. 13–14 (1439), a woman sold a girl to unknown Lombards, who deflowered her against her will and then took her to the stews in Southwark on four occasions. For cases from the Consistory Court, see Wunderli, *London Church Courts*, pp. 91–96. On prostitution in London, see Ruth Mazo Karras, "The Regulation of Brothels in Later Medieval England," *Signs* 14 (1989): 399–433, and E. J. Burford, *Bawds and Lodgings: A History of the London Bankside Brothels* (London, 1976).

52. *Memorials*, p. 140.

53. For examples, see Guildhall, Consistory Court 9064/1 14v, 22v, 58v.

54. Wunderli, *London Church Courts*, pp. 83–84. Only one defamation case appears in which a woman charged another woman with having a "woman" for a husband because he grabbed priests between the legs.

55. Ralph B. Pugh, ed., *Calendar of London Trailbaston Trials Under Commissions of 1305 and 1306* (London, 1975), p. 84.

56. Wunderlli, *London Church Courts*, p. 87, finds that large numbers of adultery cases came into the Consistory Court at the end of the fifteenth century. See also Guildhall, Consistory Court 9064/1 15v, 46, 124, 9064/3 11 (wife in adultery with husband's servant), 58v, 90, 116, 200.

57. Guildhall, Consistory Court 9064/1 10, 40v (a dress), 50 (£4 40d. for a prostitute of Lupanavi), 101 (sheaf of corn), 113 (40s.); CLRO, MCl/1/7 file 1.7 (1392).

58. *CCR*, p. 147.

59. Jacques Rossiaud, *Medieval Prostitution*, trans. Lydia G. Cochrane (Oxford, 1984), pp. 11–15.

60. P.R.O. Cl/154/60.

61. See Natalie Zemon Davis's essay "The Reasons of Misrule," in *Society and Culture in Early Modern France* (Stanford, Calif., 1975), pp. 97–123.

62. Pendrill, *London Life in the Fourteenth Century*, pp. 47–63.

63. Burke, "Popular Culture in Seventeenth-Century London," pp. 144–145. Lack of court records may simply represent laconic entries rather than lack of practice.

64. *Mercers*, pp. 418–419 (1513).

65. Ibid., pp. 444–445.

66. For a discussion of trade fights and their consequences for the city, see Pendrill, *London Life in the Fourteenth Century*, pp. 133–169.

67. J. H. Baker, "The English Legal Profession, 1450–1550," in *Lawyers in Early Modern Europe and America*, ed. Wilfrid Prest (New York, 1981), pp. 27–29. The term "apprentice" also came to denote someone already trained and practicing law.

68. *CPMR*, vol. 1, p. 213.

69. *CCR*, pp. 225–226, 134–135.

70. Ibid., pp. 156–60.

71. J. B. Threfall, "John Fressh, Lord Mayor of London 1395," *Genealogists' Magazine* 21 (1984): 291.

72. Pendrill, *London Life in the Fourteenth Century*, pp. 76–77. For an account of the alien merchants in late-fourteenth-century London, see Alice Beardwood, *Alien Merchants in England, 1350–1377: Their Legal and Economic Position* (Cambridge, Mass., 1931).

73. See, for instance, Pugh, *Calendar of London Trailbaston Trials*, pp. 95–97.

74. G. R. Owst, *Literature and the Pulpit in Medieval England* (Cambridge, 1933), pp. 460–468.

75. *La Male Regle*, in Bennett, *England from Chaucer to Caxton*, pp. 138–141.

Chapter 8

1. Steve Rappaport, *Worlds Within Worlds: Structures of Life in Sixteenth-Century London* (Cambridge, 1989), p. 294. With apprenticeship terms lengthened to ten or more years in the late fifteenth and sixteenth centuries, apprenticeship could last about a quarter of a man's life.

2. Stella Kramer, *The English Craft Gilds: Studies in Their Progress and Decline* (New York, 1927), has very little discussion of apprenticeship. Margaret Gay Davies, *The Enforcement of English Apprenticeship: A Study in Applied Mercantilism* (Cambridge, Mass., 1956), is more interested in the implications of government enforcement. Ilana Krausman Ben-Amos, "Apprenticeship, the Family, and Urban Society in Early Modern England" (Ph.D. diss., Stanford University, 1985), is a good corrective to the older trend.

3. Michael Mitterauer and Reinhard Sieder, *The European Family: Patriarchy to Partnership From the Middle Ages to the Present*, trans. Karla Oosterveen and

Manfred Horzinger (Chicago, 1982), pp. 104–105, has a brief and contradictory discussion of apprenticeship. On the one hand, the master stood *in loco parentis;* on the other hand, he was an exploiter of cheap labor. They are, however, among the few authors to discuss the relationship. Philippe Ariès, *Centuries of Childhood: A Social History of the Family,* trans. Robert Baldick (London, 1962), p. 366, has a very uninformed discussion of apprenticeship, confusing it with servitude, which is actually a very different sort of contract.

4. A. H. Thomas, Introduction, *CPMR,* vol. 2, pp. xxxii–xxxiii. By the sixteenth century, the vast majority of citizens of London became so through apprenticeship rather than by being born citizens or buying citizenship.

5. Jean M. Imray, "'Les Bones Gentes de la Mercerye de Londres': A Study of the Membership of the Medieval Mercers' Company," in *Studies in London History,* ed. A. E. J. Hollaender and William Kellaway (London, 1969), pp. 159–60, 169. Often, apprentices who were brothers were enrolled with the same master.

6. Rappaport, *Worlds Within Worlds,* pp. 304–305. This advantage meant that Londoners played a dominant role in the major guilds even while composing only one-quarter or one-third of the membership.

7. *Letter Book E,* pp. 137–138 (1320); *Letter Book F,* p. 234 (1351).

8. *Letter Book E,* p. 192; *CPMR,* vol. 5, p. 88 (1445); *CEMCR,* p. 190 (1305).

9. *CPMR,* vol. 5, p. 65 (1445); P.R.O. C1/125/2, C1/66/66; P.R.O. C1/29/180, in which a man named Baldwin Victour apprenticed his cousin and namesake.

10. P.R.O. C1/48/11.

11. A. H. Thomas, Introduction, *CPMR,* vol. 2, p. xxxi.

12. Walter S. Prideaux, ed., *Memorials of the Goldsmiths' Company, Being Gleanings from Their Records* (London, 1896), p. 15.

13. *Mercers,* pp. 89, 193. According to Imray, "'Bones Gentes de la Mercerye,'" pp. 157–158, in 1347 entry required a 2*s.* fee from the master and a similar amount from the apprentice; in 1348, the fee was raised to 20*s.,* and in 1357 to £3 6*s.* 8*d.* About 12 percent of masters and apprentices were delinquent in paying fees, but most did eventually pay them, along with a fine for delinquency. See also A. H. Johnson, *The History of the Worshipful Company of Drapers of London* (Oxford, 1914), p. 272. The Drapers set the fee at 13*s.* 4*d.* in the late fifteenth century, but reduced it to 6*s.* 8*d.* in 1512.

14. Sylvia L. Thrupp, "The Grocers of London, A Study in Distribution Trade," in *Studies in English Trade in the Fifteenth Century,* ed. Eileen Power and M. M. Postan (London, 1933), p. 255.

15. *Letter Book A,* p. 5.

16. *CPMR,* vol. 3, pp. 14–15; P.R.O. C1/67/144; *Letter Book G,* p. 308 (1373), says an eight-year apprenticeship went for 46*s.* 8*d.*

17. P.R.O. C1/208/63, C1/212/2. There was some question of who got to keep the money if the apprentice died or became unfit during the term. For instance, William Grene gave 20 marks for apprenticing his son. After a year and a half, the boy fell into a frenzy, and the master evicted him. The father wanted the money back (Sylvia L. Thrupp, *The Merchant Class of Medieval London, 1300–1500* [Chicago, 1948], pp. 214–215).

18. Thomas Reddaway, *The Early History of the Goldsmiths' Company* (London, 1975), p. 73.

19. Thrupp, "Grocers of London," p. 256.

20. Ibid., pp. 256–257; Thrupp, *Merchant Class of Medieval London,* p. 215.

21. Charles M. Clode, *The Early History of the Guild of Merchant Taylors* (London, 1888), pts. 1 and 2, p. 344. The process of drawing up the contract is described in another case. William Morton and Robert de Eye, a cutler, came to a verbal agreement, and Robert had a scrivener draw up an indenture of apprenticeship that contained clauses William had not agreed to. The contract said that William would pay the usual 4 marks for his first year, but Robert had added that he would have to pay a bond of £40 if he broke the contract. William refused and argued that his parents and friends would never have agreed to that stipulation. The mayor overturned the bond (*CPMR*, vol. 3, p. 14 [1383]).

22. George Clune, *The Medieval Gild System* (Dublin, 1943), pp. 91–94.

23. Reddaway, *Early History of the Goldsmiths' Company*, p. 147.

24. *Letter Book D*, p. ix.

25. Sixty-six served for eight years; nineteen, for nine; forty-two, for ten; eight, for eleven; eleven, for twelve; two, for thirteen; five, for fourteen; and one, for sixteen (Thomas, Introduction, *CPMR*, vol. 2, p. xxxiii).

26. Rappaport, *Worlds Within Worlds*, p. 297.

27. *CPMR*, vol. 1, pp. 235–239.

28. Reddaway, *Early History of the Goldsmiths' Company*, pp. 73, 80.

29. *CPMR*, vol. 5, index under "Apprenticeship, length of term."

30. Of sixty-five scattered cases of broken apprenticeship contracts that appear in the records of the mayor's court, Chancery petitions, and surviving company records for the fifteenth century, the average length of apprenticeship was ten years. Sixteen years for a contract was not unknown (P.R.O. C1/19/143). For the sixteenth century, see Rappaport, *Worlds Within Worlds*, p. 109; George Unwin, *The Gilds and Companies of London* (London, 1908), pp. 91–92; and Charles Welch, *History of the Cutlers' Company of London*, vol. 1: *From Early Times to 1500* (London, 1916), pp. 10–14. The Cutlers required a seven-year term with extra service.

31. Imray, "'Bones Gentes de la Mercerye,'" pp. 170–171. Only 509 out of 1,047 had apprentices.

32. *Liber Albus*, pp. 237, 330–331.

33. Reddaway, *Early History of the Goldsmiths' Company*, p. 91, says that eighty-eight took two apprentices, forty-six took three, thirty-four took four, nineteen took five, fifteen took six, fourteen took seven, seven took eight, three took nine, two took ten, four took eleven, and one took sixteen. Reddaway warns that these figures must represent underreporting because not all apprentices were registered, regardless of the regulations.

34. Johnson, *History of the Worshipful Company of Drapers*, pp. 105, 180. The variation in the number admitted each year is very interesting. In 1413, the Drapers admitted 40 apprentices; between 1423 and 1434, they admitted an average of 20 a year, but in 1441 they admitted 255.

35. Imray, "'Bones Gentes de la Mercerye,'" p. 171.

36. Reddaway, *Early History of the Goldsmiths' Company*, pp. 275–321.

37. *Letter Book M*, 12 Henry VI (founders' ordinances).

38. Rappaport, *Worlds Within Worlds*, p. 69. Those apprentices about whom information is known might expect to be masters by age twenty-eight and then have an average life expectancy of twenty-eight more years. This made the majority of the cohort he studied fifty-six years of age when they died. Many, of course, did not live that long.

39. Clune, *Medieval Gild System*, p. 91.

40. *CPMR*, vol. 2, p. 294 (1381). Roger Dane, without the consent of his apprentice, transferred the apprentice to another master (p. 212 [1376]).

41. Rappaport, *Worlds Within Worlds*, pp. 311–315; Heather Swanson, *Medieval Artisans: An Urban Class in Late Medieval England* (Oxford, 1989), p. 36. In York's Weavers' guild of the late fifteenth century, only 15 percent of the apprentices completed their terms and became free of the city.

42. Prideaux, *Memorials of the Goldsmiths' Company*, p. 7.

43. P.R.O. C1/38/40.

44. Imray, "'Bones Gentes de la Mercerye,'" p. 172. Mercers insisted that the apprentice be enrolled with the Mercers first and then with the city. In fact, they were lax about enrollment and collection of fines before 1477 to 1478.

45. *Mercers*, p. xi. According to Welch, *History of the Cutlers' Company*, vol. 1, p. 114, the guild required that the apprentices be "clean of limb and lith in their bodies without any deformity for the worship of the city."

46. Reddaway, *Early History of the Goldsmiths' Company*, p. 147; Rappaport, *Worlds Within Worlds*, p. 298; Prideaux, *Memorials of the Goldsmiths' Company*, p. 28.

47. Guildhall, 11592, Grocers' Company, Register of Freemen (1345–1481).

48. *Mercers*, pp. 105 (1477), 382 (1510).

49. P.R.O. C1/49/527.

50. *CPMR*, vol. 5, pp. 50–51. *Letter Book D*, pp. 97 ff., refers to the enrollment by wards.

51. *Letter Book G*, pp. 179–80, 211. The mayor and the aldermen agreed to the presence of guild members in addition to the master and apprentice, but a special day set aside for enrollment was not approved (pp. xii–xiii).

52. *Mercers*, pp. 89, 105, 592. According to *Memorials*, p. 258, the Furbishers threatened to deny freedom of the city to anyone not enrolling an apprentice. See also Welch, *History of the Cutler's Company*, vol. 1, pp. 141–142; *Letter Book I*, p. 134. R. R. Sharpe, in *Letter Book D*, p. x, states that more apprentices than masters were cited for failing to enroll. Taking all the cases from various court records, the failure appears to be equal for both parties.

53. Marian K. Dale, "The London Silkwomen of the Fifteenth Century," *Economic History Review*, 1st ser., 4 (1933): 324–335; Kay E. Lacey, "Women and Work in Fourteenth- and Fifteenth-Century London," in *Women and Work in Pre-Industrial England*, ed. Lindsey Charles and Lorna Duffin (London, 1985), pp. 24–82.

54. P.R.O. C1/155/10.

55. Charles Pendrill, *London Life in the Fourteenth Century* (London, 1925), pp. 75–76. The various trades that women entered included embroidery, hurer, burrither, brekegwidelmakere, dressmaking, and, most common, silk-thread making. He also remarks that girls were often put to apprentice in such trades as cordwain, drapery, and grocery. In fact, these are the occupations of the husband; it is more likely that the wife would teach the trade, but her craft is not mentioned.

56. *CPMR*, vol. 1, p. 274 (1364).

57. CLRO, MC1/2/3, 3/171; *Letter Book F*, p. 142 (1346).

58. *CPMR*, vol. 2, p. 219 (1376). In *Letter Book H*, p. 227 (1275), a paternoster maker released his apprentice for 14s. to be paid by installments of 6d. at Easter from term to term.

59. *Letter Book I*, p. 38 (1404).

60. *CPMR*, vol. 4, p. 88 (1445); CLRO, MC1/1/13, MC1/3/171.

61. Maryanne Kowaleski and Judith M. Bennett, "Crafts, Gilds, and Women

in the Middle Ages: Fifty Years After Marian K. Dale," *Signs* 14 (1989): 474–478; Judith M. Bennett, "Working Together: Women and Men in the Brewers' Gild of London, c. 1420," in *The Salt of Common Life: Individuality and Choice in the Medieval Town, Countryside, and Church,* ed. Edwin DeWindt (Kalamazoo, Mich., forthcoming).

62. "The Childe of Bristowe," in *Remains of Early Popular Poetry of England,* ed. W. Carew Hazlitt (London, 1864), pp. 113–114.

63. According to *Letter Book K,* pp. 353 (1452), 87, the statute was from 7 Henry VI; pp. 104–105 gives the petition to have the statute struck down.

64. Caroline M. Barron, "Richard Whittington: The Man Behind the Myth," in *Studies in London History,* ed. A. E. J. Hollaender and William Kellaway (London, 1969), pp. 197–99. The tale that he came to London penniless and acquired a cat that caught the rat that lived in the house that his master lived in and so won the master's daughter in marriage (a simplified version) is fictitious. He was of gentry birth, became very wealthy, and served as Lord Mayor.

65. H. S. Bennett, *England from Chaucer to Caxton* (New York, 1928), pp. 149–150.

66. Thrupp, *Merchant Class of Medieval London,* pp. 211–219.

67. Rappaport, *Worlds Within Worlds,* pp. 304–311; Thrupp, *Merchant Class of Medieval London,* pp. 218–219, makes a similar observation about the lesser companies in the fifteenth century.

68. Reddaway, *Early History of the Goldsmiths' Company,* pp. 275, 286, 288.

69. Thrupp, *Merchant Class of Medieval London,* pp. 208–210, 219.

70. Thomas, Introduction, *CPMR,* vol. 2, pp. xxxiii–xxxv; Rappaport, *Worlds Within Worlds,* pp. 77–84.

71. C. A. Sneyd, ed., *The Italian Relation of England,* Camden Society 37 (London, 1847), p. 24.

72. *Mercers,* p. xii; Imray, "'Bones Gentes de la Mercerye,'" p. 160.

73. *CEMCR,* p. 166 (1304–1305); on p. 190 (1305), when an apprenticeship did not work out, it was the apprentice's mother and stepfather who intervened. See *CPMR,* vol. 1, pp. 268–269 (1364), in which the sponsor brought the case for the apprentice. In *CPMR,* vol. 2, p. 248 (1378), a father complained of the failure to make his son free of the city; on p. 12 (1364), a master claimed that the apprentice refused to be enrolled, but the youth's mother was able to show that she and the master had agreed that the indentures should be broken, so that the master was fined; see also CLRO, MC1/1/48, in which the son had run away because he was not taught, was treated harshly, and was not fed and clothed; also, MC1/1/50, in which a mother complains that her son was not taught and then was sent to another household where he almost starved; also, MC1/2/3, in which parents of a girl intervene when her master and mistress do not feed her; MC1/3/171, in which parents complain that their daughter was not instructed; and MC1/2/3, in which parents insist that their daughter be returned.

74. *Memorials,* p. 197 (1376). The record went on to say that the apprentice was too young to make his own arrangements in any case, and the only surety the master provided was to pledge "by the cross at the north door" (P.R.O. C1/66/215, C1/24/83). See also *CLMC,* p. 54 (1352), in which the master said that the accusation was malicious, but the boy did arrange with his master to go to Ware to visit friends for a few days and he had not returned.

75. CLRO, MC 1/1/17. John Halle, from Sussex, complained that he was apprenticed in 1381 to Gregory Capell, a citizen and fuller of London, for twelve

years. In 1392, his master handed him over to Gilian Wolfhale, who handed him over to Katherine Abell the same year. Abell was suing the brother-in-law for loss of services, but Halle countersued.

76. CLRO, MC1/1/18 (1392). In P.R.O. C1/72/66, one master threatened to imprison the brother of an apprentice in order to extort money from him.

77. *CEMCR*, pp. 237–238 (1305–1306).

78. *CPMR*, vol. 1, p. 130 (1340). In one case, the agreement between master and father was close enough that they mutually mainprised the apprentice.

79. Bothe we have met with before making a petition to the Chancellor against his master, William Hill, a mercer. The plea recalls his oath in the Guildhall (P.R.O. C1/49/527). One would think that his family, his sponsor's family, and his master would be easy to find in the records, but no wills are recorded for them. On the other hand, the Mercers' Court records that a William Hill, the name of the master recorded in the petition, did ride out to meet the king and that he was one of the wealthy members of the guild, paying a variety of subsidies (*Mercers*, pp. 49, 52, 55). Other people with the name Hill also played a prominent role in the company. Bothe is a name that appears later in the century (1488) in connection with continuing to maintain chantries established by his ancestors. By this time the family had become gentlemen in Sussex (ibid., pp. 185–186). Robert Claymond, the sponsor, does not appear in the company records or in other sources, but another Claymonde (Olyver) was mentioned in 1510. The story is a composite, but it is possible that all the figures have relationships with the Mercers' Company and with families long associated with the company.

80. "Childe of Bristowe," in *Early Popular Poetry of England*, ed. Hazlitt, pp. 113–131.

81. The happy ending is a fiction. Bothe returned and was pardoned, but he left again. Claymond claimed that he had been willing to pay the bond for the first disappearance of Bothe, but not for the second one.

Chapter 9

1. Thomas Reddaway, *The Early History of the Goldsmiths' Company* (London, 1975), pp. 83–84, has reconstructed this young man's story from a lengthy record of his crimes that appeared in the court book. The shop description is on pp. 14–15, 83–84.

2. CLRO, MC1/2/5, MC1/2/116 (9 Richard II). He was getting fodder from the ditches and hauling wood. For other cases, see *Mercers*, p. 67, and *CPMR*, vol. 2, pp. 87–88, 128–129.

3. CLRO, MC1/3/290 (1450s), MC1/3/295.

4. *CPMR*, vol. 2, pp. 195 (1375), 57. See also *CPMR*, vol. 2, pp. 197, 263; CLRO, MC1/3/231.

5. *CPMR*, vol. 2, pp. 60, 194, 246, 275–276; *CPMR*, vol. 3, p. 69 (1383).

6. CLRO, *Letter Book N* (10 Henry VIII); P.R.O. C1/67/144.

7. *CPMR*, vol. 2, p. 202 (1375); CLRO, C1/3/231, in which a master moved out of the city and sold the remainder of the term, contrary to the custom of the city; P.R.O. C1/11/367, 66/244, 113/5. In this last case, the sale of contract was approved by the two masters and the apprentice, but then the first master claimed that the apprentice had done damage and must make restitution before he could move. He had him thrown into prison. The new master was also angry because he had already paid and had no service from the apprentice. On the selling of apprentice-ships and the abuses thereof, see Jean M. Imray, "'Les Bones Gentes de la Mer-

cerye de Londres': A Study of the Membership of the Medieval Mercers' Company," in *Studies in London History*, ed. A. E. J. Hollaender and William Kellaway (London, 1969) pp. 169–170. Sylvia L. Thrupp, "The Grocers of London, A Study of Distributive Trade," in *Studies in English Trade in the Fifteenth Century*, ed. Eileen Power and M. M. Postan (London, 1933), p. 255, argues that the selling of contracts was more typical of the last few years of the term.

8. P.R.O. Cl/28/171; *CEMCR*, p. 246 (1308), in which the mistress charged that the apprentice despised his food, tore his clothes, beat her and her daughter, and stole goods. Only the last charge stood up in court, but the mistress had to pay compensation for mistreating the apprentice and unfairly dismissing him. See also *CPMR*, vol. 2 (1367); CLRO, MCl/1/9 (1393).

9. CLRO, MCl/1/84, 1/2/9; P.R.O. Cl/97/65, 39/221, 64/978.

10. CLRO, MCl/2/3; *CPMR*, vol. 1, pp. 274 (1364), 243 (1355); *CEMCR*, p. 222 (1305).

11. Walter Prideaux, ed., *Memorials of the Goldsmiths' Company, Being Gleanings from Their Records* (London, 1896), p. 8; *Mercers*, pp. 662–663; CLRO, MCl/2A/1; *CPMR*, vol. 2, p. 54 (1366).

12. P.R.O. Cl/107/27; *CEMCR*, p. 222 (1305), in which another young man said he was beaten and driven out into the streets naked.

13. P.R.O. Cl/155/43, 66/235, 48/509. The master claimed that he had an apprentice, eleven-year-old Thomas Moyse, in the house and that this boy had met "one Innocent" who was twelve years old. They had tussled, and Thomas fell down the stairs and hurt his head. He had a bad swelling after two days, and the master called the doctor. Despite the doctor's cutting of the swelling, the boy died. A coroner's jury acquitted the master. The ages may not have been accurate, as both boys were young to face adult criminal charges, although the "Innocent" would have been just old enough. In any case, the family was suspicious. See also Prideaux, *Memorials of the Goldsmiths' Company*, p. 17 (1411); *CPMR*, vol. 1, p. 274 (1364).

14. *Letter Book K*, p. 17.

15. *CPMR*, vol. 3, pp. 14–15 (1382); P.R.O. Cl/231/4, 61/342.

16. CLRO, MCl/2A/2–5, 45–53, 62–72 (1379, 1426, 1442–1443), 3/1, 171 (complaint of parents of female apprentice), 339; *CPMR*, vol. 1, 237 (1350); P.R.O. Cl/60/216, in which the master held up the apprentice for a sum (presumably a bribe to make him overlook certain failings of the apprentice or else outright extortion).

17. P.R.O. Cl/107/27.

18. *CPMR*, vol. 1, pp. 15–16.

19. *CPMR*, vol. 2, pp. 8, 129, 205 (late fourteenth century).

20. P.R.O. Cl/155/43; CLRO, MCl/1/48 (1390), in which an apprentice flees because of the harshness of treatment.

21. *CLMC*, pp. 165–166.

22. P.R.O. Cl/123/28; *CLMC*, p. 25 (1350–1351).

23. *Memorials*, p. 629 (1416).

24. *CLMC*, pp. 11–12. For other examples of masters requesting letters to particular boroughs, see pp. 25, 28, 34, 38, 46, 56, 62, 67, 70, 74, 76, 82, 100–103, 106–108, 123–124, 127, 133, 136, 138–139, 143, 149–153, 158, 168–169.

25. P.R.O. Cl/64/165; CLRO, MCl/1/11.

26. P.R.O. Cl/61/353; *CLMC*, p. 65 (1354–1355).

27. *CEMCR*, p. 168 (1304); P.R.O. C1/66/257, 82/109, 9/334, 66/411. In the last case, a mason was working on a building in Havering, Essex, when a woman came up and asked if he knew where John Hall was. She promised the man a cloth if he would find Hall. He did and was rewarded with the cloth. But then the woman Hall was serving accused him of enticing away her apprentice. CLRO, MC1/2/33, 3/174 (accusation of forcefully abducting apprentice), 1/196; *CLMC*, pp. 65, 170. See also Guy Parsloe, ed., *Wardens' Accounts of the Worshipful Company of Founders of the City of London* (London, 1964), p. 1 (1497), which records a fine of 20*d.* "for egging of other mannes apprentice from his master."

28. *Letter Book C*, p. 123 (1303); Reddaway, *Early History of the Goldsmiths' Company*, p. 147; Prideaux, *Memorials of the Goldsmiths' Company*, pp. 18, 22.

29. *CPMR*, vol. 1, p. 40 (1327).

30. *CEMCR*, p. 47. He may have been doing this with the connivance of his master, or he may have been released from his apprenticeship. In any case, the jury found that he had been illegally trading.

31. CLRO, MC1/2/120. The apprentice put himself on the mercy of his master, not denying that he had done these things. See also CLRO, MC1/2A/10, 2/121; *Letter Book B*, pp. 131, 144, 250; *Letter Book C*, pp. 184–188; *CLMC*, p. 86.

32. P.R.O. C1/186/98.

33. P.R.O. C1/235/71.

34. *CPMR*, vol. 3, pp. 88–90.

35. See, for instance, *CPMR*, vol. 1, p. 276; *CPMR*, vol. 2, pp. 129, 205, 220.

36. *Letter Book A*, pp. 18–19, 38, in which 47*s.* 6*d.* could be paid in installments on a debt of £22.

37. *CPMR*, vol. 5, p. 14 (1439); *CPMR*, vol. 1, p. 268 (1364).

38. *Mercers*, pp. 109–110, 112, 134 (1479).

39. *Letter Book D*, p. 217, in which the apprentice could not work with any other mercer; *CPMR*, vol. 2, p. 129.

40. *Mercers*, pp. 251–252, 262, 316, 319–323, 333, 340, 346, 352, 358, 377, 380, 387, 402, 408, 419, 433, 435, 446–457, 463, 490, 501, 510, 512, 527, 534, 546, 560.

41. Ibid., p. 690.

42. Ibid., pp. 662–663. The case is particularly full. The part about the imitation of the master and mistress is made up, but enough hints of mutual problems are in the source itself. As it turns out, Berne had not taken sureties for either apprentice and was fined £5 for each of them (p. 671). Berne was described as out of livery in 1527 and paid only 10*s.* toward the £100 that the city needed for wheat (p. 762).

43. Guildhall, Commissary Court 9051/1 18 (1393), 9171/5 225v; Reddaway, *Early History of the Goldsmiths' Company*, p. 285, in which Richard Bradcock left one existing and two former apprentices his best and second and third best anvils, and his two last apprentices, a clenching anvil each. See also pp. 292, 294; *Husting Wills*, vol. 2, p. 42, in which a goldsmith left tools to his apprentice (p. 144, [1371]).

44. *Husting Wills*, vol. 1, p. 232 (1312); *Husting Wills*, vol. 2, p. 233 (1383).

45. *Husting Wills*, vol. 2, pp. 13, 63 (1361).

46. Reddaway, *Early History of the Goldsmiths' Company*, p. 309; *Husting Wills*, vol. 2, pp. 282 (1390), 400 (1413), in which an apprentice was released from contract three years early on condition that he faithfully serve the master's wife.

47. Reddaway, *Early History of the Goldsmiths' Company*, p. 315; P.R.O. C1/64/313.

48. *Husting Wills*, vol. 2, pp. 114, (1368), 138 (1370), which cites prayers for both master and mistress.

Chapter 10

1. Peter Laslett, "The Institution of Service," *Local Population Studies* 40 (1988): 55–60, has one of the few discussions of service. He estimates, without specific figures or an urban–rural breakdown, that 10 percent of the preindustrial population of England entered into service as part of the life course, usually between childhood and maturity.

2. Sylvia L. Thrupp, *The Merchant Class of Medieval London, 1300–1500* (Chicago, 1948), p. 151, in which a man specifies in a retirement contract that he will have servants to accompany him and his wife when they go out in the streets.

3. For a discussion of the term, see David Herlihy, *Medieval Households* (Cambridge, Mass., 1985), pp. 2–5. In the London Consistory Court records, innkeepers are referred to by the Latin title. The word appears in no other records.

4. Caroline M. Barron, "The Fourteenth-Century Poll Tax Returns for Worcester," *Midland History* (1989): 14, suggests that the title might indicate more or less training, a subject worth more research.

5. Few books exist on the topic of domestic service in the preindustrial period. One of the few, and an excellent one, is Cissie Fairchilds, *Domestic Enemies: Servants and Their Masters in Old Regime France* (Baltimore, 1984). Sara C. Maza, *Servants and Masters in Eighteenth-Century France: The Uses of Loyalty* (Princeton, N.J., 1984), is generally later in date but is also very good, particularly on the subject of expected loyalties and on the general status of servants.

6. *Husting Wills*, vol. 2, p. 75, in which an uncle leaves money toward marriage, or pp. 8–9, in which the man has both his niece and his nephew in the household.

7. Charles Welch, *History of the Cutlers' Company of London*, vol. 1: *From Early Times to 1500* (London, 1916), p. 86. The date of the will is 1349.

8. CLRO, MC1/2A/14 (1382); *CCR*, pp. 80–81, in which a brother and sister were in service in the same household. *Letter Book H*, p. 297 (1349), is a case in point. See also P.R.O. C1/46/435; we know about this case because the previous "owner" turned up and accused him of breaking the Statute of Laborers and took her away with force of arms.

9. P.R.O. C1/31/493.

10. P.R.O. C1/46/387, C1/67/160, C1/22/27.

11. CLRO, MC1/1/28 (1380); *CPMR*, vol. 1, p. 231 (1349).

12. The Statute of Laborers (1351) is discussed in Chapter 1. Briefly, it was legislation designed to fix wages and prices at the preplague level. See CLRO, MC1/2A/8, 19, 20; CLRO, MC1/3/78, in which one widow accused another in 1442 of forcibly abducting her female servant. In P.R.O. C1/180/2, William Wyngar of London, a merchant haberdasher, said that Herre Hylle, a merchant of London, took away his servant in Milk Street. Wyngar was out of town and did not know that the servant was gone for fifteen weeks.

13. *Letter Book F*, p. 198. The Pursemakers provided a fine of 40*s.* for anyone who tried to entice away the servant of another in the guild. The Glovers had a similar provision, as did the Braclers (*Letter Book G*, fol. xxxii).

14. Thomas Reddaway, *The Early History of the Goldsmiths' Company* (London, 1975), p. 82; P.R.O. Cl/46/278.

15. P.R.O. Cl/27/198. James Cusake, a baker, complained that Richard Brooke, a baker, had hired him on a four-year contract at the rate of 40*s.* a year, but had not paid him and then had him thrown into prison.

16. CLRO, MCl/1/173; P.R.O. Cl/67/160, Cl/61/564.

17. CLRO, MCl/2A 114 (1382).

18. Welch, *History of the Cutlers' Company,* vol. 1, p. 23.

19. *Liber Albus,* pp. xxxv–xxxvi. Daubers received 4*d.* a day or 1½*d.* and their table from September to November 11; 3*d.* a day or 1*d.* and table from November 11 to February 2; 4*d.* a day or 1½*d.* and table from the Purification to Easter, and 5*d.* or 2*d.* with table from Easter to the Feast of St. Michael. Information on wages is available in a variety of secondary sources. See, for instance, Douglas Knoop and Gwilyn P. Jones, "London Bridge and Its Builders: A Study of Municipal Employment of Masons Mainly in the Fifteenth Century," *Transactions of the Quartuor Coronati Lodge* 47 (1938): 5–44, and (1939): 5–46.

20. Henry Littlehales, ed., *The Medieval Records of a London Church,* Early English Text Society, o.s., 125–128 (London, 1905), pp. 71, 80.

21. P.R.O. C/66/264, Cl/28/172. Cornu left service because insufficient food, drink, clothing, and other necessities were found for him. Now he was having a hard time recovering the 5 marks. Robert Rowes, a Norman-born capper, worked from week to week and could not collect his wages (P.R.O. Cl/222/27).

22. P. J. P. Goldberg, "Female Labour, Service, and Marriage in Northern Towns During the Later Middle Ages," *Northern History* 22 (1986): 25, finds that 45 percent of the female servants in York were engaged by clothworkers and 23 percent in victualing.

23. For the percentage of males and females over fourteen described as sons or servants, see Barron, "Fourteenth-Century Poll Tax Returns for Worcester," p. 6. Her comparative data (p. 16) come from the work of P. J. P. Goldberg and Maryanne Kowaleski. For figures on York, see Goldberg, "Female Labour," p. 21. On the Continent, a few records exist that give some hint of female occupations. Of those women who headed households and paid taxes in Paris in 1292, over 25 percent were listed as household servants, compared with about 5 percent of the men. Men were more likely than women to be immigrants into Paris, whatever their occupation. In Florence in 1427, more than one-third of women heading households were listed as servants (David Herlihy, *Opera Muliebria: Women and Work in Medieval Europe* [New York, 1990], pp. 142–148, 159). Such figures, of course, do not include those women or men living in other people's households as servants. Fairchilds, *Domestic Enemies,* p. 4, finds that 15 percent of the population of Paris on the eve of the Revolution were domestics. Males predominated, especially in noble households, but increasingly the service positions became feminized (pp. 9–16).

24. P.R.O. Cl/64/1158. Goldberg, "Female Labour," p. 23, claims that twelve was the usual age of entry. When he actually does the calculations in another article, "Marriage, Migration, Servanthood, and Life Cycle in Yorkshire Towns of the Later Middle Ages," *Continuity and Change* 1 (1986): 146, the age is closer to fourteen. P. J. P. Goldberg, *Women, Work, and Life Cycle in a Medieval Economy* (Oxford, 1992), was not published in time to be included in this book.

25. P.R.O. Cl/124/32.

26. P.R.O. C1/82/65.

27. CLRO, MC1/1/1.

28. Reddaway, *Early History of the Goldsmiths' Company,* p. 151.

29. For a similar case, see *CCR,* pp. 40, 195; *CCR,* pp. 142, 80–81, in which a brewer had his chambers in the main part of the house.

30. P.R.O. C1/64//764; *CPMR,* vol. 1, pp. 220–221. Chapter 2, has more information on renting.

31. "John Russell's Book of Nurture," in *The Babees' Book: Medieval Manners for the Young,* ed. Edith Rickert (New York, 1966), pp. 48–49.

32. "How the Good Wife Taught Her Daughter," pp. 37–38, and "How the Wise Man Taught His Son," p. 46, in ibid.

33. "How the Good Wife Taught Her Daughter," in ibid., p. 38.

34. P.R.O. C1/11/114. As it turned out, the mystery man was a city official coming to arrest William. William escaped into the house, and Thomas was in trouble for interfering with official business. Thomas objected that he would not have acted so if the official had shown his badge.

35. P.R.O. C1/32/430.

36. P.R.O. C1/11/114. They claimed that the executors deprived them of it.

37. P.R.O. C1/64/1158.

38. *CEMCR,* p. 112 (1301). A number of cases, all from the late fourteenth or the fifteenth century, appear in which the servant has been enticed away or imprisoned to the loss of the master and the master then sues (CLRO, MC1/2A/8, 19, 20; CLRO, MC1/3/78, 245).

39. P.R.O. C1/46/203.

40. P.R.O. C1/46/26. He was appealing to the Chancellor to get out of prison. See also *CEMCR,* p. 213 (1305), and *CCR,* pp. 240–241.

41. *CCR,* pp. 24–25. The servant died, but the finding was that he had fallen ill from sleeping out all night, not from the beating. See also *CPMR,* vol. 2, p. 227 (1376), and P.R.O. C1/48/107.

42. P.R.O. C1/32/355, 386. For other cases of servants being sued and imprisoned under the statute, see P.R.O. C1/222/27, C1/64/231. For cases settled in the mayor's court, see CLRO, MC1/1/192.

43. P.R.O. C1/66/390, C1/46/117. It was not just young women who suffered. A young man said that he was put into prison under the statute until he paid 17s. to his master to get released (P.R.O. C1/64/906).

44. P.R.O. C1/66/210.

45. P.R.O. C1/148/67. On the slavery of female domestics, see Susan Mosher Stuard, "To Town to Serve: Urban Domestic Slavery in Medieval Ragusa," in *Women and Work in Preindustrial Europe,* ed. Barbara A. Hanawalt (Bloomington, Ind., 1986), pp. 39–55.

46. Richard M. Wunderli, *London Church Courts and Society on the Eve of the Reformation* (Cambridge, Mass., 1981), pp. 83–84, finds only a few slander cases but no allegations. Fairchilds, *Domestic Enemies,* pp. 185–188, again finds only rumors, rather than evidence that masters and male servants had sexual relations.

47. Charles M. Clode, *The Early History of the Guild of Merchant Taylors* (London, 1888), pt. 2, pp. 11–13, 20–21.

48. CLRO, MC1/1/62.

49. P.R.O. C1/66/368.

50. Guildhall, Consistory Court 9064/2 m. 48.

51. *CEMCR*, p. 59; *CPMR*, vol. 1, p. 205 (1342); *CPMR*, vol. 2, pp. 42 (1365), 278 (1380); *CCR*, pp. 149–151, in which one of the men accused of homicide was called "Malcovenaunt."

52. P.R.O. C1/66/332.

53. P.R.O. C1/61/554; *Letter Book I*, p. 114 (1413), in which a servant was confined in Newgate for "cursing and slandering" his master, an alderman.

54. CLRO, MC1/2/103. Another servant kept the keys to his master's house when he left service without warning (CLRO, MC1/2/75; *CLMC*, p. 26 [1350]).

55. *CLMC*, p. 63 (1352); P.R.O. C1/46/401, C1/46/271; *CPMR*, vol. 2, p. 33 (1365).

56. P.R.O. C1/64/1112, in which a master claimed a debt of 53*s*. 4*d*.; P.R.O. C1/64/1053, in which a master claimed that a female servant had made off with 100*s*. Her kin insisted that the money was back wages and countersued.

57. See, for instance, *CLMC*, pp. 18, 22, 26, 40–41, 44, 156, 167, and P.R.O. C1/64/906.

58. P.R.O. C1/27/373.

59. *CCR*, pp. 108–109 (1324).

60. P.R.O. C1/67/185.

61. *CCR*, p. 114 (1325). A common practice was for the master to leave London during plague periods, putting the business in the hands of a servant or factor. See, for instance, P.R.O. C1/64/323.

62. *CCR*, pp. 266–269; *CPMR*, vol. 1, p. 129 (1340).

63. *Memorials*, p. 277 (Bracers), 245 (Glovers).

64. *Husting Wills*, vol. 1, p. 221; *Husting Wills*, vol. 2, pp. 4, 5, 8, 9, 35, 48, 72, 75, 86, 111, 123, 135, 160, 178, 252, 270, 292, 306, 323, 332.

65. This remarkable case appears in a coroners' inquest preserved in *Letter Book B* and is also printed in *Memorials*, pp. 11–13. Little is made up in the story except Robin Hood, who has been re-created time after time; the earlier relationship between Symon and "Roger"; and Symon's unsavory business practices and treatment of his servants. It is an unusual case for medieval England because of the obvious planning and concealment of the body. Most homicides were done in haste, and the guilty party fled from the scene.

66. Barbara A. Hanawalt, "The Voices and Audiences of Social History Records," *Social Science History* 15 (1991): 159–175.

67. P.R.O. C1/142/18; *CCR*, p. 10 (1300). In another coroner's case, two servants of Queen Philippa fought, but the reason was not given other than an earlier argument (pp. 264–265).

68. *Calendar of Proceedings in Chancery*, 2 vols. (London 1827, 1830), p. 130 (1460).

69. CLRO, MC1/1/106.

70. Guildhall, Consistory Court 9064/2 221v., 175; *Letter Book K*, pp. 216–217 (1437), in which a couple enticed away a servant girl and sold her to be debauched against her will. In *CPMR*, vol. 5 (1445), pp. 74–75, a man tried to rape a servant girl until two men intervened.

71. *CCR*, pp. 209, 86–87.

72. *CPMR*, vol. 1, pp. 94 (1332), 161 (1344); CLRO, MC1/2/59; *CEMCR*, p. 124 (1302).

73. *CRR*, p. 196; *CPMR*, vol. 2, p. 130 (1371).

74. Welch, *History of the Cutlers' Company*, vol. 1, pp. 14, 23, 142, 174; *Mercers*, p. x; Reddaway, *Early History of the Goldsmiths' Company*, p. 91.

75. George Unwin, *The Gilds and Companies of London* (London, 1966), p. 224.

76. *CPMR*, vol. 2, p. 90 (1368).

77. Reddaway, *Early History of the Goldsmiths' Company*, pp. 108, 109; CLRO, MCl/1/112. In some respects, the guilds forced such measures because they forbade partnerships that might have made a pooling of resources into a viable shop (Welch, *History of the Cutlers' Company*, p. 142 [1485]).

78. *CEMCR*, pp. 148–149.

79. *CPMR*, vol. 1, pp. 225–226, 232–233; *CPMR*, vol. 2, pp. 54–56, 264 (1380), in which Saddler's journeymen met illegally; Reddaway, *Early History of the Goldsmiths' Company*, p. 95; Clode, *Early History of the Guild of Merchant Taylors*, pp. 61–62; *Letter Book K*, pp. xli–xliii.

80. *CLMC*, p. 52.

81. Reddaway, *Early History of the Goldsmiths' Company*, p. 95; *CPMR*, vol. 5, p. 69.

82. Unwin, *Gilds of London*, pp. 224–229, has a very good discussion of the establishment of this secondary group. For a provincial response to journeymen, see Heather Swanson, *Medieval Artisans: An Urban Class in Late Medieval England* (Oxford, 1989), p. 115. For a more complete discussion of the sixteenth-century yeomanry and journeymen, see Steve Rappaport, *Worlds Within Worlds: Structures of Life in Sixteenth-Century London* (Cambridge, 1989), pp. 215–250.

83. *Mercers*, p. x.

Chapter 11

1. J. A. Burrow, *The Ages of Man: A Study in Medieval Writing and Thought* (Oxford, 1988), pp. 12–36.

2. Ibid., p. 37.

3. "The Mirror of the Periods of Man's Life," in *Hymns to the Virgin and Christ, The Parliament of Devils, and Other Religious Poems*, ed. Frederick J. Furnivall, Early English Text Society, o.s., 24 (London, 1868; New York, 1969), p. 61.

4. Burrow, *Ages of Man*, pp. 49–50.

5. Charles Carlton, *The Court of Orphans* (Leicester, 1974), p. 14.

6. *Letter Book H*, p. 430 (1395). Her father had died in 1372.

7. *Letter Book I*, p. 239.

8. For another case, see *Letter Book H*, pp. 167, 189. *CPMR*, vol. 5, pp. 146, (1455), 1 (1437), which discusses marriage or majority as the basis for a young man to inherit. In *Letter Book I*, pp. 143, 177, 192, 201, 219 (1416–1420), all had inheritance delayed because of apprenticeship. The age of inheritance was usually twenty-four. In *Letter Book K*, pp. 186, 257 (1440), the young man got half at twenty-one; the other half would be delivered when he was twenty-six "unless he was profitably employed earlier." See also pp. 279, 349, in which twenty-eight is the age of inheritance; *Letter Book G*, pp. 136, 147 (1360s); *Letter Book H*, p. 187 (1383).

9. Thomas Reddaway, *The Early History of the Goldsmiths' Company* (London, 1975), pp. 73, 80. Of the sixty-five scattered cases of broken apprenticeship contracts that appear in the mayor's court, the Chancery petitions, and surviving company records for the fifteenth century, the average length of apprenticeship was 9.4 years, with the most common contracts for 9 or 10 years.

10. George Unwin, *The Gilds and Companies of London* (London, 1908), pp. 91–

92; Charles Welch, *History of the Cutlers' Company of London,* vol. 1: *From Early Times to 1500* (London, 1916), pp. 10–14. Cutlers may have required an extra year of service after seven years.

11. Guildhall Archives, Grocer's Company 11592. In the sixteenth century, the age of completing apprenticeship would have been closer to thirty (Steve Rappaport, *Worlds Within Worlds: The Structures of Life in Sixteenth-Century London* [Cambridge, 1989], p. 296).

12. *Mercers,* p. 121 (1479).

13. Burrow, *Ages of Man,* p. 30.

14. Information is from Letter Books. Four women were married at age nineteen, two each at ages sixteen to eighteen, and one at twenty. Only one married at twelve, and three at fourteen or fifteen. One each married at twenty-six and thirty. Other scattered references indicate a similar pattern from *Letter Book H,* p. 127 (1379), in which the girl is described as being "more than 15"; p. 186 (1403) describes the girl as well over twenty-one; and p. 357 (1402) says the girl was fourteen when she married without the mayor's permission. These are young women whose fathers were citizens of London, and they had property, sometimes substantial. They married when they were in their middle to late teens. Of course, they were much in demand as marriage partners and might have married at a younger age. Rappaport, *Worlds Within Worlds,* p. 68, thinks that in the sixteenth century, women married in their mid-twenties.

15. Margery Kempe, *The Book of Margery Kempe,* ed. Stanford B. Meech and Hope Emily Allen, Early English Text Society, o.s., 212 (London, 1940), p. 6.

16. Charles Phythian-Adams, *Desolation of a City: Coventry and the Urban Crisis of the Late Middle Ages* (Cambridge, 1979), pp. 84–85, finds that in 1523, 43 percent of the female population over fifteen was unmarried. Equivalent data do not exist for London.

17. *Letter Book H,* pp. 266 (1385), 384 (1392); *Letter Book G,* p. 181 (1364).

18. Sylvia L. Thrupp, *The Merchant Class of Medieval London, 1300–1500* (Chicago, 1948), p. 196.

19. For a discussion of age of marriage in York, see P. J. P. Goldberg, "Marriage, Migration, Servanthood, and Life Cycle in Yorkshire Towns of the Later Middle Ages," *Continuity and Change* 1 (1986): 153–154. Goldberg, "Female Labour, Service, and Marriage in Northern Towns During the Later Middle Ages," *Northern History* 22 (1986): 25–26, has made much of very slim data arguing that because the couples were closer together in age, they had "companionate marriages." His data, like other medieval English data on age of marriage, are very weak. Estimating the degree of companionship in these marriages, of course, is not possible. Mere age similarity is hardly enough.

20. *Letter Book L,* p. 8 (1462); *Letter Book G,* pp. 152–153 (1363).

21. See, for instance, *Letter Book H,* p. 169 (1381), and *Letter Book L,* pp. 83, 95, 142 (1469–1476).

22. *Letter Book D,* p. 45; *Mercers,* p. 412; Rappaport, *Worlds Within Worlds,* pp. 328–329.

23. On the canon law of marriage in England, see Richard Helmholz, *Marriage Litigation in Medieval England* (Cambridge, 1974), pp. 25–73.

24. *CLMC,* p. 161.

25. *Letter Book I,* p. 141 (1415).

26. P.R.O. C1/6/89.

27. P.R.O. C1/20/137, 26/286, 39/9, 64/271.

28. P.R.O. C1/9/199, 64/299.

29. Guildhall, Consistory Court 9064/3, 172v; Richard M. Wunderli, *London Church Courts and Society on the Eve of the Reformation* (Cambridge, Mass., 1981), p. 88.

30. P.R.O. C1/66/308, 66/353. In another case, the master had at first given permission for his servant to marry and then withdrew his permission (P.R.O. C1/64/797).

31. *CEMCR*, p. 129, in which a young man is sued by his master; *Mercers*, p. 186, in which the Mercers were more merciful when Peter Penketh married while only seven years into his ten-year contract. His master had died, and Peter had married. They allowed him to work for wages to support his wife.

32. P.R.O. C1/66/407.

33. Alison Hanham, *The Celys and Their World: An English Merchant Family of the Fifteenth Century* (Cambridge, 1985), p. 309.

34. Ibid., pp. 309–315.

35. P.R.O. C1/166/45.

36. "How the Good Wife Taught Her Daughter," in *The Babees' Book: Medieval Manners for the Young*, ed. Edith Rickert (New York, 1966), pp. 35–36, 40.

37. Ibid., p. 45.

38. *Husting Wills*, vol. 1, pp. 214–215, 241, 243, 259 (early fourteenth century); *CPMR*, vol. 5, p. 25 (1439), in which the eldest got £10 and the youngest got 10 marks.

39. Henry Thomas Riley, ed., *Chronicles of the Mayors and Sheriffs and London* A.D. *1188–1274* (London, 1863), pp. 8–9.

40. Guildhall, Archdeaconry Court, 9051/1, m. 89 (1400), 9051/2, m. 101v (1403).

41. P.R.O. C1/137/24; *Husting Wills*, vol. 1, pp. 602 (1348), 618 (1349); *Husting Wills*, vol. 2, pp. 418 (1419), 468 (1432).

42. Barbara A. Hanawalt, "The Widow's Mite: Provisions for Medieval London Widows," in *Upon My Husband's Death: Widows in the Literature and History of Medieval Europe*, ed. Louise Mirrer (Ann Arbor, 1992), pp. 21–46, has a complete discussion of the dower practice in London and widows' success in actually recovering dower.

43. *Letter Book C*, pp. 18–19 (1293–1294).

44. P.R.O. C1/22/144. See also some of the wardship cases previously discussed.

45. P.R.O. C1/71/7, in which a London clerk married a cousin of a London scrivener. The agreement was that he would get 10 marks sterling for the marriage and 10 marks in household goods. He claims to have gotten only 6 marks sterling and 26s. in household goods. P.R.O. C1/47/102 is a case of an argument over the value of "chamber plate" that was to come with the marriage of a Londoner to a knight's daughter.

46. P.R.O. C1/67/199, in which a marriage was arranged in the house of the master of a female servant; *Letter Book I*, p. 141, in which a marriage was arranged in the house of a friend and witness; P.R.O. C1/16/334, 60/142.

47. For the reading of banns and the neglect thereof, see James A. Brundage, *Law, Sex, and Christian Society in Medieval Europe* (Chicago, 1987), pp. 441–443.

48. Hanawalt, "Widow's Mite," pp. 31–32.

49. On the canon law of marriage in England, see Helmholtz, *Marriage Litigation,* pp. 25–73. On the ceremony, see Kenneth Stevenson, *Nuptial Blessing: A Study of Christian Marriage Rites* (New York, 1983), pp. 76–80.

50. Frederick J. Furnivall ed., *Early English Meals and Manners: John Russel's Boke of Nurture, etc.,* Early English Text Society, o.s., 32 (London, 1868; Detroit, 1969), pp. 358–359.

51. W. O. Hassall, ed., *How They Lived: An Anthology of Original Accounts Written Before 1485* (New York, 1962), p. 99.

52. P.R.O. C1/32/334, 216/68, 196/46, 31/351, 33/71, 64/985, 71/138, 83/86; Guildhall, Consistory Court 9064/2, ms. 159. These are but a sample of the disappointed hopes of grooms.

53. Hanawalt, "Widow's Mite," pp. 30–32.

54. For some examples, see *Letter Book H,* p. 440, and *Letter Book I,* pp. 16, 44, 196, 241.

55. Barbara A. Hanawalt, "Remarriage as an Option for Urban and Rural Widows in Late Medieval England," in *Wife and Widow: The Experiences of Women in Medieval England,* ed. Sue Sheridan Walker (Ann Arbor, 1993), pp. 141–164.

56. P.R.O. C1/19/459. This story is based on a very full and detailed petition to the Chancellor. Quotes are from the case text. The name of the bride and her background are composites. The role of the master is also a composite. The groom's pathetic tale is told in his own voice.

Bibliography

Manuscript Sources

Corporation of London
   Court of Common Pleas CP (and number).
   Husting Court Wills and Deeds
   Letter Books
   Mayor's Court, Original Bills MC1, 2, 3 (late fourteenth through mid-sixteenth
      centuries)
   Portsoken, Ward Presentments 1465–1483
   Sheriffs' Court Rolls. Box 1407–1595

Guildhall Archives
   Archdeaconry Court 9051
   Churchwardens' Accounts
     Allhallows London Wall Ms. 5090
     Allhallows Staining Ms. 4956
     St. Andrew Hubbard Ms. 1279
     St. Mary at Hill Ms. 1239
     St. Peter Westcheap Ms. 645
   Commissary Court 9171
   Consistory Court 9064
   Grocers' Company registers, warden's accounts, ordinances

Public Record Office
   Chancery Miscellanea
   Coroners' Roll Just 2/94A
   Early Chancery Proceedings C1
   Prerogative Court of Canterbury
   Probate Prob2

Chronicles and Literary Sources

Adamson, Margot, ed. *A Treasury of Middle English Verse Selected and Rendered into Modern English.* London, 1930.

Aungier, George James, ed. *Croniques de London.* Camden Society Series. London, 1864.

Bateson, Mary, ed. "A London Municipal Collection in the Reign of John." *English Historical Review* 17 (1902): 480–511, 707–730.

Bennett, H. S., ed. *England from Chaucer to Caxton.* New York, 1928.

Child, Francis James, ed. *The English and Scottish Popular Ballads.* Vol. 1. Boston, 1883.

Comper, Frances M. N., ed. *Spiritual Songs from English MSS. of the Fourteenth to Sixteenth Centuries.* Cambridge, 1936.

Crotch, W. J. B., ed. *The Prologues and Epilogues of William Caxton.* Early English Text Society, o.s., 176. London, 1928.

Douce, Francis, ed. *The Customs of London, otherwise Called Arnold's Chronicle.* Ca. 1502. Reprint. London, 1811.

Furnivall, Frederick J., ed. *Early English Meals and Manners: John Russel's Boke of Nuture, etc.* Early English Text Society, o.s., 32. London, 1868. Reprint. Detroit, 1969.

———. *Hymns to the Virgin and Christ, The Parliament of Devils, and Other Religious Poetry.* Early English Text Society, o.s., 24. London, 1868. Reprint. New York, 1969.

———. *Robert [Mannyng] of Brunne's Handlyng Synne.* Early English Text Society, o.s., 119. London, 1901.

Gairdner, James, ed. *Historical Collections of a Citizen of London in the Fifteenth Century.* Camden Society, n.s., 16. London, 1876.

Hazlitt, W. Carew, ed. *Remains of Early Popular Poetry of England.* London, 1864.

Kempe, Margery. *The Book of Margery Kempe.* Ed. Stanford B. Meech and Hope Emily Allen. Early English Text Society, o.s., 212. London, 1940.

Kingsford, Charles, ed. *Two Chronicles from the Collection of John Stow.* London, 1910.

Lester, G. A., ed. *Chronicles of London.* Oxford, 1905.

———. *Three Medieval Morality Plays: Mankind, Everyman, and Mundus et Infans.* New York, 1981.

Meyer, Paul, ed. *Les Contes moralises de Nicole Bozon, frère mineur, pub. Pour la premier fois d'après les manuscrits de Loudres et de Cheltenham.* Société des anciens textes français. Paris, 1889.

Myrc, John. *Instructions for a Parish Priest.* Ed. Edward Peacock. Early English Text Society, o.s., 209. London, 1940.

Rhys, Ernest, ed. *Stow's Survey of London.* Introduction by Henry B. Wheatley. London, 1912.

Rickert, Edith, ed. *The Babees' Book: Medieval Manners for the Young.* New York, 1966.

Riley, H. T., ed. *Chronicles of the Mayors and Sheriffs of London, A.D. 1188–1274.* London, 1863.

———. *The French Chronicle of London, 1259–1343.* London, 1863.

Rimbault, Edward F., ed. "Two Sermons Preached by the Boy Bishop at St Paul's." In *The Camden Miscellany,* Camden Society, n.s., 7. Westminster, 1875.

Robbins, Rossell Hope, ed. *Secular Lyrics of the Fourteenth and Fifteenth Centuries.* Oxford, 1952.

Rowland, Beryl, ed. *Medieval Woman's Guide to Health: The First English Gynecological Handbook.* Kent, Ohio, 1981.

Seger, Mary, ed. *A Medieval Anthology, Being Lyrics and Other Short Poems Chiefly Religious.* London, 1915.

Smith, Lucy T., ed. *Commonplace Book of the Fifteenth Century.* London, 1886.

Sneyd, C. A., ed. *The Italian Relation of England.* Camden Society 37. London, 1847.

Stevick, Robert D., ed. *One Hundred Middle English Lyrics.* Indianapolis, 1964.

Stow, John. *A Survey of London: Reprinted from the Text of 1603.* Ed. C. L. Kingsford. 2 vols. 2nd ed. Oxford, 1971.

Stubbs, William, ed. *Chronicles of the Reigns of Edward I and Edward II.* 2 vols. Rolls Series. London, 1882, 1883.

Thomas, A. H., and I. D. Thornley, eds. *The Great Chronicle of London.* London, 1938.

A Volume of English Miscellanies. Surtees Society 85. York, 1890.

Printed Record Sources

The Accounts of the Churchwardens of St. Michael, Cornhill, 1456–1608. Ed. William H. Overall. London, 1871.

Acts of the Court of the Mercers' Company (London), 1453–1527. Ed. Laetitia Lyell and Frank D. Watney. Cambridge, 1936.

Calendar of Coroners' Rolls of the City of London, 1300–1378. Ed. R. R. Sharpe. London, 1913.

Calendar of Early Mayor's Court Rolls of the City of London, 1298–1307. Ed. A. H. Thomas. London, 1924.

Calendar of Inquisitions Miscellaneous. (Chancery). Preserved in the Public Record Office. 7 vols. 1916–1937.

Calendar of Letter Books of the City of London, A–L (1275–1497). Ed. R. R. Sharpe. 11 vols. London, 1899–1912.

Calendar of Letters from the Mayor and Corporation of the City of London, A.D. 1350–1370. Ed. R. R. Sharpe. London, 1885.

Calendar of London Trailbaston Trials Under Commission of 1305 and 1306. Ed. Ralph B. Pugh. London, 1975.

Calendar of Plea and Memoranda Rolls of the City of London, 1323–1482. Vols. 1–4, ed. A. H. Thomas. Vols. 5 and 6, ed. P. E. Jones. Cambridge, 1926–1961.

Calendar of Proceedings in Chancery. 2 vols. London, 1827, 1830.

"A Calendar of the Cartulary of the Parish Church of St. Margaret, Bridge St. (Guildhall Library MS. 1174)." Ed. Anthony Dyson. *Guildhall Studies in London History* 1 (1974): 163–191.

Calendar of Wills Proved and Enrolled in the Court of Husting, London, A.D. 1258–A.D. 1688. Ed. R. R. Sharpe. 2 vols. London, 1890.

Cartulary of St. Mary Clerkenwell. Ed. William Owen Hassall. Camden Society, 3rd ser., 71. London, 1949.

The Church in London, 1375–1392. Ed. A. K. McHardy. London Record Society 13. London, 1977.

Churchwardens' Accounts of Parishes Within the City of London. London, 1969.

The Churchwardens' Accounts of the Parish of All Hallows, London Wall, A.D. 1455–A.D. 1536. Ed. Charles Welch. London, 1912.

A Descriptive Catalogue of Ancient Deeds in the Public Record Office. 6 vols. London, 1890–1915.

Documents Illustrating the History of St. Paul's Cathedral. Ed. Sparrow Simpson. Camden Society, n.s., 26. Westminster, 1880.

English Suits Before the Parlement of Paris, 1420–1436. Ed. C. P. Allmand and C. A. J. Armstrong. Camden Society, 4th ser., 26. London, 1982.

"Facsimile of the First Volume of Ms. Archives of the Company of Grocers, 1345–1523." Ed. John Kingdon. *Antiquary* 21 (1890): 266–270; 22 (1891): 7–30, 70–73; 18, pts. 1, 2 (1886).

Fitzstephen, William. *Description.* Trans. H. E. Butler. In Frank M. Stenton, *Norman London: An Essay.* Rev. ed. London, 1934.

"Lay Subsidy, temp. Henry IV (London, 1411–1412)." Ed. J. C. L. Stahlschmidt. *Archaeological Journal* 44 (1887): 56–82.

Liber Albus: The White Book of the City of London. Ed. Henry Thomas Riley. London, 1861.

Lists of Early Chancery Proceedings in the Public Record Office. 2 vols. New York, 1963.

London Assize of Nuisance. Ed. Helena M. Chew and W. Kellaway. London Record Society 10. London, 1973.

London Possessory Assizes: A Calendar. Ed. Helena M. Chew. London Record Society 1. London, 1965.

The Medieval Records of a London Church. Ed. Henry Littlehales. Early English Text Society, o.s., 125–128. London, 1905.

Memorials of London and London Life in the XIIIth, XIVth, and XVth Centuries. Ed. Henry Thomas Riley. London, 1868.

Memorials of the Goldsmiths' Company, Being Gleanings from Their Records. Ed. Walter Prideaux. London, 1896.

Munimenta Gildhallae Londoniensis. Liber Albus, Liber Custumarum et Liber Horn. Ed. Henry Thomas Riley. 3 vols. Rolls Series. London, 1859–1862.

"The Ordinances of Some Secular Guilds of London, 1354–1496." Ed. Henry C. Coote. *Transactions of the London and Middlesex Archaelolgical Society* 4 (1871): 1–59.

Records of Medieval Oxford, Coroners' Inquests, the Walls of Oxford, etc. Ed. H. E. Salter. London, 1912.

The Records of Two City Parishes: Sts. Anne and Agnes, Aldergate and St. John Zachary, London. Ed. William McMurray. London, 1925.

Rotuli hundredorum. Ed. J. Caley and W. Illingworth. London, 1812–1818.

Scriveners Company Common Paper, 1357–1628. Ed. Francis Steer. London Record Society 4. London, 1968.

Two Early London Subsidy Rolls. Ed. E. Ekwall. Lund, 1951.

Wardens' Acounts of the Worshipful Company of Founders of the City of London, 1497–1681. Ed. Guy Parsloe. London, 1964.

Secondary Sources

Alcock, N. W., ed. *Warwickshire Grazier and London Skinner, 1532–1555.* Oxford, 1982.

Alvis, F. C. *The Sixteenth-Century Long Shop Printing Office in the Poultry.* London, 1982.

Amundsen, Darrel, and Carol Jean Dries. "The Age of Menarche in Medieval Europe." *Human Biology* 45 (1973): 363–368.

Ariès, Philippe. *Centuries of Childhood: A Social History of the Family.* Trans. Robert Baldick. London, 1962.

Atkinson, Clarissa W. *The Oldest Profession: Christian Motherhood in the Middle Ages.* Ithaca, N.Y., 1991.

Baker, J. H. "The English Legal Profession, 1450–1550." In *Lawyers in Early Modern Europe and America,* ed. Wilfrid Prest, pp. 16–42. New York, 1981.

Baldwin, Frances Elizabeth. *Sumptuary Legislation and Personal Regulation in England.* Baltimore, 1926.

Barron, Caroline M. "The Fourteenth-Century Poll Tax Returns for Worcester." *Midland History* (1989): 1–29.

———. "London and the Crown." In *The Crown and Local Communities in England and France in the Fifteenth Century,* ed. J. R. L. Highfield and R. Jeffs, pp. 88–109. Gloucester, 1981.

———. *The Medieval Guildhall of London.* London, 1974.

———. "The Parish Fraternities of Medieval London." In *The Church in Pre-Reformation Society: Essays in Honor of F. R. H. Du Boulay,* ed. Caroline M. Barron and Christopher Harper-Hill, pp. 13–37. Woodbridge, Eng., 1985.

———. "Richard II and London, 1392–7." In *The Reign of Richard II,* ed. F. R. H. Du Boulay and Caroline M. Barron, pp. 173–201. London, 1971.

———. "Richard Whittington: The Man Behind the Myth." In *Studies of London Presented to Philip Edmund Jones,* ed. A. E. J. Hollaender and William Kellaway, pp. 195–248. London, 1969.

Barron, Caroline, C. Coleman, and C. Gobbi. "The London Journal of Allesandro Magno, 1562." *London Journal* 9 (1983): 136–152.

Baskerville, Geoffrey. "A London Chronicle of 1460." *English Historical Review* 28 (1913): 124–127.

Beardwood, Alice. *Alien Merchants in England, 1350 to 1377: Their Legal and Economic Position.* Cambridge, Mass., 1931.

Beaven, Alfred B. *The Aldermen of the City of London, temp. Henry III–1908.* 2 vols. London, 1908, 1913.

———. "The Grocers' Company and the Aldermen of London in the Time of Richard II." *English Historical Review* 22 (1907): 523–525.

Beier, A. L. "Engine of Manufacture: The Trades of London." In *London, 1500–1700: The Making of the Metropolis,* ed. A. L. Beier and Roger Finlay, pp. 141–167. London, 1986.

Beier, A. L., and Roger Finlay. "The Significance of the Metropolis." In *London, 1500–1700: The Making of the Metropolis,* ed. A. L. Beier and Roger Finlay, pp. 1–34. London, 1986.

Belmont, Nocole. "Levana: or How to Raise up Children." In *Family and Society: Selections from the Annales, Economics, Sociétés, Civilisation,* ed. Robert Forster and Orest Ranum, trans. Elborg Forster and Patricia M. Ranum, pp. 1–15. Baltimore, 1976.

Ben-Amos, Ilaria Krausman. "Apprenticeship, the Family, and Urban Society in Early Modern England." Ph.D. diss., Stanford University, 1985–1986.

Bennett, Eric. *The Worshipful Company of Carmen of London.* Rev. ed. Buckingham, Eng., 1982.

Bennett, Judith M. "Working Together: Women and Men in the Brewers' Guild of London, c. 1420." In *The Salt of Common Life: Individuality and Choice in the*

Medieval Town, Countryside, and Church, ed. Edwin DeWindt. Kalamazoo, Mich., forthcoming.

Bennett, Michael. "Spiritual Kinship and the Baptismal Name in Traditional European Society." In *Principalities, Powers, and Estates: Studies in Medieval and Early Modern Government and Society*, ed. L. O. Frappell, pp. 1–12. Adelaide, 1979.

Besant, Walter. *Medieval London*. Vol. 1. London, 1906.

Biddle, Martin, D. Hudson, and C. Heighway, eds. *The Future of London's Past*. Worcester, 1973.

Bird, Ruth. *The Turbulent London of Richard II*. London, 1949.

Blumenfeld-Kosinski, Renate. *Not of Woman Born: Representations of Caesarean Birth in Medieval and Renaissance Culture*. Ithaca, N.Y., 1990.

Boswell, John. *Kindness of Strangers: The Abandonment of Children in Western Europe from Late Antiquity to the Renaissance*. New York, 1988.

Brigden, S. "Youth and the English Reformation." *Past and Present* 95 (1982): 37–67.

Brooke, Christopher, assisted by Gillian Keir. *London, 800–1216*. London, 1975.

Brundage, James A. *Law, Sex, and Christian Society in Medieval Europe*. Chicago, 1987.

Burford, E. J. *Bawds and Lodgings: A History of the London Bankside Brothels*. London, 1976.

Burke, Peter. "Popular Culture in Seventeenth-Century London." *London Journal* 3 (1977): 143–147.

Burrow, J. A. *The Age of Man: A Study in Medieval Writing and Thought*. Oxford, 1988.

Cam, Helen M. "Representation in the City of London in the Later Middle Ages." *Album E. Lousee* 3 (1963): 109–123.

Camp, Anthony J. *Wills and Their Whereabouts*. London, 1974.

Carlton, Charles. *The Court of Orphans*. Leicester, 1974.

Carr, Anthony D. "Sir Lewis John: A Medieval London Welshman." *Bulletin of the Board of Celtic Studies* 22 (1967): 260–270.

Chojnacki, Stanley. "Measuring Adulthood: Adolescence and Gender in Renaissance Venice." *Journal of Family History* 17 (1992): 371–396.

Clark, Elaine. "City Orphans and Custody Laws in Medieval England." *American Journal of Legal History* 34 (1990): 168–187.

Clark, J. "Medieval Enamelled Glass from London." *Medieval Archaeology* 27 (1983): 152–156.

Clark, P., and P. Slack, eds. *Crisis and Order in English Towns, 1500–1700*. London, 1972.

Clode, Charles M. *The Early History of the Guild of Merchant Taylors*. Pts. 1 and 2. London, 1888.

Clune, George. *The Medieval Gild System*. Dublin, 1943.

Cooper, C. R. H. "The Archives of the City of London Livery Companies and Related Organizations." *Archives* 16 (1984): 323–353.

Courtenay, W. J. "The London *Studia* in the Fourteenth Century." *Medievalia et Humanistica*, n.s., 13 (1985): 127–141.

Craig, John. *The Mint: A History of the London Mint from A.D. 282–1948*. Cambridge, 1953.

Cramer, Stella. *The English Craft Gilds and the Government.* Colorado University Studies in History, Economics, and Public Law 23. New York, 1905.

Crawford, A. *A History of the Vinters' Company.* London, 1977.

Cunningham, William. *The Growth of English Industry and Commerce.* Vol. 1. 3rd ed. Cambridge, 1896. Vol. 2. Rev. ed. Cambridge, 1903.

Dale, Marian K. "London Silkwomen of the Fifteenth Century." *Economic History Review* 4 (1932–1934): 324–335.

Danneel, Marianne. "Orphanhood and Marriage in Fifteenth-Century Ghent." In *Marriage and Social Mobility in the Late Middle Ages*, ed. W. Prevenier, pp. 99–111. Studia Historica Gandensia 274. Ghent, 1989.

Davies, Margaret Gay. *The Enforcement of English Apprenticeship: A Study in Applied Mercantilism.* Cambridge, Mass. 1956.

Davis, Natalie Zemon. *Society and Culture in Early Modern France.* Stanford, Calif., 1975.

Doolittle, I. G. "The City of London's Debt to Its Orphans, 1694–1767." *Bulletin of the Institute of Historical Research* 56 (1983): 46–59.

Dummelon, John. *The Wax Chandlers of London.* London, 1973.

Dyer, C. *The Guild of Freemen of the City of London: A Record of Its Transformation and History.* London, 1982.

Ekwall, E. *Early London Personal Names.* Lund, 1947.

———. *Street Names of the City of London.* Oxford, 1954.

———. *Studies on the Population of Medieval London.* Stockholm, 1956.

Elder, Glen, Jr. "Adolescence in the Life Cycle: An Introduction." In *Adolescence in the Life Cycle*, ed. Sigmund E. Dragastin and Glen H. Elder, Jr., pp. 1–13. Washington, D.C., 1975.

———. *Adolescent Socialization and Personality Development.* Chicago, 1968.

Elias, Norbert. *Über den Prozess der Zivilisation: Wandlungen des Verhaltens in den weltlichen Oberschichten des Abendlandes.* Vol. 1. Bern, 1969.

Engelmann, George. *Labor Among Primitive Peoples.* St. Louis, 1883.

Evenden-Nagy, Doreen. "Seventeenth-Century London Midwives: Their Training, Licensing, and Social Profile." Ph.D. diss., McMaster University, 1991.

Fairchilds, Cissie. *Domestic Enemies: Servants and Their Masters in Old Regime France.* Baltimore, 1984.

Fenwick, Carolyn C. *The English Poll Taxes of 1377, 1379, 1381: A Critical Examination of the Returns.* London, 1983.

Finlay, Roger, and Beatrice Shearer. "Population Growth and Suburban Expansion." In *London, 1500–1700: The Making of the Metropolis*, ed. A. L. Beier and Roger Finlay, pp. 37–59. London, 1986.

Fischer, J. *A Collection of Early Maps of London, 1553–1667.* London, 1981.

Fitch, Marc, ed. *Index to Testamentary Records in the Commissory Court of London.* Vol. 1: *1374–1488.* Vol. 2: *1489–1570.* London, 1969, 1974.

Flandrin, Jean-Louis. *Families in Former Times: Kinship, Household, and Sexuality.* Trans. Richard Southern. Cambridge, 1979.

Flenley, Ralph. "London and Foreign Merchants in the Reign of Henry VI." *English Historical Review* 25 (1910): 644–655.

Franklin, Peter. "Peasant Widows' 'Liberation' and Remarriage Before the Black Death." *Economic History Review* 39 (1986): 186–204.

Fundley, Palmer. *The Story of Childbirth.* New York, 1934.

Goldberg, P. J. P. "Female Labour, Service, and Marriage in Northern Towns During the Later Middle Ages." *Northern History* 22 (1986): 18–38.

———. "Marriage, Migration, Servanthood, and Life Cycle in Yorkshire Towns of the Later Middle Ages." *Continuity and Change* 1 (1986): 141–169.

———. *Women, Work, and Life Cycle in a Medieval Economy.* Oxford, 1992.

Goody, Jack. *Development of Family and Marriage in Europe.* Cambridge, 1983.

Green, Alice. *Town Life in the Fifteenth Century.* 2 vols. London, 1894.

Gudeman, Stephen. "Spiritual Relations and Selecting a Godparent." *Man,* n.s., 10 (1975): 221–238.

Guide to the Archives of City Livery Companies and Related Organizations in Guildhall Library. 2nd ed. London, 1983.

Haas, Louis. "Social Connections Between Parents and Godparents in Late Medieval Yorkshire." *Medieval Prosopography* 10 (1989): 1–21.

Haine, W. Scott. "The Development of Leisure and the Transformation of Working Class Adolescence, Paris 1830–1940." *Journal of Family History* 17 (1992): 351–376.

Hanawalt, Barbara A. "Childrearing Among the Lower Classes of Late Medieval England." *Journal of Interdisciplinary History* 8 (1977): 1–22.

———. "Conception Through Infancy in Medieval English Historical and Folklore Sources." *Folklore Forum* 13 (1981): 127–157.

———. *Crime and Conflict in English Communities, 1300–1348.* Cambridge, Mass., 1979.

———. "Historical Descriptions and Prescriptions for Adolescence." *Journal of Family History* 17 (1992): 341–351.

———. "Keepers of the Lights: Late Medieval English Parish Gilds." *Journal of Medieval and Renaissance History* 14 (1984): 21–37.

———. "Remarriage as an Option for Urban and Rural Widows in Late Medieval England." In *Wife and Widow: The Experiences of Women in Medieval England,* ed. Sue Sheridan Walker, pp. 141–164. Ann Arbor, 1993.

———. *The Ties That Bound: Peasant Families in Medieval England.* New York, 1986.

———. "The Voices and Audiences of Social History Records." *Social Science History* 15 (1991): 159–175.

———. "The Widow's Mite: Provisions for Medieval London Widows." In *Upon My Husband's Death: Widows in the Literature and History of Medieval Europe,* ed. Louise Mirrer, pp. 21–45. Ann Arbor, 1992.

Hanham, Alison. *The Celys and Their World: An English Merchant Family of the Fifteenth Century.* Cambridge, 1985.

Harley, Dorothy, and Margaret M. Elliot. *Life and Work of the People of England: The Fifteenth Century.* New York, 1926.

Hatcher, John. *Plague, Population, and the English Economy, 1348–1530.* London, 1977.

Helmholtz, Richard H. "Infanticide in England in the Later Middle Ages." *History of Childhood Quarterly* 1 (1974–1975): 282–340.

———. *Marriage Litigation in Medieval England.* Cambridge, 1974.

Herbage, Peter. *A History of the Worshipful Company of Cooks, London.* London, 1982.

Herlihy, David. *Medieval Households.* Cambridge, Mass., 1985.

———. *Opera Muliebria: Women and Work in Medieval Europe.* New York, 1990.

Herlihy, David, and Christiane Klapisch-Zuber. *The Tuscans and Their Families: A Study of the Florentine Catasto of 1427.* New Haven, Conn., 1985.

Hopkinson, Henry Lennox. *Report on the Ancient Records in the Possession of the Guild of Merchant Tailors of the Fraternity of St. John Baptist in the City of London.* London, 1915.

Hughes, Susan E. "Guildhall and Chancery." *Guildhall Studies in London History* 2 (1980): 53–62.

Imray, Jean M. "'Les Bones Gentes de la Mercerye de Londres': A Study of the Membership of the Medieval Mercers' Company." In *Studies in London History,* ed. A. E. J. Hollaender and William Kellaway, pp. 155–180. London, 1969.

Ingram, M. "Spousal Litigation in the English Ecclesiastical Courts, c. 1350–1640." In *Marriage and Society: Studies in the Social History of Marriage,* ed. R. B. Outhwaite, pp. 35–57. London, 1981.

Irwin, Raymond, and Ronald Stavely, eds. *The Libraries of London.* 2nd rev. ed. London, 1961.

Jeay, Madeleine. "Sexuality and Family in Fifteenth-Century France: Are Literary Sources a Mask or a Mirror?" *Journal of Family History* 4 (1979): 328–345.

Jenks, S. "Das Schrieberbuch des John Thorpe und der hansische Handel in London 1457–59." *Hansische Geschichtsblatter* 101 (1983): 67–113.

Johansson, Sheila Ryan. "Deferred Infanticide: Excess Female Mortality During Childhood." In *Infanticide: Comparative and Evolutionary Perspectives,* ed. Glen Hausfater and Sara Blaffer Hrdy, pp. 463–485. New York, 1984.

Johnson, A. H. *The History of the Worshipful Company of Drapers of London.* Vol. 1. Oxford, 1914.

Johnson, David J. *Southwark and the City.* London, 1969.

Jones, Philip E. *The Butchers of London: A History of the Worshipful Company of the Butchers of London.* London, 1976.

———. "The City Courts of Law." *Law Journal* 93 (1943): 285–286.

———. "The Court of Husting." Corporation of London Record Office. Research Papers 2.1. 1975.

Jones, Philip E., and Raymond Smith. *A Guide to the Records in the Corporation of London Records Office and the Guildhall Library Muniment Room.* London, 1950.

Kahl, William F. *The Development of London Livery Companies.* Kress Library of Business and Economics 15. Boston, 1960.

Karras, Ruth Mazo. "The Regulation of Brothels in Later Medieval England." *Signs* 14 (1989): 399–433.

Keene, Derek. *Cheapside Before the Great Fire.* London, 1985.

Keene, Derek, and Vanessa Harding. *A Survey of Documentary Sources for Property Holding in London Before the Great Fire.* London Record Society 22. London, 1985.

Kellaway, William. "John Carpenter's *Liber Albus.*" *Guildhall Studies in London History* 3 (1978): 67–84.

Kingsford, Charles L. "An Historical Collection of the Fifteenth Century." *English Historical Review* 29 (1914): 505–515; 31 (1916): 126–128.

———. *Prejudice and Promise in Fifteenth-Century England.* Oxford, 1925.

Klapisch-Zuber, Christiane. *Women, Family, and Ritual in Renaissance Italy.* Trans. Lydia Cochrane. Chicago, 1985.

Knoop, Douglas, and Gwilyn P. Jones. "London Bridge and Its Builders: A Study of Municipal Employment of Masons Mainly in the Fifteenth Century." *Ars Quartuor Coronatorum* 47 (1938): 5–44; 48 (1939): 5–46.

Kramer, Stella. *The English Craft Gilds: Studies in Their Progress and Decline.* New York, 1927.

Kuehn, Thomas. "Some Ambiguities of Female Inheritance Ideology in the Renaissance." *Continuity and Change* 2 (1987): 11–36.

Lacey, Kay E. "Women and Work in Fourteenth and Fifteenth Century London." In *Women and Work in Pre-Industrial England,* ed. Lindsey Charles and Lorna Duffin, pp. 24–82. London, 1985.

Laslett, Peter. *Family Life and Illicit Love in Earlier Generations.* Cambridge, 1977.

———. "The Institution of Service." *Local Population Studies* 40 (1988): 55–60.

Leach, A. F. *The Schools of Medieval England.* London, 1915.

Lynch, Joseph H. *Godparents and Kinship in Early Medieval Europe.* Princeton, N.J., 1986.

Martin, G. H. "The Registration of Deeds of Title in the Medieval Borough." In *The Study of Medieval Records: Essay in Honor of Kathleen Major,* ed. D. A. Bullough and R. L. Storey, pp. 151–173. Oxford, 1971.

Masters, Betty R. *The Chamberlain of the City of London, 1237–1987.* London, 1988.

———. "The Corporation of London Records Office: Some Sources for the Historian." *Archives* 12 (1975): 5–14.

———. "The Mayor's Household before 1600." In *Studies in London History,* ed. A. E. J. Hollander and W. Kellaway, pp. 95–116. London, 1969.

Maza, Sara C. *Servants and Masters in Eighteenth-Century France: The Uses of Loyalty.* Princeton, N.J., 1984.

McDonnell, Kevin. *Medieval London Suburbs.* London, 1978.

Mcfarlane, Alan. *Marriage and Love in England: Modes of Reproduction, 1300–1840.* Oxford, 1986.

McLaughlin, Mary Martin. "Survivors and Surrogates: Children and Parents from the Ninth to the Thirteenth Centuries." In *The History of Childhood,* ed. Lloyd deMause, pp. 101–181. New York, 1974.

Metcalf, P. "Living over the Shop in the City of London." *Architectural History* 27 (1984): 96–103.

Mitchell, R. J., and M. D. R. Leys. *A History of London Life.* London, 1958.

Mitterauer, Michael, and Reinhard Sieder. *The European Family: Patriarchy to Partnership from the Middle Ages to the Present.* Trans. Karla Oosterveen and Manfred Horzinger. Chicago, 1982.

Moran, Ann Hoepner. *The Growth of English Schooling, 1340–1548.* Princeton, N.J., 1983.

Myers, Alec. *London in the Age of Chaucer.* Norman, Okla., 1972.

Nicholas, David. *The Domestic Life of a Medieval City: Women, Children, and Families in Fourteenth Century Ghent.* Lincoln, Neb., 1985.

Nightingale, P. "The London Pepperers' Guild and Some Twelfth-Century English Trading Links with Spain." *Bulletin of the Institute for Historical Research* 58 (1985): 123–132.

———. "Some London Moneyers, and Reflections on the Organization of English Mints in the Eleventh and Twelfth Centuries." *Numismatic Chronicle* 141 (1981): 71–116.

Orme, Nicholas. *English Schools in the Middle Ages.* London, 1973.

————. *From Childhood to Chivalry: The Education of the English Kings and Aristocracy, 1066–1530.* London, 1984.

Owst, G. R. *Literature and Pulpit in Medieval England.* Cambridge, 1933.

Page, William, ed. *The Victoria History of London.* Vol. 1. London, 1909.

Palliser, D. M., and L. J. Jones. "The Diocesan Population Returns for 1563 and 1603." *Local Population Studies* 30 (1983): 55–58.

Pendrill, Charles. *London Life in the Fourteenth Century.* London, 1925.

Pentikäinen, Juha. *The Nordic Dead-Child Tradition.* Folklore Fellows Communications, no. 201. Helsinki, 1968.

Phythian-Adams, Charles. *Desolation of a City: Coventry and the Urban Crisis of the Late Middle Ages.* Cambridge, 1979.

Power, Eileen. *Medieval People.* London, 1924.

Prescott, A. J. "Essex Rebel Bands in London." In *Essex and the Great Revolt of 1381,* ed. W. H. Liddell and R. G. E. Wood, pp. 37–54. Colchester, 1982.

Putnam, Bertha Haven. *The Enforcement of the Statute of Labourers During the First Decade After the Black Death.* New York, 1908.

Rappaport, Steve. "Social Structure and Mobility in the Sixteenth Century: London, pt. 1." *London Journal* (1983): 107–135.

————. *Worlds Within Worlds: Structures of Life in Sixteenth Century London.* Cambridge, 1989.

Reddaway, Thomas. *The Early History of the Goldsmiths' Company.* London, 1975.

————. "The King's Mint and Exchange in London, 1343–1534." *English Historical Review* 82 (1967): 1–23.

Reyerson, Kathryn L. "The Adolescent Apprentice/Worker in Medieval Montpellier." *Journal of Family History* 17 (1992): 353–370.

Reynolds, Susan. "Decline and Decay in Late Medieval Towns: A Look at Some of the Concepts and Arguments." *Urban History Yearbook* (1980): 76–78.

————. *An Introduction to the History of English Medieval Towns.* Oxford, 1977.

Rosenthal, Joel T. *Patriarchy and Families of Privilege in Fifteenth-Century England.* Philadelphia, 1991.

Rossiaud, Jacques. *Medieval Prostitution.* Trans. Lydia G. Cochrane. Oxford, 1984.

Russell, J. C. *British Medieval Population.* Albuquerque, N.M., 1948.

Sabine, Ernest. "Butchering in Mediaeval London." *Speculum* 8 (1933): 335–353.

————. "City Cleaning in Mediaeval London." *Speculum* 12 (1937): 335–353.

————. "Latrines and Cesspools of Mediaeval London." *Speculum* 9 (1934): 303–321; 12 (1937): 19–43.

Schofield, John. *The Building of London from the Conquest to the Great Fire.* London, 1984.

Schofield, R., and E. A. Wrigley. "Remarriage Intervals and the Effect of Marriage Order on Fertility." In *Marriage and Remarriage in Populations of the Past,* ed. J. Dupaquier, E. Helin, P. Laslett, M. Levi-Bacci, and S. Songer, pp. 211–227. London, 1981.

Schultz, James A. "Medieval Adolescence: The Claims of History and the Silence of German Narrative." *Speculum* 66 (1991): 519–539.

Segalen, Martine. *Historical Anthropology and the Family.* Trans. J. C. Whitehouse and Sarah Matthews. Cambridge, 1986.

Sen, Amartya. "More than 100 Million Women Are Missing." *New York Review of Books,* 20 December 1990, pp. 61–66.

Shahar, Shulamith. *Childhood in the Middle Ages.* London, 1990.

Sharpe, J. A. *Defamation and Sexual Slander in Early Modern England: The Church Courts of York.* Borthwick Papers, no. 58. York, 1980.

Sheehan, Michael M. "The Influence of Canon Law on the Property Rights of Married Women in England." *Mediaeval Studies* 25 (1963): 109–124.

Shorter, Edward. *The Making of the Modern Family.* New York, 1977.

Slack, P. "Metropolitan Government in Crisis: The Response to Plague." In *The Making of the Metropolis: Essays in the Social and Ecomonic History of London,* ed. A. L. Beier and Roger Finlay, pp. 60–81. London, 1986.

Smith, S. R. "The London Apprentices as Seventeenth-Century Adolescents." *Past and Present* 61 (1973): 149–161.

Speert, Harold. *Iconographia Gyniatrica.* Philadelphia, 1973.

Spence, Jonathan. *The Death of Woman Wang.* New York, 1978.

Stenton, Frank M. *Norman London: An Essay.* With translation by H. E. Butler of William Fitzstephen's *Description.* Rev. ed. London, 1934.

Stone, Lawrence. *The Family, Sex, and Marriage in England, 1500–1800.* New York, 1977.

Stuard, Susan Mosher. "To Town to Serve: Urban Domestic Slavery in Medieval Ragusa." In *Women and Work in Preindustrial Europe,* ed. Barbara A. Hanawalt, pp. 39–55. Bloomington, Ind., 1986.

Sutton, A. F. "Richard Gowle, Supplier of Mercery to Richard III and Anne Neville." *The Ricardian* 7 (1986): 238–245.

Swanson, Heather. *Medieval Artisans: An Urban Class in Late Medieval England.* Oxford, 1989.

Thomas, A. H. "Life in Medieval London." *Journal of the British Archaeological Association* 35 (1929): 122–147.

———. "Sidelights on Medieval London Life." *Journal of the British Archaeological Association,* 3rd ser., 2 (1937): 99–120.

Thomas, Keith. "Age and Authority in Early Modern England." *Proceedings of the British Academy* 52 (1976): 205–248.

Thomson, John A. F. "Piety and Charity in Late Medieval London." *Journal of Ecclesiastical History* 16 (1965): 178–195.

Threlfall, J. B. "John Fressh, Lord Mayor of London in 1395." *Genealogists' Magazine* 21 (1984): 577–585; 21 (1985): 635–642.

Thrupp, Sylvia L. "Aliens in and Around London in the Fifteenth Century." In *Studies in London History,* ed. A. E. Hollaender and William Kellaway, pp. 251–272. London, 1969.

———. "The Grocers of London, A Study of Distributive Trade." In *Studies in English Trade in the Fifteenth Century,* ed. Eileen Power and M. M. Postan, pp. 242–292. London, 1933.

———. *The Merchant Class of Medieval London, 1300–1500.* Chicago, 1948.

———. *A Short History of the Worshipful Company of Bakers of London.* London, 1933.

Tierney, Brian. *Medieval Poor Law: A Sketch of Canonical Theory and Its Application in England.* London, 1959.

Trexler, Richard. "The Foundlings of Florence, 1395–1455." *History of Childhood Quarterly* 1 (1973): 259–284.

Turner, F. Hudson. *Some Account of Domestic Architecture in England from the Conquest to the End of the Thirteenth Century.* London, 1851.

Turner, Victor. *The Ritual Process: Structure and Anti-Structure.* New York, 1969.

Unwin, George. *The Gilds and Companies of London.* London, 1908.

————, ed. *Finance and Trade Under Edward III.* Manchester, 1918.

van Gennep, Arnold. *The Rites of Passage.* Trans. Monika B. Vizedom and Gabrielle L. Caffee. Chicago, 1960.

Veale, Elspeth. "Craftsmen and the Economy of London in the Fourteenth Century." In *Studies in London History,* ed. A. E. J. Hollander and W. Kellaway, pp. 133–154. London, 1969.

Walmisley, Claude, ed. *An Index of Persons Named in Early Chancery Proceedings. Richard II (1385) to Edward IV (1467).* 2 vols. London, 1928.

Weinbaum, Martin. *London unter Eduard I und II: Verfassungs- und Wirtschaftsgeschichtliche Studien.* 2 vols. Stuttgart, 1933.

Welch, Charles. *History of the Cutlers' Company of London.* Vol. 1: *From Early Times to 1500.* London, 1916.

Welsford, A. E. *John Greenway, 1460–1529: A Merchant of Tiverton and London: A Devon Worthy.* Tiverton, 1984.

Wiesner, Merry E. "Early Modern Midwifery: A Case Study." In *Women and Work in Preindustrial Europe,* ed. Barbara A. Hanawalt, pp. 94–113. Bloomington, Ind. 1986.

Williams, Gwyn. *Medieval London: From Commune to Capital.* London, 1963.

Wimberly, Charles. *Folklore in English and Scottish Ballads.* Chicago, 1928.

Withington, Robert. *English Pageantry: A Historical Outline.* 2 vols. Cambridge, Mass., 1918.

Wood, Charles T. "The Doctor's Dilemma: Sin, Salvation, and the Menstrual Cycle." *Speculum* 56 (1981): 710–727.

Wunderli, R. *London Church Courts and Society on the Eve of the Reformation.* Cambridge, Mass., 1981.

————. "Pre-Reformation London Summoners and the Murder of Richard Hunne." *Journal of Ecclesiastical History* 33 (1982): 209–224.

Yarborough, A. "Apprentices as Adolescents in Sixteenth-Century Bristol." *Journal of Social History* 13 (1979): 67–81.

Index